Water-Cooled
VOLKSWAGEN
Performance Handbook

Greg Raven

MBI Publishing Company

First published in 1999 by MBI Publishing Company,
729 Prospect Avenue, PO Box 1, Osceola, WI 54020-0001 USA

MBI Publishing Company books are also available at discounts in
bulk quantity for industrial or sales-promotional use. For details
write to Special Sales Manager at Motorbooks International
Wholesalers & Distributors, 729 Prospect Avenue, PO Box 1,
Osceola, WI 54020-0001 USA.

Library of Congress Cataloging-in-Publication Data
Raven, Greg.
    Water-cooled Volkswagen performance handbook/Greg
    Raven.
      p. cm.
    Includes index.
    ISBN 0-7603-0491-2 (pbk.: alk. paper)
    1. Volkswagen automobiles—Performance. 2. Volkswagen
automobiles—Motors—Modification. 3. Volkswagen
automobiles—Customizing. I. Title.
TL215.V6R39   1998
629.25'04—dc21   98-51692

Edited by John Adams-Graf

Designed by Katie Sonmor

Printed in the United States of America

Acknowledgments

The author would like to thank the following persons for
their many contributions: Jeff Moss and Jeremy Wolf of
Velocity Sport Tuning, Dana Clark of Autotech
SportTuning, James Sly of *European Car* magazine, and Brad Timms
for helping with my various projects over the years.

Contents

Preface

What is it about Volkswagens? First they make history with the revolutionary "people's car," the Beetle, and next they start the whole trend toward small, front-wheel-drive cars with the Rabbit. Although these two cars could hardly be more different from one another, they both have the mystical power to inspire their owners to personalize them in one way or another. Perhaps that's why the New Beetle, with styling reminiscence of the old Beetle, but with running gear nearly identical to its water-cooled contemporaries, has proven such a hit.

As it did with the air-cooled Beetle, in the water-cooled Rabbit (and its successors) Volkswagen has provided us with a great day-to-day vehicle. Good looks, good mileage, and a solid and dependable design all add up to a car that can deliver year after year of basic transportation.

And, as with the air-cooled Beetle, this "basic transportation" is also an incredible platform for high performance. The Volkswagen chassis is light but strong, the suspension is simple and fairly easy to tune, and the powerplant seems nearly limitless in terms of what it can be made to do.

With each passing year, the new Volkswagens become more and more capable and sophisticated—and expensive. However, those of us with older Volkswagens, and a little time and money, can easily build up our own personalized "pocket rocket," a phenomenon first envisioned by the appearance of the GTi in Europe in 1976.

The aftermarket for the water-cooled Volkswagen has reached the point at which just about any type of high-performance part is available. And just as the Beetle of yore could be pumped up to do battle with the so-called muscle cars, today's Volkswagen can be injected with enough additional performance to keep it door-handle-to-door-handle with the competition.

Driving around southern California, meeting the aftermarket parts suppliers, and talking with Volkswagen enthusiasts, it becomes apparent that most enthusiasts want to build up their cars for better performance without losing streetability. For them, their hot rods are also their daily drivers. Most of the information in this book is aimed at this type of enthusiast.

On the other hand, it is hard to ignore those who are putting thousands of dollars and hundreds of hours into making their cars the ultimate machines. Therefore, I have tried to include as much of the "no-limits" information as I could get my hands on. I may not be able to promise you a win at Laguna Seca, but I can at least get you thinking about some of the things you will need to consider.

To all of you, I hope that getting there will be half the fun, and that when you get your car set up just the way you have always wanted it, it is as sweet as you hoped it would be.

Philosophy

This book concerns hot-rodding your Volkswagen. Because there is so much information and so little room to squeeze it into, I have purposely left out some of the things (such as hands-on procedures) that you will find in a shop manual.

The best shop manuals I have found are those published by the Robert Bentley Company, and I highly recommend that you purchase the one for your model and year. Used alongside this book, it will provide a very complete picture of what is happening with your car. The new Bentley manuals are laid out completely differently than the old ones, although either can prove to be a little difficult to work with. The information is there, however; all you have to do is find it. Shop manuals are valuable for another reason, and that is to keep you in touch with the basics. Before you go hot-rodding, you owe it to yourself to understand at least some of the basics about what you are changing.

For example, suppose your engine has a burnt valve, but because it hasn't been diagnosed yet, all you know is that the engine is running roughly. The easiest thing in the world is to blame that darned old fuel injection, which must be the problem because it's difficult to understand, instead of performing some simple tests to get at the root of the poor running. If you start replacing fuel injection components without addressing the true problem, the car will still run poorly, no matter how much it costs to install the unnecessary parts.

To take another example, if your suspension is out of alignment, your car will handle poorly, and the tires will wear out more quickly. Buying expensive tires will not improve the handling, and they will be that much more costly to replace when they wear out prematurely.

No matter how extreme your car gets, pay attention to the basics. Even when you are *sure* you have guessed exactly what is causing some mysterious problem, go through the well-established diagnostic steps, rather than jump to a conclusion and miss the fault entirely. Every engine—no matter how sophisticated—needs air, fuel, and properly timed spark to run, something to keep in mind when troubleshooting engine problems.

One difficulty in producing a book such as this is that the subject is still growing and evolving. Even setting aside for a moment the fact that in a couple of years Volkswagen may have a W12 engine in its top-performing cars, an author still must try to address the needs of both the Rabbit owner on a budget and the upwardly mobile young executive who could have bought a BMW but chose instead to purchase a new Golf, spend a few thousand customizing it, and pocket the difference. As much as possible I have attempted to cover both extremes and the variations in between.

I also have tried to incorporate a blend of basics, specifics, and theory. I hope the basics will keep you out of trouble, and the specifics will reduce the amount of experimentation necessary during any type of change. The theory will help you evaluate new developments in the field that are not covered in this edition and provide food for thought.

The best way to keep up with what is happening now is to subscribe to magazines that cover this field and to stay on the aftermarket suppliers' mailing lists. While advertising is designed to portray products in the best light, it is surprising how much good information you can glean from advertisements and catalogs.

Compromise

Everything ever designed involves compromise. A case in point is the automobile. If your goal is to eliminate all compromise from your car, you will be disappointed. At virtually every turn you will be confronted with a choice, a tradeoff, that involves compromising one factor for another.

Do you want the ultimate 17-inch wheel and tire combination, or do you want something that will not rattle your teeth out on the frost heaves and potholes of the turnpike? Do you want the highest amount of horsepower per cubic centimeter, or do you want to be able to use pump gas?

Hot-rodding involves more than mere maintenance, and thus can be expensive. There are no limits on the amount of money you can spend on your car. The first performance upgrades may be inexpensive, but as you get further and further from stock, you will find it takes more and more money to

proceed. High performance costs money. The limiting factor is more often your wallet than the engineering or labor.

One trap that can be difficult to avoid is the "For $100 More" syndrome. This usually grips you after you have everything apart; as you are preparing for reassembly, you find out that "For $100 More" you can have your crankshaft spiffed up, or your gears specially treated, or whatever. You will be able to tell when you have fallen prey to this syndrome when your car is taking forever to put back together because you are forever waiting for parts, yet you need more parts still and have stopped balancing your checkbook because you are afraid to look at how much money has been funneled into your project. Forewarned is forearmed.

This book was not conceived to eliminate all compromise but merely to help you examine some of the options, should you choose a different set of criteria for your vehicle than it comes with from the factory.

Caveat Emptor

Everything that involves getting out of bed in the morning can be dangerous. In particular, the car you drive off the showroom floor has a tremendous potential for havoc, personal injury and tragedy. If you want to get into trouble with your car, you do not need to make it into a hot rod first—it is ready when you are.

The aim of this book is to make the car more responsive to the wishes of the driver. A more responsive car is usually a safer car, whether we are talking about the brakes, the handling or acceleration.

However, having a high-performance car is not a license (or a demand) for its driver to behave irresponsibly. Surface streets are there to help motorists get to and from their destinations; they are not race courses in disguise. If you need to get the Call of the Wild out of your system, join a car club and rent a race track for a weekend. Maybe attend a high-performance driving school. Above all, consider the consequences of your actions. It is not only your life and health and your car that are at stake; it is the life, health, and property of innocent bystanders.

Introduction

About Your Warranty

If your car is still new enough to have part or all of its warranty in force, consider the consequences of modifying your car, if doing so will make it difficult to make a warranty claim. Even though it may seem ridiculous that the warranty will be voided by something as sensible as using a long-drain-interval motor oil, those provisos are there for your protection.

About Air Pollution, Laws, and Inspections

Air pollution is the dark side of automobile use. Fortunately, auto makers have made impressive strides in reducing auto-related air pollution through oxygen sensors, catalytic converters and vapor recovery systems. Even the basic CIS (continuous injection system) fuel injection that most Volkswagen products are fitted with runs fairly cleanly without any help at all.

In the early days, the words "air pollution control equipment" were irrevocably linked with the image of "low-performance automobiles." This image was due primarily to the way American car manufacturers approached air pollution controls, leading to a lot of "tuning tips" that involved disconnecting the pollution control equipment. With only a couple of exceptions, Volkswagen has not had the problems with pollution control equipment that the American car makers have had. In fact, disconnecting your Lambda probe can actually lose you power (and it is illegal).

It is commonly held that removing the catalytic converter is an easy and virtually free way to obtain a meaningful power increase. Many people whom I know of firmly believe this. They even go as far as to breakup the internal matrix with a long punch and refit the catalytic converter to retain the appearance. My understanding is that the modern catalytic converter is responsible for a very small power loss and probably less than that of turbulence added by an empty catalytic converter shell or worse, one with fragments. If you replace it with a straight pipe, it won't pass visual inspection (and, increasingly, emissions inspection), and the amount of horsepower you gain is simply not worth the additional pollution. There are a lot of high-horsepower cars in California, which has very strict pollutions standards, that still have their catalytic converters. In other words, the catalytic converter is not standing in the way to your quest for more street horsepower.

Whether or not you leave everything connected, if your fuel-injected car is running dirty, there is a good chance you

have missed something somewhere; you should not have to be a polluter to make horsepower. If you are running carburetors, it can be more difficult to get your motor "clean," but your car can often make just as much power running clean as dirty, or even more, and a clean engine will usually last longer. Best of all, the modern fuel injection systems used by manufacturers such as Volkswagen actually offer possibilities for squeezing more clean power from your engine than could only have been imagined a few years ago.

highway. This protects the firm from the massive penalties some states levy against anyone who tampers with pollution control devices. Before you make radical modifications, find out what the procedure is in the state where you will be licensing your car.

There are some things you can do with your motor that will not change its appearance even though they increase your horsepower. Even a large throttle body can be blended into the manifold well enough to pass just about anybody's inspection. Turbochargers and superchargers are different matters entirely. If you have your heart set on one of those, make sure it has been certified for use where you will be licensing your car.

Many aspects of engine hot-rodding are antithetical to air pollution laws. However, it is not the intent of this book to encourage anyone to modify his or her vehicle to the detriment of air quality, whether or not the modifications or the emissions are against the law. After all, everyone breathes the same air.

About Dynamometer Numbers

The dynamometer (chassis or engine) can be a wonderful tool in the search for more horsepower. You can test your theories and new products, and find out if they make more power or not—or whether they can take the abuse of wide-open throttle operation. And some things, like carburetor jetting, are almost impossible to do correctly without one.

But dynos are expensive, and few persons have one. Even if you have your own dyno, setting up for a dyno run can take a long time, and a thorough test of a new product can run into days.

In addition, not all dynos read the same, with each other or with themselves. You can imagine how results can diverge even when similar engines are tested on different dynos. These differences are compounded when dyno testing does not take into account ambient temperature and humidity. The dyno is a measuring tool. And, as you would not use a ruler that expanded and shrank due to weather conditions, you should not depend on dyno numbers that do not incorporate correction factors.

Sometimes companies guess at their horsepower figures, based on past experience, instead of spending money on a series of dyno runs. Other companies that spend the time dyno testing may come up with different numbers than a competitor just across town. Still others may hear about the results of someone else's dyno testing and "borrow" the figures for themselves. This means that you should be cautious when buying parts, and not presume that you are buying a horsepower figure.

From time to time this book gives horsepower figures. These are supplied not to show absolute numbers so much as for comparison—how much gain you get, for example, from a camshaft and an exhaust system.

If you need to buy the most horsepower you can get, find a shop that tests its products on a calibrated dyno, following established dyno procedures. You may not get a number that will beat every other number around, but at least you will know that the money you have spent has gone into making more horsepower, and not into inflating someone's ego.

To reduce tampering, many states have instituted vehicle inspections. Some states use only the sniff test, while others conduct a visual inspection as well. Many states also have established lists of aftermarket parts and products that may be used legally, making anything not on the list illegal to use. Aftermarket suppliers are obliged to print warnings along the lines of "certain parts may not be legal for sale or use on pollution-controlled motor vehicles," or "for off-road use only on vehicles that will never be operated on the highway." If you ask an aftermarket firm to install "off-road" parts, it may require you to sign a statement that the car will never be used on the

completely different sets of numbers. This is because on the chassis dyno the engine power must be transmitted to the dyno through the transmission and drivetrain, resulting in approximately 25 percent lower figures. There is no universal correction factor for calculating engine power based on chassis power, or vice versa, because of the differences among drivetrains. However, you can get a pretty close estimate with this formula:

$$\text{Engine hp} = \frac{\text{Road hp}}{0.8} + 8$$

Therefore, when your 102-horsepower GTi shows only 75 horsepower on the chassis dyno, do not panic. Use whatever number you get as a base line, and work off that for all future modifications.

About Hot-Rodding

When it comes right down to it, hot-rodding your car means making it quicker, or faster, or both. Whether you are talking about quarter-mile speed or time through a slalom, hot-rodding your car makes it perform that operation better than it did when you started.

C. Van Tune, editor of *Motor Trend*, can climb into a car he has never driven before and, at the end of a 0-60 acceleration test, guess within a couple of tenths of a second what the car ran. Most persons cannot do that, which is one reason stopwatches were invented. Lord Kelvin once said, "When you can measure what you are speaking about, and express it in numbers, you know something about it; but when you cannot measure it, when you cannot express it in numbers, your knowledge is of a meager and unsatisfactory kind: It may be the beginning of knowledge, but you have scarcely, in your thoughts, advanced to the stage of science."

Beyond the stopwatch, devices such as the Vericom and the G-analyst use accelerometers to quantify performance. These are useful tools for the enthusiast, although the price for either is a little steep. If you have a car club or a group of enthusiast friends, you may want to pool your resources. I prefer the Vericom or the G-tech, but the G-analyst will give you better information at a road course track. Both of these tools are discussed in "Accelerometers."

If you are serious about hot-rodding your Volkswagen, try to get some numbers before and after each modification. Before-and-after testing (whether with a stopwatch or on the dyno) lets you know when you have made a wrong turn or when you have overlooked something. And it makes it possible for you to go back to your mechanic or parts supplier with solid evidence that whatever was recommended did not work.

While you are doing your testing, keep in mind that you are usually going to be dealing with incremental improve-

Both engine dynos and chassis dynos work pretty much the same way. The difference is that on an engine dyno, the resistive load is connected to the flywheel. On a chassis dyno, the resistive load is applied to the drive wheels. A chassis dyno gives you a better idea how the motor will perform as installed, as it accounts for just about everything except aerodynamic drag. It is in some ways more accurate, and it is certainly easier to use, as you simply drive the car onto the rollers and let it go. An engine dyno, on the other hand, eliminates external factors and makes it easier to detect more subtle differences without worrying about transmission anomalies or whether the tires are slipping, as they can on the chassis dyno rollers.

A dyno measures the engine's ability to push against a resistive load, expressing this ability as either horsepower or torque. Dyno runs are typically performed at full throttle with the resistive load being increased or decreased to bring the engine to the rpm range that the dyno tester wants to measure. By performing a number of runs with different loads, the dyno tester can get a complete picture of the power curve of the engine.

If you test your engine on an engine dyno, and then install it in your car and retest it with a chassis dyno, you will get two

Like the Audi Fox before it, the VW Fox has the engine mounted longitudinally, but many of the modifications discussed in this book will work the same is on the A1 cars.

ments. In other words, there will not be one part that, once bolted on, gives you all the horsepower or handling you need. Often you will get a little from one modification, then a little more from another. It is the sum of all these little gains that gives you the total performance you are looking for.

About Those Who Do the Work

This book was written with the assumption that you will be doing at least some of the work on your own car. Whether you are or not, it helps to have a good relationship with your mechanic or tuner. And developing that relationship can be just about as difficult as developing the skills to be a mechanic!

If you do not have the skills of a mechanic and do not yet have a mechanic you trust, the best way to check out a shop is to have it perform some routine maintenance for you. An oil change is a good, inexpensive way to audition an unfamiliar shop. While you are there, you can find out if the shop is interested in doing custom work. Some have found it difficult to put up with temperamental hot-rodders, and will not touch such work. Others have the pioneer spirit, are just plain curious, or maybe have a hot rod Volkswagen themselves and will welcome the opportunity to do a little exploration.

Whatever you do, do not beg someone else to perform custom work for you. The chances are good that neither of you will be satisfied with the results.

About Your Budget

The number one question in the minds of enthusiasts seems to be, "What should I do to my car if I only have $_____ spend?" You can fill in the blank with whatever figure you want. The common denominator is that no one has an infinite amount of money to spend on his or her car, so somewhere the line has to be drawn.

Everybody has a different set of priorities about what they want out of their cars. Some think the handling is fine but the power is lousy, while others think just the opposite. Clearly, no one set of recommendations will suit everyone.

But that is no reason not to try.

First, enthusiasts can be divided into two groups: those who are satisfied with the way they drive and those who are not. It is no shame to admit that you could be a better driver, and many times the better driver in a worse car will beat the poorer driver in the better car. If you suspect that your driving skills could be honed, sign up with a driving school. When you graduate, you will have a significantly better understanding of your abilities, your car's abilities, how the car should be set up and what needs to be done next on the car—if anything.

If, on the other hand, you are satisfied with your driving abilities, or you have already attended driver's school, I can make some recommendations for a limited budget.

Next, it is a lot less expensive to let something wear out before you replace it. If you use a super motor oil and change

10

your dual-filter setup every 1,500 miles, you may not want to wait until you wear out your motor before you get big-bore pistons, but you get the idea. There is not much point in wasting 75 percent of the life of a set of brake pads or shock absorbers or tires unless you are really upset about the way they are performing. If you feel you just have to take near-new parts off your car, save them for later when you want to sell the car but keep your trick parts.

Something else to keep in mind is that it will be less expensive in the long run if you have an idea about what your goal is before you start hanging parts on your car. For example, there is not much point in spending the time and money required to bolt in the latest radical camshaft, and then a couple of months later have to ditch it when you bolt on a supercharger.

You may have to remind yourself of your goal from time to time, especially when you bolt on a big throttle valve and a camshaft and see only modest improvements. But you will find your patience has been rewarded when you finally get a free-flow exhaust, letting the other parts fully work for you for the first time.

Suspension upgrades are the first priority for many of the leading aftermarket tuning firms. Keep in mind, however, that an experienced driver with a stock suspension will beat an inexperienced driver using a high-performance suspension every time.

Assuming that you want more hardware instead of more driving lessons, your first choice for a pre-1985 vehicle would be a lower stress bar, followed by antiroll bars, then an upper stress bar. Chassis and suspension changes in 1985-and-later chassis made stress bars far less necessary, and some of the stock suspensions (such as in the GTi, various VR6s, and the Corrado) are pretty good as they come from the factory.

If your shocks are showing wear, do those next. A good set of low-pressure gas shocks will make those old springs seem much better than they did before. To keep the engine from seeming too sleepy, you can install an exhaust system as a start toward whatever your ultimate horsepower setup will be. (Suspension work is covered in "Suspensions and Steering"; exhausts are covered in "Exhaust Systems.")

The next step is a toss-up between further suspension work and starting in on the engine modifications. Depending on the condition of the roads where you live, the importance you place on ride quality, and the tires and wheels your car came with, you may choose more power instead of lower but stiffer springs, and tires with a better grip but harsher ride. For more on these subjects, see "Tires and Wheels" and "Bolt-on Engine Performance."

Another consideration at this step is engine longevity. Even though an oil cooler and a different fan switch do not make your car any faster, they can make your motor last longer if you live in a temperate or tropical zone. (Oil and water cooling are both covered in "Cooling.")

It is getting close to the moment of truth. How far do you plan to go in your search for high performance? With the suspension taken care of, you can start on your motor. But first you have to decide if you are going to swap for a bigger motor or maximize the displacement you have. Are you going to try forced induction, or go for porting and polishing?

And if you are going for a really big jump in horsepower, are your brakes going to be able to stop you safely? If your car has solid rotors up front, factor in the cost of new brakes to offset the higher engine output. (Brake upgrades are discussed in "Brakes.")

In summary: Make sure you can drive first; go for chassis and suspension modifications second; make wheel, tire, engine longevity, and bolt-on horsepower changes third; and do the engine and brakes together last. Creature comfort and appearance items can come any time you need them.

About Safety

There are a few things to be aware of when working on or around cars. Some of them are trivial almost to the point of being nuisances, but some can kill you if you do not keep your wits about you.

When working under the car, always use jacks stands *and* a floor jack. The floor jack serves as a safety in case the car is accidentally pushed sideways and the jack stands flop over. Always work on level ground.

If you have the use of a hoist, keep in mind that up to 60 percent of the weight of the water-cooled Volkswagen is in the front of the car. If you remove the engine while the car is up on the hoist, the weight balance will be immediately and radically transferred toward the rear end of the vehicle.

Do not run the motor in an enclosed space unless you have an exhaust line connected to the tailpipe. The red blood cells in your lungs will bond with carbon monoxide much more readily than they will with oxygen. Because of this preference, carbon monoxide will continue to displace oxygen in your bloodstream even after you step outside for a breath of fresh air. Therefore, it takes quite a while before your lungs return to normal. It is better to avoid the problem in the first place.

Be conscious of the fact that one gallon of gasoline is powerful enough to propel you, three friends, their luggage, and 2,000 pounds of car nearly 30 miles. When working around gasoline, make certain there are no open flames (water heaters, for example), electrical heaters, electric motors, or burning cigarettes. It is

When jump-starting a car do not connect both ends of the jumper cable to the battery; connect the positive end to the battery, and then connect the negative end to the chassis or engine block, away from the battery, in case it arcs across.

For maximum safety, wear safety goggles when working with a battery that is charging or when jump-starting a car. If the battery blows up, it sends hydrochloric acid everywhere. If you get acid on yourself or on your clothes, wash it off immediately. Your clothes will probably be ruined anyway, but you can save your skin if you move fast.

When the motor is running, keep your fingers, hair, test equipment leads, tools, shoelaces, worry beads, neckties, shop rags, and everything else out of the mechanism. If you get something caught between a belt and a pulley, you may be surprised how quickly things happen.

MacPherson struts, such as those found in the front suspension of your Volkswagen, must be taken apart using a spring compressor. Even when the strut assembly is out of the car, the spring is under enough compression to give it a pretty good launch if you undo the retaining nut at the end of the shock absorber piston rod without first compressing and restraining the spring.

Carburetor cleaner, brake parts cleaner, hot tank solutions and many other solvents found around cars should be kept off your bare skin. Otherwise, they will soak in through the skin and attack your central nervous system. This is not something you notice right away, but over a period of years it all adds up. Once it gets into your body, it does not leave. These solutions are also not kind to paint, so avoid contact between these solvents and your car's finish.

Another toxic compound that can move in for keeps is asbestos. This is most often found in brake pads and clutch discs, and thus in brake dust and clutch dust. Do not blow asbestos dust around the shop with an air hose. If you are going to be working around asbestos dust a lot, invest in a box of inexpensive breathing filters, the kind that painters use.

Brake fluid is toxic too and can strip your car's finish right down to the metal.

If you find yourself facing a fastener that will not budge, be patient. Make sure that you will be in control of the wrench if it slips off the fastener (cracking your knuckle open is no fun). Spray some penetrating oil on the reluctant fastener, tap it with a small hammer to set up a vibration, and then try a slow, steady application of torque.

If you change your own oil, gear lube, antifreeze, or brake fluid, dispose of the waste liquid properly. Many garages and service stations recycle oil. *Never* dump waste oil on the ground, into a body of water, down the drain, into a storm drain, or anywhere else where it will not be recycled. The toxins in even a small amount of waste oil are enough to pollute thousands of gallons of otherwise pure water.

Two additional common chemicals should be handled with care: Freon and silicone spray. Freon 12 (dichlorodifluoromethane) is a mildly dangerous fluorocarbon even before you let it enter the air intake of a running motor. By the time it reaches the end of your

also a good idea to have a fire extinguisher available. Never wash parts in gasoline.

If you have to drain your fuel tank, store the gasoline safely in a sealed container. When you loosen a fuel line on a fuel-injected car, remember that the fuel can be under nearly 92 psi of pressure. It tends to spray out and can get in your face. Also, when spraying out under that much pressure, the fuel is atomized, making it *much* more susceptible to ignition.

Speaking of explosions, your battery is a potential bomb as well. Inside the case, the chemical action that stores electrical energy also makes hydrogen gas. Remember the *Hindenburg?* Same stuff.

When working on the car, disconnect the ground strap first. (This may be a hassle, but it is very important.) If you disconnect the positive terminal first and your wrench touches ground, you will create an arc that will do its best to ignite the hydrogen in and around the battery. It is also not a good idea to smoke around a battery, or check the electrolyte level with a match. Be especially cautious around batteries that are charging, or that have just finished charging; that is when they make the most gas. Those with anti-theft radios must have the radio code on hand before disconnecting the battery.

Two engines—one in front and one in back—power this Pike's Peak runner. Su Kemper

tailpipe it can turn into phosgene gas, a chemical warfare agent. Also, if you do get Freon into the intake, shut off the engine and get some air immediately. If you spray Freon on your skin you can get frostbite within a few seconds. Finally, if you hook up the recharging system to the air conditioner the wrong way, the bottle of Freon can explode. Wear safety goggles.

Silicone spray is not quite as dangerous, but it can be costly when misused around cars that have oxygen sensors. The silicone spray bonds with the sensing surface of the sensor probe, rendering it worthless. (Even though it is not silicone-based, antiseize compound can ruin a oxygen sensor too.)

Chassis Types

When this book first appeared, Volkswagen had one chassis for the Rabbit, Scirocco, and Jetta. Now there are more than four chassis types, although for the sake of this book we won't be dealing with the Dasher, Passat, and other vehicles that are commonly perceived as not being "sporty."

Volkswagen's designations for the chassis in which we're interested are: A1, A2, A3, and A4. Even though you know what car you have, you may need to know its chassis designation to understand what hot-rodding is possible. For more details on chassis types, see "Volkswagen Chassis Information."

Chapter 1

Bolt-on Engine Performance

A surprising boost in performance can be gained through the use of bolt-on components—parts that do not require taking the entire motor apart to install. Hot-rodding works in general because even modest gains in bolt-on horsepower seem so exciting. When your engine propels your car down the road with 70 horsepower, it is not only making enough horsepower to push the car, but also making whatever power is required to overcome the internal friction of the engine, drivetrain losses, air resistance, and all the other horsepower-robbing factors involved. In fact, a substantial fraction of the total engine output can be absorbed by frictional losses, leaving less horsepower to push your car down the road. If you add even 10 horsepower through bolt-ons, none of this has to go toward frictional losses, because those are already taken care of by the existing engine output. Therefore, all the horsepower you add through hot-rodding is available for performance.

It is also surprising how much money you can waste on parts that do not do a bit of good. One way to avoid wasting money is to have a plan for what you ultimately want to do with your car. Another is to use only parts that have proven their worth, either on the dyno or on the track.

The term *bolt-on* also implies that you do not have to be an engineer to install the part. Most people can tackle the installation of a "recurved" distributor, a camshaft, adjustable cam sprocket, a larger throttle body, or an exhaust system. Most suspension pieces also fall into the bolt-on category.

Some consider a reworked head to be a bolt-on item because you can unbolt the stock unit and bolt on the high-performance unit. However, most people consider a head swap to be more than a bolt-on upgrade, for price and other reasons. If price is not a consideration, but lack of mechanical ability is, check out the "bolt-on" blowers for VR6 and 2.0-liter 8V engines in "Superchargers."

For now, consider some of the quick and simple things you can do to improve the performance of your engine, usually in just a few hours. These "bolt-ons" should be done in the order listed below.

Tune-ups

Yes, the lowly tune-up. A tune-up not only optimizes the performance of your car as it sits, but it also puts you in touch with the basics. Without getting the basics right you are wasting your money on high-performance parts. An all-too-common example of this can be seen in the case of a car that runs poorly and the fuel

This all-out motor has twin camshafts, mechanical fuel injection, combination dry sump and fuel pumps (lower left), crank-fired magneto trigger (bottom), and block-off plate for the intermediate shaft hole.

injection is the suspect. Because fuel injection seems complex and mysterious, and because it can be difficult to troubleshoot, it seems easier to replace parts that *may* be bad, based on guess-work. With the new parts, however, the engine runs as poorly as ever, because the original problem was not related to the fuel injection.

It is disheartening to realize that you have thrown away some perfectly good (and sometimes expensive) parts, spent good money on replacement parts that didn't need to be replaced, and you still need to come up with enough money to fix the original problem. You must understand the basics before you charge off into the great unknown world of high performance, and unless the engine is in an optimal state of tune, it can be difficult if not impossible to troubleshoot problems that come up.

In addition to setting the timing (including points, if you have them), adjusting the valves on the early cars, installing new spark plugs and replacing all filters, do not forget to check the distributor cap, distributor rotor, and plug wires and replace them if necessary. Plug wires get old and start "leaking" current, so the spark plugs see only a fraction of the energy from your coil. Stock plug wires work great in just about all applications. The so-called high-performance wires can help a little, but they are not strictly necessary. Also check the air sensor plate height, and center and adjust it if necessary before setting the mixture on CIS cars. Tune-up and adjustment procedures can all be found in the shop manual for your car.

A simple engine dyno for testing the engine before installation.

A typical chassis dyno for testing the engine in the car. Load is applied to the road wheels through rollers.

Every 10,000 miles, you should seriously consider adding a can of Lubro Moly Jectron and a can of Lubro Moly Ventil Sauber to the gas tank. Jectron cleans the inside passages of the fuel injection, and the Ventil Sauber cleans the fuel deposits from the backs of the valves, so your engine can breathe as freely as possible. Because these treatments can remove a lot of contaminants from the inside of your engine, it is best to use them shortly before you are going to be changing your oil and filter anyway, as a lot of the dirt they break loose winds up in the oil.

Exhausts

Depending on the year of the car and how much of the exhaust system you are willing to replace, you can find between 5 and 15 horsepower with a free-flow exhaust. For this reason, and because a high-performance camshaft will show little gain without improving the exhaust, the exhaust is high on the list.

For years it was argued that on some 1983-and-later cars, replacing the catalytic converter with a straight pipe would cause a *loss* of horsepower. Subsequent tests have shown this *not* to be the case, but removing or disabling the converter is a bad idea anyway. Not only does the converter help reduce pollution, but removal is illegal in many states. The 1983 and 1984 GTis do have an incredibly restrictive header, however, and replacing it is a big step in the right direction.

On all cars with catalytic converters, if you remove the converter for racing purposes, you may have to replace it with a resonator pipe to return the exhaust system to the state of tune at which it will work best. If your state conducts visual smog equipment inspection or a catalytic converter test, there is no resonator pipe that looks enough like a catalytic converter to pass.

There are several types of exhaust systems for you to consider. The various offerings are discussed in "Exhaust systems," as are some installation tips.

"Recurved" Distributors

The following applies only to cars without knock sensors—more about those later. In the olden days, hot-rodders would "recurve" mechanical-advance distributors to bring in more advance sooner—which brings in more horsepower as well—as long as you don't exceed the maximum amount of advance that the engine can tolerate. The recurving process is somewhat time-consuming and requires a distributor testing machine, which few shops still have. As a result, the fine art of distributor recurving is disappearing fast. Now, aftermarket performance shops sell "European curved" distributors that are actually factory-built distributors with the specs you would aim for if you were recurving a stock distributor for more performance.

Don't be surprised if you run across someone who claims that a recurved distributor is a waste of money. He may have dyno tested a recurved distributor and found that it makes no additional horsepower. This does not mean you should not consider a recurved distributor. For years, the methodology of dyno testing was not well suited to showing what a recurved distributor does. Where the recurved distributor will help is under partial-load conditions, as opposed to the maximum-load conditions typically encountered on the dyno. This will give you a seat-of-the-pants difference, and one that can be measured with a stopwatch, but not one that can be detected on the average dyno.

Both breaker and breakerless distributors can be recurved. The installation procedure can be found in "Electrical Systems."

Engine Management System Chips

In the olden days of carburetors, fuel injection seemed troublesome and difficult to tune, to those who had grown up tinkering with carburetors. As fuel injection took over, carburetors began to look troublesome and difficult to tune to those accustomed to dealing with fuel injection systems, which steadily became more reliable. This increase in reliability came in spite of their growing complexity, which was the automobile

Speed at the end of the 1/4 mile	Weight in pounds					
	1900	**2000**	**2100**	**2200**	**2300**	**2400**
80	89	94	99	104	109	114
85	105	113	118	124	130	136
90	108	134	140	146	152	158
95	149	157	165	173	181	189
100	172	182	191	201	210	220
105	204	215	226	237	248	259
110	238	250	263	276	288	300
	Horsepower needed to attain 1/4-mile speed					

Table 1: Horsepower needed to attain 1/4-mile speed

Horsepower needed to attain 1/4-mile speed. Lighter cars perform better, but removing weight from the car can be more difficult than adding horsepower.

The results of two nearly identical engines run on two different engine dynos. One dyno operator failed to correct for environmental factors.

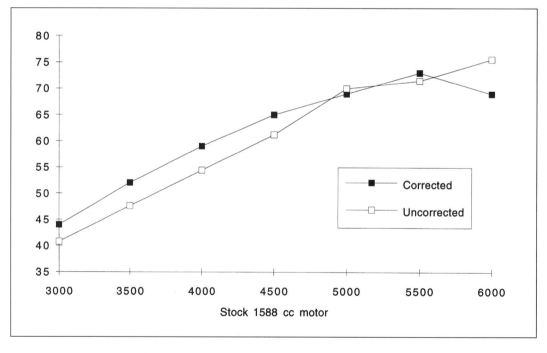

Stock 1588 cc motor

manufacturers' only way to cope with more restrictive emissions standards and consumer demands for better performance without sacrificing mileage.

Now fuel injection is just a subsystem of the all-encompassing, computer-controlled, engine management systems on modern cars. Ironically, although the average do-it-yourselfer would be completely at a loss about how to modify such a system, virtually anyone can replace the chip in the engine management computer with one provided by expert "tuners," and instantly gain more performance. If your car has an engine management system chip, you will be amazed how easy it is to completely change the personality of your engine's performance.

If you have a G-60 engine, chips are available that allow you to run more boost (by running a smaller pulley) and a more aggressive camshaft. Depending on your combination, this can give you more horsepower than a stock VR6 with no additional weight.

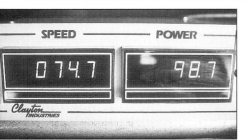

The read-out on a chassis dyno showing miles per hour and horsepower. It is up to the operator to calculate torque, engine rpm, and compensate for environmental factors.

The hows and whys of these electronic marvels are discussed in "Engine Management Chips."

Mild Cam and Valve Springs

For the sake of this discussion, a *mild camshaft* is defined as a camshaft for which it is not necessary to change the valve springs. Everybody has a different opinion on how big a camshaft the stock valve springs will tolerate, but most people agree that the stock springs are not good for much over 0.425 inch of lift. Once you get up to 0.430 inch of lift, you might run out of room.

The problem is that the stock springs vary widely in terms of how soon they go into coil bind (when the coils of the valve spring touch each other, prohibiting further compression). If you have valve springs that will not allow a high-lift camshaft, you must replace the valve springs to avoid broken springs or a ruined camshaft. Replacing the valve springs is also a bolt-on operation, but it requires some special tools, a little talent, and patience.

If you decide you do not care to chance running a bigger cam without at least first checking your stock valve springs, read the section on valve springs in "Valve Train" before you order that set of ultratrick springs for your street motor. Staying with nothing more than a mild camshaft, you can expect roughly an additional 5 horsepower over the gains possible with an exhaust system. Because of the interaction between these two items, do not install a camshaft without a free-flow exhaust.

Adjustable Cam Sprockets

An adjustable cam sprocket allows you to vary the overall timing of the camshaft relative to the rotation of the crankshaft, and is a perfect example of compromise in high performance. By advancing the camshaft, you move the torque peak lower in the rpm range; by retarding the camshaft, you move the torque peak higher in the rpm range. You get about the same amount of horsepower, but the adjustable cam sprocket allows you to move it around: When you advance the camshaft, you will show a gain of 4 or 5 horsepower up to 4,500 rpm (with a matching loss at the high end), and 5 horsepower or more from 4,000 to 6,500 rpm in the retard position (with a corresponding loss on the low end).

In spite of the big horsepower numbers that are casually talked about on cars that need to be wound out to 8,500 rpm to work, most people find that they drive their cars under 4,500 rpm most of the time. Therefore, advancing the camshaft would provide a better feel and driveability around town.

Adjustable cam sprockets won't work on the A4 four-cylinder engines because the camshaft position sensor (CMP),

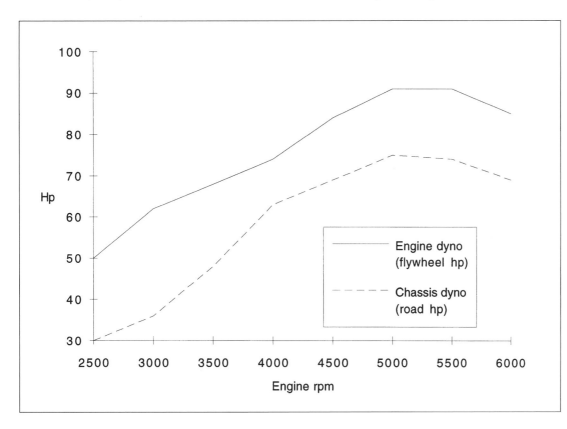

Differences are even greater when comparing engine dynos with chassis dynos. Because of power losses through the transmission, the drivetrain, and tire slip, the chassis dyno will always read lower.

The control panel of an engine dyno.

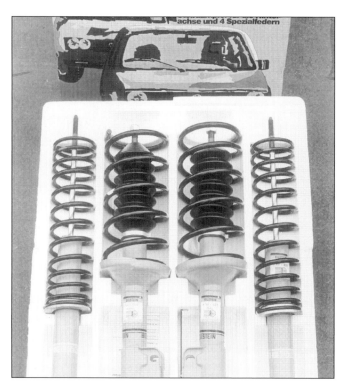

A matched kit of lower, sportier springs, with shocks to match.

which sets the timing for the fuel injection and ignition, is mounted to the back of the stock sprocket.

Installation and setup of camshafts, valve springs, and adjustable cam sprockets are discussed starting at "Installing an Adjustable Cam Sprocket."

Throttle Bodies

Installing a monster throttle body is one of the last things you need to do, even if you have an early car with the restrictor venturi that creates the vacuum needed by the EGR (exhaust gas recirculation) system to work properly. Up through the

1992 model year, the intake manifold was more restrictive than the throttle body. This makes a ported-out throttle body one of the last bolt-on pieces to buy, after you have freed up the rest of your engine's breathing. Even then you will find that a bigger throttle body works best on large, modified motors.

A more complete discussion can be found in "Throttle Bodies."

Supercharger

While a turbocharger isn't exactly a bolt-on item, a supercharger can be. Unfortunately, Autotech SportTuning no longer markets its slick supercharger for the four-cylinder engines, but if you have a VR6, or 2.0-liter four, you could be only 12 hours away from an additional 100 horsepower.

Carburetors

Should you install a set of trick carburetors on your car? Yes and no. Yes if you have a 1975 or 1976 Volkswagen with the stock carburetors. They are difficult to live with and should be replaced early in the hot-rodding process.

No, if you have fuel injection. Volkswagen fuel injection is incredibly nice. Not only is the driveability of the stock fuel injection better than that of a carburetor, but it will automatically compensate for lots of engine modifications without a squeak of protest. If you have injection on your car, hang onto it.

Unplugging the Oxygen Sensor

The Lambda sensor is viewed with suspicion by some, but unless you have gotten your engine so far out of adjustment that it barely runs anyway, the Lambda sensor is a great watchdog that makes sure your motor is getting the right amount of fuel under any given load and rpm. If you unplug it, you will lose horsepower and mileage.

The only reason you should ever defeat the Lambda sensor is if you need to run leaded gas, at which time you must remove it and the catalytic converter to avoid damaging those components.

Breakerless Ignition

If your distributor has points, consider a breakerless ignition. Breakerless ignitions can deliver a hotter spark than points can, and you have to adjust them only once. Although in some cases you can find more horsepower with a breakerless ignition, in reality a breakerless ignition gives more horsepower than a points ignition only because of its consistent timing. As points wear, the timing will change, and you will lose horsepower gradually. With a breakerless ignition there is no wear and no timing change, so your ignition always runs at peak performance.

One other benefit for those of you with older cars lies is that, if you do have a problem with your engine, such as high oil consumption or poorly set up carburetors, the plugs won't foul as quickly, so you won't have to change the plugs three or four times while diagnosing the problem.

There are a couple of good units on the market, including the Crane (formerly Allison) and the Perlux. Installation procedures can be found in "Ignitions."

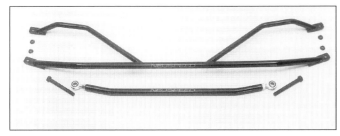

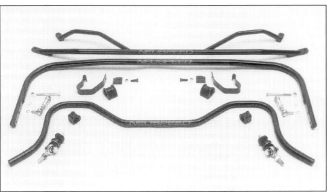

Upper and lower front stress bars for an A1 chassis.

Coils

Coils make only a very slight difference in the way the car performs, and they almost never go bad. The stock coil is fine for most high-performance applications.

"Limited-slip" Differential

Unfortunately, it's not possible to "bolt-on" a true limited-slip differential, unless you happen to be a transaxle expert, but if you're on a budget and want a little help in the traction department, check out the GTi "Minislip."

Driving School

For most of us, this should be the first performance upgrade. You don't need to spend a bundle, either. The basics can all be learned at a kart racing school. Explore the others as your budget allows.

Upper front stress bar, with beefier front and rear antiroll bars for an A2 chassis.

Each modification interacts with the stock parts and with other modifications. If you plan ahead, these interactions will work to your benefit.

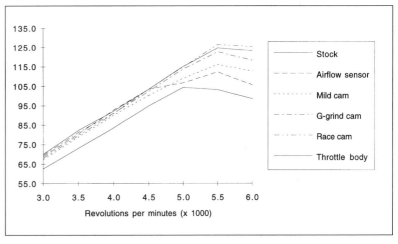

Some add-ons do boost horsepower, but make certain that new horsepower is where you can use it.

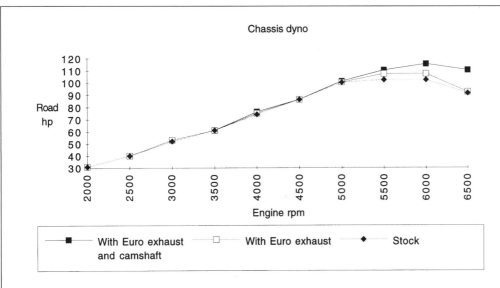

Chapter 2

Engine Swaps

Perhaps the ultimate bolt-on is a completely new engine. In the early days, there weren't many different engines to swap, so hot-rodders built up what they had, even if it meant boring the block, buying a new (and often expensive) crankshaft, with new pistons, head work, and all the extras. For the extreme enthusiast, aftermarket turbocharging was the ultimate way to go.

Now, because of a high degree of commonality among Volkswagen chassis, engines, transaxles, and other components, aftermarket suppliers have developed a lot of the components necessary to make it easier to swap in a newer, higher-performance engine, of which there are many.

Among the benefits of swapping for a more modern, higher-output Volkswagen engine, as opposed to building up your existing engine, are reliability and driveability. Reliability, because the higher-output newer engine will be less stressed than an earlier motor that has been built up. Driveability, because modern engine management computers monitor and control a great many aspects of engine performance, and the stock engines will not have the same "peaky" torque curve that an early engine would require to achieve the same output.

Of course, you have the option of building up a late-model engine before or after the swap for even more power.

Considerations

When rebuilding or building up your existing engine, you will usually have someone else doing any needed machine work, if only because most of us lack the necessary machine tools. If necessary, you can send your parts out and do something else while awaiting their return.

Engine swaps often require fabrication and innovation, and they have to happen on the spot. You can have your entire car towed or freighted somewhere if you get into trouble, but this runs into some real money.

Despite the similarities among cars, there is a wealth of small but crucial changes that must be addressed in virtually any engine swap. Some cars have the fuel injection on the left, some on the right. Different fuel injections have different wiring harnesses, and you can't just cut off the "extra" wires that your old engine didn't use. CV joints and axles changed in time with increases in engine output. Anything with an intercooler is going to demand a lot of extra installation work. Turbos put out a lot of heat, which means other components in the neighborhood must be shielded somehow. Early cars with carbure-

The 1987 VW GTi 16V.

Table 2: Chassis reference chart	
Chassis	**Volkswagen model**
A1	Rabbit, Rabbit Pick Up, Rabbit Convertible, Cabriolet, GTI, Jetta I, Scirocco
A2	Golf, Golf GTI, Golf GT, Jetta II, Jetta GLI, Jetta GLI 16V, Jetta Carat, Corrado G-60, Corrado VR6
A3	Golf III, Jetta III, GTI VR6, Jetta GLX, Cabrio
A4	New Beetle, Golf 4, Jetta 4
B1	Dasher
B2	Quantum
B3	Passat to 1997
B4	1998-on Passat from 1998 (Audi-based)

Engine swaps within the same chassis type are easiest, but swaps from newer cars are more exciting.

tors won't have the fuel tank, fuel lines, fuel pump, and fuel filter needed by fuel-injected engines (diesel cars will need different fuel system components too). And don't forget that if you increase engine output, you should increase brakes and suspension to match.

While brakes and suspension are relatively easy (if not cheap) to upgrade, one nontrivial aspect to dumping additional power (and weight, in the case of the VR6) into an early chassis is that of chassis strength. As can be seen in "Volkswagen Chassis Information," each chassis revision has seen an improvement in chassis stiffness and strength. By comparison, the A1 chassis is flexible and, in stock form, not suited to accept

The 1987 VW Scirocco 16V. Note that its fuel distributor is in the "old" location, unlike the GTi version. Pay attention to differences such as this when swapping engines.

an additional 100 horsepower and 100 extra pounds over the front axle, which is what is involved in a VR6 swap.

If you are swapping engines in a car you will be racing, be absolutely certain that the rules allow the swap. Read the rule book, and find out who in your class of racing makes the final determination. Tell that person exactly what you are doing, and make sure you are interpreting the rules correctly. If you err here, you could easily be bumped into a class in which you have no chance of winning, even with your new engine.

One final consideration is that you may be required to pass an emissions test. California is one of the strictest states in this regard, and it seems to be setting the example for other states. If your state doesn't have emissions testing now, if and when it does, it has a good chance of following the California model.

Boiled down to its essence, the law is that, in the case of an engine swap, the car must pass the emissions test of the newest component. Therefore, if you swap a 1998 engine into a 1977 chassis, the result must pass 1998 standards, which are much stricter than those of 1977. On the other hand, if you install a 1977 engine into a New Beetle for reasons of your own, the car still must meet 1998 emissions standards, which it would not do. This effectively eliminates most swaps that involve older engines in newer chassis.

It also means that if you perform an engine swap, you must retain all the emissions control equipment that came with the original engine. With the sophistication of the modern engines, this is nowhere near as onerous a requirement as it once was, and in fact the engines run best with all the sensors, computers, and other bits and pieces connected and working. This includes swaps of gasoline engines into diesel chassis.

One snag you might run into is that if you swap a VR6 into an early A2 Golf, for example, there is no test procedure for an early Golf with a six-cylinder engine. In cases such as this, you will be sent to a referee station, where they will evaluate your car, and if it meets the standards set for (in this case) the engine, they will issue you a waiver, which means that henceforth your car will be tested as if it were the car from which your VR6 originally came.

Choices

Although there are a lot of factors to consider in choosing an engine for a swap, including cost, the basic rules seem to be:

- Every A1 should have a 16V.
- Every A2 should have a VR6.

VW supplies engines for a lot of different manufacturers, and sometimes there are subtle differences. Chrysler's longitudinal mounting necessitated a slightly different pilot shaft bearing (right) compared with the VW crank on the left.

Is the new turbocharged five-valve 1.8-liter engine the wave of the future? Many tuners think it is.

• Every A3 should have a chipped 1AT (Volkswagen's new turbocharged 1.8-liter five-valve engine).

A complete breakdown of engine types and chassis assignments can be found starting at "Volkswagen Engine Information." Here is a quick summary:

Chassis	Volkswagen Model
A1	Rabbit, Rabbit Pick Up, Rabbit Convertible, Cabriolet, Rabbit GTi, Jetta I, Scirocco
A2	Golf, GTi, Golf GT, Jetta II, Jetta GLi, Jetta GLi 16V, Jetta Carat, Corrado G-60, Corrado VR6
A3	Golf III, Jetta III, GTi VR6, Jetta GLX, Cabrio
A4	New Beetle, Golf 4, Jetta 4
B1	Dasher
B2	Quantum
B3	Passat to 1997
B4	1998-on Passat from 1998 (Audi-based)

Engine swaps among cars that share the same chassis will be easiest, whether they are replacements or upgrades. For example, if you have an A2 Golf and want a VR6 engine, try to get one from a Corrado rather than from a Passat, whereas if you have an A3 Golf and want a VR6, you should get one from a GTi or GLX, rather than a Corrado or Passat.

You also have to be careful swapping engines from a Rabbit, Golf, or Jetta into a Scirocco or Corrado, due to the much lower hood line and different radiator of the latter two models. Typically, of course, the Scirocco and Corrado have hot engines already, so owners of these cars won't often be swapping in an engine from something else.

Costs

The affordability of an engine swap is something only you can determine. The best way of looking at it is in terms of what else you can get for the same money. For example, just the parts for swapping a VR6 engine into your four-cylinder A2 Golf is going to be more money than a supercharger kit, and the installation on the supercharger kit is typically less involved than an engine swap. If you're not sure about supercharging, cylinder head work, cams, manifold porting, and other go-fast mods are going to run about the same amount as a supercharger, which is still less than a VR6 swap. This doesn't mean you should never do a VR6 swap, just that you should look at all the options you have for the money you are spending.

A1 Swaps

A1 cars have the lightest weight chassis, so dropping more power into the engine compartment results in a big difference. Unfortunately, that engine compartment is smaller than the later-model cars, and the chassis have the most flex (and the smallest brakes, and so on.)

Your best performance trade-up is the 1.8-liter 16V engine from a late model Scirocco, rather than from an A2 GTi 16V or Passat 16V. (The 2.0-liter 16V engine is more work, and the 1.8-liter 16V is fine in the lighter car.) Next best is the 90-horsepower 1.8-liter GTi engine. If you want a newer engine with only a little more complexity on installation, an 8V engine from an A2 will fit if you use the A1 exhaust manifold.

The A3 "tall block" engine is about the same, again with an A1 exhaust manifold, with the addition of a longer downpipe to match the extra height of the block. The downpipe is available from Techtonics.

The Corrado G-60 engine is not recommended unless you are an ace fabricator. All U.S. G-60s came with air conditioning, which necessitates chassis surgery, and then you have to install the intercooler.

Also not recommended is the VR6, which in addition to 100 more pounds than the stock four-cylinder engine, adds much more complexity to the installation. Fabricating the motor mounts alone is torture. Few A1s are going to be worth the amount you will have to spend to get a VR6, and don't forget you will have to upgrade the suspension and brakes at the very least to get the package to work right. From a financial point of view, you are better off starting with a later model car.

If you want a late-model motor but love the early CIS, with its simplicity and flexibility, you can have the best of both worlds, assuming you are swapping in a 1992-or-earlier 1.8-liter engine from an A2. One problem you will run into is that the 1.8-liter engine has the crankcase breather mounted on the left side of the engine (facing front in the Volkswagen) where the CIS warm-up regulator is supposed to go. To get around this, you must remove the breather and use your original valve cover. Techtonics offers a kit that allows you to mount the warm-up regulator where the breather used to go (that is, where the warm-up regulator is supposed to be).

A2 Swaps

Compared to the A1, the A2 is a much better recipient of an engine swap, not only because of the larger engine compartment, but also because Volkswagen has used a wide variety of engines in this chassis. Even so, swapping the G-60 into anything except a Corrado G-60 is going to be more difficult because of the extra plumbing. Still, that leaves the 8V, 16V, and VR6.

An A2 16V swap is going to be easiest if your A2 car has the CIS-E injection, rather than the Digifant. If the VR6 is on your list, you will save yourself a lot of aggravation if you get the engine, transaxle, and other parts from a Corrado, as the wiring matches up well. The VR6 change, though, also requires modification of the shift linkage (to switch from conventional linkage to the cable shifter), and the installation of a hydraulic clutch.

The trick setup for swapping a G-60 engine into a Golf or Jetta II is to obtain the Euro-style intercooler assembly. The G-60 appeared only in the Corrado in the United States, but it was an option in the European Golf.

There is another possibility for a "half swap," involving the block from a 2.0-liter A3, and the cylinder head from a 1.8-liter. This combination gives you more horsepower, and allows you to use the earlier ignition and fuel injection, with which you can make more power than with a built A3 and Motronic. This "half swap" will not be legal in any state with pollution control laws, because the older engine almost certainly will not meet the more modern standards mandated for the A3.

A3 Swaps

Because of their relative newness, A3 models are more likely to provide an engine than receive one, although predictions are that the 1AT engine will change that. Even the standard 115-horsepower, four-cylinder, 2.0-liter engine is a strong performer. The new, shorter 2.0-liter four-cylinder from the New Beetle and A4 is also rated at 115 horsepower, making a swap senseless from a performance standpoint. On the other hand, those with the four-cylinder are justified in considering the VR6 engine for a swap. Who wouldn't want a VR6-powered Cabriolet, for instance?

As mentioned elsewhere, this may all change when the turbocharged 150-horsepower, five-valve, four-cylinder 1AT engine arrives in quantity. (A version of this engine with a larger turbocharger and higher boost is said to put out 180 horsepower for the upcoming Audi TT, and Audi is working on a future version with sequential intercoolers and still more boost that is good for 225 horsepower.) The first to try this will no doubt be those for whom the promise of up to 400 streetable horsepower is too much to resist. Even those who stop at the more realistic 200 horsepower level (easily achievable with a chip and free-flow air filter) will be attracted by the thought of having more horsepower on tap than in a stock VR6, with better fuel economy and lower weight.

On the other hand, a stock VR6 engine with a supercharger easily puts out more than 250 horsepower. Another way of saying this is that at 250 horsepower, the VR6 engine is under a lot less stress than a 1AT engine putting out that same amount of horsepower. All things being equal, this should mean that the more lightly stressed VR6 should last a lot longer than the more highly stressed 1AT engine, horsepower for horsepower. Peaky turbo engines can be thrilling to drive, but for day-in, day-out satisfaction it's difficult to beat a big, torquey, understressed engine like a VR6.

As with A2 swaps, the most difficult part of installing a VR6 will be modifying the shift linkage and installing a hydraulic clutch. It remains to be seen what the 1AT engine will cost, and how much work it will take to get the turbo plumbing installed. The move by Volkswagen to standardize wiring harnesses among cars with different powerplants will no doubt greatly ease changing over the wiring.

Diesel Swaps

There are actually two different types of diesel engine swap: One with a newer diesel engine, and the other that involves converting to a gasoline engine.

When the Rabbit diesel first came out, as noisy and slow as it was, it got great mileage and diesel fuel was less expensive than regular gasoline. Now, diesel fuel costs more than gasoline, and diesels are still noisy and slow. They do get good mileage, however, and if you put a lot of long-distance miles on your car, you may have grown to appreciate their workhouse nature.

The most straightforward swap is to install a new 1.9-liter diesel in place of the 1.5- or 1.6-liter diesel. The increase in horsepower brings an increase in power and torque (the stroke is longer in the 1.9-liter). There is also a 1.6-liter turbo diesel, but they are rare (meaning expensive) and difficult to install because of the extra turbo parts. Perhaps the ultimate diesel engine is the TDI, with even more horsepower and computer control that delivers incredible driveability and fuel economy. With 90 horsepower, which can be chipped to 110, and almost the same torque as a VR6, this engine will make even nonbelievers rethink their bias against diesel engines.

For those wishing to swap in a gasoline engine, see the appropriate section above for guidance. As previously mentioned, however, you will need to replace the fuel tank, the fuel lines, the fuel filter, add a fuel pump (and the wiring harness to run it), and swap the exhaust for one with a catalytic converter. Bear in mind that if you do swap in a gasoline engine, your car will then fall under whatever emissions standards exist in your state, whereas emissions standards for diesels are not yet in place. If you swap in a modern engine and do the job the right way, though, you won't have a problem passing a smog test.

Audi Engines

Four-cylinder Audi engines are similar to Volkswagen engines, and often Audi engines receive "trick" parts a year or two before their Volkswagen counterparts. Even so, you are better off starting with a Volkswagen engine because Audi engines are mounted longitudinally (with the crankshaft pointing in the same direction as the front of the car), while Volkswagen engines are mounted transversely (sideways). This means that virtually all intake parts will have to be replaced. Some Audi engines also have cylinder heads that will not work in the Volkswagen engine bay, which means a cylinder head change too. You can use your existing transaxle, but if you have a four-speed, you are going to want to upgrade to a five-speed with the new engine, and even if you have a five-speed, you may want to upgrade the transaxle to get different gear ratios.

None of the five-cylinder Audi engines will fit into the A-chassis Volkswagens without major surgery, if even then. The upcoming five-cylinder Volkswagen engine is a "V-5," meaning it is similar to the narrow-angle VR6 with one cylinder missing, unlike the in-line five-cylinder Audi engines, which are longer and require more space in the engine bay.

Preparation

The engine connects to the rest of the car through six main interfaces: the motor mounts and transaxle, the wiring harness (electrical), the cooling system (which in some cars includes an oil cooler), the fuel system, the exhaust, and the linkages (predominantly the shift linkage).

Although the best preparation for an engine swap is to be ready for anything, here are some more specific points to consider:

If possible, get the entire car from which you will be getting the engine. That way, you should have just about every part you need, no matter how unusual or unexpected. Otherwise, your entire swap could be held up on account of a single part that dealers don't stock because they never go bad.

If you cannot get the entire car, deal with an aftermarket supplier who knows in advance what you will need to complete your swap. As bad as it can be to get stuck part-way through a project of this scope, it can be just as bad to get close enough to completion that you can get your car running by butchering it in some fashion. This is an excellent way to destroy the resale value of your car.

Have the shop manuals for both your car *and* for the car from which you are getting the engine.

Do not cut any of the harnesses, or accept a cut harness as part of a engine swap package.

Mark all connections as you take them apart on both cars, and make diagrams if necessary to keep track of what goes where.

If you have doubts about your ability to complete the job, arrange in advance with someone who does know to provide answers to the questions that inevitably come up.

Do numerous trial-fits to ensure that everything is going to work properly. This means repeatedly putting the new engine into the car and removing it again until you have everything right.

One of the worst ways to get into an engine swap is to back into it. This usually happens when you come across an orphaned engine, and suddenly you start thinking about installing this engine into your A1 or A2. For example, you find a Passat or Eurovan VR6 engine with the automatic transaxle still attached for sale for 100 bucks. Not only is it going to be

The new Golf
Engine mounts

A2 front suspension and subframe.

more difficult to mount this engine in the engine bay because of subframe and engine mount differences, but after you remove the automatic transaxle you are going to need to buy a manual transaxle and all the parts needed to get it working in your car, and you still need to think about cooling and fuel delivery.

Engine swaps can run into some serious money even when they go right. Any unexpected additional parts you have to buy can really drive up the final tab. Be prepared to spend a lot of money for the small parts if you don't get everything you need from the donor car. Even if you buy a wrecked car, some of the parts you get may be damaged.

Engine Mounts

All four-cylinder motors mounts are close enough that swapping among them is not a problem. This commonality does not extend to the VR6, however.

When putting a Corrado VR6 into an A2 Golf or Jetta, use the subframe that came with the engine, which will bolt right in. The Corrado VR6 subframe is slightly different from other VR6 subframes in that the engine rides a little lower for better hood clearance. Putting a VR6 into a four-cylinder A3 involves cutting down an A3 subframe to gain the necessary hood clearance. The G-60 uses a normal A2 subframe.

As this is written, the new-style "pendulum" motor mounts from the A4 were so new that no one had yet experimented with them. As before, however, A4 cars are more likely to be on the donating end of an engine swap than on the receiving end, so the A2 or A3 mounts should work with A4 engines.

Transaxles

The simplest path is to use your existing transaxle, if it will handle the power. Any 8V transaxle should handle the power of any 8V or 16V, but the gear ratios will not necessarily enable you to get the most from your new engine. (For more on this, see "Gear Ratios and Shift Points.")

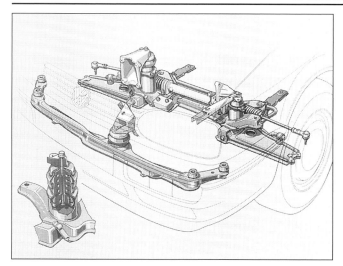

A3 front suspension and subframe.

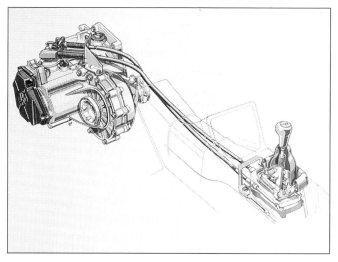

VW cable shifter.

You will almost always get a better match if you use the transaxle that came with the engine you are installing, and as a bonus, you get a newer transaxle, too.

The choice exists only with four-cylinder swaps; the G-60 and VR6 demand their own transaxle, shift linkage, and hydraulic clutch.

The Automatic Question

If you are going to the trouble to swap in a more powerful engine, chances are that you are not going to want a power-robbing automatic transaxle to go with it. If you are looking for a VR6, though, you should be aware that some of them—such as those in the Passat—came with automatic transaxles. When swapping to a VR6, you need a VR6 transaxle, which in the case of an engine from an automatic-equipped car, means buying a transaxle separately, along with all the parts to make it work: flywheel, clutch assembly, pedal assembly, cable shifter assembly, starter, and possibly a throttle body. These and other small parts can cost a surprising amount, which—once again—is why the recommendation is to get a donor car (or engine assembly) as close as possible to what you want.

Constant Velocity Joints and Axles

On the four-cylinder cars with 020 transaxles (that is, everything except the A4s), CV joint size is an important issue. Early A1 transaxles have 90-millimeter output flanges. Output flange size increased to 100-millimeter with the introduction of the 1984 1/2 and up Scirocco, the Scirocco 16V, and the 1985 GTi and Cabriolet. By 1987 the 100-millimeter output flanges were standard equipment.

If your car has 90-millimeter CV joints and you install an engine (and transaxle) with 100-millimeter output shafts, you have three options.

First, you can upgrade to axles with 100-millimeter CV joints. The catch is that A1 steering knuckles have only enough clearance for the 90-millimeter outer CV joint. To switch to 100-millimeter axles you must increase the clearance with a die grinder as needed.

Second, you can switch the output flanges from your early transaxle to the new transaxle. The flanges must be in good shape, of course, which means they have to fit tightly without wobble, and have no appreciable wear in the seal area.

Third, you can make custom axles with 100-millimeter CV joints on the inner ends, leaving the 90-millimeter CV joints on the outer ends. In most street applications, the 90-millimeter CV joints will do fine, but the harder you accelerate, the stronger the argument for 100-millimeter CV joints.

No matter which option you choose, you should check (and replace if necessary) the transaxle output flange seals while everything is out, and you should repack the CV joints. Velocity sells the special tool you need to install the seals. This is also an excellent time to check the clutch assembly, and replace it if necessary. All these jobs are a lot easier when the engine is still out, and you can easily get to everything.

Electrical

The early A1 cars are pretty straightforward in the wiring department, even with the CIS fuel injection. As the fuel injections merged with electronic ignition systems to become engine management systems, the wiring has become more complex, and less tolerant.

A1 cars have different wiring, depending on whether they were built in Germany, or in either the United States or Mexico. If you are doing the transplant on your own, label everything, and have the shop manual available for both your car and the car from which the new engine is coming. If you buy an engine from a place such as Bug World, you should consider buying the optional wiring harness for your swap.

In 1990, Volkswagen switched to a more modular wiring system worldwide. Called Central Electric II, it enabled Volkswagen to produce different models on the same assembly line. While it probably isn't what Volkswagen had in mind, it also facilitates engine swaps among cars with Central Electric II. The connectors are coded for easy identification.

The A4 literature refers to Central Electric features, as well as Controller Area Network Bus (CAN-Bus) electronics, which should also make it easier to perform engine swaps.

Cooling System

When installing a larger engine into an earlier car, you can preempt cooling problems by installing the radiator that goes with the new engine. This also helps eliminate problems in finding hoses to reconnect the engine to the radiator. This is especially important when swapping in a VR6 engine.

Fuel System

Generally speaking, the fuel system is easiest to deal with when putting a four-cylinder engine into a car that originally had a four-cylinder. A3 engines swapped into A2 cars follow this rule well, but A1 cars can be different, as the fuel distributor on some of the early cars is on the left side of the engine bay, rather than the right side.

This poses a difficult problem because the fuel lines are what are known as "hard lines," that is, they are not flexible. In order to make the swap work, you may have to bend and move the lines to their new positions. The key here is to take your time. One false move and you can crimp the line, which could necessitate replacing the line completely. Professionals bend lines such as these by inserting a coil spring inside the line to keep it from collapsing, while using special tools known as mandrels to bend the line. If you have these tools, your job will be easier, but it is possible to bend the lines without them.

As to the question of where you should move the lines, you can always look at the car from which you are getting your engine to see where the factory runs them. In the end, however, you will probably have to improvise somewhat.

When installing a VR6 into a four-cylinder car, the hot tip is to use the fuel tank and lines from the VR6 car.

Exhaust

If your engine swap involves similar engines, the exhaust won't be too big of a problem. For others, the easiest way to handle the difference in exhaust systems is to use one of the "adaptor" exhausts available, such as those from Techtonics. Their 16V adaptor exhaust for the A1 cars, and VR6 adaptor exhaust for the A2 cars, compensate for differences in height and flow between the new engine and the exhaust that came with the original chassis.

Linkages

The big change in linkages comes with G-60 or VR6 swaps, as the transaxle that comes with these engines is shifted by cable (rather than by a more traditional linkage of rods), and the clutch is hydraulically actuated. To install the cable shifter you remove the old shift lever, shift rods, and linkage and replace them with their cable-shifting analogs.

The mount for the hydraulic clutch master cylinder must be welded in, and you will have to run the plumbing from the master cylinder to the slave cylinder on the bell housing. Bleeding the clutch system is similar to bleeding the brakes.

Chapter 3

Engine Basics

For a lot of do-it-yourselfers, engine swaps present too many problems (aside from cost), so if you have good mechanical skills but aren't sure about your ability to customize existing parts, fabricate special pieces, or solve the myriad of challenges that arise in most engine swaps, then you either have to rebuild your existing engine or buy a direct replacement.

Replacement Engines

Exchanging your existing engine with a new, used, rebuilt, or modified engine based on the same block is about as simple as any project this size is going to be. As with an engine swap, label everything you disconnect, draw yourself diagrams to show where wires, lines, and hoses originally attached, and take out the old engine. As the saying goes, installation is the reverse of removal.

When you go shopping for a replacement engine, you will notice that many firms sell complete engines. Two terms commonly used in connection with these engines are *short-block* and *long-block*. A *short-block* is the block with a crank shaft, an intermediate shaft (in engines that have them), an oil pump, pistons, connecting rods, and all bearings. In other words, it will include everything below the cylinder head, with the possible exception of the oil pan. A *long-block* will have all of these items, plus the cylinder head (with valves, seats, springs, and so on), camshaft, and cam belt. If you are short on time, patience or mechanical ability, buying a short- or long-block is one way

A micrometer set, inside mikes and depth mikes can put a big dent in your budget, especially if you are only building one engine. Start off with some dial calipers and Plastigage and add more pieces as you need them.

of getting your car on the road with a minimum of fuss.

One of the best things about an engine exchange is that you can install a bored and stroked engine with the same ease as a stocker. Compared to an engine rebuild where you have to either do or arrange for all the machining (and make the decisions about what gets machined in the first place), this almost qualifies as bolt-on performance.

Table 5: Bore vs. Stroke

	Stock bore and stroke	Stock stroke with 1mm larger bore	Stock bore with 1mm larger stroke	Stock bore with realistic stroker crank
Bore	79.50	81.50	79.50	79.50
Stroke	86.40	86.40	87.40	90.50
Displacement	1715.53	1802.93	1735.38	1796.94

Bore versus stroke: Engine size goes up much faster as the bore is increased than when the stroke is increased.

Tools and Techniques
Cleanliness

If, on the other hand, you want to build your own engine, one of the most important things you can do is to keep everything clean. Not so the parts look clean at 20 feet, but really clean. The cleaner you keep everything during the assembly process, the longer your engine will last once you get it together. If your car is running, take it to the "quarter wash" and clean the outside before you break it down. If your car isn't running, buy a can of special-purpose cleanser from the auto parts store and hose down the engine and engine compartment before you start.

As you disassemble the engine, note the condition of bearings, cam lobes, seals, gaskets, rings, piston skirts, and all points of wear. If your engine is trying to send you a message, this is where you will find out what that message is.

Unless you work with engines to the point that you recognize all the internal parts on sight, it is a good idea to clean all parts as you remove them, and then bag and label them for later. This is especially important on a long-term project, where you know it is going to take you longer than a week to tear down and rebuild your engine.

In looking over the steps outlined here, especially the steps on cleanliness, you might feel overwhelmed by the details involved in building a high-performance engine. Keep in mind that the procedures mentioned are for a worst-case situation. In other words, you can usually get away without doing some of them. But the more you follow the recommendations, the better off you will be, especially if your previous motor died a horrible death or if you are planning on going all-out with the motor you are building. The more you pay attention to the details during the assembly process, the better chance your engine has for survival, especially in highly stressed applications.

Blueprinting

Two terms that are used a lot are balancing and blueprinting. *Balancing* is the process of making all reciprocating and rotating parts weigh the same so the engine will spin as smoothly as possible. *Blueprinting* refers to the process of measuring and machining the various engine components to match the "perfect" dimensions called for in the blueprint when the part was designed.

A leakdown test is the next step beyond the compression test, and it requires special equipment.

Blueprinting is necessary because not all parts are manufactured precisely as intended. When Paul and Karl Hacker bought a pair of Scirocco 16Vs for the Firestone Firehawk series, for example, a tear-down revealed that one of the rod journals was larger than the specifications allowed. Had they attempted to race with that crankshaft, they would have had a tough time winning—or even finishing. Blueprinting will not always show up flaws this serious, but for maximum performance you want to have everything as close to perfect as you can make it.

If you are going to be measuring everything, you are going to need tools to measure with. After you purchase a machinists rule and a couple of micrometers, however, your passion for acquiring more measuring instruments will probably be somewhat dampened. After all, this is money you could be spending on parts!

A good example of a tool you probably will *not* buy right away is a set of inside micrometers. These are expensive and can be difficult to use properly. If you have a good set of outside micrometers and a good feel for measuring things, you can get by with a set of snap gauges, but there is something even less expensive that seems to work just about as well: Plastigage™.

Plastigage

Plastigage is the brand name of a soft, round material that comes in several different sizes and can be used for checking inner clearances, such as between crankshaft journals and rod bearings. The Plastigage itself is a precise diameter, so that when it is crushed flat the width of the crushed Plastigage can be predicted and used to determine the amount of clearance.

Different sizes of Plastigage are different colors, and each package has markings on the outside to help you determine the measurement you are seeking.

Table 3: Leakage and engine condition	
Percent of leakage	**Engine condition**
2 — 10%	Okay
10 — 20%	Marginal
20% and higher	No good

Guidelines for evaluating leakdown readings.

Compression readings and engine condition		
Gauge reading	Probable cause	Indicated condition
First pulse 90 psi; subsequent pulses build to normal reading	Normal	Good
First pulse low; subsequent pulses build to normal reading	Slow compression leak	May start hard, but should run near-normal
First pulse low; subsequent pulses build to low reading	Large compression leak	May not start. Will run poorly
First pulse medium; subsequent pulses add a little; final reading less than normal	Excess camshaft overlap	May start hard, but should run okay with dynamic compression
Pulses read low, medium, or high, but fall between strokes	Stuck or leaking check-valve on compression tester	Clean or replace check valve
No reading, even though engine seems to have compression	Broken compression tester	Run to store for new gauge

Guidelines for evaluating compression test results.

When using Plastigage, never place it in such a position that the weight of a component will be resting on it, or you will get a false reading. For example, do not put the Plastigage over the crankshaft bearing shell and then lay the crankshaft on top of the Plastigage. Lay the crankshaft in first, then lay the Plastigage on the journal, then carefully install and torque down the bearing cap.

Never move a part during the measuring procedure, or use oil around the Plastigage, as the reading will be distorted.

Leakdown Testing

For engine diagnostic work, another valuable tool is the leakdown tester. The leakdown tester helps you determine the integrity of the combustion chamber by pressurizing the chamber and then telling you how much of that pressure is leaking out. Low leakdown means that the rings, valves, and head gasket are sealing properly, and that there are no cracks between the combustion chamber and the block or head. A leakage figure in the middle range (10 to 20 percent) means it is time to tear down the motor and fix whatever is wrong. Due to the nature of leakdown testing, a compression gauge cannot be used to give comparable readings.

If leakdown testing shows an unacceptable amount of leakdown, try to locate the source of the problem before you pull the engine apart. Intake valve leaks will be audible through the intake manifold. Exhaust valve leaks can sometimes be heard through the tailpipe. Head gasket leaks and cracks in the head or block will show up as bubbles in the coolant, so remove the radiator cap before you pressurize the cylinder. Bad rings will produce leaking sounds audible at the oil filler cap.

Leakage and Engine Condition

Always check leakdown with the engine at TDC (top dead center) for the cylinder you are checking. Remember that when you pressurize the cylinder, the engine is going to want to spin if the piston is not exactly TDC, so any wrench you have on the end of the crankshaft to turn the motor is going to go flying. If you have the transmission in gear and the wheels are touching the ground, the car is going to want to move. In short, observe all the common safety precautions.

In addition to being a good diagnostic tool, leakdown testing can be performed on an engine that is not running.

Compression Testing

The compression tester is not as useful as a leakdown tester for diagnostic work, but is much easier to use. When using a compression tester, remember to disconnect the ignition so you do not get a shock. Also keep in mind that compression readings are dependent on the speed at which the engine cranks over, so if the start or battery is not in good shape or the engine and motor oil are cold, you will get low compression readings.

If you perform a compression test along with your normal maintenance schedule, you will be able to catch downward performance trends before they become bigger problems. Also watch the reading of the very first compression stroke. If it is in the neighborhood of 80 to 90 psi, there is a good chance that the leakdown percentage will be low. If the first compression stroke gives a low reading that then builds up to a normal reading, you may have some leakage.

When inspecting a car for purchase, at least do a compression test. If you note anything that appears to be out of the ordinary, perform a leakdown test, too, to get a clearer picture of the condition of the engine, or have your car checked on an engine diagnostic analyzer to determine if the problem is serious or easily repairable.

Increasing Engine Size

Bigger engines make more horsepower. Although forced induction (examined later in "Forced Induction") can make a smaller engine act more like a bigger engine, in most cases the straightforward approach to enhanced performance comes from more cubic centimeters in the motor.

In the search for more cubes, you can increase the bore, or increase the stroke, or both. The difference between these alternatives can be seen in the formula for calculating engine displacement:

$$\text{Displacement} = \frac{\pi \times B \times B \times S \times C}{4 \times 1000}$$

In this formula, B equals the bore in millimeters, S equals the stroke in millimeters, and C is the number of cylinders. Every increase in the bore increases the displacement by the square of the increase divided by 4 (the 1,000 is there to convert the answer to cubic centimeters). An increase in the stroke increases the displacement only by the amount of the increase divided by 4.

This simple device plugs into the spark plug hole and whistles as the piston approaches TDC.

The basic components for building up an engine: stroker crank, bigger pistons, and reworked head and rods. The reworked intermediate shaft is a must with the stroker crank.

A 1-millimeter increase in the bore will yield more of an increase in displacement than will a 4.1-millimeter increase in the stroke. It would also be less expensive to bore the block for the larger pistons than it would be to buy the long-stroke crankshaft and pistons to match. Furthermore, larger bores have more room for the combustion chamber and bigger valves, allowing better breathing. Therefore, if you are in search of a larger-displacement engine, bigger-bore pistons are a less expensive way to go.

This is not to say that longer strokes are not desirable. The Volkswagen block will allow only about 3 millimeters of over-bore before you start running out of room. If you are still looking for more displacement, you can get it with a long stroke crankshaft. In a turbocharged application, a radical overbore is not the best idea because you run into cooling problems, so again the answer is to lengthen the stroke.

As the stroke becomes longer (relative to the connecting rod), the engine makes more torque lower in the rpm range, which is one of the reasons the 86.4-millimeter crankshaft with 144-millimeter rods is more driveable than the 80-millimeter crankshaft with 136-millimeter rods. Even though the 144-millimeter rods are 8 millimeters longer, the rod/stroke ratio is 1.67, as opposed to the other motor's 1.7 ratio.

In theory, virtually any combination of bore and stroke is possible. In practice, some combinations are more common than others. Unless you have a pressing need to hit a specific displacement, stick with the common combinations. They are a lot less expensive.

Four-Cylinder Displacement Options

Bore	Stroke					
	73.4	80.0	81.0	86.4	92.8	95.5
75.0	1297	1414	1431	1527	1640	1688
76.5	1349	1471	1489	1588	1706	1756
79.5	1457	1588	1608	1716	1843	1896
81.0	1513	1649	1670	1781	1913	1968
82.5	1569	1711	1732	1847	1984	2042
83.0	1589	1731	1753	1870	2008	2067
83.5	1608	1752	1774	1893	2033	2092
84.0	1627	1773	1796	1915	2057	2117
84.5	1646	1795	1817	1938	2082	2142

Metal Preparation

This section often refers to different types of metal preparation. Brief explanations of the different techniques follow.

Magnafluxing

Magnafluxing is a method of detecting flaws in metal components that would not otherwise be visible to the naked eye. It works only on ferrous materials, such as steel and cast iron.

The component to be Magnafluxed is placed in a very strong magnetic field while it is being bathed in a special fluorescent solution. Under an ultraviolet lamp, the trained operator can tell by the way the fluorescent solution forms patterns on the metal where the flaws are.

Everything from stress risers (microscopic cracks that form on sharp machined edges) to subsurface cracks can be detected this way, often saving a lot of money and hard work that would otherwise go into further preparation of a faulty component (a crankshaft, for example), to say nothing about the cost of the damage that would be done when the part breaks, or of the cost of losing a race.

Nitriding

Nitriding involves heating a piece of ferrous metal in a salt bath. The salt attaches to the surface of the metal, making it much more resistant to scratches and other damage.

Tuftriding is a special version of the nitriding chemical and heat-treating process. It uses molten cyanide salts and 1,000-plus-degree Fahrenheit temperatures to reduce surface friction, increase wear resistance and increase component strength. After being Tuftrided, the top few thousandths of an inch of the part has an iron carbide outer surface, beneath which is an intermediate diffusion zone. Under the diffusion zone, the metal is unchanged.

Shot Peening

Shot peening is bombarding a piece of metal with thousands of pieces of cast-steel or cast-iron shot of various sizes and hardnesses, depending on the end result required. When a piece of shot hits the surface of the metal, the upper layer of the metal (0.005 to 0.010 inch deep) is stretched slightly. This

A3 2.0-liter engine as found in the 1994 Golf and Jetta.

This Bertil Racing 1800 features dual-sidedraft Weber 34s, 13:1 compression, Bosch crank-triggered ignition, and solid lifters to make 180 horsepower. Note the boxed strut towers and the alternator drive off the camshaft.

causes a compressive stress in the surface of the metal that can be much higher than the normal tensile stress found within the part. The two stresses offset each other, resulting in increased fatigue and crack resistance.

The ability of shot peening to change residual tensile stress to beneficial compressive stress is particularly good on machined or ground surfaces. Areas of concentrated tensile stress, such as notches and fillets in crankshafts and gears, also can be made stronger using shot peening.

After shot peening, the metal surface is usually not processed any further, except for the application of a coating of oil to prevent corrosion. Heat treatments of any sort, for example, reduce or eliminate the effectiveness of shot peening.

Moly Impregnation

Moly impregnation is *not* done by adding a can of liquid molybdenum to your oil. Moly impregnation is done after the parts have been painstakingly cleaned and the surface prepared to accept the moly. So-called dry moly (molybdenum disulphite, or MOS_2) is used, going deep into the pores of the metal. In this compound, the molybdenum is bonded to the metal by the sulfur. Sulfur also has a high affinity for hot metal, so if you lose lubrication, even on a microscopic area, the sulfur will bond to it, carrying the moly with it.

Molybdenum construction is similar to that of a deck of cards. If you place a deck of cards on the table and press down hard, you can still slide the cards relative to each other. The molybdenum disulphite fills in all the dips and valleys in the metal, presenting a smooth and low-friction surface to other moving parts.

Moly impregnation is a multifunction coating in that it not only aids lubrication, but also helps dissipate and radiate heat. In the combustion chamber, for example, this means that less of the heat will soak into the head, block and piston. What heat does soak in is quickly and evenly spread out to reduce detonation-causing hot spots. Simultaneously, the soaked-in

Here's one way of doubling your displacement: Add an engine in the rear. Su Kemper

heat is being transferred to the coolant (in the head and block) and into the oil (from the underside of the piston). The lubricity of the moly even retards carbon build-up.

Treated parts come out black from the excess of moly that is applied, but after a running-in period, the excess will rub off, leaving the part looking similar to an untreated part. The moly is still in the pores of the metal working, however. Moly impregnation does not change tolerances, although with the increased lubricity of the metal, tolerances can be reduced if desired.

Gun Kote

Gun Kote is the name of the process developed by Kalgard to coat metal with a phenolic resin that contains molybdenum disulphite and other ingredients for the purpose of promoting cooling. The difference between Gun Kote and moly impregnation (which is also a Kalgard process) is that the Gun Kote is not used in areas of friction.

The back side of a 1.6-liter block.

The back side of a 1.7-liter VW block (the Chrysler blocks say "1.7").

The back side of the 1.8 block. Note the larger oil return hole at the center front of the block, and the additional oil return hole on the right front.

The almost-flat pistons work in the 16V because of the shape of the combustion chamber. The "grooves" in the tops of the pistons provide valve head relief.

For best results, all boring and honing must be done with a torque plate on top of the block and with the main caps bolted on.

Zirconium Oxide Coating

Zirconium oxide was developed for the space industry. When applied to aluminum it reduces heat transfer, as a result of the lower heat conduction of zirconium oxide (0.53 BTU/hour/feet) compared with the heat conduction of aluminum (139 BTU/hour/feet). The coating is applied using a special process that mixes powdered zirconium oxide with superheated plasma gas that is sprayed onto the aluminum. The coating, which also goes by the name of Turbokoting, is three layers thick, adding a substantial 0.015 to 0.018 inch to the surface.

If you are under budget on your engine work, Turbokoting is for you. Pistons cost about $50 each to coat, and the cylinder head will run around $300. For this reason, I recommend this only for highly stressed turbo motors, and then only if the coating is properly applied.

So far there have been no real problems with the coating flaking off and destroying the turbo (although any coating of this type has the potential for doing so), but it is a good idea to take some 220- or 320-grit sandpaper and lightly scuff the finished coating.

Another reason that this does not get an unqualified okay is that it does not remove or reduce the heat of combustion, it just keeps it from soaking into the coated surface. This heat still has to go somewhere. In a turbo motor, if you can get it all going out the exhaust port you will have better turbo efficiency and better throttle response. The problem is that some of the heat also gets to the rings, the cylinder walls, the valves, and so on.

For less than an all-out motor, you probably will not want to get involved in the research and development it would take to discover the pros and cons of using this coating in your application.

Blocks
Differences among Blocks

Undecided between building up your old block and buying a complete short- or long-block that promises all new parts? For some parts the newer they are the better. However, in this case a seasoned block has the advantage over a brand-new casting. Because of the metallurgy and construction of a block, things tend to shift around a bit as the block settles in dimensionally. If you need to replace a motor that is completely worn-out, you may not have a choice. Otherwise, go with a good used block, especially if you are going to do a lot of prep work on the block itself.

If you are buying a used block for a project and Volkswagen has a block that was used in a motor similar to the one you are building up, try to get that block. For example, if you have a normally aspirated car but want to build up a supercharged engine,

Table 6: 4-cylinder displacement options						
Bore	**Stroke**					
	73.4	**80.0**	**81.0**	**86.4**	**92.8**	**95.5**
75.0	1297	1414	1431	1527	1640	1688
76.5	1349	1471	1489	1588	1706	1756
79.5	1457	1588	1608	1716	1843	1896
81.0	1513	1649	1670	1781	1913	1968
82.5	1569	1711	1732	1847	1984	2042
83.0	1589	1731	1753	1870	2008	2067
83.5	1608	1752	1774	1893	2033	2092
84.0	1627	1773	1796	1915	2057	2117

Displacement in cubic centimeters for all cylinder combinations of bore and stroke. Not all combinations are possible or desirable.

Removing casting flash and making room for a stroker crank. Tape protects the bearing bores.

try to find a G-60 block. It is easy to identify because it has two freeze plugs on the flywheel end, and the knock sensor mounts in a different location than other blocks. There is also a hole in the block at the front pulley end in front of cylinder one, which is covered by a plate. This allows better circulation of coolant around that side of the cylinder wall, which may help keep your engine alive that much longer.

Preparation

Preparation involves many diverse activities, such as making sure you have all the parts you will need, having all the proper tools, getting all the machine work done in the right order, having the right information available, and so on. Read through all the following steps even if you do not plan on performing them on your engine. Any engine would benefit from all these steps, but not everyone has all the time and money needed to complete them. If you are going to take short cuts, at least be aware of what you are missing.

Clearancing the block (and other pieces) for a big crankshaft will be another step in the preparation for some of you. That step is covered later in "Crankshafts."

Using a sawn-off intermediate shaft to check the intermediate shaft outer bearing.

Initial Cleaning and Inspection

The very first thing to do with any block, new or used, is to give it a thorough cleaning with soap and water. Many coin car-washes have an engine cleaning area that is good for jobs like this. If you are really dedicated, you can take out the oil galley plugs and clean the galleys too.

It is not necessary to hot tank the block. If you feel better with a hot-tanked block, be aware that you will need to replace the intermediate shaft bearings when you are through. Intermediate shaft bearings come both finished and unfinished. Get the finished ones and save yourself having to hone the bearings to size.

Once the block is clean, perform a visual inspection to see if everything looks good enough to proceed. If you are going to be subjecting the engine to lots of stress, have the block Magnafluxed at this point, as well.

Using the other half of the sawn-off intermediate shaft to check the inner bearing.

Freeze Plugs

You can take out the freeze plugs for the cleaning process, but the factory freeze plugs are better than any available aftermarket plugs, so this is not recommended unless your freeze plugs are rusting out. Use brass freeze plugs if you need replacements.

If you plan to be doing hard racing where everything gets knocked about, you have probably thought about drilling and tapping the freeze plug holes for threaded plugs. That is one

Forged crankshafts can be identified by the forging seam that runs through the centerline.

The manufacturing process of a cast crankshaft creates no seam.

Crankshaft oil galley plug.

Align the drill with the oil galley.

The stock oil galley plugs rarely fall out, but they must be removed for proper cleaning. Centerpunch the oil galley plug before drilling.

way of doing it, but it takes forever to do, and the time is much better spent doing something else. Instead, use a punch to stake the freeze plugs in place. They will stay put, and you can use all your "extra" time to measure everything once more.

Stress Relieving

To stress relieve the block, the main caps are bolted up and torqued to spec. Then the block is heated to 1,050 degrees Fahrenheit and baked for two hours. Next the temperature is reduced in 200 degree steps, letting the block bake for one hour at each step. Once it reaches 500 degrees, the block can be air-cooled. After stress relieving, you will need to buy new main bearing cap bolts; do not use the ones that were baked with the engine. This procedure is not usually performed on Volkswagen motors.

Deburring

Deburring is done with a hand grinder, and the goal is to eliminate all casting flash, small pockets of sand (from the casting procedure), and roughness from the block. Some engine builders overdo this, making the entire inside of the engine as smooth as a used bar of soap. This much grinding creates stress

risers all over the block, necessitating shot peening, heat-treating or some other step to neutralize it. Unless you want to go to this much trouble, all you need to do is get rid of all the loose stuff that might float out of, or away from the block while the motor is running. However, a shot-peened block would be very durable, and would earn you the admiration of those who know. Even a little deburring goes a long way, however.

While you are going over the block, you should also chase all the threads with a tap lubricated with light oil to make sure they are clean. After the block has been decked (if necessary), chamfer all threaded holes, especially the head bolt holes. Chamfering the bolt holes removes the top thread, so it will not be pulled above the surface of the block when you torque the bolt, which helps ensure a flat surface for the head gasket.

Align Boring

For most uses, it is sufficient to install the crankshaft in the block and see if it turns easily. If you have any doubts about the integrity of your block, or if you are going to be racing with this engine, you should next align bore the crankshaft mains. Align boring removes all doubt about whether or not the crankshaft bore is true and straight, as long as the machine shop does the job right.

Once you are satisfied that the crankshaft bore is straight, you can check the block for trueness.

Truing

With your crankshaft properly sized, your rods machined, the pistons sized, and the block align bored, you can check the squareness of the block. This means measuring from the crankshaft to the top of the block on the outside two cylinders to ensure that the top of the block is parallel with the centerline of the crankshaft. This is different from checking the deck height of the pistons, which comes later.

Using a new set of bearings, install the No. 1 and No. 4 rods and pistons. Bring each up to TDC while measuring with a dial indicator on a magnetic base. Indicate as close to the center of the piston as possible, to eliminate errors that would result if one side of the piston gets cocked in the cylinder bore.

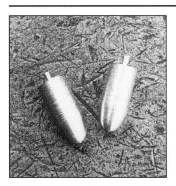

Inexpensive aluminum plugs for closing off the oil galleys after cleaning the crankshaft galleys.

When you have finished, the end of the plug should be recessed slightly below the surface of the crank.

Installing an aluminum oil galley plug.

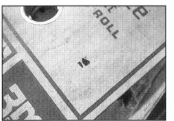

These chunks of grime were found behind just one oil galley plug on a used (but not abused) crankshaft.

consider O-rings instead of head gaskets. Installing O-rings involves cutting grooves around every opening in both the head and the block (around water passages, bolt holes, cylinder bores and so on), and installing metal O-rings. As you might guess, the work required for this is substantial, and it is almost never necessary on a properly prepared block running less than an insane amount of compression or boost. If you are blowing out head gaskets, check everything else one more time, including your exhaust gas temperature before you decide to install O-rings. It is extremely rare to find a Volkswagen engine application that requires O-rings.

Another part of the truing process is checking to see that the cylinder bores line up with the centerline of the crankshaft. If the cylinder bores are not lined up, the pistons will not apply force against the crankshaft in the most efficient manner. Typically, this checking (and any needed adjustment) is performed by the shop that does the cylinder honing. Note that in the VR6 engine, the bores are offset from the crankshaft centerline by 12.5 millimeters, which is compensated for by the special crankshaft, which has adjacent rod journals offset from each other by 22 degrees.

Cylinder Honing

Honing the piston bores is necessary when the bore is worn from use and must be made cylindrical again. If you are not sure of the proper method for measuring the cylinder bore, refer to the shop manual. Honing is probably not a procedure you will tackle by yourself, but the more you know about it the better able you will be to discuss the matter with the machine shop that does it.

When honing the cylinder bores, it is important to install the main bearing caps and to use a torque plate on the cylinder head mating surface. The torque plate is a heavy piece of steel with holes in it that correspond to the cylinder bores and the head bolts. It bolts to the top of the block and is tightened to the same torque that the head would be.

If the measurements are the same, and your straight-edge says the top of the block is flat, you're done. If the measurements are off, you may need to have the block machined, but first, double-check the crankshaft, the connecting rod center-to-center length, and the piston pin height. There are lots of areas where something could be off, which would lead you to think that the block is crooked. Alternately, you could measure the distance between the centerline of the crankshaft and the top sealing surface of the block. This eliminates potential problems with the other components (although any discrepancies in the crank, rods, or pistons will later show up as differences in deck height), but it can be difficult to measure from the crankshaft centerline. To actually do the measurements, use a large set of dividers, which you can even fabricate if necessary.

If the block needs to be machined to bring it into square, make sure that the gasket surface is not polished too smooth. The head gasket will seal better if there is some surface roughness.

For stock purposes, the factory head gasket works fine. For big-bore applications, use a big-bore head gasket. Most tuners who sell big-bore kits also sell a head gasket to match.

If you are running a turbo motor with a lot of boost and you find yourself blowing out head gaskets no matter what,

Although it means more work, it's better to tap the galleys for pipe plugs. Note that this is a welded stroker.

With only four counterweights, the factory cast crankshaft is easy to identify.

The late-model A1 crank nose (right) is much sturdier than the early version.

By installing both the main bearing caps and the torque plate, you are placing the block under approximately the same stresses it will see in use. Thus, when the cylinder bores are honed, they will be much closer to round than if they were honed without taking these preliminary steps.

When opening up the cylinder bores for larger pistons, the rough hone should be done to within 0.0025 inch. To finish hone the cylinder bores, use a 625 stone if you are going to be using chrome rings, and an 820 stone if you are going to be using moly rings. The honing isn't as critical with iron rings, which are more standard replacement rather than high-performance rings.

Always hone each bore to match the piston that will be used in that hole. Measure each piston carefully, and number it to correspond with the bore it will be run in to prevent mix-ups.

VR6 crankshaft.

Once the bores are honed to size, check the piston ring gap while the torque plate is still bolted up. Do not file the ring gap with the ring in the cylinder bore. After removing the torque plate, use fine sandpaper to chamfer the top of the cylinder bore. Work carefully so you do not wind up sanding on your newly honed cylinder bore.

Cylinder Boring

Boring is needed when the cylinder is worn beyond limits (including when it is worn to the point that there is a ridge around the top of the cylinder), or when you want to punch out the block for larger pistons.

Boring takes special tools, so this is another job for the machine shop. When you get the block back from the machine shop, though, the cylinders will not need any further work (including deglazing).

There are limits on how much any given block can be bored. The 1.6- and 1.7-liter blocks can go to 82.5 millimeters with care, and the 1.8 blocks can go up to 83 millimeters. Be aware that one of the limits with the 1.8 block is in the placement of the oil squirters. Oil squirters on the 2.0-liter blocks are moved back, which allows up to 84.5-millimeter bores. Your pistons must still be clearanced to allow the spray from the oil squirter to hit the bottom of the piston at BDC. This is the same for 2.0-liter blocks from the 16V engine as with the 2.0-liter tall block from the A3 built before August 1995.

Deglazing

Another process that is sometimes referred to as honing is breaking the glaze on the cylinder walls. You can do this yourself using a hand drill motor and a deglazing tool, which you can sometimes rent from specialty shops. This procedure is done only when the cylinders are in good shape, are the right size, and just need a little preparation before installing new rings.

Before starting the deglazing procedure, look at the cylinder walls. You will see a cross-hatch pattern that is created when the factory finishes the cylinder bores, and unless your cylinders are very worn (that is, too worn for mere deglazing) you will see the remnants of this cross-hatch pattern. Your goal is to duplicate this pattern in the deglazing.

Set the drill motor to a medium speed, coat the deglazing tool with some light oil or brake parts cleaner, and move the deglazing tool in and out of the cylinder bore in time with the rotation of the tool, so you get that 30-degree cross-hatch, just like the factory. Move the tool through the full stroke, so the top, bottom, and middle of the cylinder bore are as even as possible. It takes less than a minute per cylinder bore; any more and you may be removing metal in the wrong places.

Once done, you should have a nice, evenly rough surface that will help your rings seat quickly and completely all around the cylinder bore.

Finish off by flushing the cylinder bore with solvent (such as brake parts cleaner in an aerosol can), and then lightly oil the bores to prevent oxidation.

Final Cleaning

After you have done all the machining and before you begin to assemble the motor, do one final cleaning of the block. Start with solvent and finish with detergent and warm water. Scrub everything, especially the inside of the cylinder bores, and blow the block dry with compressed air or wipe it dry with paper towels. Compressed air is better than paper towels because the towels can shred, leaving little scraps behind. If you do not have access to an air compressor, how-ever, you can use paper towels if you are careful. Cloth towels leave behind lint, and should be avoided.

All threaded holes should be chased with a tap to clean out the garbage that gets into them. If your tap cuts into the metal while you are cleaning the threads, the tap is too big— do not use it. A good investment is to buy some undersize taps, such as those that come three-to-a-pack for cutting threads precisely (finish tap, first undersize, rough cut). They are not available at every hardware store, but they can be purchased at industrial supply houses that cater to machinists.

You are not done yet, however. The honing process imbeds metal particles deep in the pores of the metal, and nei-ther the solvent nor the soap and water got it all out. Take cheesecloth and SAE 10 oil, and clean the cylinder bores as if they were gun bores. The first few times, the patches will come out dirty. Persevere. Eventually they will come out clean.

Also, go to a gun shop or a sporting goods store and buy two bore bristles and two cleaning rods, one each for a .410 shotgun and a .22 rifle. Get a couple of boxes of patches in both of these sizes too. These will allow you to clean the oil galleys thoroughly. Again, clean them as if they were gun bores. Do not quit until the patches come out clean.

After the final cleaning, coat the entire block with a light preservative such as WD-40, and wrap it in a large trash bag to keep out dirt and moisture. At this point, you can either send the block out for moly impregnation and water jacket treatment, or just set it aside until it is time to assemble the motor.

With 10 bolts, the VR6 crank does not need dowel pins for high-performance use.

Crankcase Oil Jets

Crankcase oil jets are small squirters mounted in the block, pointing up at the bottom of the piston. When the engine oil pressure reaches approximately 30 psi, oil is sprayed on the underside of the pistons to help transfer some of the heat away. These are standard equipment on the 16V, VR6, and A4 4-cylinder motors. The 4-cylinder A3 engines had them up until July 1995. A3s built after August 1995 do not.

These squirters can be retrofitted to pre-16V blocks, as the oil galley that feeds the oil squirters is there waiting to be tapped into. Machine shops have been doing this same service for high-performance Beetle and Porsche motors for years. If you fit these to your block, you will also need to upgrade your oil pump to feed them, and your pistons must be machined so that at BDC the piston skirt allows clearance for the oil, so it can reach the underneath side of the piston.

Bolts Versus Studs

With the exception of the "stretch" bolts used in some Volkswagen engines, which are designed to be used once and then replaced, the stock Volkswagen fastener is a good quality piece. For a true high-performance engine, however, there is a better way to go: precision-ground 8740 chrome alloy fasten-ers from Race-Tech Engineering or ARP. The stock 8V head bolt is good for 135,000 psi tensile strength at best, the stock 16V head bolt is good to 146,000 psi at best, and the stock 16V main bearing cap bolt is good to 164,000 psi at best. In comparison, the lowest failure point for the corresponding Raceware or ARP fastener is 190,000 psi.

It gets better. When you torque a head bolt, you are turning one end of the fastener, hoping that this torque is transmitted to the other end, so the fastener will turn against the friction of the threads in the block and provide the clamping force needed to keep your head gasket from blowing out. If the bolt is stretched, if the threads aren't perfect, or if there is liquid (or some other obstruction) in the hole, the torque you apply at the top of the bolt may not be transmitted faithfully to the threaded end.

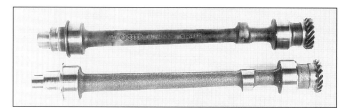

When using a stroker crankshaft, the stock intermediate shaft (top) must be clearanced at the distributor drive to allow the crankshaft to swing by.

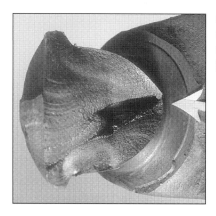

Offset grinding on this welded stroker created a weak point, with predictable results.

With studs, you install the stud into the block by hand, so you know if it seats properly or not. Once you get the studs installed, you lower the head gasket and cylinder head onto the studs (no more sliding the head around on the gasket attempting to line up the holes), install the chrome alloy washers, and torque the nuts at the tops of the studs. This results in much more accurate clamping force from fastener to fastener, and the added strength means the head is staying put. They were worth their weight in gold in the early diesels.

The stock bolts seem to work okay on the 8V and 1.8-liter 16V engines, but the 2.0-liter 16Vs have a problem with the head working loose and coolant weeping out the back of the block. This is a good application for head studs, as are all VR6s, which have enough problems in this area to justify going through the extra work it takes to retorque the studs.

Main bearing cap studs work the same. They are really a great way of keeping your motor together.

If you aren't taking your engine apart, you can still install Raceware studs, if you replace one bolt at a time. With head studs, you must drain the coolant, but Race-Tech sells a special tool for spinning the studs into place. Head stud and main bearing cap stud kits are available from Race-Tech for all water-cooled Volkswagens, including the VR6. ARP offers head stud kits for 8V and 16V engines, and main bearing stud kits for all four-cylinder engines.

Crankshafts

There are three types of crankshafts: billet, forged, and cast. Billet cranks are cut from a billet of steel and are incredibly expensive. Unless you are building an all-out race engine, you won't need one. Forged crankshafts can be much stronger than cast crankshafts, and for years were the only crank to consider for serious high-performance use.

Cast cranks appeared in the 1978 Rabbit, 1978 Scirocco, and in the 1979 Dasher. Although they are not fully counterweighted, they are fine for most hot street machines—unless you need a longer stroke for more cubic inches. While not as strong as a stock forged crankshaft, there are some applications where a cast crank is acceptable.

Techtonics found that some of its customers who broke modified forged crankshafts were not able to break a cast crankshaft. Forged crankshafts are modified by welding metal on the outside of the rod journal, and then offset grinding the journal for greater stroke. Given enough offset, machining the rod journal can sometimes cut to within a couple of millimeters of the oil hole. This creates a weak area in the crankshaft, on the side of the journal that takes a lot of stress at the bottom of the stroke. The cast crankshaft does not have the inherent strength of a forging, but at least its oil holes are in the right place.

Volkswagens are famous for *not* having crankshaft problems, as the lower end of the block is very sturdy, with five main bearings (seven, in the case of the VR6) that prevent crank flex. A cast crankshaft might well fit into your budget better than a welded or forged crankshaft of the desired stroke. An unwelded, forged crankshaft is still the way to go for best strength.

If you choose a cast crankshaft for your high-performance application, have it shot peened or Tuftrided. Shot peening can increase the fatigue strength of a cast crankshaft by as much as 50 percent, and Tuftriding can improve strength by up to 88 percent. In many cases, this additional strength permits a cast crank to be used where it would not otherwise work.

Differences among Crankshafts

In addition to metallurgy and stroke, you should be aware of two other differences among crankshafts. First, the rod journals on 1.6-liter and 1.7-liter crankshafts are smaller at 46 millimeters than those on diesel, 1.8-liter, and later crankshafts, which are 47.758 millimeters. When you buy an aftermarket crankshaft, be sure to find out what rods you have to use with it.

Volkswagen also introduced a 1.7-liter crankshaft in 1983. The cam belt drive sprocket no longer is indexed to the crankshaft with a Woodruff key, instead using a different crankshaft snout and cam belt drive gear. It can be very irritating to get everything put together to that point, only to find that no dealership for miles around has the new-style gear. ("They never break, so why stock–em, right?") Get this detail taken care of at the same time you get the crankshaft.

In the 1.6-liter and 1.7-liter blocks, if you use a 90.5 cast crank and 136-millimeter connecting rods, you will have to clearance the underside of the pistons to allow the counterweights to swing by. In the 1.8-liter blocks, the 91-millimeter cast crank works just fine with the 144-millimeter rods—no clearancing is required.

Preparation

There are many steps to preparing a crankshaft, although not all of them will be needed in all cases. The following are descriptions of all the steps that can be done to a crankshaft. Some are important any time you have the crankshaft out of the car, while others can be classified as solutions for problems that may exist.

Measuring the Crankshaft

Much time, effort, and money can be spent on a crankshaft to make it better, so make sure before you start that the crankshaft you have is worth all the hard work. The first step is to measure all the journals to make sure that the crankshaft is the right size and that the journals are round. Remember to measure each journal twice, the second time at 90 degrees from the first measurement. Be very gentle with the crankshaft and the micrometers. The last thing you want to do is nick a journal with the sharp edge of a micrometer.

Magnafluxing

Note that a marginally cracked crankshaft can still ring like a bell, so the sound test is not really a test at all but merely an indication of whether to proceed with Magnafluxing or to throw the crankshaft away. (Note: Because of the stress risers induced by welding, no welded crankshaft will pass Magnaflux inspection.)

Indexing

The four-cylinder Volkswagen crank is a "flat" crankshaft, which means that after it is drop forged or cast, it is machined to its final size. As a result, the rod journals are very rarely out of alignment. It would not hurt to check, but if you choose not to, you need not lose any sleep over it.

VR6 crankshafts, on the other hand, are heated and twisted after drop forging to get the roughed-out rod journals into the approximate location where they need to be. The crankshaft blank is then machined to final size. Manufacturing tolerances being what they are, the throws might not be in the right place on every crankshaft.

The process of checking and correcting the alignment of the rod throws is called indexing, and is best left to a crankshaft specialist.

Cross-drilling

Cross-drilling is something that started with the big American V-8s to ensure positive lubrication of the main and rod journals through 360 degrees of crankshaft rotation. By cross-drilling the cranks, manufacturers were able to use flat-faced lower bearings instead of bearings that incorporated an oil groove, which provided more surface area on the bearing to take the pounding of the crankshaft.

There must be something to it. The stock Volkswagen crankshaft comes cross-drilled, as should any aftermarket crankshaft you buy.

Stroking

Stroking refers to changing the distance between the centerline of the crankshaft and the centerline of the connecting rod journal. Although it usually refers to an increase

The stock three-piece bearings are a trick way to go, but if you can't find replacements the standard one-piece bearings will work.

in this distance, it can also refer to a decrease, or a de-stroking.

There are two ways to stroke a crankshaft. The first is to offset grind the existing journals and use connecting rods with smaller big ends. The second is to weld extra material to the journal before offset grinding. For the Volkswagen, this second method is by far the most popular.

Welding the extra metal onto a journal tends to warp the crankshaft. Fortunately, on four-cylinder cranks there are two journals on opposite sides of the centerline, so there should be two equal pulls on each side of the crankshaft. Just to be on the safe side, however, a welded crankshaft should always be checked for straightness.

Whenever the stroke of the crankshaft is changed, the connecting rods, the pistons, or both must be changed. For example, if the stroke is increased using the same rods and pistons, it could result in the top of the piston protruding above the top of the engine block. To bring the top of the piston down, you must use shorter rods or pistons with the pin located closer to the top of the piston, or both. In-between-length rods will be difficult to come by and expensive, but there are many pistons available with the correct pin height for long-stroke crankshafts.

Sometimes you have to get inventive to achieve the stroke you want. For example, in a 1.6-liter engine, the stroke of the diesel crankshaft is 80 millimeters. You could offset grind the rod journals to 46 millimeter to gain an 81.5-millimeter stroke and pick up a little displacement. You will then have to use the 1.6- or 1.7-liter rods, and you will need to either deck your pistons or live with the increased compression. You could do the same on an 86.4-millimeter crankshaft, taking it out to 88-millimeter and then changing to the early rods and decking the pistons to match.

Knife-edging

Normal counterweights have square edges. This is the cheapest and easiest way to manufacture the crank, but for high-rpm applications knife-edging is recommended. Knife-edging takes mass out of the crankshaft, promotes oil draining off of the crank, reduces the surface area of metal that must pass through the oil in the crankcase, and minimizes oil splash as the rod journals dip into the crankcase. These last two are important because at high rpm the crankshaft can actually beat

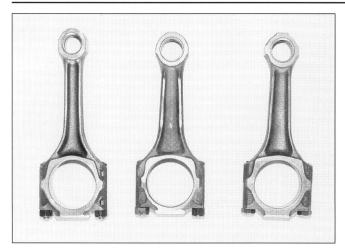

From left to right: a 1.8 rod, a 1.6 rod, and an Audi rod.

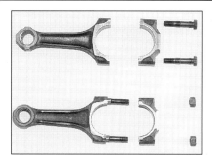

An exploded view of the 1.6 rod and the Audi rod.

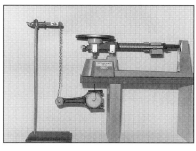

Using a triple-beam balance to weigh the rods end-for-end.

air into the oil. This foamy oil may remain thick enough to prevent your oil pressure light from coming on, but not thick enough to protect your bearings. Note that the antifoaming agents in all modern motor oils are not enough to prevent oil aeration in all situations. This is one of the reasons why real race cars have dry sump oil systems, which can be constructed to break down the air bubbles so the bearings receive oil that is free of air.

Checking for Straightness

It does not take much of a bend to make the crank whip around pretty good at 7,000 rpm. To check for straightness, place the crankshaft in the bearings and check each main bearing surface with a dial indicator. Any reading of more than 0.001 inch means the crankshaft should be straightened. Straightening is done by a special hammering process; bending it straight creates stress risers. Darrell Vittone of Techtonics says that if the crankshaft turns easily when the main caps are bolted down, it is probably straight enough to run with.

Increasingly, the trend is to forged crankshafts in the desired stroke to start with. They are more expensive, but would you really want to weld, regrind, and straighten your 90.3-millimeter VR6 crank to stroke it out to 95.6 millimeters?

Nitriding

Nitriding (or Tuftriding) can extend the life of a crankshaft by up to five times, owing to the wear resistance it imparts to the bearing surfaces. In addition, Tuftriding can almost double the strength of the crankshaft, and friction over a Tuftrided surface is cut nearly in half. Just as important, the crankshaft is not made brittle by this process. Before Tuftriding, all sharp edges should be radiused and smoothed down.

Shot Peening

Because shot peening leaves a slightly rough surface, the journals and thrust surfaces must be masked off so the shot peening does not ruin them. Masking tape does not work for this purpose; shot peening requires adhesive-backed rubber to repel the steel shot from sensitive areas. When taking a crankshaft in for shot peening, be sure to specify which surfaces are to be treated and which surfaces are to be left as is.

In addition to the throws, the fillets (where the journal joins the throw) are also shot peened, as this is a high-risk area for breakage.

Before shot peening, all sharp edges should be radiused and smoothed down. Only limited polishing can be performed on shot-peened surfaces.

Balancing

Balancing is not something that happens only to crankshafts. For proper balance, all reciprocating and rotating weights attached to the crankshaft must be balanced, too. Reciprocating weights include the pistons, the piston pins, the piston rings, and the small end of the connecting rod. Rotating weights include the big end of the rod, the rod bearings, the flywheel, the pressure plate, and the front pulley or pulleys.

In a stock motor, the components are balanced exceptionally well compared with other production line motors. If you are building a race engine or changing any of the components, take these parts out to be balanced before assembling your motor. Record all balance weights in case you must later replace a component. Knowing the existing weights will make it unnecessary to rebalance the entire motor just to accommodate one changed component.

Clearancing

When moving up to a larger-stroke crankshaft, you have to ensure that the rod journals and counterweights don't hit anything else inside the block, such as the inside of the block, the intermediate shaft, and so on. This is one of the reasons why trial-fitting everything is so important before final assembly.

Clearancing the inside of the block can be tedious work. It was bad enough with the air-cooled Volkswagen and their magnesium cases, but the cast iron of the water-cooled blocks

1.8-liter connecting rod small-end bushings are relieved across the top for better pin oiling.

A variable-length rod for determining optimal piston pin height in custom pistons.

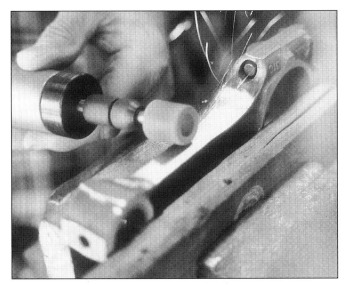

Always grind rods lengthwise. Shot peen afterward to relieve grinding stress.

is a real pain to grind away. Grinding by hand does allow you to remove only what needs to be removed. The more metal you can safely leave, the stronger your block will be.

Set the crankshaft into the block on used bearings and note areas of interference. You are looking for roughly .040 inches of rotational clearance and roughly .015 inches of back-and-forth clearance. You can reduce the amount you have to take out of the block (and other components) by clearancing the big ends of the rods. You don't want to take too much out of the rods, of course, but taking the corners off the big ends can really reduce the amount of grinding you need to do on the case. Any clearancing on the rods must be done *before* they are balanced.

Cleaning

Cleaning the outside of the crankshaft is no problem, but cleaning the inside of the oil galleys can be a real chore. You will need to drill out the existing plugs, and then either replace them with aluminum plugs or drill and tap the holes for threaded plugs.

If you are using a crank that has been in use for a while, do not bypass this step. Removing the plugs makes it possible to get into the oil galley for a thorough cleaning that is just about impossible any other way. This is vitally important with a used or reground crankshaft because centrifugal force packs grime into the outer ends of the oilways (behind the plugs), and the only way to get it out is to remove the plugs. On engines that were not well cared for, baked-on oil residue will have narrowed the oil galleys (kind of like hardening of the arteries). On a reground crankshaft, an abrasive compound can be hiding anywhere and can be removed only by taking out the oilway plugs or installing the dirty crankshaft in your engine, at which time the stuff will magically float out and get into everything. On a new crankshaft the odds are better that the oil galleys will be clean, but it does not take very long to run a brush through the galleys, and it is better to be safe.

The easier of the two methods is to use aluminum plugs. Centerpunch the existing plug and drill it out with a 6-millimeter drill. Run your bore bristle and patches through all the oil galleys until the patches come out clean.

Insert the aluminum plugs pointed end first, and hammer them in with a ball peen hammer until the top of the plug is flush with the surface of the crankshaft. To finish off, take a punch with a rounded end or a rod with a small-diameter ball bearing welded to it, and keep hammering until the plug is slightly concave. If you follow this procedure, you should never have to worry about the plug coming loose.

If you plan on frequent crankshaft cleaning or you do not trust hammered-in plugs, you can drill and tap the oil galleys for 1/16-inch pipe plugs. Make sure to Loctite the plugs in after cleaning!

Whatever you do with the oil galley plugs, double-check them before buttoning up the motor. Pressed-in plugs may come out in operation, resulting in a puzzling lack of oil pressure.

Chrome Plating

One trick for making a very smooth and very tough journal is to chrome plate it. The plating adds metal and increases the diameter of the bearing surfaces, so the journals must be ground undersize with that in mind before sending the crankshaft to the plater.

Another consideration with chrome-plating is that plating cracks can propagate into the base metal in a process known as hydrogen embrittlement. These cracks reduce the strength of the part and can cause failure unless the part is properly prepared for chroming.

For crankshafts, the hard compressive surface left by shot peening has proved to be very resistant to cracking. Before sending any highly stressed part out to have chrome plating, electroless nickel plating, or cadmium plating applied, have the part shot peened.

With the inherent durability of the Volkswagen crankshaft, chrome plating is not needed for any but the most extreme uses.

Moly Impregnation

In a perfect world, you would never need to moly coat crankshaft journals, because the bearings are supposed to ride on a soft carpet of oil—never touching the journal.

Every time you turn off the motor, however, the oil coating goes away and the crankshaft settles downward, eventually resting against the bottom bearing surface. When the starter motor is engaged, those first few seconds can be tough while the crankshaft turns in the bearings waiting for lubrication. This is where moly impregnation comes in handy. Theoretically, it would also help if there were ever a strong enough load to push the oil film aside, such as might happen if the engine detonated heavily.

Because of the nature of molybdenum, impregnation can be of benefit to untreated, polished, or chromed crankshafts.

Bearings

There is nothing trick to know about the bearings, although there is something to watch out for if your main journals have been ground undersize. The Kolbenschmidt main thrust bearings come 0.1-millimeter too thick and must be dressed down to set the end play. A flat piece of glass or marble with 600-grit wet-or-dry sandpaper on it works well for this. After you get the size right (0.07 to 0.17 millimeters), make certain that you have a mirror finish on the thrust surface.

If this sounds like a lot of work, specify Brazilian bearings instead of the Kolbenschmidts. The Brazilian bearings come properly sized.

No matter what bearings you use, *always* set the end play on any motor you put together.

Flywheels

When your car is all apart, you can mark the true TDC on the flywheel so you will have no trouble finding it in the future.

To find the true TDC, you must first dead-stop the motor. To do this, you must have the crankshaft bolted into the block,

Ground and polished rods.

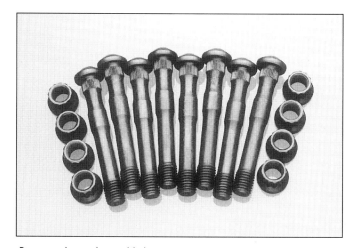

Raceware heavy-duty rod bolts.

with the connecting rod and piston for cylinder No. 1 installed. Bolt a piece of metal (the dead-stop) across the top of the No. 1 cylinder bore, so that it interferes with the piston near the very top of the stroke.

Now rotate the engine in one direction until the piston touches the dead-stop. Doing this even gently can flat-spot your bearings, so use old bearings to do this, or if you have the tools, use a dial indicator to detect TDC instead of a dead stop.

Make a temporary mark on the flywheel corresponding to the factory mark on the transmission housing. Now rotate the engine back the other way until the piston again touches the dead-stop. Make another mark on the flywheel opposite your same point of reference. Halfway between these two points of reference is the TDC for your motor. If the factory's TDC mark is off from the TDC of your motor, mark the true TDC with a chisel or a centerpunch, and then fill the mark with white paint so it will show up when you illuminate it with the timing light.

Having an accurate TDC mark will become critical later on when you time the camshaft and set the ignition timing.

For a street car, there is not much else you will need to do to the flywheel unless it is damaged or out of balance.

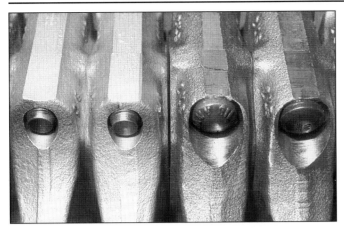

The Audi rods (left) have more metal in the area at the base of the beam.

It is not necessarily a good idea to lighten the flywheel, because the car will not idle as nicely and the flywheel helps dampen vibrations that develop in the motor. You will also get a better launch off the line with a heavier flywheel, because it stores energy better than a light flywheel. Without the flywheel there to smooth things out, broken crankshafts and worn-out bearings become more commonplace.

If you are racing a lightweight car in short races where power is everything, you will want to lighten the flywheel so the engine does not have as much mass to spin up when you press on the accelerator pedal. The trade-off will show up in engine longevity, but that is racing. Weight removed from the outer rim of the flywheel gives the most bang for the buck, but leave enough metal there to soak up the heat generated when the clutch slips. If you do not have enough metal there, the flywheel will develop hot spots, reducing its effectiveness. On one of the early 1.5- or 1.6-liter 190-millimeter flywheels, lightening the flywheel saves about 5.5 pounds of static mass, which, due to rotational inertia, translates into quite a saving. A lightened 210-millimeter flywheel saves just over 2.5 pounds. A lightened 228-millimeter flywheel from a G-60 saves about 5 pounds, and a lightened 228-millimeter flywheel from a VR6 saves about 4 pounds. You can lighten your own, or Velocity sells late-model flywheels that have already been machined and balanced. Neuspeed sells aluminum flywheels, which are lighter still, but which won't have the same longevity as a properly lightened and balanced steel flywheel.

For four-cylinder motors that will see extreme duty, the flywheel can be dowel-pinned to the crankshaft, just as is done with Type 1 Beetle motors. And, as with the Type 1, dowels are placed between the flywheel holes, for a total of six dowels. You want the dowels to take the torsional stress instead of the flywheel bolts, so make the holes a 0.0015-inch interference fit on the dowels. G-60 cranks have more bolts than four-cylinder cranks and don't need to be dowel pinned. VR6 cranks have more bolts still, and don't have need (or room) for dowel pins.

Rods
Choices

By varying the ratio between the rod length and the crankshaft stroke, you can determine some of the characteristics of the motor. This ratio is calculated by dividing the center-to-center length of the connecting rod by the diameter of the crankshaft stroke.

Generally, you want the ratio to be between 1.5:1 and 1.9:1. As the ratio gets closer to 1.5:1, the engine will produce torque lower in the rpm range with a flatter overall curve. As the ratio gets closer to 1.9:1, the engine will produce more horsepower in the upper rpm range and will have a peakier torque curve. With a high-ratio motor you can get more area under the curve, but the driveability will be nicer with the low-ratio motor (especially in conjunction with a short camshaft).

Here's why:

Because of the geometry of the rod swinging around on the end of the crankshaft journal, the piston in a long-rod (high-ratio) engine will linger a tiny fraction of a second longer at TDC and BDC (bottom dead center) than it will with a low-ratio short rod. Because of this "extra" dwell at the top of bottom of the stroke, the piston will move more quickly between TDC and BDC. The faster speed creates more suction over a shorter period of time, making valve timing less critical. The engine also seems to run more smoothly with longer rods.

With a short-rod (low-ratio) engine, valve timing is more critical because the piston accelerates and decelerates more slowly to and from TDC and BDC. The benefit is that the piston spends less time near peak velocity compared to the long-rod engine.

Note, however, that the length of the rod determines only the acceleration to and from TDC and BDC, not the maximum piston speed, which is determined by rpm and crankshaft stroke. If you are having a problem with piston speed being too high, using a shorter rod will not help; you need a shorter stroke or a lower rpm limit. It is doubtful that you will ever have to consider any of this when putting together your engine.

The Volkswagen motors use four different-length rods. The 1.5-, 1.6-, and 1.7-liter motors all use a 136-millimeter rod with a 22-millimeter piston pin, and the 1.8-liter motor uses a 144-millimeter rod with a 20-millimeter piston pin. The diesel uses the 136-millimeter rod with a 24-millimeter piston pin. If your dream is to play around with offset bushings on a short rod, here is your golden opportunity. In 1993 Volkswagen's "tall block" engine uses 159-millimeter rods, and starting in 1998, the reduced-height A4 2.0-liter uses 141-millimeter rods.

Preparation

It is the job of the connecting rods to transfer the movement of the piston to the crankshaft, and in a high-output motor they are asked to do a lot. The more you ask of your engine, the more important it becomes to condition the rods.

Thinner rings flutter less at high rpm. The 82.5-millimeter piston weighs less than the factory piston for the 1,600 engine.

These Techtonics pistons are well made, yet inexpensive. The piston dish area can be varied to adjust the compression ratio. Note the "bridge" area beneath the pin bore for strength. Even at 82.5 millimeters, these aftermarket pistons weigh less than the factory 79.5-millimeter pistons.

The raised edge around the center dish creates a squish area in the combustion chamber to boost turbulence and promote air/fuel mixing.

Magnafluxing

Magnafluxing the rods can be done at either of two times, depending on how much preparation you are planning. If you are leaving the rods basically stock, Magnaflux them after the initial cleaning. If you are going all the way, Magnaflux them after grinding and polishing but before squaring, balancing, or shot peening.

Checking the Length (Center-to-Center and Squaring)

Both of these operations are best carried out by a machine shop that has the proper tools for measuring and correcting any problems. The center-to-center length must be the same for all rods so that the compression ratio and deck height will be the same from one end of the block to the other. Squaring prevents side loads on the rod, crankshaft, and wrist pin. Even a small amount of out-of-squareness will lead to side motion in the rod— enough in some cases to hammer the wrist pin clip right out of the piston.

If you have either too much or too little deck height with your combination of stroke, rod length, and piston pin height, the center-to-center length can be adjusted by offset honing the small-end bushing. This is good for only a millimeter or so, but it is there if you need it.

Grooving Small-end Bushings

The 1.8-liter and later small-end bushings have a groove that earlier bushings did not have. The groove is located at the top of the bushing in such a way that oil that enters the pin oiling hole is distributed almost halfway down both sides of the piston pin.

This would be difficult to machine by hand, but it could be duplicated in a mill. I have seen few problems caused by insufficient piston pin oiling, but Volkswagen does not include extra-cost items like this unless it has found a benefit.

Lightening

The Volkswagen rod is a stout piece and can stand to lose some weight without sacrificing strength. If you are using a very light piston assembly, the rod can be lightened still further. A lot of the weight will come off the small end, although you do not want to remove so much metal that you endanger the strength of the rod. Unless you do this for a living, be happy with balancing the rod and let someone else find out how much metal is too much to take off the rod.

Polishing

All Volkswagen rods come with a seam that runs along the side of the beam. This seam is created during the forging process. Although it is not necessary, this seam can be ground down while you are rounding off all the other sharp edges on the rod.

Always grind in the same direction as the length of the rod, never crosswise. Your final grinding should be fairly smooth, and the grinding marks should be polished with 400-grit sandpaper.

Because grinding creates a lot of tensile stress on the surface of the metal, all ground and polished rods must be shot peened. If you cannot afford shot peening, do not waste your time polishing the connecting rods. A rough forged connecting rod is stronger than a polished but unpeened rod. If you can afford shot peening but are in no mood to polish your connecting rods, shot peening the rough forging will provide you with a stronger rod than stock.

Balancing

Balancing is done after clearancing, lightening, and polishing, after the bushings have been replaced and sized, after the big end has been sized, and after any other operation that adds weight to or removes it from the rod. The purpose of balancing the rod is to get the center of mass at the same place for all four rods.

You will need a weighing scale that is capable of reading to a gram. For best accuracy, the rod must be hung as close to horizontal as possible. This means fabricating a set of jigs, one for the big end of the rod and one for the small end. The weight of the jigs is not critical because you are only comparing small ends with small ends, and big ends with big ends; at this point

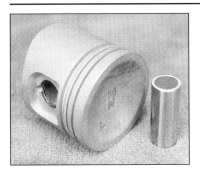

These special pistons with sodium-fitted pins are used in ITB (Improved Touring, Class B) racing.

Forged pistons. They're light, but skirt flex could be a problem without reinforcement under the pin bores.

The 1.7 pistons (left) can be replaced with Euro 1.6 Heron pistons for higher compression.

you are not concerned with the overall weight of the rod itself. Of more importance is making all the small ends weigh the same and all the big ends weigh the same.

You can only take metal away, so find the lightest rod end and grind the others to match. First weigh all the rods end for end, noting the weights on a piece of paper. You now have eight numbers. Compare the small-end weights only with the other small-end weights, and the big-end weights only with the big-end weights.

Once you have picked out the lightest small end and the lightest big end, grind the other small ends to match the weight of the lightest small end, and then grind the big ends to match the weight of the lightest big end. All grinding should be done off the pads at the top and bottom of the rod. If you go too far with one, make that your new "lightest" rod and grind the others to match.

As a bonus, when you are done the overall weights of all your rods will be the same.

Shot Peening

Shot peening is done only after all the metal has been removed by the grinding, polishing, and balancing operations. Do not have the insides of the holes or the rod bolts and nuts shot peened, just the outside of the rod itself. You *can* shot peen rough rods, and you *must* shot peen polished rods. An untreated polished rod is actually weaker than a stock (rough) rod.

Rod Bolts

As with the head bolts and main bearing cap bolts, the stock rod bolts are satisfactory, but for real peace of mind, use the chrome alloy equivalents. It will be one less thing to wonder about at 7,500 rpm. Raceware and ARP connecting rod bolts are available for the 1.6-liter, 1.7-liter, 1.8-liter, and 2.0-liter four-cylinder engines (except Corrado). Race-Tech also has rod bolts for the VR6. Race-Tech even has replacements for the Audi-style rods, which are often used in Super Vee racing. These precision-ground 8740 chrome alloy rod bolts are good for up to 220,000 psi. If you've ever seen the mess that a failed connecting rod bolt can make of an engine, you will appreciate the strength and quality of aircraft quality fasteners.

Pistons

There are two basic types of pistons: cast and forged. The stock pistons are cast, as are many of the better replacement pistons for normal and hot street uses.

Then why use forged pistons? In some high-stress applications, such as in full-race engines or engines with a turbocharger, it can be difficult to control the thermal expansion of a cast piston. A forged piston will give you greater strength without a weight penalty.

The drawback is that a forged piston expands much more than a cast piston, so it must have more clearance when installed. The more clearance there is between the cylinder wall and the piston, the more the piston can rock from side to side, upsetting the seal between the ring and the cylinder wall. When forged pistons are run loose, they are noisier and can use more oil than cast pistons.

Piston-to-wall clearance for a cast piston is 0.001 inch. You can run a forged piston as tight as 0.0015 inch, although 0.002 through 0.005 inch are more common clearances. The spec for Mahle and Kolbenschmidt forged pistons is 0.0025 inch; TRW pistons are often run at 0.0045 to 0.0055 inch. At 0.0015 inch you will not get appreciably more noise than with properly set up cast pistons, but you have to know what you are doing to run them that tight.

Choices

Typically, you will buy pistons these days as part of a package that may include a crankshaft. If you have a 1.6-liter A1, however, be aware that American Volkswagens used pistons that were nearly flat on top, incorporating only a shallow dish. European 1.6s used a piston with a deep dish on top. These differences were due to the differences in cylinder head design and are explained in the section on cylinder heads. You can get either style in both cast and forged pistons.

In choosing new pistons, you can opt for pistons that directly replace the stock ones, pistons that raise the compression ratio but leave the displacement the same, pistons that increase the displacement but leave the compression ratio the same, or pistons that increase both the displacement and the compression ratio.

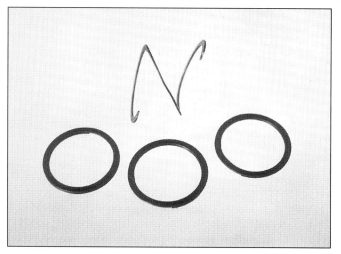

Spiralok wrist pin clips are unnecessary in all but the highest performance motors.

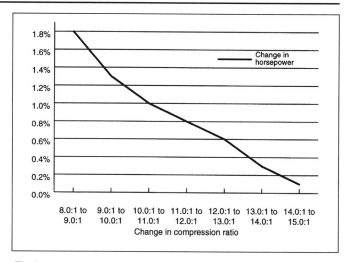

The lower your compression ratio is to start with, the bigger the gain from increasing it.

Increasing the cylinder bore does more than increase the displacement; it also creates more room for unshrouding the valves. The third benefit, as mentioned earlier in the section on techniques, is that installing bigger-bore pistons is a less expensive way of increasing displacement than going to a longer-stroke crankshaft.

Pistons to be used in blocks with oil squirters must have the skirts clearanced so that when the piston is at BDC, the flow from the oil squirter can reach the underneath surfaces of the piston.

Speaking of piston skirts, they have gotten shorter over the years, which is good because it means less weight, but the longer skirts help keep the pistons square in the cylinder bore, and the fuller skirts flex less. Careful attention to piston geometry can help keep the piston square in the bore, and some pistons are designed with reinforcements under the piston pin hole that strengthen the piston.

Piston Pins

Everything at the end of the piston rod (piston, piston rod, pin clips, rod end, and rings) is part of the reciprocating assembly. Therefore, the lighter the assembly is, the lower the acceleration and deceleration forces will have to be when the assembly stops, changes directions, and starts moving again (at TDC and BDC).

For street use, piston pins must not be too light because of the need for durability in this high-stress area. However, very high rpm race engines can benefit from lightened pins. Because of their lighter weight and greater strength, forged pistons can use lighter pins than can comparable cast pistons. The strength of the forged piston also allows the use of shorter (and hence lighter still) piston pins. In turbo applications, it is better to stick with heavier piston pins for durability.

For most street machines, the stock wrist pin clips work fine. For heavier-duty use, the Spiralok clips are better, but they are also much more difficult to remove. If your desert racer keeps hammering out the clips no matter what type you try, there are always Teflon buttons, although the block is stiff enough that they are rarely needed.

Compression Ratio

The higher the compression ratio, the better the thermal efficiency; hence, the better the engine output and the lower the fuel consumption.

This is due to the smaller volume of the combustion chamber:

During the exhaust stroke, the cylinder is evacuated more effectively, and the fresh cylinder charge has fewer residual noncombustible gases.

During the compression stroke, the fuel and air particles are more densely compressed, they get hotter, and fuel droplet atomization is increased, permitting more rapid and complete combustion.

During the power stroke, both the pressure of the hot gases and their temperature are reduced, so the cooler exhaust gases dissipate less heat.

And the combustion chamber has a smaller cooling surface, so heat losses through the cylinder walls and head are correspondingly less.

For each point of extra compression, you get increased power output and better fuel economy, up to about 15.0:1, although by that time you have long since stopped using pump gas. After 15.0:1, you start to lose more from pumping losses than you gain in efficiency. Raising the compression ratio does not increase horsepower in a linear relationship. Instead, a little less horsepower is gained with each additional point of compression.

The negative sides of compression are that when the compression gets too high, you run into motor-destroying detonation, and you generate more oxides of nitrogen (NO_2).

Checking Compression Ratio

If all you do when you rebuild your motor is freshen things up, you should not need to check your compression ratio. If you surface the head or the block, reshape the combustion chambers, change the height of the valve heads in the combustion chamber or install a set of big-bore pistons, however, you need to check that you are getting the compression ratio you want.

Most people can understand why the compression ratio has to be checked when they add or take away metal in the combustion chamber, but many do not realize that an increased compression ratio also results from increasing the piston bore.

The formula for calculating the compression ratio is:

$$\text{Cylinder displacement} = \frac{\pi \times \text{bore} \times \text{bore} \times \text{stroke}}{4 \times 1000}$$
$$= \frac{3.14159 \times 79.5 \times 79.5 \times 86.4}{4000}$$
$$= 428.88$$

In this equation, CD equals cylinder displacement (the swept volume of the cylinder), PV equals piston volume, HV equals head volume, and HGV equals head gasket volume. Therefore, before you can calculate your compression ratio, you need to know the bore, the stroke, the volume of the head, the volume of the piston, and the compressed thickness of the head gasket.

Let's say you know the bore (79.5 mm, for example) and stroke (86.4 mm) of your motor; the formula for calculating cylinder displacement is:

$$\text{Compression ratio} = \frac{\text{CD} + \text{PV} + \text{HV} + \text{HGV}}{\text{PV} + \text{HV} + \text{HGV}}$$

Now you need to determine the piston volume, or the amount of space in the cylinder when the piston is at the top of its stroke. Lower the piston in the cylinder and smear a *light* coat of white grease around the top of the cylinder. Turn the crankshaft until the piston comes up to TDC for the piston you are checking. If necessary, rock the crankshaft back and forth slightly to be sure you have TDC. As the piston rises in the cylinder, the white grease will seal the rings against the cylinder wall, making the cylinder liquid-tight. Wipe away any excess grease from the top of the piston.

You now need a piece of Plexiglass with a small hole in the center, and a graduated burette.

Apply the white grease to the surface of the head surrounding the cylinder you wish to measure. Place the Plexiglass over the cylinder so the hole is over the piston. The white grease must completely seal the Plexiglass to the top of the block.

Fill the burette with light oil and note the volume of the oil. Now decant the oil through the hole in the Plexiglass until the cylinder is filled and there are no air bubbles underneath the Plexiglass. Note the volume of oil in the burette, and subtract the second reading from the first reading. This is the volume of the piston.

Again using the piece of Plexiglass, the burette, the oil, and the white grease, it is time to measure the volume of the combustion chamber in the cylinder head. Before you start, do a test run to see that the valves are liquid-tight. If not, open the valve enough to smear some white grease on the mating surface. The spark plug must be installed.

With the sealing surface of the head facing up and horizontal, place the Plexiglass on the head using the white grease as a sealant, and decant oil into the combustion chamber until there are no bubbles beneath the Plexiglass. Note the difference in readings in the burette, and calculate the combustion chamber volume.

Because you already know the head gasket compressed thickness, the next step is to calculate head gasket thickness displacement. The formula for this is:

$$\text{Head gasket displacement} = \frac{\text{thickness} \times \text{bore} \times \text{bore} \times 0.00314158}{4}$$
$$= \frac{1.75 \times 79.5 \times 79.5 \times 0.00314159}{4}$$
$$= 8.68684$$

Plugging the figures you have obtained for cylinder displacement and head gasket volume into the formula, this is what you get:

$$\text{Compression ratio} = \frac{428.88 + 26 + 27 + 8.7}{26 + 27 + 8.7}$$
$$= \frac{490.58}{61.7}$$
$$= 7.95$$

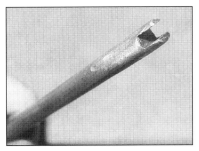

A 3/8-inch bar stock with a slot in the end makes the perfect preoiler for a new engine.

Thus, the compression ratio for this particular engine is thus 7.95 to 1. Compression ratios should be checked on both stock and nonstock motors to ensure longevity and avoid detonation.

Increasing and Decreasing Compression

To Increase Compression	*To Decrease Compression*
Mill the cylinder head	Mill top of piston
Use thinner head gasket	Use thicker head gasket
Increase bore	Decrease bore
Raise valve seats	Sink valves deeper in head
Reduce valve pockets	Increase valve pockets
Increase rod length	Shorten rod length
Use piston with lower pin	Use piston with higher pin
Offset-bush rod toward small end	Offset-bush rod toward big end
Fill combustion chamber	Open up combustion chamber

Clearances

With big valves, high-lift camshafts, and reduced deck height, you need to check the piston-to-valve clearance before assembling the motor. Modeling clay works well for this. Put a piece of the clay on top of the piston, and turn the motor over with the head bolted down (with the head gasket), and with the cam belt and cam timing set as you are going to run the motor. For checking purposes, set the valves to the tight end of the specification to give yourself a little leeway. The closest point should be on the exhaust stroke just before TDC, when the intake valve begins to open.

Remove the clay and note where the valve made an impression. Carefully cut through the thinnest point of the impression and measure the thickness of the clay. This is your piston-to-valve clearance.

You are looking for 0.125 inch of clearance at the minimum point. If you have less, you should have

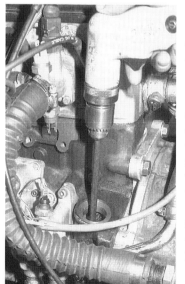

Priming the engine before that all-important first start-up. Even on a warm day, 80 psi is not unusual using this method.

valve pockets cut. To determine the centerline for the valve pockets, remove the valves, temporarily replace the head, and mark the centerline of the valve stem on the piston (at TDC) by inserting a long, thin punch down through the valve guide. The pistons can then be removed and machined.

Coatings

The pistons absorb a lot of heat from the combustion process, especially in race and turbo applications. One way to cut down this heat transfer and the possibility of detonation is to coat the tops of the pistons with zirconium oxide or impregnate them with molybdenum.

Zirconium oxide coating and moly impregnation differ slightly in where the material is applied and in how they work. Zirconium oxide is applied only to the top of the piston to reflect heat. Moly is applied to the entire piston to reduce friction, even out temperature across the surface of the component, and reflect heat away from the part.

Temperature flow is a property of moly that reduces hot spots by transferring heat quickly from high-temperature areas to low-temperature areas. But the moly also reflects heat away from the part, so there is less heat to transfer across the surface of the part. In a piston, this would mean a lot of the heat from the combustion process would be kept from soaking into the piston in the first place. What heat did soak in would be evenly distributed across the surface of the piston. This lower amount of heat would then be quickly radiated into the oil by the moly applied to the underside of the piston. There would also be less frictional heat in the piston because the skirts are treated.

One other benefit of moly impregnation is that the moly tends to shed carbon, so carbon build-up in the combustion chamber will be reduced.

Remember, if you treat one component in the combustion chamber, you should treat all the components to avoid heat overload of any untreated components.

For most people, coatings are too expensive to justify in all but the most high-performance applications.

Rings

For normal applications, the standard thicknesses of rings are fine. If you are building a very high-rpm motor, you will need to use thinner rings. Thinner rings wear more quickly, but at high rpm, a thin ring does not have as much momentum as a thick ring, so it can change direction easier. A thin ring also has less friction against the cylinder wall, so less power is lost. If you are experiencing a lot of blow-by with a high-rpm, high-compression motor, try using a thinner ring to reduce ring flutter.

A typical forged piston, for example, might use a 1.5-millimeter top ring, 1.5-millimeter second ring, and 4.0-millimeter oil control ring, compared with the stock GTi rings at 1.5, 1.75, and 5.0 millimeters. Mahle pistons for Super Vee racing use 1.2, 1.2 and 4-millimeter rings, and even rings as thin as 1.0, 1.0, and 3.0 millimeters. In general, as engine performance increases, the rings get thinner.

Hollow dowel pins for locating the head gasket on assembly.

The dowel pins go in the rear oil return holes.

If you need to increase the gap, remove the ring from the bore. Clamp a file in a vise and file the ring from the outside in, *never* the other way around. Make sure you file the ends at right angles to the top and bottom ring surface. When the gap is right, dress the ends of the rings with 400 grit sandpaper.

For street use, the stock ring gap settings are fine. Compression rings must have 0.30 to 0.45 millimeter of end gap; oil scraper rings must have 0.25 to 0.45 millimeter of end gap. For racing use, stay toward the upper limit of the ring gap specification.

Before sliding the pistons and rings into the bores, position the ring end gaps as follows: Line up the expander ring of the oil control ring set with the axis of the wrist pin. Position the top and bottom oil control ring rails 1 inch to either side of the axis of the wrist pin. Then align the second ring gap with the gap in the top oil control ring rail, and align the top ring gap with the gap in the bottom oil control ring rail. Do not line up the ring end gaps, as this will cause a loss of compression and an increase in oil consumption.

Motor Mounts

Stock motor mounts in the A1 are a little soft for high-performance use. There is a wealth of heavy-duty motor mounts out there, all the way from hardened rubber to polymer to solid metal. In the pre-1985 cars, the stock front motor mount was too loose to allow the use of tube headers, and even the cast-iron European header had a problem now and again as a result of all the flex allowed by the stock motor mounts.

Even if you have a ball joint type of exhaust, you should switch up to a heavy-duty front motor mount to reduce wheel hop and improve traction during hard launches. The Techtonics front mount is made of material similar to the stock mount, but with a different cross-section so it fits the cup better. This gives you the benefits of a stiffer mount without an undue amount of extra vibration. Harder front mounts will chatter your teeth out.

The different design of the A2 and A3 front motor mounts requires a different approach. The weight of the engine presses down on the top of the mount, lifting up only under acceleration. Therefore, you can leave the top part of the mount and replace just the underneath portion with a solid piece, such as the urethane kits sold by Velocity. One benefit of leaving the stock mount on top is that vibration from the engine in the "rest" position is minimized.

As this is being written, the new "pendulum" style mounts of the A4 are so new that there are no aftermarket replacements, and it looks as though none will be needed. The system seems to work fine up to at least 240 horsepower.

The side motor mounts can be checked by sliding a floor jack under the motor and lifting up a little. If the mount is worn out, the motor will move a lot before it is caught by whatever is left of the motor mount. If your side motor mount is worn out and you have not replaced your front motor mount, do so. A better front motor mount will take some of the load off the side motor mount.

Assembly

As you assemble the motor, constantly be on the lookout for anything that will cause the engine to self-destruct once it is all together, even if this means cleaning parts you *know* are clean and double-checking measurements you *know* are right.

In addition to making sure all clearances and procedures are correct, you will need to lubricate many of the parts so that the initial start-up procedure does not ruin them. For bearings, use a good grade of motor oil, with a little moly paste mixed in if you wish. If you use a heavy grease, paste, or oil, you will not be able to feel if a clearance is too loose, nor will grease or paste move out of the way fast enough to let oil into the bearings once the motor is running.

For cam lobes and the tops of the cam followers, use moly cam lube, usually available in little tins. Here it is okay to use paste, because these parts are splash oiled. The moly lube is to

Sawed-off cylinder head bolts are handy for aligning the head gasket when reinstalling the cylinder head.

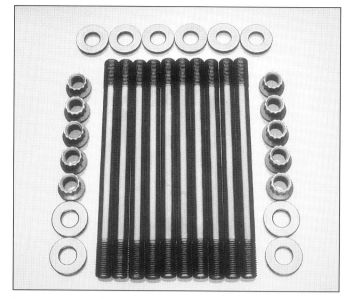

Raceware head stud kit to replace the stock head bolts.

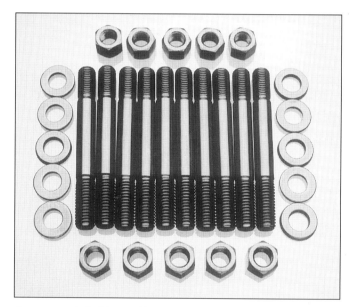

Raceware main bearing stud kit.

be applied *only* to the top of the cam follower and to the camshaft lobe. Do not coat the cam follower skirts with moly lube, grease or anything else except motor oil. Heavy grease might prevent the cam follower from rotating, leading to extreme wear or failure of the shim, the camshaft lobe, or both.

For cylinder walls, use a light coat of WD-40. This will allow the rings to seat quickly and without galling. The only problem with using WD-40 is that it does not stay on the cylinder walls very long, so start the motor as soon after assembly as possible.

If you will not be starting your motor soon after you assemble it, use something a little heavier than WD-40 on the cylinder walls, such as a thin coat of motor oil. Motor oil will not drain off as fast and will thus protect longer than the thinner WD-40.

With the engine on an angle the way it is, it can be a real trick to get the block, the head gasket, and the cylinder head all lined up when it comes time to bolt everything together. The block dowel pins you see advertised are one way of addressing this problem. Or you can take a couple of old head bolts and saw an inch or so off the threaded end to use as guides. To make it easier to get them out after the head is on, cut a slot in the top to fit a screwdriver blade. They may not be as elegant as dowel pins, but they work just as well and are reusable.

Before attempting to put the head on the block, screw these guides into two of the rear cylinder head holes. A couple of turns will do. Then slip on the head gasket and ask a passerby to help gently lift the head into place.

After centering the head and getting a couple of head bolts started, slip a screwdriver down the hole, unscrew the line-up studs, and then fish them out with a magnet.

The most difficult part of this procedure is sawing the head bolts. Plan on going through a couple of hacksaw blades if you do this job by hand; a cutoff saw would work well here. Do not be dissuaded by the prospect of hard labor, however. This is a very important step in the life of your motor.

Before you put the head back on, you must remove all traces of dirt, grease, and—especially—water from the cylinder head bolt holes. The only thing you want between the cylinder head bolt and the threads in the block is a light coat of motor oil.

One last thing to be on the lookout for when tightening the head bolts is the way they feel. It is fine to trust the torque wrench, but sometimes a head bolt will start to fail as you torque it down. One clue that this is happening is that you will have to turn the head of that bolt more than the others. If you suspect something is odd, stop and replace the head bolt with a new one of the same type. Head bolts come in many different types, so do not mix them.

Speaking of torquing head bolts, the pattern for future instructions seems to be to specify an initial low torque setting and then a certain number of degrees to turn the fastener beyond that point. This is important because the engineer knows the pitch of the bolt, knows how much stretch should be in the bolt, and can precisely calculate how much the bolt has to be turned to get that stretch. These instructions will allow you to avoid dealing with the frictional and tolerance differences among head bolts and block threads, to say nothing of the calibration of the torque wrench.

Pressurized lubricant for prelubing your engine before initial start-up.

The only problem is that a special tool is required to gauge the exact number of degrees the bolt has been turned. This tool is available in Germany for nearly $150, but Snap-On markets a similar device that retails for much less.

Start-up

Again, most engine damage occurs on start-up, before the lubricant can circulate to protect the engine. Just image what happens when you start a brand new engine! Fortunately, there are several things you can do to make the initial start-up less traumatic for your motor.

On A1, A2, and A3 four-cylinder engines, the very best thing you can do is to fill the oil galleys with pressurized oil before you turn the key. If you have access to a cutoff saw, cut about 8 inches of 3/8-inch bar stock and notch the end of it to fit over the drive tang of the oil pump (with the distributor removed). You can then chuck up the bar stock in a drill motor and manually prime the oil galleys using the oil pump. Hold on tight to the drill motor, however, because when the oil is at room temperature and the pressure builds, you will run into strong resistance. This method is so effective that Darrell Vittone ships one of these tools with each motor he sells. Remember that you must have the flywheel bolts in place in the crankshaft before you pressurize the oil system, or oil will pour out of the bolt holes. This method won't work on the VR6

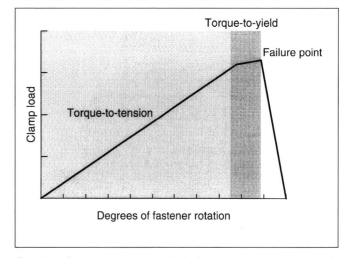

Torquing a fastener to a given tension is the most common practice, and it allows fasteners to be reused. Torquing to yield obtains maximum usage from the fastener, but because it has stretched beyond its recovery point, it must be replaced each time.

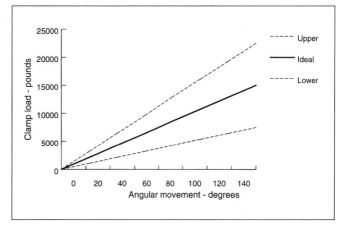

If your torque wrench is off by a certain percent, the error grows as the fastener is tightened.

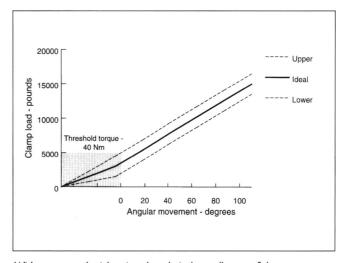

With torque-angle tightening, the relatively small error of the torque wrench is not magnified as the fastener is tightened, so clamping load is attained more reliably.

A Euro-only small-displacement 16V.

Front view of the V5 engine.

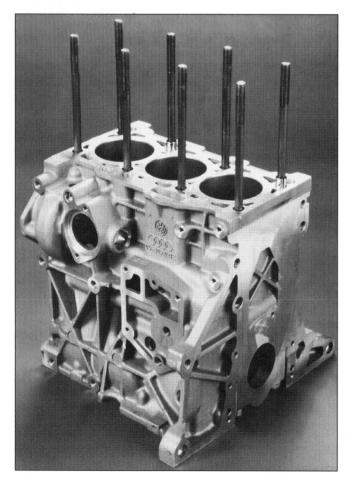

You may be glad you don't have to hot-rod this three-cylinder VW Lupo engine, but the head studs mean this little powerhouse can withstand some serious compression ratios.

engine, which drives the rear-mounted intermediate shaft off the rear of the crankshaft, or A4 four-cylinder engines, which no longer have an intermediate shaft (the oil pump is driven off of the front of the crankshaft). On these engines, it is best to connect a pressurized preluber to the oil galley at the oil pressure sender and prime the oil circuit that way.

The worst way is to use the starter motor and crank the engine until oil pressure builds up. During those first few moments of low rpm and virtually no oil pressure, all your new parts grind against each other without lubrication.

Whichever approach you take, make sure that the ignition and fuel delivery are both ready to go so that when you hit the starter the engine fires right off.

Now a word about the break-in oil, the oil you have been working so hard to get into the engine before you engage the starter motor for the first time. In the past, the practice was to use a poor-quality oil, such as something with a rating of SB, for the break-in period. (The *B* in SB does not mean that the oil is for break-in use. It just happens to be the rating of the oil.) Use normal SF- or SG-rated motor oil, which will protect your engine better during the break-in period.

Once the engine is running, do not let it idle. Run it up to about 2,000 rpm and run it for about 20 minutes. This will allow plenty of time for the parts to get to know one another. After 20 minutes, shut it down and recheck everything to make sure that nothing has wandered out of spec. If you are worried that the cam followers are not rotating, shut the motor off after about 5 minutes and check them for unusual wear patterns. Otherwise, let the motor go the full 20 minutes.

On the off-chance that your rings do not seal, there is a trick you can use to help them along. Find an empty stretch of road and shift into third at the appropriate speed. Accelerate hard from about 1,200 rpm to about 4,500 rpm, and then let the car coast down against the motor's compression until you reach 1,200 rpm again. Then do the whole procedure over. After a few runs (no more than 10) your rings should be seated—and a good thing, too, considering how badly the car has been smoking! If not, you did something wrong somewhere along the line, and it is time to think about tearing down the engine to fix it.

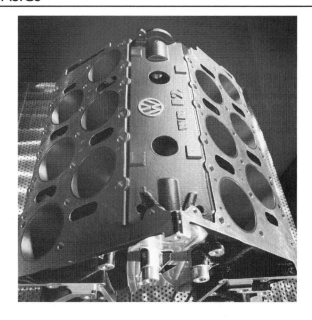

Two VR6 engines side by side, sharing a common crank, make the W12 engine.

V5 engine installed.

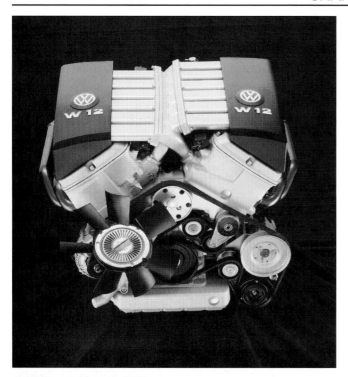

Compact and potent, the W12.

The cylinder banks for the W12 are offset just slightly, so the crankshaft journals are ground offset to match.

The side view of the W18 clearly shows the third cylinder bank, as well as an output shaft right where the two in-line three-cylinder engines mate up.

Is this four-valve head from the W12 destined for the VR6 or V5?

Chapter 4

Cylinder Heads

The head plays a dominant role in the performance of the motor. Every bit of air and fuel that your engine needs to make horsepower flows through the head at least twice, and the better it flows the more horsepower you will make.

For many years the standard two-valve head on the Volkswagen was a single-port-face design, meaning the intake manifold is on the same side as the exhaust manifold. This is not ideal for performance. In fact, some typical high-performance tricks will not work on this head. The 1993-and-later four-cylinder heads and all the four-valve heads are cross-flow designs.

Two-Valve Heads

The Volkswagen comes with six different styles of two-valve heads. All the early two-valve heads have the intake manifold and the exhaust manifold on the same side. Finally, in 1993, Volkswagen introduced the "cross-flow" head, which has the intake manifold on the opposite side of the engine from the exhaust. This configuration not only makes possible much better airflow (and performance), but also helps reduce the amount of heat transferred from the exhaust to the intake, for a denser incoming air charge.

Carbureted

The head for the carbureted Volkswagen looks very similar to the early fuel-injected head in most respects, except that there are no holes for the injectors. The combustion chamber is in the head. You cannot modify a carbureted head for a fuel-injected application.

Early Fuel-Injected

As it appeared on the 1.6-liter motors, this head differs from the carbureted head in that there are threaded openings above each intake port into which the fuel injector fits. The combustion chamber is in the head.

In flow bench testing done by Greg Brown for Autotech SportTuning, it was discovered that the stock port started losing airflow after 0.330 inch of valve lift. The stock camshaft at that time offered 0.406 inch of lift, so going to a still larger camshaft without head work is not the hot tip. Gains from switching camshafts in this head are the result of different lobe profiles and lobe centers.

As it sits, this head is good for making 85 to 90 horsepower with bolt-on accessories.

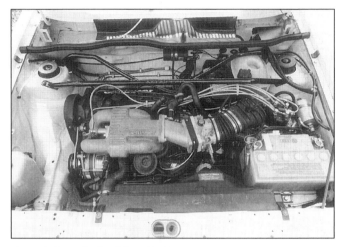

An early four-valve head from Oettinger.

Heron

As previously mentioned, the European GTis used this flat bottom head in combination with deep-dished pistons. This head is very distinctive, and you should not have any difficulty identifying it. The combustion chamber is in the piston. There are threaded openings for the fuel injector nozzles.

In most cases, the pistons that mate with this head cannot be interchanged with those from an American head without changing the head too. The exception is that the pistons from the 1.6-liter GTi bolt into the 1.7-liter motor, raising the compression ratio to 9.2:1. Other than this, you will normally use flat-top (or shallow-dished) pistons with American-style heads and the deep-dished pistons with the Heron heads.

GTi

All the preceding heads share a common valve spacing. When Volkswagen made the bore bigger in 1983, it made good use of the extra room in the cylinder by spacing the valves 1 millimeter farther apart.

This is a great head right out of the box, with big valves, straight ports, and good valve spacing, so for most applications you can use it as is. You can see gains from bigger valves and porting, but you will pay a lot and not get much in return.

These heads have an additional oil return hole at the front of the head between cylinders 3 and 4 (you can see the bump from the outside of the head), and the original front oil return

It takes a lot of skill and a flow bench to come up with ports such as these.

The factory camshaft splash guard for the later cars fits the early cars, too, and works just as well.

hole was enlarged. To make this head work in cars with earlier blocks, the additional oil return hole must be filled in, and the enlarged front oil return hole must be welded up and then drilled to match the smaller-size hole of the earlier heads.

GTi with Air-shrouded Injectors

This head is similar to the GTi head, with the addition of a passage that feeds air in around the injector for better atomization. For maximum value, this head must be used with the air-shrouded injector assemblies. It would be very difficult to modify a non-air-shroud head to work with air-shrouded injectors.

The injectors for this head also have a brass insert instead of plastic. The injector itself has a plastic shroud, a directional shield, and an additional circlip to hold the sealing O-ring in position.

Hydraulic

In 1985, Volkswagen added hydraulic lifters to its already great cylinder head. These heads are easily identified by the No. 4 cam bearing cap, which was removed to make room for

This special valve guide installer is a must when manually inserting valve guides. The tool is designed to apply pressure to the thicker shoulder area of the valve guide to eliminate distortion of the guide wall.

an oil squirter, and by the oil feed hole in the lifter bore to feed the hydraulic lifter. The addition of the oil squirter makes it mandatory to use the plastic splash guard, which made its first appearance in this engine. A hydraulic follower is easy to identify as such by putting your thumb inside the follower and your finger on the top, and squeezing. If it is a hydraulic cam follower, it will compress.

If you are looking for maximum performance from your head, be aware that not all Volkswagen heads are of the same quality. Some early Mexican heads have reduced port flow, shrouded valves and poor alignment of the valve stem centerlines. More recent Mexican heads have been improving, and they should soon be every bit as good as other Volkswagen heads.

No matter where it comes from, check your cylinder head for flow, valve shrouding, and valve centerline before you invest time and money in it. If it is too far off, purchase a good used head and start with that.

If you are racing your car in a class that does not allow changes outside of blueprinting, you can gain 0.5 point of compression by shaving the head to its lowest limit. This is no good for street motors, because if you ever need to mill the gasket surface there will be no more metal left and you will have to replace the head. Remember that shaving the head retards the camshaft timing, which can be reset, if desired, with an adjustable cam gear.

1996 2.0-Liter Heads

During the 1996 model year, Volkswagen modified the 2.0-liter heads to reduce combustion noise and exhaust emissions and boost performance and economy. The intake port is a "swirl" design for better mixing of the air and fuel, and the port is offset from the axis of the intake valves for even more mixing as the incoming air/fuel charge enters the combustion chamber. The cam profile has been altered to match. As a result, these heads show big performance gains with porting and polishing and a performance camshaft. Bump the intake valve size from 40 to 42 millimeters, and the exhaust valve from 33 to 34 millimeters, and this head really starts to perform.

Head Gaskets

First, the obvious: If you are going to all the trouble of building your own motor, buy a quality head gasket, and if you have bored out the block for bigger pistons, make sure you get a head gasket with bigger openings to match.

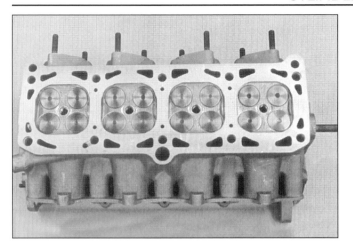

An early Oettinger four-valve head with a more traditional design, requiring different pistons.

The VW four-valve head. Note the squish area alongside the intake valves.

You won't be able to do this with the extremely large bores, such as 84.5-millimeter pistons, so you will have to buy the largest head gasket you can find, and use pistons that have been relieved around the edges to clear the head gasket.

The hot tip about head gaskets in general is laminated metal. They cost a little more, but they really hang in there.

Four-Valve Heads

Consider for a moment what happens inside the engine when it is operating. When the intake valve is open the intake air column rushes into the cylinder, drawn by the low pressure created in the wake of the receding piston. So far so good. Then the valve closes. The air column tends to want to stay in motion, but with the valve shut it has nowhere to go, so it stops. By the time the intake valve begins to open again, the air column is stopped and wants to stay where it is.

Even if it were still in motion, the air column would have precious little opportunity to express itself for the first few degrees of crankshaft rotation. At the beginning of the intake cycle, the camshaft is able to open the valve only a small amount. No matter how strong the airflow of the head is when the valve is fully open, what counts is what happens the rest of the time—when the valve is only partially open. And when the valve is just beginning to open, there is not much room for the intake air column to get by the head of the intake valve.

This problem is addressed by using two smaller intake valves for each of the bigger valves. The greater circumference of these four small valves compared with the two big ones not only helps breathing, it gives more surface area on the valve seat for the valves to cool off.

The flow is what you are after, however. For example, look at what happens in two heads when the valves are 1 millimeter off the seats. The first head will have one intake valve, and the second head will have two intake valves.

Using a 40-millimeter valve in the single-valve head, the curtain area (the opening through which the air can flow) is 1.26 millimeter^2. Using two 34-millimeter valves to do the same job results in a curtain area of 1.82 millimeter^2, more than

44 percent larger. This shows how the critical low- and partial-lift figures can be much higher with a four-valve head than with a two-valve head.

Two-valve and Four-valve Curtain Areas

Valve Size	Curtain Area of Single Valve	Curtain Area of Double Valves
40	1.26	2.51
39	1.19	2.39
38	1.13	2.27
37	1.08	2.15
36	1.02	2.04
35	0.96	1.92
34	0.91	1.82
33	0.86	1.71
32	0.80	1.61
31	0.75	1.51
30	0.71	1.41
29	0.66	1.32
28	0.62	1.23
27	0.57	1.15
26	0.53	1.06
25	0.49	0.98

The tradeoff comes in a loss of air velocity. At high rpm this is not a problem, but the normal response curve of a four-valve engine shows that low-end torque suffers relative to high-end torque. This is one of the reasons Volkswagen went to such extraordinary lengths in the design of its intake manifold for the 16V.

A four-valve motor has two other benefits not yet mentioned: reduced valve component weight and less need for a radical camshaft. Even though there are more valves, springs, and retainers to actuate, the weight of each individual assembly is lighter than that of its larger counterpart in a two-valve head. This reduced weight makes it much easier to control

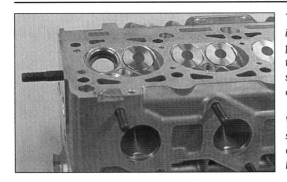

The view through the intake port on the VW four-valve head. With twin valves and a nice, straight port, airflow is assured.

VW four-valve head showing the knife-edged camshaft bearing surfaces.

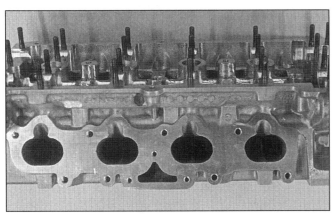

The intake ports of a VW four-valve head.

valve movements, thus making is possible to hit higher rpm without suffering from valve float. This is further helped by the fact that less valve movement is needed, so a tamer camshaft can be used and still get the proper amount of air into the cylinder. Because the valves are lighter, however, the valvetrain will tolerate a more radical camshaft, if desired. The best of both worlds.

Confusingly, Volkswagen refers to engines equipped with its four-valve head the 16V. It's confusing because their new engines are 20V engines. This could be either five-valve four-cylinder engines (which they are), or four-valve five-cylinder engines (which is consistent with the way the current engines are designated). This designation also forces you to "do the math" to calculate the number of cylinders. The 16V head has two intake and two exhaust valves per cylinder, exotically shaped intake ports, siamesed exhaust ports, and room for two camshafts. Inside the head are five camshaft bearings for each camshaft, plus an oil squirter. Because there are twice as many cam followers, the followers from adjacent cylinders nearly touch, leaving no room for the lower half of the camshaft bearings. These bearings narrow down to a knife-edge at the very bottom, but all the load is in an upward direction, so this is not a problem. Because of the number of valves, the spark plug is in the middle of the cylinder head. The camshaft belt drives the exhaust cam; the intake camshaft is driven by a chain at the opposite (flywheel) end of the camshaft from the belt drive. The entire head is one casting.

The 2.0-liter 16V is similar to the 1.8-liter, with slightly different port sizes and other minor changes. This makes it convenient

for those who want to bore out their 1.8-liter blocks from 81 millimeters to 83 millimeters, increasing the displacement from 1,781 cc to 1,870 cc, as they can use the readily available 2.0-liter head gasket. (This goes for anyone doing a head swap too). Both blocks have roll pins for locating the head gasket, but in the 2.0-liter engine they are slightly offset from where they were in the 1.8-liter engine. Because the roll pins are really not needed after the cylinder head is bolted on, you can tap them down into the block with a hammer so the 2.0-liter head gasket will work on the 1.8-liter block.

The 1.8-liter 16V head has bigger intake ports and smaller exhaust ports than the 2.0-liter 16V head, so it makes more power. You can gain somewhere between 10 to 15 horsepower swapping your 2.0-liter head for a 1.8, or you can port your 2.0. Obviously, the 2.0 head is not a performance upgrade for the 1.8-liter 16V engine.

Five-Valve Heads

In Europe, Volkswagen sells a number of five-valve engines, both normally aspirated and turbocharged. Eurosport is looking into the prospect of using these new heads atop older blocks.

Porting and Polishing
Using a Flow Bench

A flow bench allows the engine builder to isolate the head from the rest of the motor to see just what contribution it is making. By sucking air through intake ports and blowing air through exhaust ports with the valve at various distances off the valve seat, the engine builder can experiment with different port shapes and dimensions without having to assemble the entire motor and run it on the dyno. A probe inserted into the port shows where there are areas of fast-moving air (low pressure) and areas of relatively dead air (high pressure).

Through careful shaping of the port, the flow can be improved by eliminating or reducing discontinuities in the air path. By measuring the differential between the air pressure entering the head and the air pressure exiting the head, the overall efficiency of the port can be determined. As a rule of thumb, for every additional cubic foot per minute (cfm) of airflow through the port, you should realize an additional 0.4 horsepower per cylinder. On a 1.6-liter cylinder head, porting increases the airflow by nearly 10 cfm on top of the 14.6 cfm gained by utilizing GTi valves. This translates to a theoretical potential of 124 to 129 horsepower, compared with the stock theoretical potential of 85 to 90 horsepower.

Estimating Airflow by Horsepower

Horsepower	Airflow (cfm)
1	0.69
2	1.39
3	2.08
4	2.78
5	3.47
6	4.16
7	4.86
8	5.55
9	6.25
10	6.94
11	7.63
12	8.33
13	9.02
14	9.72
15	10.41
16	11.10
17	11.80
18	12.49
19	13.19
20	13.88
21	14.57
22	15.27
23	15.96
24	16.66
25	17.35
26	18.04
27	18.74
28	19.43
29	20.13
30	20.82
31	21.51
32	22.21
33	22.90
34	23.60
35	24.29
36	24.98
37	25.68
38	26.37
39	27.07
40	27.76
41	28.45
42	29.15
43	29.84
44	30.54
45	31.23

Estimating Horsepower by Airflow

Airflow (cfm)	Horsepower
1	1.4
2	2.9
3	4.3
4	5.8
5	7.2
6	8.6
7	10.1
8	11.5
9	13.0
10	14.4
11	15.8
12	17.3
13	18.7
14	20.2
15	21.6
16	23.0
17	24.5
18	25.9
19	27.4
20	28.8
21	30.2
22	31.7
23	33.1
24	34.6
25	36.0
26	37.4
27	38.9
28	40.3
29	41.8
30	43.2
31	44.6
32	46.1
33	47.5
34	49.0
35	50.4
36	51.8
37	53.3
38	54.7
39	56.2
40	57.6
41	59.0
42	60.5
43	61.9
44	63.4
45	64.8

When evaluating add-ons it can be helpful to estimate current and promised airflow. This chart works for complete motors as well as add-ons. For example, a stock 1,600-cc motor in a good state of tune requires about 54 cubic feet per minute to make 78 horsepower. To gain 10 percent more power (8 horsepower), you need to increase airflow more than 5 cubic feet per minute.

On the other hand, if you know the airflow, you can estimate the horsepower. This chart works for complete motors as well as for add-ons. A stock 1,600 head flows about 61 cubic feet per minute. Therefore, the most you could expect with bolt-on modifications would be about 88 horsepower.

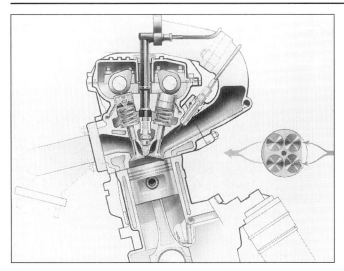

This cut-away view of the VW four-valve engine clearly shows the port design, the 25-degree intake valve angle and the squish area, as well as the piston oil squirters down below.

There are many ways to port a head for more power. The optimum port is the smallest port that will flow the most air; *small* so the velocity is high, and *flow* so the air gets into the combustion chamber where it will do some good. Although no set formulas or procedures work on all heads and all ports, the more a tuner uses a flow bench, the better chance he or shehas of understanding what the head needs to work right.

It is critical to remember the concept of the optimum port when working on 16V heads, which flow more air by virtue of their twin valves. It is easy to open up the ports to the point where you lose air velocity, and thus performance. In general, nowhere should the cross-section of the intake port be larger than the size of valve(s) it feeds.

If you want to try porting yourself, be careful. You can easily grind through into the water jacket, or otherwise damage the head if you are inexperienced. Practice on a junk head before you try to port your only cylinder head.

The flow bench gives calculated numbers that indicate what the head should do. It is very helpful, but in the final analysis the only thing that matters is how much horsepower the head makes when it is in the car.

Unshrouding the Valves

If you have your head ported and polished, part of the procedure is to unshroud the valves. On a stock valve job, for the first few thousandths of an inch of valve lift, the airflow past the head of the valve is obscured by the ledge of metal that runs around the valve seat. Unshrouding the valves involves removing this lip so the air can flow unimpeded into and out of the cylinder.

Valves
Sizing

There is a formula that can help you figure out what is best for your application, and it works by matching the valve size to the engine displacement. First you figure out the intake valve size, and from that you calculate the exhaust valve size in millimeters.

In this equation, S equals the stroke in millimeters and B equals the bore in millimeters.

To see how this works, consider a 1,588-cc motor. The bore is 79.5 millimeters, and the stroke is 80 millimeters. You expect to rev the engine to 6,000 rpm. This gives you:

$$\text{Diameter (in inches)} = \sqrt{\frac{\text{rpm} \times S \times B \times B}{2,286,000}}$$

Thus, the theoretical intake valve is 36.4 millimeters in diameter. This is 2.6 millimeters larger than the stock valve. The theoretical exhaust valve is 85 percent of the size of the intake valve, or about 31 millimeters.

In dyno tests with various size engines, this formula seems valid for most high-performance street applications.

Selecting

With the introduction of the GTi motor in 1983, the stock factory steel valves (40-millimeter intake, 33-millimeter exhaust) became popular in aftermarket applications. Not only are they the right size, the right length, the right material, and long lasting, they are also available through most dealerships, as well as from many aftermarket suppliers. These valves are highly recommended for all street applications.

These steel valves are even good in the early 1,600 heads, where the additional flow bumps the performance capabilities of the head up to 100 to 115 horsepower without any other modifications to the ports.

In some applications, however, you might need a valve that is a different diameter or length than this (or any other)

Table 11: Increased air flow due to porting		
	CFM	**Theoretical hp**
Stock	54.9	85-90
GTI valves	69.5	108-113
Porting	79.4	124-129

Airflow and horsepower at .462 lift: 1,600-cc head. Blueprinting, balancing, and so on are nice, but you must get the engine to breathe, which means head work on the early heads, as shown by these results of flow-bench tests by Greg Brown for Autotech SportTuning.

Table 8: 2-valve and 4-valve curtain areas (mm²)		
Valve size	Curtain area of single valve	Curtain area of double valves
40	1.26	2.51
39	1.19	2.39
38	1.13	2.27
37	1.08	2.15
36	1.02	2.04
35	0.96	1.92
34	0.91	1.82
33	0.86	1.71
32	0.80	1.61
31	0.75	1.51
30	0.71	1.41
29	0.66	1.32
28	0.62	1.23
27	0.57	1.15
26	0.53	1.06
25	0.49	0.98

The much larger curtain area of two small valves compared with one big valve allows the engine to breathe much better; even at 1 millimeter lift off the valve seat.

In hydraulic lifter heads, the No. 4 cam bearing has been replaced with an oil squirter.

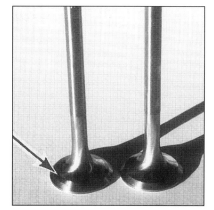

This extra cut on the back side of the valve allows better airflow but reduces longevity.

stock valve. If so, you can buy either steel valves, which do many things very nicely, or stainless steel forged valves.

Stainless steel valves (when made properly) are stronger than steel valves. All stainless steel valves are one-piece valves, because the metallurgy involved is not conducive to making two-piece valves. The factory steel valves are all one piece as well, but not all aftermarket steel valves are. Stainless steel is more elastic than steel, so it can take more of a bend without breaking or taking a set. Those of you with turbo motors will be glad to hear that stainless steel valves seem to be more burn resistant too.

They are not perfect, unfortunately. Stainless steel valves are more expensive than steel valves, and are slightly softer, so they will require refacing and replacement more often. It is also possible for the chrome plating to come off the stems of poorly made stainless steel valves, at which point the valve guide takes a real beating.

The stainless steel valves that are commonly available are slightly longer than a stock-length valve. If you need a stock-length valve, you will have to machine down the end of the stem to match the distance between the valve seat and the cam follower (assuming the stainless steel valve has been made with enough material above the keeper groove to allow machining).

Some people install special matching seats that stick out into the combustion chamber by the same amount that the valve stems are too long. This would allow you to unshroud the valves without having to port and polish the head or rework the combusting chamber. However, this increases your compression ratio and reduces your piston-to-valve clearance, and creates hot spots in the combustion chamber—which can lead to preignition.

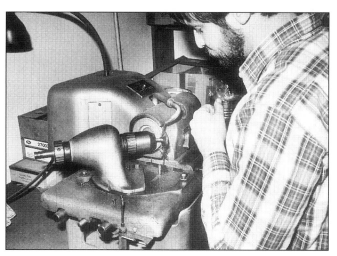

Resurfacing a valve.

Another way of improving flow is to use valves with smaller-diameter stems. The standard stem is just under 8 millimeters, and valves are available from the aftermarket with 7-millimeter stems. These require changing your valve guides, seals, retainers, and keepers, though, so only those looking for all-out performance will be interested.

Warning: Sodium-filled valves must be treated with special handling, because the sodium is under high pressure. Do not grind or break the stem of a sodium-filled valve. Do not

Two-step lapping compound, with coarse compound on one end and fine polishing compound on the other end.

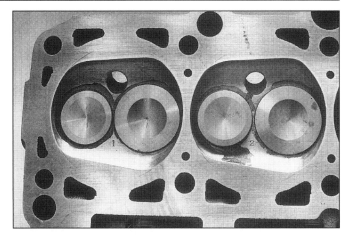

Polishing is done to the combustion chamber. At the same time, the valves are unshrouded, and the combustion chamber volumes are all made equal.

dispose of a sodium-filled valve with the rest of the scrap metal, as doing so will then present a danger to others.

Cutting Valve Angles

The proper angle for the valve face is 45 degrees. Low-lift flow on the exhaust port can be improved by performing an additional 60-degree cut on the *margin* of the valve (the area between the stem and the seat face), but it would come at the expense of longevity. Stick with a single cut at 45 degrees for street motors.

Valve Seats

As with some of the other procedures in this book, working with valve seats is not something you should tackle on your own unless you plan on making a living at it. Valve seats can be tricky to work with, and if you make a mistake your engine will not run right, at the least. The worst that can happen is that the seats will fall out of the head while the motor is running, ruining your whole day.

Although anybody can have a seat come out of the head, it is more prevalent with the "high-performance" heads you see advertised at "too-good-to-be-true" prices. The low prices can be enticing, but head work is so important to the overall performance of the motor that you will be money ahead getting a good-quality head and passing up the bargains.

Valve seats have an ID (internal diameter) measurement and an OD measurement (valves have an OD measurement only). The ID measurement gives you an idea how much air will flow through the seat. The OD measurement gives you an idea how much trouble it is going to be to fit the seat in your head.

One reason Volkswagen went to the different valve spacing on later heads was to fit more valve. The 1,600-cc heads will not accept much more than a 40-millimeter intake seat. Even at that you can hit the water jacket in the center cylinders, which can crack the head. These cracks will ooze coolant into the combustion chamber after you shut the car off, and if extreme enough will allow combustion gases into the coolant.

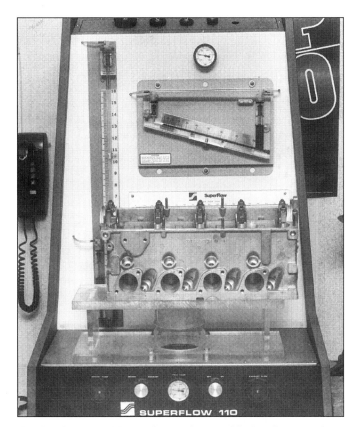

Flow-bench testing, while not always indicative of final performance, does show the engine builder things that may not reveal on a dyno.

If your 1,600 with big valves runs rough after one hour of sitting, it may not be the fuel injection. Pull the radiator cap off and run the motor to see if the cooling system is building up unusual pressure when cold. Let the motor warm up, then pull a spark plug and check for coolant in the cylinders. If you see a little green puddle, head for the store and pick up some Alumiseal. If that does not work, consider upgrading to an 1,800-cc head modified to work on your block. Not only are

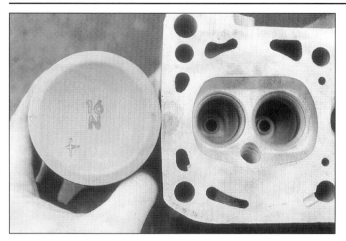

U.S.-style head with matching pistons. The combustion chamber is in the head.

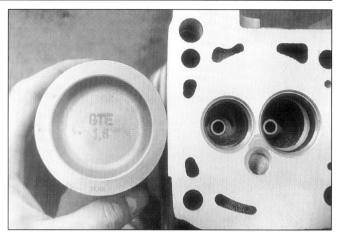

European-style head with matching pistons. The combustion chamber is in the crown of the piston.

Stock 1,600 combustion chamber showing the valve shrouding.

Hydraulic head, showing the two front oil return holes.

the stock valves the size you want them, but the ports are far superior right out of the box.

Cutting Valve Seat Angles

The way the valve seat is cut is as important as the way the port is shaped, because it has to let air past smoothly, it has to provide a sealing surface for the valve, and it has to act as a heat sink, as well.

To accomplish all these tasks, the valve seat has three different angles ground into it. The first angle blends the seat into the port. It is called the bottom cut and must be 60 degrees.

The seat, where the valve touches, must have the same angle as the valve face, or 45 degrees. On the intake valve, the width of the seat contact area is 2 millimeters. On an exhaust valve, the seat contact area is 2.4 millimeters wide.

The width of the contact area is critical. If it is too thick, there will be too many square millimeters of seat against which the valve face will ride. Unless you are changing valve springs too, the valve spring pressure will be spread out over a greater surface area. The valve spring will not be able to pull the valve closed tightly enough to seal, and eventually the valve will burn.

To blend the airflow over the seat into the combustion chamber, one final cut must be made at 30 degrees.

If you are going to be porting and polishing your head after installing new valve seats, the new seat must be rough cut to 0.25 millimeter smaller than the finished diameter.

Lapping the Valves

Lapping the valves involves coating the mating surfaces of the valve and seat with a special lapping compound (a paste that has fine abrasives in it), and rotating the valve while it is in contact with the seat. To rotate the valve, you can either use the traditional suction cup on the end of a stick on the head of the valve and push the valve closed, or you can slip some stiff rubber tubing over the stem of the valve and pull the valve closed while you lap. You don't want to get any compound into

The air port for the air-shrouded injectors on a 1984 GTi head.

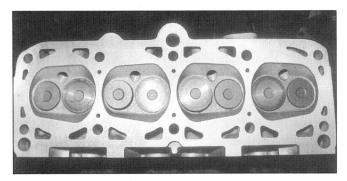

This late-model head has been modified to work on an early block by welding up the right front oil return and reducing the diameter of the front center oil return.

the valve guides, of course, and you must clean up afterward to ensure none of the grit stays in the motor.

Some machinists will tell you that with the new valves and valve seat cutters available, you no longer have to hand-lap your valves. It is tempting to believe this because valve and seat surfacing equipment is pretty good these days, and hand-lapping can be a lot of work.

The trouble is that many machine shops are not as careful as they should be, and you may wind up with a valve that does not sit on the seat quite right. This results in small leaks that start out by simply robbing you of horsepower, but that can progress to the point where the valve will burn and you must do the job over again.

If you are after professional results, take a few minutes and hand-lap your valves. After all, it is your engine, and you want it to live for a long, long time. Lapping the valves is also important in racing classes where you cannot do anything to the motor other than blueprinting.

It does take time to disassemble the head to lap the valves, but once you get set up, the work goes quickly. If the machining was done correctly, the valve and seat faces will have a nice, even coating of lapping compound on them almost immediately. If there is a problem, you will have to judge

whether it is better to return the head to the machine shop so they can fix it, or to use the course lapping abrasive to rub out the flaw and then final lap with the finish compound.

Valve Guides

The best-wearing and longest-lasting valve guides are made of silicon-bronze alloy. These are readily available from most automotive supply houses. The valve guides in the Volkswagen motor are relatively short, so they should be checked carefully for wear when you have the head apart. A tight fit is necessary to help cool the valve and to make sure the valve closes properly on the seat each time it comes down.

After installing new guides, always run a guide reamer through them for good measure.

Selecting a High-Performance Head

When buying a head, or having yours reworked, here are some questions to ask:

What valves are used? Stock valves are good because you can easily obtain replacements, in the event of a failure.

What springs are used? For high-performance use, you want dual (inner and outer) springs. Also, find out if the springs have been treated in any way (such as shot peening) to extend their longevity.

How much lift will they accept? If the springs will not allow as much lift as the camshaft needs, they will go into coil bind. At the least, the springs will fail. At worst, the coil bind will be so bad that it will wipe out the springs, the camshaft, and the followers.

Are the valves set up for a stock-base circle camshaft? Valve length is governed by the base circle of the camshaft you are using. If you have a reground or exotic race camshaft, the base circle may be smaller than stock, which means the valves must be longer to compensate. Alternately, you can't use a stock-base-circle cam if the valve lengths have been set for a cam with a reduced base circle.

Is the head flow tested? It is possible that whoever did the head was able to do a good porting job without flow testing the head, but flow testing removes all doubt. If the head has not been flow tested, find out how much extra it would cost.

Is the installed height of the valve spring checked? Springs are specified to run at known "installed heights," that is, the compressed length of the spring when the valve is closed. If the installed height is wrong, you might run into coil bind, or there may not be enough spring pressure to keep the spring from bouncing off the seat when it closes.

Do the seats have a three-angle cut? Any good head should have three-angle cuts on the valve seats for maximum flow.

Have the valves been lapped? It only takes a couple of extra minutes to check while the head is disassembled.

Camshaft Bearing Problems

Another problem I hope you never have to deal with is that of bad camshaft bearings. The Volkswagen engine has no bearing shells for the camshaft to ride in; it spins directly in the head material itself.

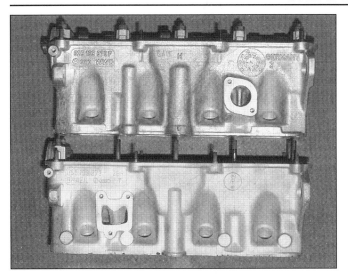

Intake valves from left to right: 34-millimeter (1,600 and 1,700), 38-millimeter (Mexican 1,800), 40-millimeter (GTi), and 41-millimeter (Oettinger 2021 kit).

To make room for air conditioning, the water return port was moved from the right side of the head (bottom) to the left

Normally the camshaft bearings should last well over 100,000 miles. If the oil gets very dirty they can become scored, however. Camshaft bearings will also be turned into hamburger if you reassemble the engine with the head gasket on upside-down, or if you torque the bearing caps on backward.

If the bearings are damaged, they can be surfaced and the camshaft bore rehoned to size. If there is greater damage, the camshaft bearing saddles will have to be machined for bearing inserts. Rimco is the place to get this done, and it is also the place to buy the camshaft bearing shells if you need them.

Miscellaneous Tips and Techniques
Valve Cover Studs

One of the best things you can do for early heads is to upgrade the valve cover gasket studs. This goes double if you have a very early head that uses bolts to hold the valve cover on. The new-style studs have a shoulder in the middle. After removing the old studs (or bolts), Loctite the new studs in. Between the shoulder and the Loctite, you can crank on them to make them stay.

With the new-style studs, you can use the new-style gaskets that have larger holes. These seal better than the early style gaskets because the shoulder prevents the valve cover nuts from being tightened down so far that the gasket is flattened. This does not increase the performance of the motor, but it does keep it cleaner and make it nicer to work on.

Oil Splash/Blow-by Guard

Another easy modification for the early cars comes straight from Volkswagen. Starting in 1985, the company began installing a black plastic splash guard that sits atop the camshaft bearing studs, under the valve cover. This simple device cuts down the amount of oil splash that can cause valve cover gasket and oil fill cap leaks, and it also helps separate out the oil in the blow-by.

If your air filter is getting saturated with motor oil, you should install one of these. It even seems to help the performance of aftermarket valve covers in this respect, although none of the aftermarket valve covers I have ever seen seal, handle blow-by, provide oil cooling, or fit as well as the stock valve cover. An aluminum valve cover may look good, but the stock unit does everything a valve cover needs to do.

Preventive Maintenance

The only problem with the camshaft splash guard is that it obscures the view of the intake and exhaust lobes for cylinder No. 1. This makes it impossible to quickly check the position of the cam (or the condition of the inside of the head) by removing the oil fill cap.

If you do not have a camshaft splash guard, check the inside of the head any time you have your valve cover or oil fill cap off. Are the surfaces clean and shiny, with a light coat of oil? Or are they caked with black or dark brown sludge? If the inside of the head is not clean down to the bare metal, you are doing something drastically wrong, and your engine is going to get revenge some day.

That caked-on gunk is oxidized oil. Oil oxidizes either because it is old and abused, or because it has been overheated.

Checking installed valve stem height with a special setup tool, the Pad Saver.

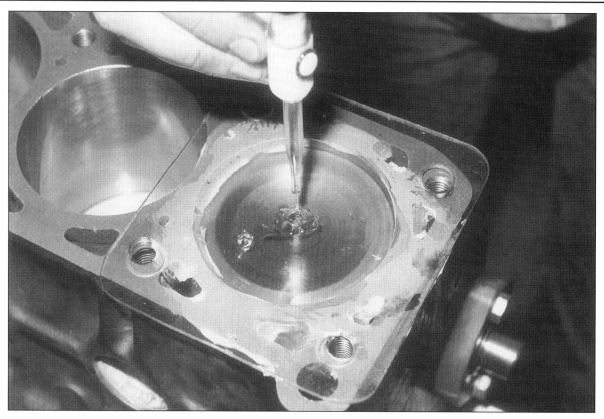

Measuring the volume of the piston.

Measuring the head volume.

Welding an old valve to the valve seat . . .

. . . allows you to knock the seat out from behind.

This fully prepped head shows extensive work to the ports and combustion chamber. The plugged cooling passages identify this as a head for an alcohol-burning engine.

A ported VR6 head. The differences in port shape are due to differences in runner length, as one row of cylinders is closer to the port side than the other.

Either way, you have to do something about it before your engine dies a horrible death.

Go to the auto parts store and get some oil and an oil filter. While you are there, pick up a can of carburetor cleaner. Berryman's Chem-Tool is a good product, but keep it away from your paint.

Take some old rags and the carb cleaner, and clean off as much of the gunk from the inside of the head as you can, taking care not to let too much of the carb cleaner get into the oil drain-back holes. When you are finished, drain the oil, change the filter and pour in the new oil.

Repeat this procedure every 1,000 to 1,500 miles until the head is clean inside. Your car will run much cooler, and your oil will protect your engine longer when it no longer has to fight the existing oil sludge from the minute you pour it in the crankcase.

Moly Impregnation

As described at the end of the section on engine tools and techniques, moly impregnation can help a camshaft, crankshaft, cylinder bore, or piston skirt. But the inside of the head?

According to the people who do this sort of thing, it works, and works well. By coating the inside of the head, heat flow is improved across the surface of the combustion chamber, helping eliminate hot spots and thus cutting down on preignition. Used in combination with coated pistons, moly impregnation keeps more heat in the combustion chamber and out of the motor.

As nice as this all sounds, it is not something everyone will want to do. The Volkswagen motor runs fine without it, so this is another technique that is relegated to the race-only category.

Chapter 5

Camshafts

As with many aspects of the Volkswagen motor, the stock camshaft is very well thought out, providing a good example of what to look for in an aftermarket camshaft. The stock profile integrates all the design parameters you expect in a camshaft while paying heed to emissions requirements, and it does a good job of balancing performance against pollution. However, there is a lot more performance to be had from other camshaft profiles.

Theory

In an *ideal* world, the camshaft would open the intake valve only when the cylinder was ready to accept a fresh air/fuel mixture, and close when the cylinder was filled. The exhaust valve would open after the complete combustion of the air/fuel mixture and close after the exhaust gases had left the cylinder. The intake valve would then open again, repeating the cycle.

The real world operates quite differently and is far more complicated, making the camshaft that much more important.

Camshaft Operating Parameters

A vast number of characteristics are embodied in camshaft design. And if you are to get the most from your engine, every single aspect of the camshaft must be taken into consideration.

There are two main parameters that determine cam performance, not counting the effects of intake and exhaust efficiency: *when* the valves open and close and *how much* they open. These two main parameters can be broken down into nine separate categories, each of which interrelates with the next. To these nine categories I have appended three additional categories specific to the Volkswagen engine.

Intake Opening and Closing

Of the four cam-controlled events mentioned earlier, it is widely acknowledged that intake valve closing is the most important. The sooner the valve is closed, the sooner cylinder pressure will begin building up, boosting low-end torque.

Intake opening is set by the range of operating rpm of the engine. The sooner you can open the intake valve, up to a point, the more time the engine will have to fill the cylinder with the fresh air/fuel mixture. At low rpm, opening the intake too early results in a rough idle and poor off-idle response, because the air/fuel mixture mixes with the exhaust gases that are still trying to get out of the cylinder. At higher rpm, opening the intake valve early allows the exiting exhaust gases to

A 16V cam setup showing the drive chain for the intake valve.

pull the air/fuel mixture into the cylinder, and the engine will breathe better.

Exhaust Opening and Closing

After the spark plug ignites the air/fuel mixture, the piston is forced downward by the expanding gases. This is called the power stroke, and it ends when the exhaust valve opens. The sooner the exhaust valve opens, the shorter the power stroke. On the other hand, you do not want to delay opening the exhaust valve for too long, because after a point there is not enough energy left in the expanding gases to continue to create meaningful force against the piston, but there is enough residual force to help flow the spent gases out the exhaust port. By opening the exhaust valve at just the right time, you can take advantage of this residual energy to help evacuate the cylinder. Because the exhaust valve is usually left closed until long after the point at which the combustion gases are contributing to the power output, the exhaust valve opening has the least effect on torque of the three main valve events (intake closing, intake opening, and exhaust opening).

The exhaust valve usually does not close until after the intake valve has begun to open. This promotes intake breathing to some extent, and the cooler temperature of the intake charge helps take some of the heat out of the exhaust valve to keep it from burning.

In conjunction with the intake opening parameter, the exhaust closing parameter allows you to calculate valve overlap.

69

Duration

Duration is the measurement in crankshaft degrees between when the valve opens and when it closes. For example, if the intake valve opens at 7 degrees BTDC (before top dead center) and closes at 49 degrees ABDC (after bottom dead center), you add the number of degrees between the opening of the valve and TDC (7 degrees) to the number of degrees between TDC and BDC (180) and the number of degrees between BDC and the closing of the valve (49).

$$\text{(Intake open to TDC)} + \text{(TDC to BDC)} +$$
$$\text{(BDC to intake closed)} = \text{duration}$$
$$7 + 180 + 49 = 236$$

In this case, the duration is 236 degrees. What is not so obvious is why the duration is often measured at 1 millimeter, instead of directly off the surface of the camshaft lobe, or off the follower or valve face with the valve clearance properly set.

There are three reasons for this: One, Volkswagen measures its camshafts at 1 millimeter. Two, for the purposes of engine builders, there is not much airflow past the valve at low lifts (when the valve is just starting to open or almost completely closed). And three, the transition area on the cam lobe between when the valve is closed and when the valve is being forced open is called the clearance ramp.

At running tolerance, these ramps are critical for proper valve and lifter control. For setting up an engine, they are worse than worthless, because they might not have anything to do with the working profile of the cam. Therefore, to make calculations based on a duration that is not 100 percent usable is misleading. By measuring duration at the cam at a figure such as 1 millimeter, however, you can predict the performance of an installed cam in an engine after all the tolerances are taken up, the valve is open enough to allow meaningful airflow, and the ramps are out of the way.

When either valve is open, the engine cannot make any compression, so long-duration camshafts are found only in engines that see high rpm and need to breathe more than they need dynamic compression. This type of motor would usually be built with lots of static compression (which is derived mathematically), so there would be some compression left when the engine was running.

Camshaft Checking Height and Duration

Checking Height	Intake Open	Intake Close	Duration
.001	58	98	336
.010	40	77	297
.020	22	58	260
.030	13	50	243
.040	9	46	235
.050	6	42	228

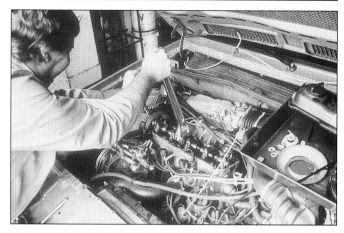

Counter-holding the cam when removing the cam sprocket bolt with the motor in the car. To avoid marring the cam lobe you might want to use a rag between the crescent wrench and the camshaft.

A custom setup for degreeing camshafts, making use of a junked head.

Lobe Centers

The lobe center is the number of camshaft degrees between the centerline of the intake lobe and the centerline of the exhaust lobe. The lobe centerlines are imaginary lines through the axis of the cam that bisect the cam lobes at their point of highest lift.

If you know the opening and closing times of both the intake and exhaust valves, you have all the information you need to calculate lobe centerlines and lobe centers. Taking numbers from the sample camshaft, remember that the intake opened at 7 degrees BTDC and closed at 49 degrees ABDC. When you added these two numbers to the 180 degrees there are between TDC and BDC, you got

$$7 + 180 + 49 = 236$$

This is the total time the intake is open. Assuming the lobe is symmetrical (see the later section on lobe profile), you can divide this number by 2 to get the exact midpoint of the lobe, or the lobe centerline.

$$236 \div 2 = 118$$

This is the number of crankshaft degrees between the lobe centerline and the opening (or closing) of the valve. To find out where this lies in relation to TDC, subtract the number of degrees that the valve is open BTDC from the lobe centerline value.

$$118 - 7 = 111$$

This gives the number of crankshaft degrees between TDC and the lobe centerline. Running the numbers for the exhaust lobe, you will find the lobe centerline value to be

$$\frac{9 + 180 + 47}{2} - 9 = 109$$

Now that you have the lobe centerlines in crankshaft degrees, you can calculate the lobe centers, which are always expressed in camshaft degrees. Add the two centerline values together and divide by 2 (because the crankshaft turns twice for each time the camshaft turns once). This gives

$$\frac{111 + 109}{2} = 110$$

The lobe center for this camshaft is 110 degrees (at the camshaft). As discussed earlier, the lobe center determines how much time the intake and exhaust valves will be open at the same time. The closer together the lobe centers are, the longer the two valves will be open simultaneously, all other factors being equal.

Valve Overlap

Overlap is the time (expressed in degrees of crankshaft rotation) that both the intake and exhaust valves are simultaneously open in the same cylinder. Overlap is a function of the lobe centers and camshaft duration:

$$D - 2L = O$$

D represents the duration, L represents the lobe center and O represents the overlap. Therefore, the sample camshaft with 236 degrees of duration and 110 degrees of lobe center has 16 crankshaft degrees of overlap.

As the lobe centers are spread farther apart, overlap is reduced. Engine power range is narrowed, becoming concentrated toward the upper end of the rpm curve. This is because of the later closing of the intake valve.

Moving the lobe centers closer together increases the overlap and increases cylinder pressure (because the intake valve is closing earlier), but it also increases exhaust scavenging. Too much overlap will lead to increasing portions of the incoming air/fuel mixture being scavenged (pushed out the exhaust without being burnt), which negatively affects the brake-specific fuel curve.

Engines run with a lot of cam overlap usually have more static compression built into them to compensate. In a CIS-

Because this is a permanent fixture, it makes sense to go to the extra effort to adapt a Beetle degree pulley.

injected motor, the proper amount of valve overlap for all-around performance is found in camshafts with about 108 to 110 degrees of lobe center. Any more overlap (less lobe center) than that will create a rough idle, as pressure pulses from the exhaust cycle affect the intake tract, causing the air sensor plate to flutter. The newer Motronic cars have a sensor that tells the computer how much air is flowing "backward" in the air intake, so the fuel injection doesn't read that as incoming air and meter too much fuel but you still have to use a cam with moderate overlap.

As the rpm increases, this ceases to be a problem and advancing the camshaft (either by grinding advance into the camshaft or with the use of an adjustable cam sprocket) can mitigate air sensor plate flutter. Early carbureted Golfs used 114-degree-lobe-center camshafts, and Super Vees with mechanical (not CIS) injection used 100-degree-lobe-center camshafts.

In all cars, the greater the overlap, the less vacuum the engine will pull at idle.

Cam Timing

There are two ways to alter cam timing. The first is to grind the amount of advance or retard into the cam itself. The figures that are important in calculating camshaft advance or retard are the intake valve opening and exhaust valve closing specifications. If the intake duration is the same as the exhaust duration, and the intake opening figure is the same as the exhaust closing figure, then there is no advance or retard ground into the cam, and it is said to have a split overlap.

To determine the amount of advance or retard ground into a cam with equal intake and exhaust duration but unequal intake opening and exhaust closing figures, subtract the smaller of the two figures from the larger of the two figures, and divide by 2. This gives you the amount of advance or retard in crankshaft degrees. If the intake opening figure is larger, the cam is advanced. If the exhaust closing figure is larger, the cam is retarded.

The sample camshaft is one illustration of this. It begins opening the intake at 7 degrees BTDC and closes the exhaust at 9 degrees ATDC. From this you can immediately see that the cam is ground with a slight amount of retard in it. How much?

$$\frac{7-9}{2} = -1$$

This camshaft is ground with one crankshaft degree of retard.

Sometimes the intake duration and the exhaust duration are unequal. In that case, subtract the smaller duration from the larger duration and divide by 2. Then subtract this figure from each end (opening and closing) of the larger figure. You will have one adjusted duration and one unadjusted duration. You can then determine the amount of advance or retard as outlined earlier. This gives you an approximate figure, at which time you will need to put in some time on the dyno to accurately evaluate whether or not the cam will work in your application.

Lobe Profile

Each cam lobe has two sides. One opens the valve and one closes it. Normally, it is sufficient if the shapes or profiles of both sides are the same. Also, it is normally sufficient if the profiles of the intake lobes are the same as those for the exhaust lobes. However, that is not the only way to do it.

Asymmetric cams are found with different profiles for opening the valve than for closing it. This is normally done to allow the cam to pop the valve open at a maximum rate and then allow for a more leisurely closing to prevent valve float (uncontrolled or false motion in the valvetrain).

A dual-pattern cam, on the other hand, is one in which the profile of the intake lobe is different than that of the exhaust lobe. A dual-pattern cam is a special-duty design, and most applications work well without going to dual-patterns.

A flat spot ground into the bearing surface of the camshaft allows a little oil to squirt out onto the cam follower for better lubrication. This is not needed except in very high-performance applications.

A typical adjustable cam sprocket.

Adjustable cam sprockets are a necessity on a twin-cam motor, both for setting cam timing and for setting overlap.

Lift

Lift is measured at the cam, and is defined as the difference between the cam base circle (the point on the camshaft with least lift, usually directly oppose the cam lobe) and the highest part of the camshaft lobe, which is also known as the toe or nose. Because the lift of the camshaft is measured at the nose of the camshaft, there is no need to worry about the 1-millimeter checking height that is so important when talking about duration and timing.

Lift determines how much the camshaft will open the valve. Stock cams are often relatively mild, and the Volkswagen motor will accept a much higher lift cam than the factory puts in. However, the factory valve springs will accept only a certain amount of lift before the coils of the spring start touching each other, a condition known as coil bind. (See the following section on valve springs.)

You can check the lift on a solid-lifter camshaft yourself. You need some way of measuring the camshaft accurately (a set of outside micrometers or a dial caliper will do the trick). On hydraulic camshafts and some full-race camshafts, the ramps extend down to the point where you will be measuring, which will throw the numbers off. To measure these, put the camshaft between centers and use a dial indicator to check the lift. First set the dial indicator so

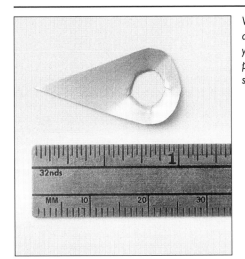

With a pair of scissors and an aluminum can, you can make a pointer for the cam sprocket.

The pointer eliminates erroneous readings when dialing in the camshaft.

that the indicator end has enough travel to stay in contact with the surface of the lobe throughout 360 degrees of rotation. Next, turn the camshaft so that the indicator is on the nose (high point) of one of the camshaft lobes and take a reading there. Rotate the camshaft 180 degrees to a point directly opposite your first reading, and take a second reading there. Subtract the second reading from the first, and you have your lift.

To measure the lift on a solid-lifter camshaft, first take a measurement from the nose of one of the camshaft lobes to the opposite side of the cam, as shown in the illustration. Write this number down. The next measurement must be taken at 90 degrees from your first measurement. Subtract your second measurement from the first to get the lift of the cam. For example, if the first measurement is 1.925 inches and the base circle is 1.5 inches, the lift of your camshaft is 0.425 inch.

Camshaft Lift in Millimeters and Inches

millimeters	inches	millimeters	inches
9.00	0.354	11.25	0.443
9.05	0.356	11.30	0.445
9.10	0.358	11.35	0.447
9.15	0.360	11.40	0.449
9.20	0.362	11.45	0.451
9.25	0.364	11.50	0.453
9.30	0.366	11.55	0.455
9.35	0.368	11.60	0.457
9.40	0.370	11.65	0.459
9.45	0.372	11.70	0.461
9.50	0.374	11.75	0.463
9.55	0.376	11.80	0.465
9.60	0.378	11.85	0.467
9.65	0.380	11.90	0.469
9.70	0.382	11.95	0.470
9.75	0.384	12.00	0.472
9.80	0.386	12.05	0.474
9.85	0.388	12.10	0.476
9.90	0.390	12.15	0.478
9.95	0.392	12.20	0.480
10.00	0.394	12.25	0.482
10.05	0.396	12.30	0.484
10.10	0.398	12.35	0.486
10.15	0.400	12.40	0.488
10.20	0.402	12.45	0.490
10.25	0.404	12.50	0.492
10.30	0.406	12.55	0.494
10.35	0.407	12.60	0.496
10.40	0.409	12.65	0.498
10.45	0.411	12.70	0.500
10.50	0.413	12.75	0.502
10.55	0.415	12.80	0.504
10.60	0.417	12.85	0.506
10.65	0.419	12.90	0.508
10.70	0.421	12.95	0.510
10.75	0.423	13.00	0.512
10.80	0.425	13.05	0.514
10.85	0.427	13.10	0.516
10.90	0.429	13.15	0.518
10.95	0.431	13.20	0.520
11.00	0.433	13.25	0.522
11.05	0.435	13.30	0.524
11.10	0.437	13.35	0.526
11.15	0.439	13.40	0.528
11.20	0.441	13.45	0.530

Camshaft lift in millimeters and inches.

Camshaft pulley degree equivalents

Teeth	Degrees	Teeth	Degrees	Teeth	Degrees
0.5	4.09	15.5	126.82	30.5	249.55
1.0	8.18	16.0	130.91	31.0	253.64
1.5	12.27	16.5	135.00	31.5	257.73
2.0	16.36	17.0	139.09	32.0	261.82
2.5	20.45	17.5	143.18	32.5	265.91
3.0	24.55	18.0	147.27	33.0	270.00
3.5	28.64	18.5	151.36	33.5	274.09
4.0	32.73	19.0	155.45	34.0	278.18
4.5	36.82	19.5	159.55	34.5	282.27
5.0	40.91	20.0	163.64	35.0	286.36
5.5	45.00	20.5	167.73	35.5	290.45
6.0	49.09	21.0	171.82	36.0	294.55
6.5	53.18	21.5	175.91	36.5	298.64
7.0	57.27	22.0	180.00	37.0	302.73
7.5	61.36	22.5	184.09	37.5	306.82
8.0	65.45	23.0	188.18	38.0	310.91
8.5	69.55	23.5	192.27	38.5	315.00
9.0	73.64	24.0	196.36	39.0	319.09
9.5	77.73	24.5	200.45	39.5	323.18
10.0	81.82	25.0	204.55	40.0	327.27
10.5	85.91	25.5	208.64	40.5	331.36
11.0	90.00	26.0	212.73	41.0	335.45
11.5	94.09	26.5	216.82	41.5	339.55
12.0	98.18	27.0	220.91	42.0	343.64
12.5	102.27	27.5	225.00	42.5	347.73
13.0	106.36	28.0	229.09	43.0	351.82
13.5	110.45	28.5	233.18	43.5	355.91
14.0	114.55	29.0	237.27	44.0	360.00
14.5	118.64	29.5	241.36		
15.0	122.73	30.0	245.45		

Camshaft pulley degree equivalents: Using this table, you can get to within a couple of degrees when measuring or degreeing your camshaft.

Area Under the Curve

Although this might remind you of the calculus class you took in high school, you are not going to have to work out first derivatives and integrations. Picture instead two camshafts that both open and close the intake valve at the same crankshaft degrees. If one camshaft has a lift of 0.410 inch and the other has a lift of 0.425 inch, the second camshaft will have a great deal more area under the curve than the first, even though the durations are the same.

If the cam grinder so desires, he could reduce the duration on the second cam by some extent and still have more area under the curve than with the lower-lift cam. In theory, whenever the area under the curve is increased, the engine's ability to breathe should improve.

Base Circle

One thing that prevents some reground and aftermarket camshafts from interchanging directly with the stock unit is the base circle. It is possible (sometimes even desirable) to grind the cam on a different base circle than the factory cams. On a replacement cam with a smaller base circle, the valve stem will need to come up higher toward the camshaft (by being longer or by having the valve sunk deeper into the head), all the adjustment shims will need to be thicker to compensate, or you will need to use lash caps between the end of the valve stem and the cam bucket.

When people were first starting to do high-performance work on Volkswagens, there were no high-performance camshafts or valves available. If you wanted a hot camshaft, you reground the one you had. Grinding reduced the base circle of the camshaft, requiring different valves or the use of lash caps.

A reduced-base-circle camshaft has one advantage over the stock-base-circle camshaft. By reducing the base circle and leaving the nose of the camshaft alone, you get much more lift than is possible with a stock base circle. With this extra lift, however, comes the necessity of changing the valves, followers, and springs, in addition to machining the head to make the followers and springs work. None of this will be required for any reasonable street machine, and only the most radical race engines need make use of it.

Thus, for most of us, a stock-base-circle camshaft is the only way to go, if for no other reason but that if your state passes smog inspection legislation, with stock-length valves you can slide your old stock camshaft right back in there. (You did save it, didn't you?)

Billets

Many companies tout the fact that their camshafts are "chill-hardened" German billets for the ultimate in wear resistance. A chill-hardened camshaft is cast in a special mold that chills the hot metal quickly on the outside, causing the carbon in the metal to form a tough facing surface while the inside is still hot. This combination makes for a very good cam billet.

There are other ways of making a cam billet, however. Often, American billets are cast from a material called Proferal (short for Process Ferrous Alloy). Proferal is cast using more traditional sand-casting, which is less labor intensive and thus less expensive than chill-hardening. Controversy has arisen because the early Proferal formulation gave spotty results in some applications. It takes only a couple of camshafts going flat to start the word around, and that is what happened. If you do find a Proferal billet, it should have additional chrome for increased wear resistance (compared to the problem billets from the late 1980s), which makes it acceptable for Volkswagen camshafts.

Selecting a Camshaft
Fuel-Injected Camshafts

If you have a normally aspirated CIS fuel-injected car, selecting a camshaft is fairly easy. Be conservative in your selection, and if possible drive a car fitted with the camshaft you

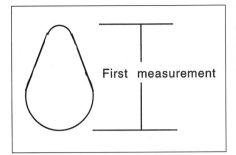

First measurement

When trying to determine the lift of your camshaft, use your dial caliper to measure this distance first.

Next, measure the base circle as shown here. If you have a hydraulic or high-performance camshaft, the ramp will already be starting here, so your calculated lift figure will be off by a couple of thousandths on the low side.

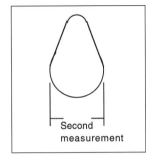

Second measurement

have your eye on before you buy. If others tell you a certain camshaft is not very good for street use, believe them. There are definite limits to what a fuel-injected motor will accept.

I find that more of my driving time is spent with the car at idle than at redline. Therefore, a camshaft with good idle characteristics is more important that a camshaft that gives me 5 horsepower more above 6,500 rpm. You must also free up the exhaust flow before a hot camshaft will do you much good.

The most camshaft you can run in a 1.6- or 1.7-liter engine with stock springs and CIS measures about 0.425 inch of lift with a 108- to 110-degree lobe center. The 1.8-liter engines have been known to run 0.435 inch of lift. Use too much lift, and you run into problems with valve springs; more overlap than that, and the back pulse in the intake manifold will cause the airflow sensor in the fuel distributor housing to flutter, destroying horsepower. The DigiJet, Digifant, and Motronic injections are also intolerant of too much overlap, as can be seen in the Motronic VR6, which has almost 5 degrees of negative overlap.

Cams designed for use with hydraulic lifters are different from those designed for solid lifters. The biggest difference with the hydraulic-lifter camshafts is that the ramps start very early, to preload the lifter so it will be locked up by the time the flank of the camshaft comes around.

For those with 16V motors, the intake camshaft is easiest to change, gives the most bang for the buck, and is still driveable. You can get more horsepower by changing the exhaust cam, too, but this moves the power peak to a much higher rpm. (For even more big-end horsepower, see the discussion of intake manifolds in chapter 3.)

Generally speaking, cams from U.S. aftermarket suppliers such as Autotech and Neuspeed are designed with an eye to driveability, and may even be "smog legal" (certified for use in states with strict pollution control laws). Cams from German suppliers such as Abt and Schrick tend to be more "all-out."

Don't buy your camshaft without considering other modifications you may be making to the engine, however. For example, in a VR6 application, the Schrick 260 cam and either the stock manifold or a slightly-larger-than-stock manifold are a nice combination, especially in a heavier car. However, if you want a bigger cam such as the Schrick 268 cam, consider coupling it with the Schrick Variable Geometry intake manifold, which has more horsepower at 2000 rpm than the 260 with a smaller, non-variable manifold, and 35 to 40 more lb/ft of torque at 3500 rpm. The peak horsepower is about the same, but where the smaller cam and manifold drop off rapidly after the horsepower peak, the 268 and the Variable Geometry manifold drop off more gradually, which makes driving (and gearing) that much easier. The Schrick Variable Geometry manifold works great with smaller cams, too, of course.

Carburetor Camshafts

If you have a carbureted motor, the first thing to remember when selecting a camshaft is do not overcam—just as with a fuel-injected motor, but for slightly different reasons. Overcamming kills bottom-end power and will result in poor idling. Unless you are racing, most of your daily driving is done at relatively low rpm, so you want to preserve or improve the low-end torque as much as possible.

You can check for possible overcamming on solid-lifter engines by loosening the valve adjustment 0.010 to 0.015 inch. If your engine runs better with more valve lash, you have too much cam for the rest of your engine in your application. When running a single carburetor, one of the CIS-style camshafts would be a good choice. With two or more carburetors, you can get more radical.

Second, measure your cam at 1 millimeter. The reasons behind this are covered earlier. Many cams are advertised with measurements taken at the valve, or at a 0.004-inch clearance, or whatever. Do not trust these claims. Measure everything at a clearance of 1-millimeter so you know you are comparing apples with apples. Then, before you install the cam you have selected, double check the measurements to ensure the figures you were quoted are right.

Third, the more overlap you use, the more static compression the engine will need to make horsepower. This is because no compression is being built up during the overlap period, so all compression must come from that part of the piston travel remaining after both valves finally close. (Also remember that moving the lobes closer together is better for high-rpm applications, and spreading the lobe centers boosts low-end performance.)

Fourth, the more carburetor, head work, and exhaust efficiency you have, the more camshaft you can run. Just remember to match the camshaft to the other components after you have decided on the other components. In the Volkswagen motor, it is a lot easier to change camshafts to match your other components than it is to port the heads to allow the camshaft to work properly. A stock exhaust will diminish any benefit from a camshaft change. Change your exhaust first.

Fifth, if you have a choice between two cams that each

A quick-and-dirty method for setting the camshaft to TDC uses a straightedge.

Table 12: Camshaft checking height and duration

Checking height	Intake open	Intake close	Duration
.001	58	98	336
.010	40	77	297
.020	22	58	260
.030	13	50	243
.040	9	46	235
.050	6	42	228

Camshaft checking height and duration: Camshaft specifications depend on the checking height, and there is no way of correlating specs from one checking height to another.

make about the same horsepower, but one is noisier than the other, choose the quieter one. Popping the valve open quickly usually results in more power, but you pay for it in engine longevity. Unfortunately, most people find out which cams are noisy the hard way—they install one. Also beware of any camshaft that requires a different clearance than the stock camshaft's when used for hot street performance.

In any case, the camshafts for a water-cooled Volkswagen may not be less expensive than those for a Chevy or Beetle, but you do not have to take the motor apart to try one out.

Supercharger Camshafts

For a supercharger, studies done by Volkswagen for its then-prototype G-lader showed that the best combination of power and emissions could be had with minus seven crankshaft degrees of overlap. In other words, the exhaust valve is almost completely closed when the intake valve starts opening. This reduces the tendency of the blower to force the incoming air/fuel mixture right out the exhaust port.

Volkswagen also shortened the intake valve closing time to 26 degrees ABDC, splitting the difference between the maximum torque point at 1,300 rpm and the maximum power point at 6,000 rpm. Closing the intake valve earlier would have picked up the bottom-end torque only about 1 percent, and a later intake valve closing would have improved maximum power even less. Tests showed that the short intake duration was more than made up for by the cylinder charging of the supercharger. That is what you call a good compromise. The negative overlap reduced hydrocarbon emissions by more than 50 percent, compared with emissions at 3 crankshaft degrees of overlap.

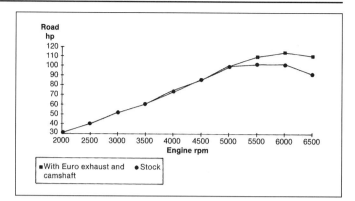

The 16V horsepower improvements are all on the big end when adding the Euro exhaust and exhaust camshaft. Porting the intake manifold would increase the horsepower peak further, but at the expense of low-end torque and driveability.

When the G-lader finally appeared in street form in the Corrado G-60, the cam specs were different, but the production camshaft still had no overlap.

Other Concerns

Engines with solid lifters won't accept more than about 0.430 inches of camshaft lift without modifications. This is one reason why the so-called 426 cams were so popular. If you want a really high-lift cam, install the new cam in the head with at least one intake and one exhaust valve, using very light "setup" springs (which you can buy at virtually any hardware store), and rotate the cam 360 degrees. If the lobes hit the cylinder head, you will have to clearance the edges of the lifter bores with a die grinder. If the valve spring retainer hits the valve stem seal, you will have to use low-profile Teflon seals. If the coils go into coil bind, you will have to buy high-performance springs.

The 1996 and later 2.0-liter engines use a single valve spring, which may be good for reducing friction and drivetrain weight, but won't accurately track a high-performance camshaft. You'll have to replace them with dual springs and matching retainers, such as those available from Techtonics.

Cam Sprockets

At this point, you may be wondering about cam sprockets, adjustable and otherwise. Adjustable cam sprockets allow you to move the torque curve of the engine around by altering the timing of valve events. Advancing the timing of valve events means that the intake valve opens sooner and the exhaust valve closes sooner, helping low-end torque. Retarding the cam does just the opposite and helps move the torque toward the big end.

If you have trimmed your head down and decked the block, the centerline of the camshaft will be that much closer to the centerline of the crankshaft, retarding your cam timing. An adjustable cam sprocket will help you recover the relationship between the cam and the crank, or to run the camshaft slightly advanced for better low-end torque.

An adjustable cam sprocket is also handy on a big-cam, small-lobe-center motor, and on an automatic transmission

Rabbit. Advancing the small-lobe-center camshaft allows you to recover some smoothness at idle, and advancing the automatic camshaft helps fill in that flat spot off idle.

Some adjustable cam sprockets come with 4 degrees of adjustment on either side, some with 6 or more. The more adjustment there is, the easier it will be to set up your cam timing, but you only need 4 degrees, because each tooth on the cam sprocket is worth a little more than 8 degrees. By skipping teeth and setting the cam sprocket, you can come up with just about any combination of advance or retard you need (whether or not it runs).

If you are going to play around with cam timing, just remember that you are only rarely going to detect less than 2 degrees of difference.

As helpful as an adjustable cam sprocket is in degreeing the camshaft, the Volkswagen SOHC (single overhead cam) motor is very difficult to set up for checking the phase relationship

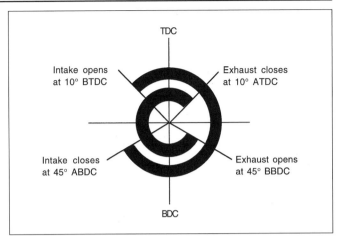

This is the way camshaft events are typically depicted. In this cam, the duration is 239 degrees at 0.050 inch, and the lobe center is 107 degrees. Although you cannot tell from this chart, the lift of this particular camshaft is 0.432 inch. To relate this chart to the four engine cycles, start at the point labeled "Intake opens." As you follow around clockwise, the cylinder starts taking in the fresh air-fuel mixture soon after the heavy line representing the intake valve crosses the thin vertical line labeled TDC. Notice that the intake valve opens before the motor actually starts taking in air and fuel, that the intake valve does not close until after the piston has passed BDC. Leaving the intake valve open these few extra degrees allows the engine to make use of the momentum of the incoming air/fuel charge. After the intake valve finally does close at "Intake closed," the compression stroke starts. Neither valve is open at this point, and you must follow around the circle clockwise past TDC again until you get to the point labeled "Exhaust opens." Notice that once again this happens before the piston has reached BDC. By opening the exhaust valve early, the motor can take advantage of the weak but still expanding gases to evacuate the cylinder. The exhaust valve stays open past TDC, again making use of the momentum of the outgoing air. It is time to start the cycle again, but wait! We need the intake valve open. Fortunately it has already started opening before waiting for the exhaust valve to close. Both valves open at the same time is called the overlap.

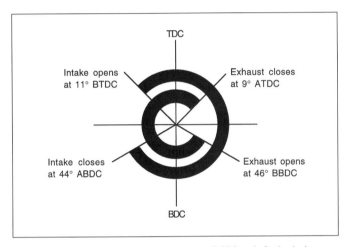

Although the duration is still 239 degrees at 0.050 inch for both the intake and the exhaust, and the lobe center is still 107 degrees, the intake valve is being opened 1.5 degrees (crankshaft) advanced. Because the intake valve is closing earlier, and the compression stroke starts sooner, the torque curve is moved lower in the rpm range.

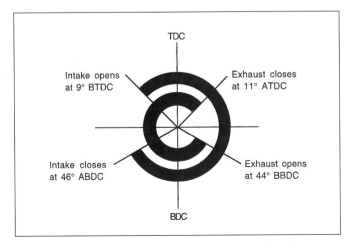

Here is the same camshaft again, only now the intake valve is being opened 1.5 degrees (crankshaft) retarded and the intake valve is closing later. Retarding the camshaft moves the torque higher in the rpm range.

between the camshaft and the crankshaft. The DOHC (double overhead cam) motor is a different story, because you can drop the dial indicator down through the spark plug hole. The procedures for checking camshaft specifications and for degreeing the camshaft to the crankshaft are explained later.

If you decide to stick with the stock cam sprocket, be aware that not all of them are perfectly marked when they come out of the factory. They may have the TDC dimple off to one side or another, relative to the sprocket tooth. The section on checking the camshaft specifications also explains how to check the TDC mark on your camshaft.

Cam Belts

The cogged cam belt Volkswagen uses is a surprisingly rugged component. Neglectful owners have seen many thousands of miles pass beneath their oil pans without the belt needing replacement or service of any kind. For a high-performance motor, *especially* in a big-valve motor where the valves

Dead-stop made from a bolt and a spark plug housing.

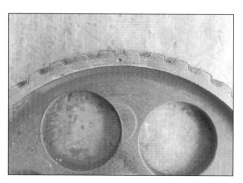

Check the cam adjustment mark to ensure it is in the center of the tooth.

For 1985, Volkswagen ground the backs of the camshafts this way, then changed back to the standard cam heel in 1986, so it apparently makes no difference.

Here is a cam nose starting to go flat, as can be seen from the sharp edge at the side of the lobe.

can contact the pistons when the belt breaks, changing the belt is inexpensive insurance.

The following directions will work for changing a belt with or without the installation of an adjustable cam sprocket on an 8V engine.

Installing an Adjustable Cam Sprocket

Remove the upper portion of the cam belt cover. Remove the oil cap so you can see the camshaft. Now turn the motor so that it is at top dead center for the number 1 cylinder. The easiest way to do this is to find an area of level ground, then put the car in top gear, let off the brake, and push or pull the car until both lobes on the camshaft for the number 1 cylinder are sticking up where you can see them. You will also be able to see the following:

• The little dimple on the outer rim of the cam gear lines up with the top edge of the head.

• The zero mark on the flywheel falls under the timing mark on the transmission housing.

• The distributor rotor points toward the mark on the side of the distributor housing.

Remember this alignment; you will need to duplicate it later. Once you have everything the way you want it, reapply the parking brake, leaving the transmission in gear. This helps hold the crankshaft in the right place.

Remove the alternator belt, the air conditioner belt, and any other belt or contraption that stands in the way of getting the lower portion of the cam belt cover off, and remove the cam belt cover. This allows you to see the timing marks on the crankshaft pulley that line up with the dimple on the intermediate shaft pulley. This alignment is hard to see from above without the use of a mirror and a flashlight. Everything should be lined up, but it does not hurt to double check.

A word of caution: Never try to turn over the motor by putting a wrench on the camshaft pulley bolt. The cam belt was not meant to put up with that, and it probably won't.

Locate the idler pulley that is used for adjusting the tension on the cam belt. Before you loosen the clamping nut, make sure you have something to grab the idler pulley adjustment nut with when the time comes to retension the cam belt. Early cars require a 27-millimeter wrench or an adjustable-end wrench of suitable size. Cars from 1986 on require a special spanner wrench. Schley Tools makes one that is sold by many of the aftermarket suppliers. If you are properly equipped, loosen the idler pulley and pull the belt off the cam sprocket.

You can remove the cam sprocket whenever you wish, but it is easiest to do it while the camshaft is still held down by the cam bearing caps. The best way to do this is to hold one of the camshaft lobes with an adjustable-end wrench. Wrap the lobe with a rag first, and make sure that the faces of the wrench jaws do not have any dings in them that could damage the camshaft lobe. Then use a 19-millimeter box-end wrench to loosen and remove the camshaft sprocket pulley bolt. Do not expect the cam belt to hold the pulley while you are breaking the bolt free.

Wiggle the cam sprocket off the end of the camshaft. If you are going to replace the camshaft at this time, go to the section on installing a camshaft and follow the procedure there.

As you are sliding the sprocket onto the camshaft, watch behind the sprocket to make sure that the Woodruff key is not being pushed out of the keyway. If it is, reseat it and lower the front end of it a little to prevent the sprocket groove from catching on it. If this still does not work, you may have to remove the Woodruff key and dress it down with a file until there are no burrs on it. Replace the camshaft sprocket bolt and, holding a lobe with an adjustable-end wrench as before, tighten it to 58 lb-ft.

The next task is to reinstall the cam belt. If your belt has many miles on it, this is a good time to replace it with a new one.

Measuring valve spring tension and compressed length.

This rifle-drilled Oettinger camshaft is also cross-drilled at the bearing journals.

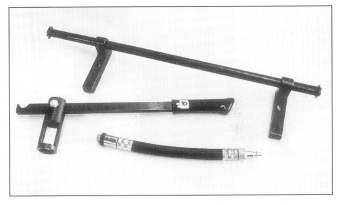

You need a couple of special tools to change valve springs in the car, including a spring compressor and some way of pressurizing the cylinder.

Unless something unusual has happened, the crankshaft should be in the same place as before. Chances are that the intermediate shaft has turned, however, and the camshaft needs to be set back in place. To set the camshaft, align the dimple in the sprocket with the top gasket surface of the cylinder head where the valve cover sits. If you are replacing the stock sprocket and you cannot locate the dimple on the sprocket, check to see if you have installed it wrong-side out. If you have, the sprocket will be too close to the valve cover, and it will rub when the motor is started.

Aligning the crankshaft and the intermediate shaft is done with a mirror, as previously explained. It is impossible to align these sprockets and then put on the belt. Put the belt on and see how close you are. It usually takes a couple of tries to get these sprockets all lined up.

Once the sprockets are in line, loop the belt up to the camshaft sprocket. The tension side of the belt is the side closest to the front of the car, so work from that side. Have your 19-millimeter wrench handy to jiggle the cam pulley bolt to line up the teeth on the belt with those on the sprocket.

After you get the cam belt on, turn the motor over twice and recheck all your settings. You may need to make a couple of tries before you get it right. Use the idler pulley to tension the cam belt, as described in the shop manual.

Installing an 8V Camshaft

For a bolt-on application, this section assumes that you do not want to change the valve springs. If you do, the procedure for changing springs can be found in "Replacing Valve Springs in the Car," page 88.

Removal

Remove the cam sprocket, as described earlier in "Cam Sprockets." After you have the sprocket removed, remove the valve cover and save the gaskets for later. Stuff rags into the oil return holes to make it more difficult to drop things into the motor. If you have a 2.0-liter cross-flow engine, you must first remove the upper portion of the intake manifold. Use rags to cover the runners in the lower intake manifold to prevent anything from falling in.

The cam sprocket is held from turning on the end of the camshaft by the Woodruff key, a small half-moon-shaped piece of metal that fits in a cutout in the camshaft and in a groove in the camshaft pulley. Remove the Woodruff key, taking care not to damage it, because you are going to reuse it.

If you cannot grab the Woodruff key with pliers or a pair of sidecutters, take a small punch and tap down on one end of the Woodruff key. The back side is rounded, so it will scoot right out. Do whatever it takes to keep track of the Woodruff key, as finding a replacement for it can be a long and wearisome task.

It is now time to remove the camshaft.

Five camshaft bearings are used to hold the camshaft in (four in a hydraulic head). You will notice that some of the camshaft lobes are pointing up and some are pointing to the sides or down. The ones pointed down are pressing against the valve springs, which are pressing back. If you loosen the bearings one at a time

Camshafts for 8V engines with solid lifters											
	Cking height	Intake		Exhaust		Lift		Duration		Lobe Center	Overlap	Advance (+) or retard (-)
		opens @ BTDC	closes @ ABDC	opens @ BBDC	closes @ ATDC	Int.	Exh.	Int.	Exh.			
Autotech GTi	0.050	2	47	42	6	0.423	0.423	229	228	110	8.50	-2.00
Hör Sport	0.050	14	49	54	9	0.436	0.436	243	243	110	23.00	2.50
Neuspeed 272	0.004	26	66	66	26	0.432	0.432	272	272	110	52.00	0.00
Neuspeed G	0.004	29	69	69	29	0.425	0.425	278	278	110	58.00	0.00
Schrick 276	Unk.	28	68	68	28	0.445	0.445	276	276	110	56.00	0.00
Schrick 288	Unk.	36	72	72	36	0.461	0.461	288	288	108	72.00	0.00
Schrick 304	Unk.	46	78	78	46	0.484	0.484	304	304	106	92.00	0.00
Schrick 320	Unk.	58	82	82	58	0.508	0.508	320	320	102	116.00	0.00
VW 1300	1 mm	6	32	42	0	0.354	0.354	218	222	107	4.00	3.00
VW 1500	1 mm	3	37	43	7	0.394	0.394	220	230	108	5.00	-2.00
VW 1600	1 mm	2	48	42	8	0.406	0.406	230	230	110	10.00	-3.00
VW G grind	1 mm	7	48	45	9	0.423	0.423	235	234	109	16.50	-1.00
VW N grind	1 mm	3	44.5	46	8	0.406	0.425	228	234	110	7.75	-2.50

Because of differences in checking heights direct comparisons among published specifications is impossible.

and pull them off, the force of the valve spring pressing against the cam lobe can be enough to snap the camshaft in two.

Make sure the camshaft is still at TDC. If you are working on a solid-lifter head, remove bearing cap 5, bearing cap 1 and bearing cap 3, in that order. On a hydraulic head, remove bearing caps 1 and 3. With the remaining bearing caps (2 and 4 on a solid-lifter head, 2 and 5 on a hydraulic head), you want to gradually loosen the four nuts a little at a time, using a diagonal pattern to maintain even pressure on the camshaft. It takes a little while to do it this way. If you find yourself getting impatient, step back, take a deep breath and when you have calmed down continue on.

Check to see that the bearing shells are coming up as you loosen the nuts. Sometimes the bearing shell will get cocked on the studs, so that you can take the nuts all the way off and the bearing shell will still be tight against the head. If you see a bearing shell that is not moving, stop loosening the bolts. Grab the bearing shell with a big pair of pliers and rock it gently until it gets straightened out before proceeding.

Once all the cam bearing nuts have been removed and the shells lifted off, the camshaft can be lifted out. Keep the bearing shells in order and facing the right way. You may want to mark them in some way so that you can tell which shell goes where and in what direction it points.

Remaining in the head are the cam follower buckets, with a shim atop each one. The valve springs are hiding beneath the cam followers. If you are going to change the valve springs, see "Replacing Valve Springs in the Car."

Installation

If any dirt or grime got into the works while you were wrestling with the camshaft, clean it up now. Smear cam lube on the shims and coat the cam bearings with clean motor oil. Do not put cam lube on the cam bearings.

Clean your new camshaft thoroughly. Wipe the camshaft seal sealing surface with clean motor oil, and carefully slip the camshaft seal on. If the camshaft seal looks worn or has tens of thousands of miles on it, you might want to replace it at this time. It generally does not leak, but new ones are not expensive and you have already done all the labor to get to it, so why not?

Coat all exposed surfaces of the camshaft lobe with cam lube. Any camshaft you buy should be sold with cam lube. If not, do not proceed until you have acquired some. It is critically important that the camshaft be properly lubricated the first time it is run. Wipe the cam bearing journals with clean motor oil, and set the camshaft in the head with the lobes for the No. 1 cylinder pointing up.

Because of the downward-pointing lobes, the camshaft is not going to want to sit squarely in the bearings. You still should be able to install the cam seal in the proper place, however, if you have the lobes for the No. 1 cylinder pointing up.

Table 15: Camshafts for 8V engines with hydraulic lifters

	Cking height	Intake		Exhaust		Lift (inches)		Duration		Lobe Center	Overlap	Advance (+) or retard (-)
		opens @ BTDC	closes @ ABDC	opens @ BBDC	closes @ ATDC	Int. (inches)	Exh. (inches)	Int.	Exh.			
Hör Sport	0.050	2	42	46	-2	0.449	0.449	224	224	112	0.00	2.00
Neuspeed 260	0.004	20	60	60	20	0.420	0.420	260	260	110	40.00	0.00
Neuspeed 268	0.004	21	67	67	21	0.440	0.440	268	268	113	42.00	0.00
Neuspeed 278	0.004	28	68	68	28	0.453	0.453	276	276	110	56.00	0.00
Schrick 268	Unk.	21	67	67	21	0.441	0.441	268	268	113	42.00	0.00
Schrick 272	Unk.	26	66	66	22	0.449	0.449	272	268	111	50.00	2.00
Schrick 276	Unk.	28	68	68	28	0.453	0.453	276	276	110	56.00	0.00
Schrick 288	Unk.	34	74	74	34	0.461	0.461	288	288	110	68.00	0.00
VW GTI 1985	1 mm	2.5	38	42	2	0.401	0.402	221	224	109	2.75	0.25

The stock base circle of 8V hydraulic cams is 1.340 inches, as opposed to the 1.500-inch base circle of stock solid-lifter cams.

Table 16: Camshafts for 16V engines

	Cking height	Intake		Exhaust		Lift (inches)		Duration		Lobe Center	Overlap	Advance (+) or retard (-)
		opens @ BTDC	closes @ ABDC	opens @ BBDC	closes @ ATDC	Int.	Exh.	Int.	Exh.			
Autotech Sport	0.050	12	60	66	18	0.400	0.430	252	264	114	24.00	-3.00
Kent 258	0.050	Unk.	Unk.	Unk.	Unk.	0.404	0.404	214	214			
Kent 278	0.050	Unk.	Unk.	Unk.	Unk.	0.435	0.435	234	234			
Schrick 260	Unk.	16	64	64	16	0.441	0.441	260	260	114	32.00	0.00
Schrick 268	Unk.	22	66	66	22	0.453	0.453	268	268	112	44.00	0.00
Schrick 276	Unk.	28	68	68	28	0.453	0.453	276	276	110	56.00	0.00
Schrick 284	Unk.	34	70	70	34	0.457	0.457	284	284	108	68.00	0.00
Schrick 300	Unk.	45	75	75	45	0.472	0.472	300	300	105	90.00	0.00
VW Euro int.	0.050	13	57			0.378		206				
VW US int.	0.050	Unk.	Unk.			0.366		196				

Camshafts for 16V engines.

Place the cam bearing shells in their proper positions.

Note that the bearing caps will go on backward, but only just. If you manage to hammer them on the wrong way, the bearing caps will pinch the cam journals, and the misaligned bearing will form a lip that will scrape lubricant off the cam bearing journal as the camshaft turns. The results will be disastrous, as it will ruin both the camshaft and the cylinder head. You should not have to force anything.

Also because of the downward-pointing lobes, not all of the bearing shells will seat down far enough to get a nut started. Start the ones you can and tighten them enough so the others can be started, then tighten all the nuts evenly, just as you loosened them. Torque the nuts to 14 lb-ft.

Install the Woodruff key in the keyway. Tap it all the way down into the keyway, and align the top of the Woodruff key parallel to the axis of the crankshaft.

Table 17: Camshafts for G-60 engines

| | Cking height | Intake | | Exhaust | | Lift (inches) | | Duration | | Lobe Center | Overlap | Advance (+) or retard (-) |
		opens @ BTDC	closes @ ABDC	opens @ BBDC	closes @ ATDC	Int. (inches)	Exh. (inches)	Int.	Exh.			
Autotech	0.050	-1	41	39	-2	0.421	0.409	220	217	111	-1.50	0.50
Schrick 268	Unk.	21	67	67	21	0.441	0.441	268	268	113	42.00	0.00
VW G-60	1 mm	0	40	40	0	Unk.	Unk.	220	220	110	0.00	0.00
VW G-lader	1 mm	-7	26	48	0	Unk.	Unk.	199	228	110	-21.50	-3.50

Camshafts for G-60 engines.

Table 18: Camshafts for VR6 engines

| | Cking height | Intake | | Exhaust | | Lift (inches) | | Duration | | Lobe Center | Overlap | Advance (+) or retard (-) |
		opens @ BTDC	closes @ ABDC	opens @ BBDC	closes @ ATDC	Int. (inches)	Exh. (inches)	Int.	Exh.			
Abt								180	180	90	0.00	0.00
Schrick 268	Unk.	18	70	68	20	0.453	0.453	268	268	115	38.00	-1.00
VW	1 mm	-8	48.2	37	3.2	Unk.	Unk.	220	220	113	-4.80	-5.60

Camshafts for VR6 engines.

The camshaft sprocket can now be reinstalled. The procedure for doing this is described in "Cam Sprockets." After you have reinstalled the cam sprocket and belt, you need to check the valve adjustment.

With the engine cold, the intake valves should be adjusted to 0.006 to 0.010 inch, and the exhaust should be adjusted to 0.014 to 0.018 inch. Try not to scrape all the cam lube off the lobes, and touch up any areas that look barren before you put the valve cover back on. If you can, reuse the old gasket and seal for now. They only need to last another half-hour.

Replace the alternator belt, but do not reinstall the lower cam belt cover just yet. You are going to run the motor for a few minutes and then recheck the adjustment of the valves, so you do not need to have everything in place now. Snap the distributor cap back on, and tighten down anything else you loosened up, or that is flopping around and could cause a problem once the engine is running.

The most critical time in a camshaft's life is the first few minutes. The cam lube is there to help a little, but with the pressure of the valve springs, the cam really needs to run for a few minutes until all the rough edges are knocked off. Ideally the motor would start immediately instead of being cranked over for long seconds or even minutes.

Once started, the motor should be run at high idle (2,000 rpm) for 20 minutes. Have someone else hold open the throttle so you can check out the cam belt adjustment. If the adjustment is too loose the belt will be flopping around, and if it is too tight the idler pulley will be making a complaining noise. If you are very careful, you can get in there with your wrenches and adjust the belt tension while the motor is running, but this is dangerous. Work cautiously.

While this is happening the motor will also be growing nice and warm. After the break- in period, you can remove the valve cover and adjust the valves to their hot running specifications: intakes at 0.008 to 0.012 inch and exhausts at 0.016 to 0.020 inch. Double-check that the cam is timed properly to the crankshaft and the intermediate shaft.

When everything is okay, put back *both* cam belt covers, all V-belts, and the valve cover with the new gaskets you bought just for this occasion. Now comes the fun part, when you get to take your stopwatch out and see how much improvement you picked up. Whatever the result, be sure to recheck the valve adjustment at 500 miles.

Installing a 16V Camshaft

It is only natural to assume that a camshaft change on the dual overhead cam 16V will be twice as difficult, but it is not. Changing the exhaust camshaft on a 16-valve engine is more difficult than changing the single camshaft on an 8-valve engine, but fortunately for us, the intake camshaft is the only one that most enthusiasts will want to change. Testing has

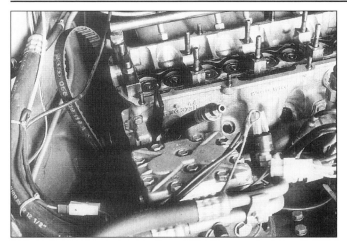

With the camshaft removed, the air pressure hose is screwed into the spark plug hole to keep the valves closed after the keepers are removed.

After jarring the keeper loose from the retainer, the lever is used to push down on the spring so the keepers can be removed.

shown that the stock exhaust cam and cam timing are pretty well optimized. The intake cam, while no less suited for the majority of all driving needs, can be exchanged if more power is desired at high rpm.

Changing a 16V intake cam isn't difficult, but there are a couple of tricks that make the job much easier.

Removal

1. Prepare the intake plenum and runners for removal.

Only the intake plenum (the top portion of the intake manifold with the runners) needs to be removed for this operation. Remove the intake air boot from the throttle housing. Remove the hose from the idle air valve to the intake air boot. Disconnect the electrical connection for the charcoal canister control valve. Disconnect the vacuum hose from the rear of the intake manifold. Remove the support bolt from the rear of the intake plenum. Disconnect the throttle cable, and any other miscellaneous wires, hoses, and clamps. Remove the spark plug wires and lay them aside. If you think you will have trouble remembering where everything goes, make a sketch before you start tearing things apart.

2. Remove the intake plenum.

Remove the five nuts that hold the intake plenum to the lower portion (the lower portion bolts directly to the cylinder head), and lift the intake plenum back and up to remove it.

3. Remove the valve cover.

Remove the cam belt cover, then remove the nuts that secure the valve cover to the cylinder head. Lift off the valve cover.

4. Check the camshaft alignment.

Camshafts on the Volkswagen 16V engine are timed by aligning two dots on the left face of the sprockets. Check the alignment so you will have a better idea what to look for when you install the new camshaft. If you cannot see the alignment marks, check that the engine is exactly at top dead center. You may need to wipe off the sprockets to see the markings.

5. Remove the No. 1, No. 3, and No. 5 cam bearing caps.

The camshaft must be removed in steps. In this step, remove only the center cap and the two end caps. Place them out of the way in the same order they are installed on the engine, so you can put each back into its original position on reassembly.

6. Slowly remove the No. 2 and No. 4 cam bearing caps.

Because some of the cam lobes are depressing cam followers, there is considerable preload on the camshaft. Gradually and evenly loosen each of the remaining four nuts on the two remaining cam bearing caps. Watch to see that the camshaft does not become cocked in the cam bore, and that it is being gently pushed upward by the force of the valve springs. Place these cam bearing caps aside as you did with the others from step 5 above. Note: Failure to follow this procedure can result in a broken camshaft or damaged cam bearings.

7. Remove the No. 5 cam bearing cap rear stud.

If you were removing both camshafts, you would repeat the above steps for the exhaust cam and lift both camshafts out together. However, we are leaving the exhaust camshaft intact. In order to disengage the intake camshaft from the drive chain, you must get a little slack, which is normally impossible due to the presence of the studs that hold the cam bearing caps. Double-nut the rear stud for the No. 5 cam bearing cap and temporarily remove the stud from the cylinder head.

8. Lift out the intake camshaft.

With the cam bearing stud out of the way, the camshaft should easily lift out. Try not to rotate the engine at this point so as not to lose the camshaft alignment. You are now ready to install the new camshaft.

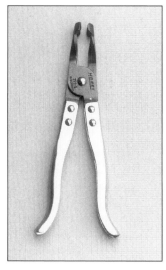

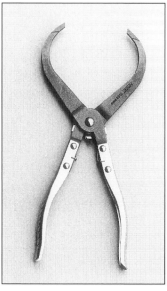

Special pliers such as these are extremely valuable when removing valve guide seals.

These tongs reach around the camshaft to grab the valve adjusting shim on solid lifter cars.

Lash caps for use with solid-top followers. The one on the left has been ground to fit.

Viton valve guide seals.

Valve spring retainer cut to allow spring height measurements.

Installation

1. Coat the lobes of the new camshaft with assembly lube.

The first few minutes are the most critical in the life of a new camshaft. A light coating of assembly lube (usually moly paste or moly paste mixed with a little motor oil) helps protect the camshaft against extreme wear while the load surfaces are burnishing in.

2. Install the camshaft.

Engage the sprocket of the intake camshaft with the drive chain, and lower the camshaft into position. Check that the alignment marks on the sprockets are directly opposite each other, in line with the top surface of the cylinder head. This will be difficult because the camshaft will not be sitting down in the cam bore, but do the best you can.

3. Install the No. 2 and No. 4 cam bearing caps.

Lubricate all five cam bearing journals with motor oil, and install the cam bearing caps for the No. 2 and No. 4 journals only. Install the washers and nuts, and gradually and evenly tighten the cam bearing nuts a little at a time so that the camshaft is gently lowered into position.

Note: The diagonal cut at the top of the cam bearing cap faces forward. Failure to replace the cam bearing caps the right way will lead to binding, camshaft failure, and cylinder head damage.

4. Check the camshaft timing.

With the camshaft down in the cam bore, it will be easier to determine if the camshafts are timed. If the timing is off, loosen cam bearing caps No. 2 and No. 4 as described above in Step 6 of Removal. Reposition the camshaft and reinstall cam bearing caps No. 2 and No. 4 as described above in step 3 of "Installation." Note: Do not rotate the engine at this time.

5. Install cam bearing caps No. 1, No. 3, and No. 5.

If the camshafts seem to be timed, install the remaining three cam bearing caps in their original positions.

6. Check camshaft timing.

Once you have all five cam bearing caps installed, rotate the crankshaft two complete revolutions (720 degrees), bring the engine to top dead center, and recheck camshaft timing. The engine must be exactly at TDC, and you must observe the alignment marks carefully. The camshafts rotate in the same direction, so the camshaft timing marks can appear to be aligned even if the timing is advanced or retarded. If the intake cam timing is advanced, the marks will appear to be in alignment above the level of the top of the cylinder head. If the intake cam timing is retarded, the marks will appear to be in alignment below the level of the top of the cylinder head. Either way, the marks will appear to be in alignment so check them carefully, and make sure the engine is at TDC when you do so.

7. Replace the valve cover.

Install a new valve cover gasket and torque the eight nuts to 7.5 lb-ft.

8. Replace the intake plenum.

Torque the five nuts to 15 lb-ft. Torque the rear support bolt to 15 lb-ft as well.

9. Reconnect all lines and hoses.

See step 1 of "Removal."

10. Start the engine and hold at high idle.

In order for the camshaft to break in properly, the engine must be started quickly and run above 2,000 rpm for 20 minutes. If the engine does not start immediately, stop and figure out why. Continued grinding on the starter is very bad on a new camshaft.

Note: If the car refuses to start, or if it does start but runs with a loud rattling noise, it is possible that you have not timed the camshafts correctly. Remove the intake plenum and valve cover and double-check the timing before proceeding with the break-in procedure.

One of the possible trade-offs for more horsepower on the top end is a loss of low-end torque. You can compensate for some for some of this loss by advancing the cam timing two or three degrees on the 1.8-liter engines. On the 2.0-liter engines, consider a chip change.

Installing a VR6 Camshaft

There are a lot more steps to installing a VR6 camshaft than are involved in an 8V or 16V swap, as at the very least you will need a special tool (VW 3268) to align the camshafts on reassembly, and you should replace the O-ring seal on the chain tensioner. You also should have your wits and your shop manual about you.

Removal

1. Remove the intake manifold cover and upper intake manifold, covering the intake runners in the lower intake manifold with rags to prevent anything from falling in.

2. Remove the cylinder head cover.

3. Turn the crankshaft to TDC. If your car has a manual transaxle, engage first gear and set the parking brake to prevent engine rotation.

4. Remove the upper timing chain tensioner from the side of the engine, and then the sprocket cover.

5. Use a 24-millimeter open-end wrench to hold each camshaft at the hexagonal area provided on the cam, and remove the sprocket mounting bolts.

6. Wire the cam chain up so it won't fall into the engine, and remove the cam sprockets. Do NOT allow the crankshaft to rotate as the pistons will run into the valves. Note that each cam has a groove that aligns the sprocket to the cam and that this groove is facing up.

7. Remove the "front" cam (the shorter of the two). First, remove the outer bearing caps, and then slowly and evenly remove the four nuts holding the two inner bearing caps, allowing the cam to rise slowly as it is pushed up from below by the pressure of the valve springs. Note the direction of the arrow on the bearing caps for later.

8. Remove the "rear" cam (the longer of the two). First, remove the center bearing cap, and then gradually remove the outer bearing caps. Note the direction of the bearing caps for later.

9. Remove all traces of old sealant from the sprocket cover.

Installation

1. The engine must still be at TDC.

2. Lubricate the bearings and lobes of the new camshafts, and put them in place with the sprocket alignment grooves facing up.

3. Install the outer two bearing caps for the "front" (shorter) cam, gradually and evenly tightening down on all four nuts to slowly draw the camshaft into position. The arrows on the bearing caps point away from the transaxle.

4. Install the center bearing cap for the "front" cam.

5. Install the center two bearing caps for the "rear" (longer) cam, gradually drawing the camshaft down into position as before.

6. Install the outer bearing caps for the "rear" cam.

7. Torque all bearing cap nuts to 15 lb-ft.

8. Align the camshafts using special tool VW 3268, by sliding it into the slots on the back ends of both camshafts simultaneously.

9. Reinstall the sprocket and distributor drive (where fitted) for the "rear" (shorter) cam, tightening the bolt hand-tight. Mind that the sprocket mates with the alignment groove in the end of the cam.

10. Engage the chain on the sprocket so that there is no slack in the chain where it goes down toward the crankshaft. (It actually connects to the intermediate shaft.)

11. Remove all traces of moisture and lubricant from both the camshaft position sensor wheel and the center of the cam sprocket where it contacts the camshaft position sensor wheel.

12. Install the remaining sprocket into the chain, and bolt it and the camshaft position sensor wheel to the end of the camshaft so that a. there is no slack in the chain between the sprockets, b. the sprocket mates with the alignment groove in the end of the cam, and c. there is no moisture or lubricant between the sprocket and the sensor wheel. The bolt should be hand tight.

13. Lubricate the threads and the underneath sides of the heads of the sprocket mounting bolts.

14. Remove the camshaft alignment tool.

15. Hold each camshaft with your 24-millimeter open-end wrench and tighten the lubricated cam sprocket bolts to 74 lb-ft.

16. Clean all traces of old sealant from the mating surfaces for the sprocket cover, including any that may have gotten into the small holes in the mating surface.

17. Reinstall the sprocket cover, using a nonhardening sealant, such as Hylomar on the mating surfaces. (Volkswagen also sells a special adhesive, part No. AMV 18800101.)

18. Lightly oil the new upper tensioner O-ring, and install the tensioner. If the tensioner has expanded, use a thin piece of wire to press down on the relief valve in the end of the tensioner until the piston retracts. Torque the tensioner to 22 lb-ft.

19. Rotate the crankshaft 720 degrees (two full turns), until it is again at TDC.

20. Check to see that the special tool VW 3268 will still slide into place in the slots at the backs of both camshafts simultaneously. If not, you have to start over.

21. Reinstall the coil, cylinder head cover, upper intake manifold, intake manifold cover, and so on.

Checking Camshaft Specifications

Any cam you buy should come with a cam card that will tell you all the vital information about the cam (except how it will run in your motor!). For hot street performance you may not need any of this information, but if you are looking for every last bit of horsepower in your engine, you are not only going to have to understand the figures, you are going to have to know how to ensure that the figures on the card relate to the camshaft you are installing. This means checking the cam.

One problem you will run into when checking out cams is that not everybody uses the 1-millimeter clearance in measuring camshafts. It can be very frustrating trying to determine the actual difference between two cams when different clearances are used in specification sheets, and there is no easy formula for translating one to the other. The solution to this problem is to measure the camshaft yourself.

Darrell Vittone has made up a special dial indicator that allows him to check the camshafts without taking them out of the head. This works very well with the hydraulic lifters because the lifter is always pushing up to touch the camshaft. With a solid lifter, he has to replace the valve spring with lighter units from a hardware store (to avoid damaging the valve springs through a coil bind), and insert an extra shim to take up the clearance between the camshaft and the lifter. This is simple compared with having a head set up specially to check camshafts or taking off the head.

The setup I used was a specially modified cylinder head out of a junk yard, but any cylinder head will do as long as you can bolt in the camshaft you want to check. For this setup, remove all the intake and exhaust valves, and reinstall the followers for cylinder No. 1 with light-gauge springs underneath them so they will still track the camshaft lobe. Only solid lifters will work for this checking procedure.

With either of these methods you need a degree wheel to bolt to the end of the camshaft. Because no one makes a degree wheel for this application, you will either have to modify a Type 1 crankshaft pulley, or get a one-size-fits-all stick-on degree wheel. Your choice will in part dictate the construction of the

pointer needed to show where on the degree wheel the camshaft is. I made my pointers out of a soft drink can. It took about five minutes, and I "drilled" the hole with a center punch.

You can also use a stock pulley. It will be aggravating to use and not quite as accurate, and you will have to be careful with your counting and math, but if you are only doing one or two camshafts it might be easier than rigging up a custom degree wheel.

The trick with the stock pulley is that it has 44 teeth, meaning that each tooth is worth 8.182 degrees. It does not matter if you count from the center of a tooth or from the edge, as long as you are consistent. Most of the time you are going to have to guess at degree values that fall between teeth.

Camshaft Pulley Degree Equivalents

Teeth	Degrees	Teeth	Degrees	Teeth	Degrees
0.5	4.09	15.5	126.82	30.5	249.55
1.0	8.18	16.0	130.91	31.0	253.64
1.5	12.27	16.5	135.00	31.5	257.73
2.0	16.36	17.0	139.09	32.0	261.82
2.5	20.45	17.5	143.18	32.5	265.91
3.0	24.55	18.0	147.27	33.0	270.00
3.5	28.64	18.5	151.36	33.5	274.09
4.0	32.73	19.0	155.45	34.0	278.18
4.5	36.82	19.5	159.55	34.5	282.27
5.0	40.91	20.0	163.64	35.0	286.36
5.5	45.00	20.5	167.73	35.5	290.45
6.0	49.09	21.0	171.82	36.0	294.55
6.5	53.18	21.5	175.91	36.5	298.64
7.0	57.27	22.0	180.00	37.0	302.73
7.5	61.36	22.5	184.09	37.5	306.82
8.0	65.45	23.0	188.18	38.0	310.91
8.5	69.55	23.5	192.27	38.5	315.00
9.0	73.64	24.0	196.36	39.0	319.09
9.5	77.73	24.5	200.45	39.5	323.18
10.0	81.82	25.0	204.55	40.0	327.27
10.5	85.91	25.5	208.64	40.5	331.36
11.0	90.00	26.0	212.73	41.0	335.45
11.5	94.09	26.5	216.82	41.5	339.55
12.0	98.18	27.0	220.91	42.0	343.64
12.5	102.27	27.5	225.00	42.5	347.73
13.0	106.36	28.0	229.09	43.0	351.82
13.5	110.45	28.5	233.18	43.5	355.91
14.0	114.55	29.0	237.27	44.0	360.00
14.5	118.64	29.5	241.36		
15.0	122.73	30.0	245.45		

Install the camshaft and degree wheel, taking care not to cock the followers in their bores. Stand the cylinder head on its side (or stand it on its end, if that is easier), and mount your dial indicator holder so you can put the shaft of the indicator through the valve guide until it rests against the bottom of the follower. Note that you cannot indicate off the head of the valve, because with the valve installed the follower does not press up against the camshaft. You are trying to eliminate all clearance between the follower and the camshaft lobe.

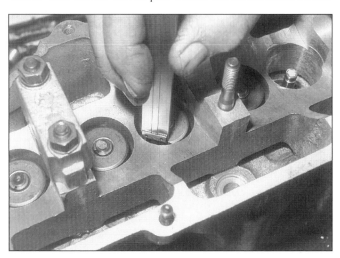

Measuring valve spring installed height.

Whichever measuring device you choose, degree wheel or sprocket, you will have to zero it relative to the pointer. There are two zero positions for every pair of intake and exhaust lobes on any camshaft. One zero position is somewhere on the heel of both camshafts; the point where both heels are touching the followers simultaneously. In this position the lobes will be facing away from the followers in a V shape.

The second zero position is 180 camshaft degrees from this position, more or less. On camshafts with equal duration for both intake and exhaust, this zero can be found using either one of the following two methods.

Method I

Put a dial indicator on both the intake and exhaust cam followers, zeroing them on the heels of their respective lobes, then turning the camshaft so the leading flank of the exhaust lobe and the trailing flank of the intake lobe are touching the followers.

Watch both dial indicators as you turn the camshaft slowly back and forth. You will see that there is one point at which the lift on both followers is the same. This is the second zero position. Note the degree reading or place a light mark on your sprocket.

Now remove the sprocket or degree wheel and install it backward. Find the zero position again and note the degree reading. If it is not exactly 180 degrees opposite your first mark, add 180 to your second reading, and then split the difference between your first reading and your second reading. This calculated figure is the TDC point for that pair of cam lobes. If you used the lobes for cylinder No. 1, you will more easily be able to time the camshaft to the crankshaft, as described later.

Method 2

(Four-cylinder only) Turn the engine over until the lobes for cylinder 1 are visually close to TDC. Lay a straightedge across the lobes for cylinder 1 and, using a dial caliper, measure from the straightedge to the gasket sealing surface on the top of the head. If the distance from the straightedge to the front scaling surface is the same as the distance from the straightedge to the back sealing surface, the camshaft is at TDC. You can now set up your degree wheel and pointers.

The camshaft chart shows that not all the numbers come out nice and even. Some variations are due to the grind of the camshaft and some are due to slight differences in manufacturing tolerances. This chart is not the last word on camshaft specifications, but it does provide an indication of what to expect from some of the available grinds. If it shows a couple thousandths of an inch more or less lift, or is off a degree or two here or there, do not be concerned. The important measurements are the ones on the camshaft you are installing.

Timing the Camshaft to the Engine

Degreeing the camshaft is nothing more than making sure that the camshaft opens when you think it is opening, relative to the pistons. This procedure is carried out with the cylinder head bolted up to the block just the way it will be when the car is running, with the cylinder head gasket and everything (you can

A cut-away view of the installed-height measurement.

leave out the spark plugs). You want the distance from the centerline of the crankshaft to the centerline of the camshaft to be set before you start, or you will have to redo your work later on.

If you have not yet dead-stopped the No. 1 piston and marked the flywheel as described in the sections on crankshaft and flywheels, do so now.

You will need to make a special tool. This will require an old spark plug, and either a bolt and matching tap or some threaded rod and a welder. Knock the porcelain and both electrodes out of the threaded base of the spark plug, and insert either the rod or the threaded bolt (after preparing the base by cutting threads with the tap). I prefer the bolt because my welding is not so good, and the movable dead-stop is more versatile.

Bring your engine up close to TDC and screw in the dead-stop tool. Thread the bolt down until you feel it touching the top of the piston. Turn the motor up gently until it stops, and lightly mark the flywheel relative to some easy-to-remember point on the transmission housing. Now turn the motor back the other way until the piston again gently touches the dead-stop. You must do this gently because it is very easy to flat-spot a rod bearing doing this. Lightly mark the flywheel again opposite that same point on the transmission housing. Half the distance between these two points is the true TDC of the engine.

You now have both your engine TDC and your camshaft specifications. Remove the dead-stop and turn the engine to TDC. If the timing belt is not installed, install it now. Check your camshaft degree wheel and see where the camshaft is relative to the crankshaft. You can now adjust this relationship. Remember, when looking at the adjustable camshaft sprocket, turning the center of the sprocket counterclockwise relative to the belt advances the camshaft timing, and turning the center of the sprocket clockwise retards the camshaft timing.

Valvetrain
Valve Springs

The stock valve springs are fine up to 7,200 rpm in motors up to 1982 (somewhat less in the GTis), and even can be used in some high-performance applications. The more you intend to ask

From left to right are stock solid adjuster, stock hydraulic adjuster, aftermarket solid-top follower and 35-millimeter Alfa follower.

of the valve spring, however, the more desirable it is to check it, or to replace it with a heavier-duty spring.

The one problem you are most likely to come up against is running the valve spring into coil bind. Coil bind occurs when the valve spring is compressed so tightly that the coils touch each other. This is very fatiguing for the spring and will result in early failure. Worse, beyond a point the spring will not compress any more because the coils are solidly up against one another, and the camshaft will have a tough time swinging over the nose. When this happens you can get accelerated wear on the camshaft nose, a motor that will not turn over, or a broken camshaft.

The problem is that the stock valve springs are very close to their operating limit when used with a camshaft with 0.425 inch of lift. Often you can install a 0.425- or 0.430-lift camshaft on top of your stock springs and drive the car for years. Sometimes, though, your valve springs will be binding up and you may not know it until something wears out, refuses to turn over or breaks. Unless you enjoy gambling, have the springs checked on a spring tester.

The reason that the high-performance springs work where the stock springs do not is that they have fewer coils, with more space between each coil. This allows room for the spring to be collapsed farther, but it is also harder on the spring. Fewer coils mean a stiffer spring, and the coils must be able to flex deeper than those in a spring with more coils. The combination of extra stiffness and more flex fatigues the valve springs, so they can fail earlier. In a street application this is nothing to worry about, but in a race motor you should definitely check your spring tension often until you get an idea about how long your springs will hold tension.

Valve Spring Preparation

For the last 45 years or so, valve springs have been shot peened by automobile manufacturers even for stock applications. Just about any valve spring that you buy should be shot peened by the time you get it. The only other thing you may want to do is give the valve springs a moly impregnation treatment. This reduces the operating temperature and greatly extends their life. You may not see the benefits in a mild street rod motor, but in an all-out motor this would be a real plus.

It is very nice to have access to a valve spring compressor to check your valve springs. The first check is to see that the valve springs will produce the proper seat pressure when installed at the specified height.

The second check is to see that there will still be 0.010 inch of clearance (checked with a feeler gauge) between the coils at full lift of whatever camshaft you have chosen.

The third check is to match the inner springs with the outer springs to balance out the total spring pressure. For example, an outer spring with less tension than the other outer springs would be matched up with an inner spring with more tension than the other inners.

Never compress a valve spring to the point of coil bind, either in the valve spring checker or in the cylinder head. This weakens the spring and will hasten the onset of failure.

Replacing Valve Springs in the Car

Although it sounds as if it would be more difficult to replace the valve springs with the head in the car, it can actually be easier. When the head is off the car, you have to find some way of holding it down while you wrestle with the valve springs. When the head is on the car, the head bolts and the block usually keep the head from wandering around.

You will need a valve spring compressor either way. If you plan to do the job in the car, you will also need an adapter that will allow you to pressurize the combustion chamber while you work, and an air compressor to supply the air.

Remove the camshaft as described previously. You should now be confronted with the camshaft followers sitting in their bores. Lift out each camshaft follower, and store the followers out of the way in the same order they sit in the head. You now will be able to see the top of the valve stem and the spring retainer.

Remove all the spark plugs. Install the cylinder pressurizer adapter into the spark plug hole for cylinder No. 1, and turn the engine so the piston is at TDC for that cylinder. If the car is on the ground and not on a hoist or jack stands, make sure the transmission is in high gear with the parking brake on. Connect the air supply to the cylinder pressurizer adapter. If the cylinder you are pressurizing is not exactly at TDC, the air pressure will try to turn the engine (and move the car).

The air pressure pushing on the underside of the valve will keep it against its seat while you work above. For this reason, you can work on only one cylinder at a time.

Warning: If you take off the valve spring retainer without pressurizing the cylinder, the valve will drop into the cylinder, and you may have to take off the cylinder head to retrieve it. Turning the crankshaft so that the piston for that cylinder is at TDC prevents the valve from falling into the cylinder, as you will still be able to grab the stem and pull it back. If the force of the air pressure turns the crankshaft so that the piston is at BDC, you have lost your safety net.

Bolt the fulcrum bar of the valve spring tool to the top of the head. Use the valve spring tool to push down on the spring retainer so you can remove the split keeper.

In a perfect world you would push down on the valve spring tool and the retainer would cleanly move away from the keeper, allowing you to fish the keepers out with a magnet. Life being what it is, however, the retainer and the keepers will often be stuck to one another. If you find this to be the case, you will need to jar them apart.

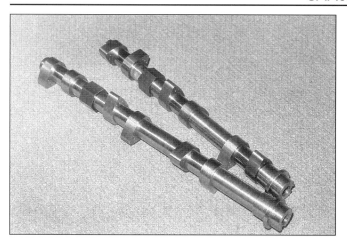

Rifle-drilled VR6 camshafts from Abt.

Cam billet before grinding.

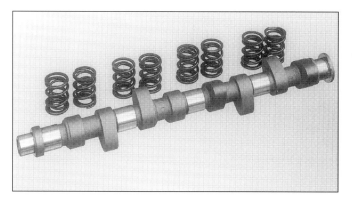

High-lift aftermarket cam with matching replacement springs.

Apply a 19-millimeter impact socket on a 6-inch extension to the valve retainer, and tap on the end of the extension with a soft-face hammer. The shock will usually separate the retainer from the keeper. Do not pound too hard; it does not take a lot. By the way, the loud popping sound you hear each time you hit the retainer is air escaping from the cylinder through the slight opening in the valve. Once you have jarred the retainer apart from the keepers, you can proceed with the valve spring tool.

Unless you have very tiny fingers, you will find that a magnet is quite helpful in fishing out the keepers once you have depressed the valve spring retainer enough so that you can get the keepers out. With the retainers and the keepers out of the way, you can remove the stock springs and install the springs you want. Put the retainer back, and using the valve spring compressor, push down on the retainer and slip the keepers back into place. Use long, thin needle-nose pliers for this job, because space is tight and the keepers can be slippery.

On four-cylinder engines, cylinders 1 and 4 are up at the same time, and cylinders 2 and 3 are up at the same time. On the VR6, cylinders 1 and 6, 2 and 5, and 3 and 4 are up at the same time. This makes it quite easy to replace the springs for pairs of cylinders. Do not forget to completely install the springs for one cylinder before moving on to the next cylinder, and do not forget to pressurize the cylinder before removing the retainer and keepers.

Once you have replaced all the valve springs, coat the skirts of the camshaft followers with oil and slip them back into the bores they cam out of. Do not coat them with grease. Oil allows them to rotate so they will not wear prematurely.

Valve Spring Installed Height

If you have done a valve job on your head, are using different-length valves or have gone for a different valve spring, check the valve spring installed height. Any of these factors can affect the distance between the valve spring seat and the valve spring retainer.

If the valve springs have been checked with a spring tester, installing them at the correct height will ensure that the distance is small enough (compressing the spring enough) to get the right seat pressure when the valve is closed, and large enough to keep the spring out of coil bind when it is all the way open.

Owing to the construction of the Volkswagen head, checking the valve spring installed height can be more trouble than it should be. One easy way to check is to use an old valve spring retainer with a piece cut out of it. Assemble the valve, retainer and keepers using a super soft spring (which you can buy at a hardware store). It is then a simple matter to measure from the top of the retainer to the valve spring seat and subtract the width of the retainer to arrive at the installed height. If you buy a set of high-performance springs, be sure to get the installed height measurement as well.

If the installed height is smaller than spec, you will have to machine the head or use thinner valve spring seats. If it is bigger, you will need to use shims to reduce the distance. Shims are readily available at many parts houses and machine shops. They come in different thicknesses, and the ones you want measure 1 1/4 inches OD and 7/8 inch ID.

Measuring the spring to get the proper seat pressure is a short cut. A better way to do this would involve even more special tools. After assembling the valve with the spring and retainer, one tool would press down on the tip of the valve, giving a read-out of the amount of pressure being exerted. A dial indicator on the head of the valve would show the precise moment the valve came off the seat. This would give you the installed height spring pressure directly. Apparently there is a tool expressly for this purpose, but measuring the springs has worked well for decades.

Once you have everything measured, you can assemble the head with the valve springs, and double-check your work.

Valve Guide Seals

Early on, Volkswagens had a problem with valve guide seals. The original valve guide seals would become hard as a result of heat, and would then allow up to a quart of oil to be sucked into the engine every 250 miles. The motor would run fine and the plugs never seemed to foul, but there was always the danger of running out of oil and ruining the motor. Volkswagen eventually issued a recall and replaced all the problem valve guide seals, but this is something to remember in case you come up against a motor that is using oil and you cannot figure out where it is going.

When oil gets past the valve guide seals (or piston rings), you lose horsepower. This is because oil lowers the octane rating of gasoline, taking between 10 and 15 percent off the peak horsepower. Between losing horsepower and putting your engine at risk, you can do without faulty valve guide seals. If yours are leaking, replace them as soon as you can.

There are three types of valve guide seals. The first is the original type made of rubber; even if you wanted these, you probably could not find any. There are some black rubber seals floating around that are supposed to be the new, improved version of the old-style stem seal, but they are to be avoided. The second type is a Teflon seal, easily spotted because it is white with a silver metal control ring wrapped around it. The third type is called Viton, which is usually green and feels like a very supple rubber seal.

Both the Teflon and Viton seals are effective at reducing oil flow down the valve guides. The Teflon seals, in fact, may be too effective; excessive wear shows up on the valve stem and valve guide, probably as a result of the great sealing job the Teflon seals can do.

The Viton seals will take nearly as much heat as the Teflon seals, but allow some oil to remain on the valve stem for lubrication. If heat is destroying your viton valve guide seals, you have other problems that need to be fixed as well.

If you find you must use the Teflon seals for whatever reason, be very careful when installing them not to scratch the inner sealing surface. The Teflon will flow around small sharp edges, but if you scratch the inner surface too deeply you will have to replace the seal again or put up with oil consumption.

The only other thing you might want to check with valve seals will only apply when you run a camshaft with more than 0.430 inch of lift. With a high-lift camshaft like this, the valve spring retainer can sometimes run into the valve stem seal. If you anticipate this problem, you can buy special shortened versions of the valve stem seals.

Changing valve stem seals in the car involves doing everything already discussed for changing the valve springs, with the additional step of removing the old valve stem seal and installing the new one. To remove the old seal you will need a pair of special pliers that are made just for this task. To replace them you can use a special valve stem seal installer, but I use a Craftsman 10-millimeter deep socket. It is a pretty close fit, it works fine, and it is less expensive than the special tool.

When you buy the valve stem seals, try to get the little plastic installation covers that slip over the ends of the valve stem to protect the inner sealing surface of the seal. Not everybody will have these, but if you find them, get them.

Most installation covers are too long to use as-is, but you can trim them back enough that once the valve stem seal is in place, the installation cover can be removed. The installation cover sometimes seems more fragile than the seal itself, so after the seal is past the keeper grooves, take the installation cover off so it does not get damaged. You usually get only a couple of these, and they have to last through eight or more seal installations.

Retainers

The stock retainers are a "lifetime" piece, meaning they will never break or wear out, so a lot of hot-rodders use them without thinking about them. For ultimate engines, though, they are a little heavy, so replacing them with titanium retainers can save a lot of weight in the valvetrain. Titanium retainers don't last as long as steel, though, so be ready for the higher price and the fact that you may have to replace them eventually.

Followers

The valve adjustment method on the Volkswagen is another great example of a compromise. Instead of requiring a screwdriver and a wrench so that anybody could set his or her own valves, it requires a spring depressor, special pliers, and a whole lot of shims—and that adds up to a lot of money.

However, by using shims the valves really stay adjusted. At the normal 15,000 mile interval, it is unusual to have to adjust more than two or three valves if they have previously been properly adjusted. That is about as maintenance-free as you get without using hydraulic adjusters.

The stock followers and shims are rugged enough for most applications, but they do fall short when you are using a very high-lift race cam. Once the difference between the base circle and the top of the lobe gets too great, the camshaft lobe has a tendency to strip the shims out of the pockets and (sometimes) hit the head next to the lifter bore.

To overcome this, you can change over to a camshaft follower with a larger top. One setup that many people use is the 35-millimeter solid-top follower. To adjust these you have to have the camshaft installed. Using feeler gauges, make measurements on all the camshaft lobes. From this measurement subtract the amount of clearance you are running. The number you get will be the thickness of the lash cap you will need to install on the end of the valve stem underneath the camshaft follower. Remove the camshaft and fit the caps, then reinstall the camshaft and double-check all your measurements.

For racing, these followers are not only a way to make a big camshaft work, they are also lighter than the stock shim-and-bucket setup. The stock setup weighs about 71 grams. The solid-top followers and lash caps come to about 43 grams. This substantial weight savings will make it possible to increase the redline further without getting into valve float.

If you cannot bring yourself to give up the convenience of the stock Volkswagen adjuster, you have damaged the camshaft follower bores, or you need to clearance the head anyway before you can swing that big camshaft around, you can enlarge the camshaft follower bores to 37 millimeters and use Fiat camshaft followers. These look almost identical to the Volkswagen-style camshaft follower except that the shim is 33 millimeters across instead of 31 millimeters. Of course, then you have to buy shims from your local Fiat dealership instead of from Volkswagen or your normal aftermarket supplier. Super Vees use 37-millimeter and 39-millimeter Alfa Romeo one-piece cam followers, both of which necessitate the use of lash caps.

Again, none of these alternative types of camshaft follower are necessary in a street motor. When used in a race motor, increasing the bore for the oversized followers has the added advantage of simultaneously clearancing the cylinder head so the toe of the camshaft can swing by without hitting.

Adjusting the Valves (Solid lifter engines only)

If you turn the engine over by hand (as opposed to using a remote starter switch), it is easier to be methodical about the order in which you adjust the valves. If you do use a remote starter, buy a grease pencil from an art or welding supply store. After checking or adjusting each follower, touch the grease pencil to the gasket sealing surface of the hot cylinder head. Always adjust the valves with the engine hot unless the engine is not in running condition If you adjust the valves with the engine cold, remember that the clearances are slightly less: 0.006 to 0.010 inch on the intake side, and 0.014 to 0.018 inch on the exhaust.

As said earlier, the valves generally do not go very far out of adjustment. If they do, you will need a special lever to depress the camshaft follower bucket, special pliers to remove the current shim, and a set of replacement shims.

The procedure for adjusting the valves can be found in the shop manual. In addition, here are a couple of tips: First, the shims sometimes do not want to come out of the camshaft follower buckets. If this happens to you, examine the camshaft follower bucket depressor lever to make sure it is not interfering with the shim. If it is, grind it down, making certain you leave enough of the lever surface to press down on the camshaft follower bucket.

Even if the lever is not hitting, the shim still may not come out easily. This can be partly because of the suction that develops between the two parts (the motor oil creates a seal), and partly because of interference between the shim and the bucket. Many nonfactory shims are just a little larger in outside diameter than the factory shims, and they can get really stuck in the camshaft follower buckets.

One thing that often breaks a stuck shim loose is air pressure. Put a rag over the head so you do not blow oil everywhere, and direct the airflow from a high-pressure air nozzle at and around the shim. Sometimes you will get the best results from pointing the stream of air between the shim and the heel of the cam. This creates a venturi effect with low-pressure air that can suck the shim out. Sometimes, aiming the air stream at the edge of the shim will allow some air to get underneath the shim and lift it out. When a shim gets stuck like this, you may have to try a couple of different techniques.

When you are buying replacement shims, make sure that the shims are stock factory shims or their equivalent. Cadmium-plated shims can shed their coating. Buy the best shims, because if a shim goes bad it takes the camshaft lobe with it.

After you have checked and adjusted all the valves, the grease pencil markings will wipe right off the gasket surface. If you have not yet brought your oil deflector, this is the time to do so. Install the new seals (the red one at the pulley end, and the blue one at the transmission end) and then fit the valve cover gasket. The gasket will seal fine without any sealant. Tighten down the valve cover, and you are done.

Lubrication

Almost any major brand-name oil is good enough to keep your engine alive. You may find that some synthetics soften engine seals and cause leaks, but not all oils—not even all synthetics—do this, so you just have to find one that works for you.

In fact, it has gotten to the point where when you hear someone say they have a problem with their motor oil not providing proper lubrication, it is more often the case that other factors are involved. For example, one of the most critical times in the life of any motor is the break-in period. The worst trouble spot is the camshaft. (This goes for breaking in new camshafts in old engines too.) Although some camshaft failures are due to inadequate lubrication, more of them are due to improper installation, including not matching the valve spring installed height to the demands of a high-lift camshaft. Once the valve springs go into coil-bind, it doesn't matter what brand of oil you are using.

Barring unforeseen problems such as this, the trick with conventional motor oils is to change them early and often. Changing your oil accomplishes many good things. It makes you check the oil level when you refill the crankcase; draining the old oil removes contaminates from the engine (both volatile and non-volatile); new oil contains all the additives your engine needs for friction reduction, antifoaming, and other important oil modifiers; and while you are performing the oil change, you might notice something wrong and catch a problem before it becomes a disaster.

Some synthetics promise longer drain intervals. If you use one of these oils with an extended capacity filter, such as the Mecca, you can run into problems, because the additive package in motor oil is used up. Even if the oil level looks good, and you have high-quality filtration, motor oils won't work right after their additives are used up. At the very least, change your filter every 3,000 to 5,000 miles. When you "top off" the engine to replace the oil you lose when doing this, it goes a long way toward replenishing the additives.

Oil Pumps

The stock pump provides adequate oil pressure not only when the motor is new, but after there is some wear in the bearings. If you have a solid-lifter engine, the stock oil pump will work fine for you. If you have a hydraulic-lifter engine, the oil pump is already larger to handle the increased demand, and if your block has crankcase oil jets, the oil pump is larger still.

Going to a larger oil pump when there is no need to do so

A simple screen-element oil filter.

A spin-on screen-element oil filter.

actually hurts performance. The larger pump requires more horsepower to do its job, and because it is pressurizing oil that just blows out the by-pass valve, it turns some of that horsepower into unnecessary heat.

If you choose to replace your oil pump, be cautious of non-brand name pumps. Some Brazilian pumps, for example, are not made with tolerances as close as they need to be. Good German pumps are made by Melling and Febi.

To be on the safe side, always check your oil pump tolerances, whether the pump is old or new. The procedure and specifications are shown in the shop manual, but for high-performance work you want your pump clearances to be on the low side of the specs. For example, the backlash should be closer to 0.05 than to 0.20 millimeter, and the farther the axial clearance is under 0.15 millimeter, the better.

If you are planning on installing a stroker crankshaft, you may have to clearance your oil pump, or buy a preclearanced pump.

Oil Pans

Considering how hard your motor works, the early factory oil pan with 3.7-quart capacity looks like a great expression of minimalist design. Lots of cars came with them, however, as the factory did not change over to the 4.7-quart design until 1981. Even before the factory enlarged the oil pan, the aftermarket was offering a variety of different sumps.

Extended Oil Pans

Although you lose a minor amount of ground clearance with an extended oil pan, you gain several benefits if you can manage to keep it off the pavement. First, the greater mass of oil absorbs more heat, so your engine runs cooler. Second, the greater amount of oil will trap and hold more contaminants, keeping them away from your expensive engine parts.

If you have a pre-1981 car, consider exchanging your 3.7-quart oil pan for the stock of 4.7-quart pan found on the 1.7-liter cars.

Baffled Oil Pans

Installing baffles in the oil pan is usually done for one of two reasons. First, the baffles may direct the hot oil past a cooling area in the pan before allowing it to feed into the oil pump pickup point. More commonly, however, baffling will be done to prevent the oil pump pickup from being left high and dry during hard acceleration, lateral, or otherwise.

How important is this? Essential.

The factory 3.7-quart pan had a built-in oil pocket at the bottom, so although baffles were difficult to install, they also were not as necessary. With the introduction of the 4.7-quart pan (and other extended-capacity oil pans) it became much easier for the oil to get out from under the oil pump pickup in high-g maneuvers. Factory oil pump pickups started coming with plastic oil baffles in the mid-1980s to help prevent oil pump cavitation during cornering. There is also a factory surge baffle that fits the 1.8-liter A1 and A2 oil pumps, although it doesn't fit all aftermarket oil pans. You could achieve better results with a baffled oil pan, but the plastic baffles work well enough that most won't need a truly baffled pan, and they can be added to the earlier cars.

If you do need a baffled pan for your pre-A4 four-cylinder engine, Autotech sells one with an adjustable windage tray, and Schrick and Neuspeed offers aluminum pans that also promote oil cooling.

Surprisingly, there isn't much out there for the VR6. If you have the lowered suspension, the super wide tires, and commonly experience high-g side-loading, get yourself some sheet metal and small hinges from the hardware store, and baffle your own pan. It doesn't take very much hard running with the oil pressure light on to wipe out a set of bearings.

Windage Trays

It may be hard to believe that oil can slow your car down, but it sometimes can. Under hard running, the crankshaft may trail long fans of oil, or worse, it may splash around in hot, frothy oil. Knife-edging the crankshaft can help, but for a real solution you need a windage tray.

The windage tray sits between the crankshaft and the sump, as close to the crankshaft as possible without hitting it (many of the baffled oil pans have windage trays built in). As the crankshaft swings by the windage tray, the tray scrapes off the excess oil.

This also reduces the tendency of the oil to foam or froth, first because the crankshaft does not whip oil around in the pan as much, and second because as the oil drains down through the holes in the windage tray, the Coriolis force separates the air bubbles from the

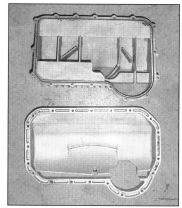

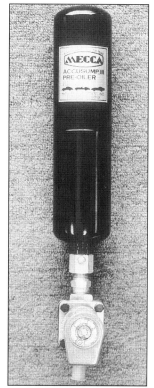

The top of the Oettinger wet sump is the windage tray; the bottom contains baffles.

The Mecca Accusump is a spring-loaded reservoir that stores oil under pressure, both for prelubrication and for low-pressure situations while the motor is running.

An extended aluminum oil pan from Oettinger.

oil. (The Coriolis force is what causes drain water to circle the drain in your bathtub: counterclockwise north of the equator and clockwise south of the equator.) At high rpm, you can appreciate the importance of pumping only deaerated oil to your engine, especially considering that your oil pump does not pump air nearly as well as it pumps oil. If you are running a high-rpm, high-compression engine and are finding a lot of oil in your air cleaner or spill tank, consider a windage tray for part of the solution.

Over the years, many tuners have offered windage trays. Currently, one of the best is a stock Volkswagen part (available from Velocity Sport Tuning and others) that mounts in place of the stock pan gasket.

Other Considerations

If you go with a cast-aluminum oil pan such as those offered by Volkswagen Motorsport, Neuspeed, or Schrick, be aware that they will crack instead of bend if you smack them on something. And they are expensive.

A sump guard is the ticket for oil pan protection. Just make sure the guard you buy will fit around your extended oil pan. Most of the aftermarket pans are patterned after the late model stock unit, and the sump guard is a Volkswagen piece, too, so you are pretty safe there.

If an aluminum pan is not to your liking, choose a steel pan carefully. Too many of the aftermarket pans are manufactured so poorly they barely bolt up. Even if you find one that fits, do not buy an oil pan with chrome on it unless you show your car instead of driving it. Chrome does not dissipate heat nearly as well as the thin coat of flat-black paint that Volkswagen uses on the stock pan.

Finally, A4 four-cylinders have a different oil pan altogether, which bolts both to the engine and the transaxle. This strengthens the engine/transaxle subassembly, but it also means none of the earlier pans will work on the new engines.

Dry Sump

For the ultimate racing machine, a dry sump is the only way to go. It is called a dry sump because the pan underneath the crankshaft is not used to store the oil. That task falls to a separate reservoir located elsewhere in the car. The Porsche 911 has had a dry sump system standard since its introduction in 1965.

• A dry-sump system requires five components:
• A dry-sump reservoir to hold the oil
• An oil pump to supply pressurized oil to the motor for lubrication
• An oil pump to scavenge the oil from the oil pan and send it to the oil reservoir (multiple pumps are often used, with separate pickups in different parts of the oil pan)
• An oil pan to direct the oil to the oil pickup, keeping the oil off the rotating parts
• Oil lines to and from the reservoir, pumps and engine

This system provides more effective and thorough lubrication under extreme conditions, and allows better oil cooling. It also reduces the amount of oil in the sump; the less oil there is, the less it will be able to aerate or cling to the crankshaft. In addition, the reduced height of the oil pan allows the motor to be moved closer to the ground for a better center of gravity.

Most racing motors that use dry sumps run stacked pumps. One belt drives all the oil pumps (one for pressure and the others for scavenge) and the fuel pump for the mechanical injection. One benefit of using this setup (besides not having to have separate drives for everything) is that if the belt breaks, robbing the engine of lubrication, the motor instantly runs out of fuel too.

Magnetic Drain Plugs

Magnetic drain plugs have been available for transmissions for years and were even a stock item with some air-cooled trans-

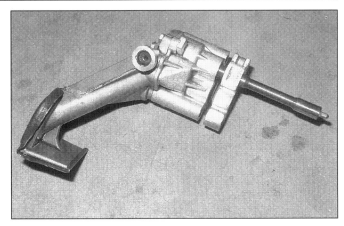

Because of the extra depth of the Oettinger wet sump you must use this extended oil pump. Note the turned-down shaft and the spacer.

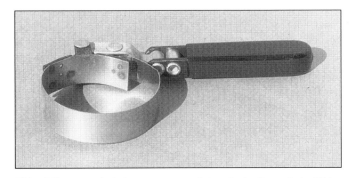

This oil filter wrench design seems to work best in the four-cylinder VW.

missions. But they never quite made it over to the water-cooled engines, even though these engines have a lot more ferrous metal than do air-cooled engines.

If you do not plan on running a Preluber, using a magnetic drain plug is an inexpensive way of keeping an eye on what is wearing off inside your engine. The plug also traps and holds particles that would otherwise cause trouble.

Prelubrication

As you go through the sections on installing a new camshaft and starting a rebuilt motor, you might get the idea that in addition to everything else you do when cranking over a fresh engine, you also cross your fingers and hold your breath, hoping against hope that everything will go all right. It wouldn't hurt to do that *every* time you start the motor, even after it is broken in.

Studies show that a lot of engine wear occurs during start-up. When a hot engine is shut off, the heat-thinned oil drains off the parts into the sump. When it comes time to start the engine, the oil is all in the bottom of your engine, doing no good whatsoever. In the long seconds that it takes for that oil to completely pressurize the oil galleys and start protecting your engine, a lot of damage has been done.

The Preluber from Lubrication Research and Accusump III from Mecca help eliminate start-up damage by pressurizing the oil

Filter element efficiency

Particle size	Screen filter 1	Screen filter 2	Paper filter
10 microns	11%	14%	18%
20 microns	14%	17%	70%
40 microns	20%	40%	94%
90 microns	29%	48%	90%

Filter element efficiency: Paper-element filters work better than screen-type filters in street applications, both in efficiency . . .

Table 21: Filter element capacity

	Screen filter 1	Screen filter 2	Paper filter
Maximum contaminents	2.26 grams	6 grams	60 grams
Time until by-pass valve opens	3.5 minutes	9.5 minutes	110 minutes

. . . and in capacity, especially considering the low by-pass valve setting of some screen filters.

galleys to 50 psi before the starter motor is engaged. This means that as soon as the crankshaft and camshaft start rotating, they ride up on a cushion of oil instead of scraping on the bearings.

The Preluber is designed around a small motor that powers a separate oil pump. The Accusump III is a straight-ahead mechanical device, using a spring-loaded piston to pressurize the oil. After the Accusump III provides start-up lubrication it resets itself using normal engine oil pressure, so it is always ready to go.

For racing use, the Accusump III can be triggered by low oil pressure to provide emergency oil pressure on a temporary basis. The Preluber, on the other hand, could be called upon to provide oil pressure in the event of an oil pump failure (not a very likely happenstance, but possible). The only problem with either system is finding the space to put it. Neither is what you would classify as dainty.

Filtration

The key to maintaining oil protection is keeping the oil clean. If you change your oil every 700 miles, it is not going to make much difference which filter you use. The rest of us have to worry about filter quality, especially those of us using long-drain-interval synthetics.

Proper oil filtration means that all the primary wear particles—tiny pieces of metal (that have worn off the inside of the motor), sand (from when the engine was cast), grit (that comes in through the air cleaner), and carbon (from imperfect combustion)—are removed from the oil before they have the opportunity to do any damage. If these contaminants are not caught they act as abrasives, wearing away the motor.

The metallic particles that are worn off of your engine parts by the primary wear particles are called secondary wear particles. They join their friends, the primary wear particles,

The Mecca oil filter.

The Frantz by-pass oil filter.

and create more friends, the tertiary wear particles. Then they create more friends, and *they* create more friends and so on. You can thus appreciate how important it is to catch those first wear particles immediately.

To trap these contaminants, there are two basic types of oil filter: full flow and by-pass. There are different ways of constructing and plumbing both of these types, but the principle of operation remains the same for both.

Full-Flow Filters

The oil filter that comes on the Volkswagen is a full-flow filter. It is so called because in theory all oil supplied to the engine must pass through the filter first. This can be very important when a catastrophic engine failure threatens to send thousands of metal particles to every corner of your motor, including the hard-to-clean oil cooler. A full-flow filter is the only type that has a chance at minimizing the effects of an engine disaster.

Because all the oil in a full-flow system passes through the filter, inside the filter is a by-pass valve in case the filter element or elements clog, collapse, or just plain fail. This ensures that the motor will also continue to get lubrication when the oil is too cold to flow easily through the filter element.

In most cars, the by-pass valve is the filter's worst enemy because it spends a lot of time in the open position, allowing unfiltered oil to circulate through the engine. This is not the case with the Volkswagen.

The Volkswagen OEM (original equipment manufacturer) oil filter by-pass valve is set to open at around 32 psi of pressure differential (the difference in pressure between the oil coming from the oil pump and the oil going to the motor), according to the Volkswagen factory specification. This is in contrast with the by-pass valves on many American car filters, which are set to open at between 7 and 9 psi of pressure differential.

A small malfunction can create the 7 to 9 psi differential required to open the by-pass valve in an American car, but there must be something seriously wrong for the stock Volkswagen by-pass to open at 32 psi of differential. However, the whole system is designed with the by-pass valve in mind, just as other systems are designed with their lower pressure by-pass valves in mind. Because of this, always make sure that your oil filter has a 32 psi by-pass valve. The Mann filters used by the factory meet this specification as do the better aftermarket filters such as the Fram PH2870A.

By-pass Filters

Now regarded by many as a curiosity, a by-pass filter is in some ways a mirror image of the full-flow filter in the sense that the strong points of the by-pass filter are the weak points of the full-flow filter, and vice versa. The by-pass filter is so called because it taps into the oil system and bleeds off oil a little at a time. Working in this way, it takes several minutes for most of the oil in the system to pass through the by-pass filter at least once.

The main disadvantage to the by-pass filter is that it offers no protection against catastrophic engine failure. If a bearing were to disintegrate, metallic particles would be pumped through the engine, impregnating the good bearings with shrapnel and scoring the crankshaft, camshaft, and other vital engine components. The by-pass filter would have caught only a small percentage of the particles by the time the damage was done.

In other areas, the by-pass filter excels. Whereas unrestricted oil flow is paramount with a full-flow filter, oil flow is of almost no concern with a by-pass filter. As long as oil flows through it, it will filter. When the element becomes clogged the filtering action stops, but there is no danger of oil starvation to the engine as a result. In fact, while a full-flow filter performs worse as it fills up with contaminants, the by-pass filter actually filters better. Because pressure differential is not a factor in the performance of the by-pass filter, it can use restrictive elements that filter much smaller containments than a full-flow filter element. It is its ability to filter superfine particulates from the oil that makes the by-pass filter worth the investment.

By-pass filters can also be much easier to service. This is because low flow, cavitation, aeration, and other factors that are detrimental to the operation of a full-flow filter are of secondary or no importance with the by-pass filters; therefore, they can be mounted for convenience sake. Unlike with a full-flow filter, air in the oil lines of a by-pass filter does not mean the motor is running dry.

One concern with the by-pass filter is its source of oil. Because it bleeds oil off a high-pressure oil galley, it appears to the engine that there is an oil leak. The "leak" in this case drips back into the crankcase, but still, pressure is lost. The Society of Automotive Engineers recognized this problem and developed a specification for by-pass filter feed lines. All oil going to the by-pass filter must pass through a 0.062 inch restrictor. This prevents

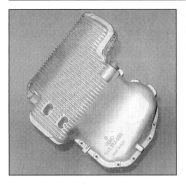

A European Dasher pan looks impressive with its deep, cast fins and front-and-back protrusions....

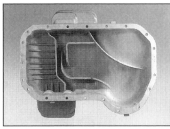

... Inside, however, the baffles are for cooling, not for oil control during high-g maneuvers.

With the flat-bottom factory oil pan, the stock oil pump needs baffles for oil control, such as this stock clip-on unit.

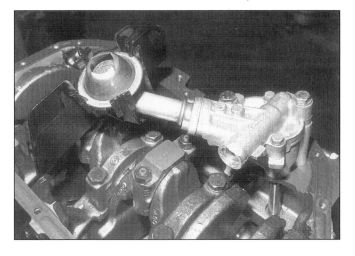

the by-pass filter from bleeding off too much oil from the main pressure circuit.

Filter Elements

Both full-flow and by-pass filters must have some sort of filtration material (the element). There are many types of filtration material, but they can be broken down into two categories: surface and depth.

Surface elements are the most common. They are usually resin-coated pleated paper through which the oil passes. The resin coating adds strength and integrity to the material used in the element. The advantages of the pleated paper filter are its low cost, large surface area, and moderate restrictiveness. It is, however, susceptible to blow-out if subjected to high pressure or to too much water in the oil system.

Another type of surface filter is the stainless steel screen. The screen is removable from the housing, allowing the screen to be cleaned and returned to duty indefinitely. As with other types of elements, as the screen fills up it starts catching smaller and smaller chunks of contamination. Screen-type elements

offer very low initial restriction, and are often used where it is important to be able to inspect the element to see what contaminants are in the oil.

The weave of the steel threads and the opening size of the weave determine the maximum-size particle that can pass through. The common screen size is 60 microns, which is pretty large for a dirt particle in your engine. The screen can trap smaller particles with irregular shapes, although it can also miss skinny chunks if they thread their way through the mesh.

The size of the weave of the screen also determines how much pressure drop there will be across the filter element. Typically, a 60-micron screen-type filter will have between 2.5 and 3.5 psi of pressure drop. Finer screens would generate unacceptably high pressure differentials, and so are not commonly used (although they are available).

One area in which the screen-element filters do excel is in initial flow characteristics (the amount the filter will flow when clean). This sounds good on paper, but in reality it is unimportant. Just about any filter element with a few square inches of element will have a higher initial flow characteristic than the nipple that holds the filter to the filter mount. Having the capability for more flow is nice, but it is not needed.

Another plus for the screen-element filters is that they are readily disassembled for inspection. Some racers like this because they no longer have to carry around cases of oil filters.

In other areas, the screen elements do not fair so well. One of the worst features of the screen element is that it has poor single-pass efficiency. This means that oil must pass through the element several times before the particles are removed. It is vitally important to your engine that the filter have good single-pass efficiency so it will trap and hold as many of the contaminants as it can the very first time the oil passes it, and every subsequent time.

Screen-element filters also have smaller filter elements than the normal spin-on filter. Typical screen-element filters have between 64 and 136 square inches of filtration media, but neither is close to a good-quality paper-element filter such as the Fram PH2870A filter, with nearly 300 square inches of filter media.

Depth elements come in many varieties, but all offer the same basic thing: thicker element material. They do this with a penalty, however, and that is usually higher resistance. For this reason, depth filtration is popular on by-pass filters, which can have much more tolerance to flow restriction than can full-flow filters.

Because of its relatively large pressure drop, toilet paper (as used in aftermarket filters that have been on the market for years) makes a poor full-flow element. It performs reasonably well as a depth-type by-pass element, however, and the price is certainly right. Oil is fed into the end of the roll, making it easy to scan a used element for debris. Because of the amount of paper in a roll of toilet paper, it also has a fair capacity for trapping water, although water will channel between the layers, reducing the effectiveness of the filter. Even this tendency can be mitigated through the use of tight rolls of toilet paper, as opposed to the "extra fluffy" brands.

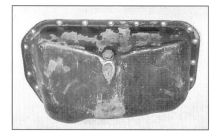

Early stock oil pan. Angled sides forced oil toward the oil pickup.

A typical aftermarket oil pan with built-in windage tray and baffles.

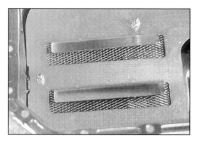

Angled flaps catch oil off the crankshaft. Screen deaerates the oil before it gets to the sump.

One-way doors trap oil around the oil pump pickup.

The piston oil jets in a 16V block.

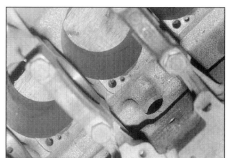

This G60 block has been bored out to the limit, leaving just enough metal for the oil jets and galleys.

One state-of-the-art depth element can be found in the Mecca line of oil filters. Mecca elements feature its exclusive synthetic depth element—and no pressure valve. These filters are able to run without the pressure valve required in almost every other full-flow filter because they give only a half-pound drop, they can flow over 15 gallons per minute, and their element can trap and hold a lot of particulates without loosing effectiveness.

If you are nervous about not having a pressure relief valve in your filter, Mecca also sells a differential pressure gauge that will tell you exactly when to change the filter. Even though the Mecca element is supposed to be good for up to 10,000 to 15,000 miles of street use, the differential gauge is a good idea.

Filter Housing Shape and Mounting

The housing shape? Yes, the housing shape. The stock Volkswagen oil filter hangs from the filter mount. This allows heavy particles to drop to the bottom of the housing and (with any luck) stay there. Any spin-on-type filter will benefit from this, so the only problems you will have are with oddly shaped or mounted by-pass filters.

Selecting a Filtration System

When it comes to figuring out how well each filter will do its job, you get conflicting stories from all sides. According to Frantz, 58 percent of engine wear particles are 10 microns or less in diameter. Fram, on the other hand, claims that its dyno tests prove the most damaging contaminants lie in the 20-40 micron range.

Naturally, the manufacturer of each type of filter claims that its is the best. The biggest push comes from manufacturers of

screen-element filters. They claim particulate filtration down to five microns, but their claims are not borne out in oil filtration tests conducted to the SAE HS-J806B standard. At a flow of 16.5 gallons per minute (just over five times the flow rate of the Volkswagen motor), both the screen-type filters filled up quickly and failed to trap high percentages of particulates, as stated in their sales literature. Typically, these filters do not have the proper by-pass valve for the Volkswagen application.

Mecca claims eight microns for its element. James Sly once conducted an impromptu test of the Mecca filter that seems to bear out this claim. A turbocharger bearing in his motor unexpectedly disintegrated, creating enough scrap metal to clog the Mecca filter. He was alerted to this fact by the dual oil pressure setup on the 1984-and-later Volkswagens. Subsequent examination of the motor revealed no damage!

Filter Element Efficiency

Particle Size	Screen Filter 1	Screen Filter 2	Paper Filter
10 microns	11%	14%	18%
20 microns	14%	17%	70%
40 microns	20%	40%	94%
90 microns	29%	48%	90%

Without having to go to the effort of sorting out the claims, you can conclude that for maximum filtration you would use a high-quality full-flow filter such as the Fram (or the Mecca), with a by-pass filter. With a dual-mode setup like this, the extra cost of the filters is more than made up by the savings in engine wear.

If inspecting the filter element for wear particles is important to you, buy a case of spin-on filters (to get a volume discount) and purchase an inexpensive 3 1/2-inch tubing cutter.

Even if the performance of all the different types of full-flow filter were the same, I would still use the traditional paper-element spin-on filters; I do not enjoy washing filters out, and I prefer filters with seams that do not leak.

Filter Element Capacity

	Screen Filter 1	Screen Filter 2	Paper Filter
Maximum contaminants (grams)	2.26	6	60
Time until by-pass valve opens (min.)	3.5	9.5	110

Oil Additives

There are nearly as many oil additives available as there are oils to put them in. Most of these additives are friction modifiers, viscosity modifiers, or "boosters" that replenish the detergents and dispersants in the oil to extend oil life.

Of the friction modifiers, the three most common are molybdenum compounds, graphite, and polytetrafluoroethylene (PTFE), better known as Teflon. Molybdenum, as explained in "Moly Impregnation," has a high affinity for metal. Moly is also attracted to hot spots in the engine. Once the moly attaches itself to the metal it is very difficult to remove, so even though it is not oil, it is an excellent lubricant.

Graphite was once popular as an additive, but since has lost its status. Graphite is quite slippery but it does not have the same metal affinity as moly, and thus has fallen by the wayside.

Teflon, from Du Pont Chemical, is also well-known as the slippery coating in frying pans, but like graphite it has no natural affinity for metal. To get Teflon to stick to metal, the metal first must be painstakingly cleaned, and that is not going to spontaneously happen in your motor. Du Pont was not satisfied that its product would perform as advertised, so it forbade the use of the trademarked Teflon name, even though it still sells it as PTFE.

Viscosity improvers make your oil thicker, and are usually the same consistency as cold honey. This is just about the last thing you want to put in your motor.

Detergency packages claim to replenish the additive package that most oils come with from the refinery. Typical of this type of product are claims to boost the TBN (total base number) of the oil. Boosting the TBN is no problem. However, the TBN of the oil is not the only thing that determines good lubrication. In fact, none of the detergents or dispersant additives, as important as they are, are lubricants. And after a point, too much of these nonoil components does you no good, if indeed the additives are not detrimental (which in some cases they are).

The last couple of years have seen a huge boom in the business of marketing oil additives that claim to do everything better than PTFE additives, with dramatic TV infomercials to convince you of their merit. It's tough to test these products to see if they help your engine last 500,000 miles, and few are willing to drain

For extreme use, this sump guard provides a lot of protection.

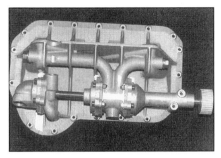

Dry-sump setups for the VW are rare. This Oettinger combination dry-sump and oil pan bolts to the bottom of the windage tray.

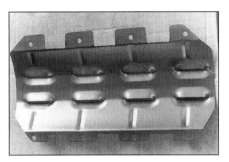

This simple windage tray integrates with the stock oil pan.

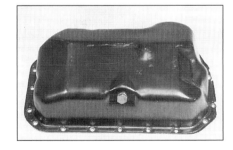

A late-style stock oil pan. Note the relative flatness of the bottom of the pan.

out their oil and drive a couple hundred miles to see if they live up to their unbelievable claims of being able to protect your engine even when it has long since run out of oil. For what it's worth, a nonscientific test shows that they don't make any noticeable difference during start-up, and fuel mileage is not helped at all, which is contrary to what you would expect.

Keep in mind that most of the current additive technology (both from the refinery and from the aftermarket) is keyed around petroleum-base stocks. Ten years ago, synthetic oil manufacturers were having a tough time figuring out what additives to use, how much of them to put in, and how to keep them in solution. The situation has improved a lot in the last few years, but if you are using a synthetic and considering an additive, first make certain that the additive will work with your synthetic. If not, you will merely contaminate your expensive oil without seeing any gain from the additive.

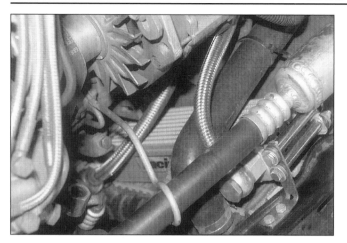

There's just enough room for this aftermarket oil cooler.

The Preluber external oil pump.

The best thing to do is to use a good oil, keep it clean, and change it on an appropriate schedule. If you want to use an additive, try moly. The rest you can live without.

Oil Analysis

One way of keeping tabs on the condition of your oil, and monitoring engine wear in the process, is to have your oil analyzed. The analysis itself is conducted in special laboratories. In return for an oil sample and a few dollars, the lab will send you a sheet telling you how much of each element it found in the sample, along with an explanation of what it all means.

Although you could wait until you suspect something is wrong in your motor before you send that first sample in for testing, it is far better to put yourself on a schedule and then stick to it. That way, you will have a better idea of the rate of wear on various components. For best results, also send in a sample of clean, fresh oil of the type you use. The lab probably has a fair idea about what is in clean oil, but it would not hurt to make sure it has a good base line for your car.

Oil analysis is used mostly to find out what engine components are shedding metal, and for this it seems to work well. If you are building race engines or doing maintenance on a fleet of cars and you need to know ahead of time when an engine is going to have a problem, oil analysis can be a good tool. Oil analysis can also be good for those using extended-drain-interval synthetics.

Oil analysis doesn't seem to be the science it should be. Stories are common about customers sending in multiple samples of the same oil, labeled differently, and getting back wildly different results.

For most people, changing the oil and filter regularly costs about the same amount, is a lot less trouble, and leaves no room for doubt as to the outcome.

Chapter 7

Air and Fuel

It is critically important to get the right air and fuel mixture delivered to the cylinder. The stoichiometric ratio (the ratio at which combustion is most efficient) takes place when there is a 14:1 air-to-fuel ratio, but maximum power is obtained with up to 10 percent less air, although economy suffers. For best economy the mixture should have 10 percent excess air, but at that point you lose some power and engine temperatures will be higher because of the slower rate of combustion. The best idle is obtained with 30 to 40 percent less air.

Therefore, the best fuel delivery system is one that runs slightly fat at idle, slightly lean at part-throttle, and a smidge rich under acceleration.

When working with either carburetors or fuel injection, a vacuum leak will throw everything off. Even small air leaks can radically alter the behavior of a motor. Keep all vacuum lines connected and in good repair (you can use the new silicone vacuum line in place of the fabric-covered rubber), and periodically check to see that there is no unwanted air leaking in at manifold joints, or through vacuum-operated devices and accessories.

Modifications for Digifant and Motronic injections are covered in "Engine Management Chips."

Tools and Techniques

In the old days, good mechanics could listen to the motor, spit on the exhaust manifolds, and tell you how to adjust the carbs. These are difficult skills to develop, however, which is why the rest of us rely on the wide range of tools we have at our disposal.

Infrared Gas Analyzers

The simplest of the high-quality diagnostic machines is the two-gas analyzer. This sniffs the exhaust and tells you how many hydrocarbons (HC) there are, and the percentage of carbon monoxide (CO).

High HC means that the fuel is not being burned. This could be because one of the spark plugs is not firing or because the valve overlap is so great that the fresh air/fuel mixture is being blown right out the tailpipe. High CO means that the mixture is running rich.

With the stiffening of air pollution laws, two-gas analyzers are being replaced by four-gas analyzers. In addition to HC and CO, the four-gas analyzers measure oxides of nitrogen and carbon dioxide.

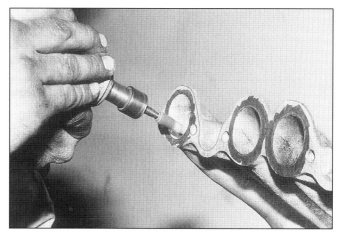

To match port the intake manifold to the cylinder head, use the intake gasket as a template and grind both the manifold and the head to the same exact opening.

This injector remover makes it easy to overcome the resistance of hardened CIS O-rings.

Computer Diagnostic Analyzers

The next step beyond the four-gas analyzer is a computer diagnostic analyzer. These new computerized analyzers monitor virtually everything of any importance that is going on in the motor, and then give you a print-out of what was found.

Neither the computer analyzer nor an infrared gas analyzer is likely to be within your budget, but if you cannot determine what is wrong with the way your car is running,

101

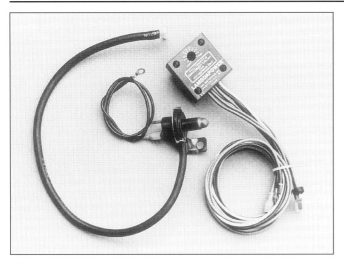

The Lambda Power improves the driveability of pre-1985 Volkswagens.

This tool allows you to remove and replace the Lambda sensor.

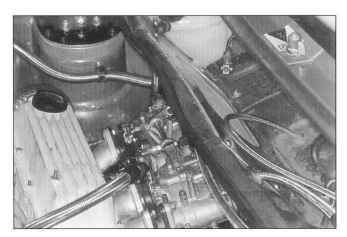

Running the velocity stacks through the firewall taps into cooler air for more horsepower on this carbureted engine.

spending a few minutes with one of these machines can be very revealing.

Exhaust Gas Temperature Readings

EGT (exhaust gas temperature) readings can give you a very accurate picture of what is occurring during combustion, but because it is difficult to connect the sensors, not many people take the time to do it.

For best accuracy, the thermocouple should be as close to the exhaust port of the head as you can get it. Ideally you would have one thermocouple per port in a carbureted application, with either four gauges (one for each cylinder) or one gauge that can be switched to read the temperature in selected cylinders.

A fuel-injected car should run quite evenly across the cylinders, so one thermocouple should work fine unless you are running at the ragged edge and are losing pistons or valves to heat. Because the thermocouple could break off, on turbo motors you should run the thermocouple *downstream* of the turbine. This location will throw your numbers off to the low side, but this is better than running pieces of metal through your turbine.

If you have a Lambda-equipped car with the exhaust emission test pipe (the one with the light blue silicone plug on the top), putting the thermocouple where the test pipe normally mounts will save you some drilling. If the thermocouple threads do not match the threads for the test pipe, make an adapter for the test pipe before you drill and tap the hole for the thermocouple, so you can reinstall the test pipe later.

Whichever method you choose, the EGT should stay between 1,300 and 1,400 degrees Fahrenheit for hard running (idle temperature will be right around 625 degrees Fahrenheit). This is best checked on the dyno, where you can run the engine at full throttle under load. It does not matter if your car is carbureted, fuel-injected, turbocharged, or supercharged; the EGT should be within this range whenever you are running gasoline. Colder temperatures mean the mixture is too rich, hotter temperatures mean the mixture is too lean.

Fuel Injection

The K-Jetronic fuel injection (1976 through 1981) is a simple design. All air entering the engine is metered as it pushes past the airflow sensor plate. The more air that enters the engine, the more that air pushes up on the plate. The plate is connected to a fuel-metering rod with laser-cut orifices on it.

As the rod is pushed higher in the fuel distributor, more of the orifice is uncovered, and more fuel is sent out the fuel lines to the injectors. The warm-up regulator applies a counterforce (called control pressure) to the top of the fuel-metering rod. The shape of the cone through which the air must pass as it pushes around the air sensor plate, along with the control pressure from the warm-up regulator, determines how high up the fuel-metering rod can rise, thus controlling the amount of fuel (the air/fuel mixture) that enters the engine.

For cold starts, the warm-up regulator temporarily reduces the amount of control pressure so the fuel-metering rod can rise higher in the fuel distributor for the same amount of air intake, richening the mixture. Also during cold starts, an auxiliary air valve allows more air to enter the engine by by-passing the throttle, increasing the idle.

The controlling systems of the Lambda sensor (introduced 1980) and KE-Jetronic injections (1985) are somewhat more sophisticated, but the basic principle is the same in that the

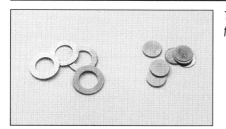

The two styles of CIS fuel distributor shims.

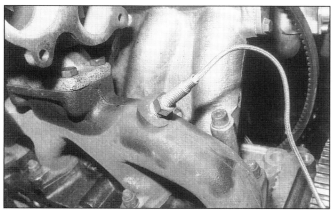

Use the emissions sniffer port for the EGT probe.

fuel is metered in direct relation to the flow of air past the air sensor plate by mechanical means.

In 1988 Volkswagen started to get away from CIS with its Digifant II injection (Digifant I in the Corrado in 1990), where injection behavior is determined in part by computer. This trend continued in 1990 with the KE-Motronic (which is relatively easy to modify by replacing a computer chip) and with the Motronic system in 1992. In these computerized systems, airflow into the engine is measured, resulting in a value that is fed to the computer. The computer takes the airflow and other factors into consideration, and opens the injectors to admit fuel into the engine based on preprogrammed values. Because the computer chip can be programmed with different built-in values, aftermarket suppliers are able to either get more power from the stock engine (with different programming), or compensate for the addition of certain engine modifications that fundamentally alter the operation of the engine (such as a supercharger). Because these engine management systems are capable of controlling so many aspects of engine performance, they typically control ignition as well as fuel delivery.

Tools and Techniques

The CIS fuel injection has two major adjustments: idle speed and idle mixture. Everything else is pretty much automatic. Because of the simplicity of the system, the adjustment does not wander around much (on the later cars the idle mixture adjustment hole is sealed up!), so you will find that the most workout these adjustments get is when you are trying to troubleshoot a problem. On the early cars with EGR, you need a two- or four-gas analyzer to set the fuel injection adjustment; on the later model cars with the Lambda sensor you can get close with a dwell meter.

Locate the small two-connector plug (it is a white plastic male plug with two female connectors in it) near the right front strut mount inside the engine compartment. One wire will be brown and the other should be light blue or gray with a white stripe. You will need a dwell meter (for example, a Snap-On MT-926) for this procedure.

The ground lead for the dwell meter is clipped to the brown wire, and the other lead from the dwell meter is clipped to the light blue or gray wire. You can make a special plug-in adapter that will allow you to make this connection easily, or cut off a couple of inches of an old Audi 100LS shift cable, which is the exact size needed for a tight fit in the female connectors. Then connect the dwell meter to these exposed leads.

Select the four-cylinder setting on your dwell meter. When the car is cold, the dwell reading should be 45 degrees. You can calibrate your dwell meter by unplugging the Lambda sensor momentarily, since 45 degrees is the system's default setting. There should be no variation in this reading.

As the motor warms up, the dwell reading should drop to around 20 degrees. This is the enrichment kicking in to give you a smooth idle until the engine is up to full operating temperature.

With the motor hot, the reading should be in the neighborhood of 45 degrees, with 7 degrees of leeway on either side. Forty degrees translates to about 1 percent carbon monoxide, which is right where the car should be run. Higher percentages of CO mean the car is running richer, lower concentrations mean the car is running leaner.

A better way, if you can afford it, is to buy one of the monitors that attach to the oxygen sensor and show you how rich or lean the mixture is. RB Racing, K&N, Haltech, and others sell great units for less than $200. For even more information, "wide band" monitors are available, but they cost more.

To make the adjustment you will need a long 3-millimeter Allen wrench. The mixture adjustment access hole is located on the air sensor housing, between the air sensor plate opening and the fuel distributor. If you have a later car on which this hole has an aluminum plug or a wedged-in ball bearing, you will need to open up the access hole before you can make the adjustment. Unfasten the air sensor housing and turn it wrong-side up. With a small punch, knock the plug or ball bearing upward (away from where the air filter would be). It should pop right out.

Screwing the mixture adjustment screw clockwise richens the mixture; counterclockwise leans it out. Always adjust from lean to rich and work in small steps, allowing the system to stabilize before making further adjustments.

Do not rev the motor with the adjustment wrench in the adjustment hole.

There are several different procedures for adjusting the fuel injection on different-year cars. Consult the shop manual for the correct procedure for your car. After making the adjustment, seal the adjustment access hole so air and dirt cannot get in.

If everything is working right, this should do it. Because this adjustment does not often wander too far off the original setting, think twice before making any major changes. If you

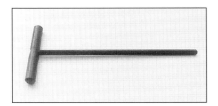

CIS mixture-adjusting wrench.

This aftermarket throttle body comes pretapped for microswitches.

Injector O-rings must periodically be replaced when they stop sealing effectively.

Check the injector housing for tightness, and seal the threads to prevent air leaks.

housing (you will have to unclip the air filter housing to do this) and push up on the air sensor plate until you hear gasoline squeaking from the injectors.

Do not get too carried away with this, as you can flood the motor. You need do it only long enough to get the fuel into the injector lines. After that, the fuel injection should be able to clear itself. In a pinch, you can even use this to get your car running again if it vapor locks in the heat.

Tweaks

The CIS fuel injection system is so elegant that there is not much you can do to optimize it. The airflow cone is essentially a mechanical computer, and it does a pretty good job of handling fuel delivery for such a simple piece. The best results come from watching what Volkswagen does and then figuring out why. Be suspicious of quick fixes—the K- and KE-Jetronic systems are pretty well dialed in.

If you are more familiar with carburetors than with fuel injection you might want to richen up the mixture to get more gas into the system. This looks simple enough to do: Insert a 3-millimeter wrench into the CO adjustment access hole and crank away. The only problem is that this adjustment predominantly regulates the idle mixture. The running mixture is governed by the profile of the cone that the airflow sensor plate rides up and down in, as mentioned earlier.

For a while, the rage was shimming the fuel distributor to get the system pressure as high as possible, while using an Audi 5000 warm-up regulator to get the control pressure as low as possible. I spent hours tracking down shims (there are two different styles), installing warm-up regulators and shimming fuel distributors. When I was all done we could only bench race the new setup because we did not have a dyno at our disposal. If we had dyno tested these changes (as Darrell Vittone later did), we would have found that there was no measurable difference between the stock setup and the trick setup. As it was, with the absence of factual information, it was not very difficult to convince ourselves that the car ran faster!

One tweak does seem to work, but it applies only to 1985-and-later CIS-equipped cars with the new fuel injection (the one without the warm-up regulator). I stumbled across this on a pair of brand-new Volkswagens that Paul and Karl Hacker were then racing. The Hackers are extremely competitive and managed to come home winners fairly often, so when they complained that their cars were down on horsepower at high rpm they were not simply making excuses. We went over those cars with a fine-toothed digital voltmeter and a fuel pressure gauge and found absolutely nothing out of specification.

It turns out that in addition to the regular CO adjustment, there is another basic adjustment to the fuel distributor: control plunger height. The only problem is that it is difficult to get to and adjusting it is a cut-and-try procedure.

Here is how it works: Adjust the CO percentage as you normally would. Remove the fuel distributor and measure the distance between the tops of the seating pads (where the fuel

get completely out of the ballpark, unplug the Lambda sensor and the idle stabilizer (if you have one), and lean out the mixture until the car stumbles, then richen it back up until it runs smoothly. If your car is in good shape, you will hear the difference. Then go back and plug everything in and try again. If you still cannot get it, you may have one or more bad components, and it is time to consult your mechanic.

One technique that might save you a few hours of time is bleeding the air from your fuel injection system. If you have any of the fuel lines apart for any reason, the system may not be able to prime itself once you get everything back together. To purge the air from the system you will need to bridge the fuel pump relay using a jumper wire. With the fuel pump running, reach underneath the airflow

Intake air for the GTi 16V comes from behind the right headlight.

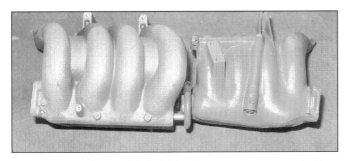

The late-style intake manifold (right) has larger runners compared with earlier units.

distributor sits) and the roller on the airflow sensor plate lever. The distance should be within 0.1 millimeter of 19 millimeters.

If it is not, adjust the height by turning the CO percentage adjusting screw until it is. Reinstall the fuel distributor and check to see how much sensor plate clearance (upward movement before the lever contacts the fuel distributor plunger) there is. If the clearance is okay, readjust the CO and idle, and check to see if this has solved your problem. If the clearance is not okay, remove the fuel distributor.

On the bottom of the plunger of the fuel distributor is a slot into which a screwdriver will fit. This is the stop screw of the control plunger. Turning the stop screw clockwise increases the clearance, turning it counterclockwise decreases the clearance. A quarter-turn results in about a 1.3-millimeter difference in sensor plate position.

Reassemble, readjust the CO percentage and idle speed, and recheck the performance.

Even when this adjustment is perfect, you could still experience poor response. Now, however, you know where to tinker with the adjustments to approach the problem. For example, for lean running you might set the sensor plate at the lower limit in the housing and set the sensor plate basic adjustment at the tight end of the adjustment to get the control plunger as high into the fuel distributor as possible.

Another tip for those of you who race is to drill out the screen in the banjo bolt on the inlet side of the fuel distributor (next to the differential pressure regulator). VW Sports recommends that you drive the car for 1,000 miles before you do this, however, and I would not recommend this for any street car.

Black Boxes

A "black box" is slang for any type of subsystem about which you don't know *how* it works, but you know what it does. Autotech's Power Module for Volkswagens equipped with KE-Jetronic (which includes many of the A2 cars) is one such device, and there are others. Developers of these devices have come up with some imaginative ways to get more fuel into the engine while retaining the benefits of the "closed loop" fuel management system built into the basic injection.

Those who sell these devices swear they work. I have personally tested only a couple of units, and so far the results have been underwhelming. If you wish to try one of these devices, make sure you test your car beforehand to establish a performance baseline, against which you can compare performance with the unit installed. If the car is faster, then the device works for you. See "Analysis Methods" for a more complete discussion of vehicle performance testing.

Throttle Bodies

As was covered in the chapter on bolt-on performance, a ported throttle body works best in combination with other

The stock 60-millimeter fuel distributor.

A thick-rim 80-millimeter fuel distributor. Note the "67 K" decal.

A thin-rim 80-millimeter fuel distributor.

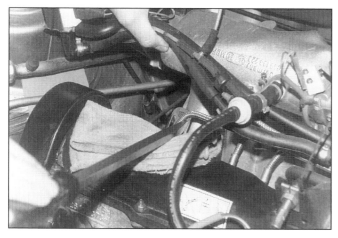
Removing a stubborn CIS injector.

modifications that free up the breathing of the engine, and thus is one of the last modifications to make. For maximum effect, match port the intake manifold to the new throttle body, and don't use the adaptor plate that comes with some throttle bodies for A1 and A2 engines. On some manifolds, the aluminum is not thick enough to allow the manifold to be match ported, making it necessary to weld additional metal to the outside of the throttle body.

After all this work, the throttle body will flow between 1 and 2 percent more air than the stock unit (at full lift in a big-valve head with a high-lift camshaft). If you are looking for the one big change that will turn your stock car into a road-mauling tire burner, this is not it. If you have exhausted all other possibilities and are looking for incremental gains of any magnitude, read on.

There are two styles of throttle body: the single-butterfly style and the dual-butterfly style, often referred to as "progressive" because a small butterfly opens first for good driveability at small throttle openings, while an additional, larger butterfly comes into play at larger throttle openings.

The single-butterfly throttle bodies are difficult to drive because even small amounts of throttle opening reveal a large cross-section through which air can flow. This makes poking along in traffic anything but smooth. On the VR6, of course, Volkswagen uses a single-butterfly throttle body, but it shapes the venturi within the throttle body so that even with a single butterfly, the response is somewhat progressive.

Porting the VR6 throttle body involves removing the "progressive" sections of the housing, so you will lose driveability. There are plenty of incorrect ways to port the VR6 throttle body, but there are well-done units available, such as the one from Velocity, which takes the stock 63.8-millimeter bore and pushes it out to 68.3 millimeters. Any well-done porting job will also lower the profile of the butterfly axle.

If you are mounting the throttle body on a pre-Lambda car, you will have to disconnect and plug the EGR vacuum line. If you are not sure if your car has EGR or not, look into the throat of the throttle body. If there is a restrictor on the small

side of the throttle body, you have EGR. The restrictor is there to increase vacuum to run the EGR system. Later cars without the EGR system did not need this extra vacuum, and the restrictor was eliminated.

If you have a throttle body with a restrictor and want to see if there is anything to be gained by removing the restrictor, there is a trick to removing it. The restrictor is held in by the EGR vacuum port. If you grab the vacuum port with a pair of pliers, you will crush the port. Find a nail that just fits inside the port and insert it before grabbing on with the pliers. This allows you to remove and replace the port without ruining it. Once you get the restrictor out, replace the port and put a rubber vacuum plug over the end to prevent leaks.

Anytime you are working on the intake tract, it is vital to ensure that there are no vacuum leaks. This means mating surfaces must be spotless, and you must use new gaskets. When connecting the throttle linkage, leave a little slack at first, then ask a friend to push the accelerator pedal fully to the floor (engine off!) while you watch to see that the throttle butterfly is opening up all the way. If not, tighten the throttle cable. If it is opening all the way but the accelerator is not all the way down, the cable is too tight and must be loosened. There's no sense in installing a big throttle body and then not making sure it opens properly.

Intake Manifolds
Two-Valve Manifolds

As just mentioned, the A2 fuel-injection manifolds are of completely different design than the A1 manifolds, and the A3 cross-flow manifolds are more different still. On the earlier manifolds the runners can be the most restrictive part of the intake system. This was not discovered until Darrell Vittone noticed that you could saw the top off of the intake manifold plenum and airflow would not improve. Intake manifold porting was born.

The difficulty of intake manifold porting is reflected in the prices that tuners charge for it. The benefits that accrue from manifold porting vary from engine to engine, so you might want to think twice about how much you need those few extra horsepower before deciding to have your intake manifold opened up. For a ported and polished head with big valves and a high-lift, Darrell found you can expect roughly 10 percent more flow through a ported manifold using the stock throttle body, with roughly 5 percent more airflow available on top of that when a match-ported aftermarket throttle body is bolted up.

One alternative to porting your own manifold is abrasive flow machining, which forces a viscous, rubbery compound with abrasive grit in it through the ports, machining them in the process.

The stock intake manifold from the A3 cross-flow engines flows enough for as much as you can get out of the fuel injection. Your best bang for the buck will be in match porting the lower half of the intake manifold to the cylinder head ports. Anything beyond that seems to be a waste of time. They make more horsepower out of the box than the noncross-flow heads, but with a little work the early heads (and CIS fuel injection) have more potential for horsepower than the A3 cross-flow and Motronic injection.

Four-Valve Manifolds

Six months before the 16V was introduced in the United States, Germany sent Volkswagen of America some samples of the new motor. Volkswagen of America took one look at the dyno sheets and spotted a major problem: The horsepower peak was somewhere between 6,500 and 7,000 rpm. This might have been great for the Autobahn, but it was next to useless in the United States.

Therefore, Volkswagen reduced the size of the intake runners from 50 millimeters to 40 millimeters on cars sold in the United States. This picked up the velocity and the low-end torque at the expense of ultimate top-end horsepower, but made the cars much more driveable.

The larger manifolds are available from many of the aftermarket suppliers, however, although the combination of the larger runners, free-flow exhaust, and high-performance exhaust camshaft make engine response peaky. Even though the Euro manifolds can be expensive, it's a lot easier to buy one than to port your existing manifold.

VR6 Manifolds

Properly done, manifold porting seems to help the VR6, especially when the displacement has been increased. One of the trickest VW manifolds ever is available for the VR6 in the form of the Schrick Variable Geometry intake manifold, which has one mode for low-range driving, another mode for high-range driving, and adjustments for both the cross-over point and cross-over reaction speed. If you have been paying attention to the ads for the world's more expensive cars (including the Porsche 928S, and—more recently—certain Japanese luxury sedans), you'll see that this type of technology is on the cutting edge. This is essentially a better, much less expensive version of the discontinued Volkswagen Motorsport VSR manifold.

CIS Air Sensor Housings

One thing we have learned from Volkswagen is that the small-plate airflow sensors are not the hot tip for pre-1985 high-performance motors. This is something that we have also verified on the dyno. The small airflow sensor housing has a 60-millimeter plate in place the 80-millimeter plate used in the other Volkswagens, so it is easy to see the difference at a glance. If you have a small-plate airflow unit, switch over to a unit with the bigger plate for better results.

Of the big-plate units used in the United States, there are two versions with slight differences between the two. On the dyno, Darrell Vittone found that the unit with the thinner (3.2-millimeter) lip around the top made more horsepower in a normally aspirated motor than the unit with the thicker (6.35-millimeter) lip.

You usually have to remove the air boot to make the identification, although many of the thick-lip units also have a black sticker on the outside that reads "67 K." The thick-lip air sensor plate housing runs a little richer than the thin-lip version, making it a better choice for supercharged motors that need a bit more fuel.

In further tests, Darrell found that even at full throttle on the dyno, the air sensor plate is not at the maximum height it could be. In other words, the stock injection is good to nearly 170 horsepower in a normally aspirated motor. (Callaway Turbosystems felt safe using the stock CIS injection to only 130 horsepower in a turbo application.) You can check this yourself the same way Darrell did—cut a section out of the boot and replace it with a sturdy piece of clear plastic. This does not necessarily mean there is a lot more fuel waiting to be used. At the extreme end of actuator arm travel, there is proportionately less additional fuel available, owing to the geometry of the arm itself.

The early European GTis had a completely different airflow housing, with steeper walls. This has led some tuners to speculate that it might be possible to develop an inexpensive slip-in plastic insert that would change the fuel flow characteristics for the better. Another possibility is to use a housing from another similar car to get more fuel. An early 924 fuel distributor and airflow housing, for example, is sized to feed a 1.9-liter motor.

Air Filters

Some tuners sell low-restriction air filters with the claim that they increase horsepower. Theoretically, this sounds good. If you are considering one, do some back-to-back time/speed runs, first with a paper-element air filter installed and next with the element removed completely. (Do this in an area that is not dusty.) If you find enough of a difference to justify the expense, go for it; however, the results of numerous tests with stock motors, big-displacement motors and turbo motors show no increase in performance with the air filter completely removed, let alone with a different type of filter element in place.

Fuel Filters

It is much more critical that you change your fuel filter with fuel injection than with carburetors. The reason lies with the difference in fuel pump output pressure. When the fuel filter in your carbureted car fills up, the engine will starve for fuel and simply stop running. At 4 to 5 psi of fuel pressure, not much will be drawn through the dirt-clogged filter.

When the filter in a fuel-injection system fills up enough to restrict fuel flow, the pressure differential across the filter can far exceed the total pressure of a carbureted fuel pump's output. This is why you sometimes find trash in the fuel injectors and fuel distributor in spite of the four-micron rating of the Bosch fuel filter.

Unfortunately, there is no way of telling when the fuel filter is full, and it takes only one contaminated tank of gas to fill it up. About the only thing to do is play the odds and change the filter at the 15,000 mile service.

Hot-Start Problems

All CIS-injected cars can fall prey to the dreaded "hot-start" syndrome. It usually happens on a hot day, and the symptom is that you cannot restart your car 20 to 30 minutes after shutting it off. You can crank and crank and crank, but the car simply needs to cool down before it will go again. If your car was built before 1980, the chances are very good that you have experienced this.

There are several ways of approaching this problem. If you need only an ad hoc solution, you could activate the fuel pump and manually raise the air sensor plate until you hear the fuel squeaking out of the injectors. For more permanent solutions, you can look at both prevention and cures for this problem.

One preventive measure involves lowering the underhood temperatures so the fuel does not cook out of the fuel lines in the first place. This might involve installing a cooler fan switch and an oil cooler. I did both of these on my Scirocco and still had a problem, until I changed to a high-quality synthetic oil, at which time the problem was almost totally eliminated.

Curative measures include performing a comprehensive CIS test and fixing whatever you find to be wrong. If everything tests out okay and your car was built before 1980, change over to the Volkswagen part No. 431.133.441C fuel accumulator and the injectors to match. (The late-model fuel accumulator holds a higher pressure, and can cause the early style injectors to leak down. You have to replace both at the same time.) The injectors you are looking for have production numbers higher than 829.

A CIS test of your system after you have installed these parts should reveal a 10-minute leakdown residual pressure of 2.6 bar, and a 20-minute leakdown residual pressure of 2.4 bar.

If this fails, you can install a hot-start pulse relay kit, available from your Volkswagen dealer. This kit automatically pulses the cold-start injector upon starting to purge the system of fuel vapors. If you have a late-model car and are experiencing starting difficulties, this relay should be checked along with the rest of the CIS system.

A quick alternative would be to wire up an additional ground wire for the cold-start valve, so you could activate the cold-start valve with a button in the passenger compartment whenever you wanted. However, if you elect to cure your hot-start problem this way you may often flood the engine, something that is extremely difficult to do with the stock fuel injection.

CIS Fuel Injectors

Tests have shown that even the stock CIS injectors will flow enough fuel to make almost 400 horsepower. For best performance, test a batch of injectors for spray pattern and use the ones that have the best misting action. The best way is to have an injection tester, which also will allow you to force through solvent to clean the injectors. These are expensive, however, so it is more likely that you will remove the injectors, point them into a can, activate the fuel pump (use a jumper wire across the fuel pump relay slot in the fuse board), and raise the airflow sensor by hand. Be very cautious doing this, because you are

An exhaust gas temperature gauge lets you know if the air/fuel mixture is off.

Even though it is a single-butterfly throttle body, the stock unit on the right is shaped in such a way to lend it some of the driveability of a progressive throttle body. The ported unit on the left sacrifices this in favor of more airflow. Note the shaping of the butterfly axle in the ported unit.

spraying atomized fuel around, and if you ignite it with a spark or flame, you will have a major fire on your hands in moments.

Testing can take a while because even new-out-of-the-box, many injectors will squirt a stream out of one side of the orifice instead of evenly atomizing the fuel. I am not aware of anyone checking the difference this makes on a dyno, but it is no secret that properly atomized fuel burns much better than liquid fuel droplets.

This is the reason Volkswagen went to the air-shrouded injectors in 1985. By adding another air port behind the injector, it was able to get better mixing of the fuel with the incoming air charge. Unfortunately, the way Volkswagen implemented this change makes it just about impossible to retrofit to an early model head, and whatever gains there are cannot be worth the cost of changing heads.

Without air-shrouded injectors, your motor will run just fine. For that last little bit of performance, however, check the spray pattern and the opening pressure on the injectors you are using. If they look sick (for example, if they are dribbling or streaming), test several new Bosch injectors to get four that all open and close at the same pressures and have nice spray patterns.

Electronic Fuel Injectors

Testing electronic injectors is much more difficult because you need both fuel pressure and a way to trigger the injector; an injector tester is almost mandatory. One of the drawbacks of sophisticated engine electronics is that the injectors don't have as much range as the CIS type. If you suspect your injectors, or if you are building an engine that will require much more fuel than stock (such as supercharged, turbocharged, or nitrous injected engines), APS offers high-flow "balanced and blueprinted" injectors that are not only matched for flow and spray pattern, but which also have lighter-weight components inside for quicker response.

Injector O-rings

If your car has some miles on it, there is a good chance that the fuel injector O-rings have become hardened, and they may be leaking vacuum. This will be noticeable only at idle (and when you are trying to adjust the mixture!), but it must be attended to.

The injector O-rings fit into plastic or metal inserts that are threaded into the head. Remove the inserts, clean them up and replace them with a little sealant on the threads. The old O-rings can become so hardened that you will have to cut them off with side-cutters, but the new ones will slide right on with a little push. The shop manual recommends soaking new O-rings in gasoline for a few minutes before installation.

Repairs

The Bosch CIS injection requires special troubleshooting tools and techniques that are beyond the budget of all but the most serious enthusiast. For repairs, then, you often will be dealing with a mechanic.

Not all mechanics were raised on fuel injection, and some do not have the proper tools to work on it. If neither you nor your mechanic can figure out what is going on with your Bosch fuel-injected motor, help is at hand. Bosch has established a network of authorized service centers across the United States. The centers must meet minimum requirements for fuel injection test equipment and product knowledge, and can replace components under warranty when needed.

If your car is equipped with Volkswagen's Digijet, Digifant, or Motronic system, the diagnostic equipment is expensive and troubleshooting can be complex. Seek aid from the dealership or a qualified repair station.

Special Fuels and Fuel Additives

With all the talk about the poor quality of fuel these days, it is not surprising that the market is flooded with octane boosters of every type. Save your money; none of them show any improvement on the dyno. If you are concerned about fuel quality, always buy a name-brand product from a busy station. Most people with fuel contamination problems have, coincidentally, always bought the cheapest gas they could find.

There seem to be hundreds of fuel additives available, and you can do without most of them. Two that do work are Lubro Moly Jectron and Lubro Moly Ventil Sauber. Jectron cleans the fuel system from the inside out (including the injectors), while the Ventil Sauber cleans deposits from the backs of the intake valves, restoring airflow.

Lubro Moly claims that an engine can accumulate enough deposits in the fuel system and on the backs of the valves to require treatment in 10,000 miles. You may not have to do it

that often, but it's not bad for an average figure. If you've never cleaned your engine with products such as these, wait until you are low on fuel and are about ready to do an oil change. Doing the cleaning when low on fuel gives the engine a "hot shot" of cleaner to help dissolve deposits. You'll want to wait until it's time to do an oil change because some of the gunk from the injection and valves will get past the piston rings, and contaminate the oil. If you do an oil change right after running the cleanser through the fuel system, you can get rid of the contaminants once and for all. There are no significant differences in what should be done for newer style injectors.

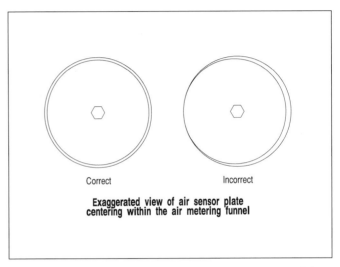

Correct   Incorrect

Exaggerated view of air sensor plate centering within the air metering funnel

Centering the air sensor plate on CIS cars ensures that the edge of the plate won't catch on the housing, causing starting problems.

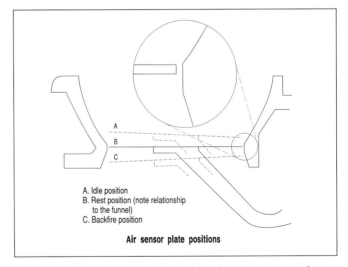

A. Idle position
B. Rest position (note relationship to the funnel)
C. Backfire position

Air sensor plate positions

The height of the air sensor plate must fall within a narrow range for good off-idle response.

Chapter 8

Forced Induction

When discussing forced induction, many of the experts disagree, sometimes on minor points, sometimes on major ones. And the sparks really fly when a turbocharger expert is in on the same conversation with a supercharger expert.

Forced induction is not the only answer to the question of how to get higher performance, but turbochargers have become very popular. In spite of this, or maybe because of it, there are also some exciting developments in superchargers. Most students of automobile history will recognize this trend as another of a long series of pendulum swings, but it is difficult not to get caught up in the excitement of the moment.

Theory

As air is drawn into the engine by the pressure differential between atmospheric pressure and the vacuum created in the wake of the receding piston, it encounters many impediments such as throttle butterflies, valve guides, valve stems, and so on. The air itself also drags along the walls of the intake tract. All of this adds up to a system that is not 100 percent efficient. In some race motors, 100 percent efficiency can be had over a narrow rpm range, but a race motor would be a real handful to coax into a parking space, and rush hour would be very dramatic.

In the effort to improve the volumetric efficiency of the stock motor (the ability of the motor to completely fill the cylinder with air), the traditional hot rod approach is to port and "polish" everything in sight, install a big cam, stick in big valves, bump up the compression and stand back.

If, however, instead of depending on the difference between the ambient air pressure (14.7 psi at sea level, less as altitude increases) and the slight vacuum created by the piston to *suck* air into the cylinder, we were to *shove* air into the motor, it would be less critical to port, polish, cam, or valve the engine to get the volumetric efficiency up to where we wanted it.

Supercharging is the generic term used to describe this forced induction of air into the combustion chamber. Forced induction is accomplished with one of two devices, one called a mechanical supercharger and one called an exhaust gas turbocharger. Both of these devices require energy from the motor to run. The increase in horsepower comes because the increased efficiency of the motor more than makes up for the small horsepower loss.

Although forcing more air into the cylinder raises the compression ratio of the motor, this is not the only reason forced

The G-lader. The inner scroll is on the left at the bottom, the two halves of the outer scroll are at the top, and the twin eccentrics are at the bottom right.

A simple turbocharger with no intercooler. It makes less horsepower, but is easier to install.

induction makes horsepower. In a typical high-compression motor, the piston compresses the air/fuel mixture into the relatively small combustion chamber for ignition. Force-fed motors typically run with lower compression to start with, meaning that when the piston comes up to compress the air/fuel mixture, it does so into a larger volume. In theory, a low-compression

110

An intercooled turbocharger for pre-1985 cars.

A intercooled turbocharger for the 1985-and-later four-cylinders.

engine, therefore, is a perfect candidate for forced induction because the supercharger will create a high-compression mixture in the larger combustion chamber volume. With more air and fuel to burn, the power stroke will be longer and will make more horsepower than it would with a smaller, equally dense air/fuel mixture in a high-compression motor.

In practice, turbo motors built this way tend to be very peaky in their response. The Porsche 930 is one example. With its low compression and big turbo, low-end response seems nonexistent, but hang onto your hat when the tachometer hits 3,500 rpm.

Both forced-induction devices also cause the engine to run hotter. Although there are several reasons for this, the main one is that compressing air also heats it. The more air is compressed the hotter it gets, whether you compress it with a turbocharger, a mechanical supercharger or a trash compactor.

You can calculate the approximate theoretical temperature rise before starting if you know in advance how much boost you plan to run. For example, consider a system with six pounds of boost.

The first thing to calculate is the pressure ratio. This is found by adding the amount of boost to the ambient air pressure and dividing by the ambient air pressure. (For the ambient air pressure at altitudes other than sea level, refer to the chart.)

In this example, taken at sea level, you come up with

$$\frac{14.7 + 6}{14.7} = 14.08$$

With the pressure ratio, you can calculate the temperature increase constant, which is expressed as $r^{0.238}-1$ (the pressure ratio raised to the 0.283 power, minus 1). This gives a temperature increase constant of 0.100.

You also need to know the ambient air temperature in Rankine. Rankine is another temperature scale similar to centigrade and Fahrenheit, only in Rankine, water freezes at 491.69 degrees. Fortunately, 1 degree of temperature change in

Rankine is the same as 1 degree of temperature change in Fahrenheit, so to convert Fahrenheit to Rankine you simply add 459.69 to the temperature in Fahrenheit (it is OK to round it off to 460).

With an ambient air temperature of 70 degrees Fahrenheit, the temperature in Rankine would be 530. Now multiply the ambient temperature by the temperature increase constant to get the approximate theoretical temperature increase:

$$530 \times 0.100 = 53 \text{ degrees Fahrenheit}$$

Notice that the result comes out in degrees Fahrenheit. This means that the outlet temperature of the sample system running 6 pounds of boost will be 53 degrees warmer than when it went in, for a total temperature of 123 degrees Fahrenheit.

You are not done yet, however, because this is the temperature increase under perfect conditions—in other words, with a compressor that is 100 percent efficient. To approximate the temperature rise under real-world conditions, divide the theoretical temperature increase by the compressor efficiency. If your turbocharger is 65 percent efficient, as an example, you get

$$\frac{53}{0.65} = 81.4$$

An aftermarket turbo with built-in wastegate.

The calculated real-world increase in temperature is therefore 81.4 degrees for a calculated real-world outlet temperature of 151.4 degrees. As this example shows, the trend is toward higher outlet temperatures as the efficiency of the supercharger decreases.

Turbo Heat Gain Due to Compression

Pressure Ratio	Turbocharger Compressor Efficiency								
	40%	50	55	60	65	70	75	80	85%
1.00	70	70	70	70	70	70	70	70	70
1.05	88.4	84.7	83.4	82.3	81.3	80.5	79.8	79.2	78.7
1.10	106.2	99.0	96.3	94.1	92.3	90.7	89.3	88.1	87.0
1.15	123.4	112.7	108.9	105.6	102.9	100.5	98.5	96.7	95.1
1.20	140.1	126.1	121.0	116.7	113.2	110.1	107.4	105.1	103.0
1.25	156.3	139.1	132.8	127.5	123.1	119.3	116.0	113.2	110.6
1.30	172.1	151.7	144.2	138.0	132.8	128.3	124.4	121.0	118.0
1.35	187.4	163.9	155.4	148.3	142.2	137.1	132.6	128.7	125.2
1.40	202.3	175.8	166.2	158.2	151.4	145.6	140.6	136.1	132.3
1.45	216.8	187.5	176.8	167.9	160.4	153.9	148.3	143.4	139.1
1.50	231.0	198.8	187.1	177.3	169.1	162.0	155.9	150.5	145.8
1.55	244.9	209.9	197.2	186.6	177.6	169.9	163.3	157.4	152.3
1.60	258.4	220.7	207.0	195.6	185.9	177.7	170.5	164.2	158.7
1.65	271.6	231.3	216.6	204.4	194.1	185.2	177.5	170.8	164.9
1.70	284.6	241.7	226.0	213.0	202.0	192.6	184.4	177.3	171.0
1.75	297.2	251.8	235.3	221.5	209.8	199.9	191.2	183.6	176.9
1.80	309.7	261.7	244.3	229.8	217.5	206.9	197.8	189.8	182.8
1.85	321.8	271.5	253.1	237.9	225.0	213.9	204.3	195.9	188.5
1.90	333.8	281.0	261.8	245.8	232.3	220.7	210.7	201.9	194.1
1.95	345.5	290.4	270.4	253.7	239.5	227.4	216.9	207.7	199.6
2.00	357.0	299.6	278.7	261.3	246.6	234.0	223.1	213.5	205.1

There are three main reasons why the increase in intake charge temperature is so important. First, a hotter intake charge requires higher octane or a special ignition system to combat detonation. Second, the higher the intake charge the hotter the engine runs, which not only can cook the motor but can also contribute to detonation and preignition. Third, the hotter the intake charge the lower the density of the air charge—and the whole reason for using forced induction was to have a denser intake charge. Cooling the intake charge is primarily the job of an intercooler, as discussed later.

An air-to-air intercooler.

Turbochargers

Turbochargers use exhaust gas to spin a turbine wheel. This turbine wheel connects with a shaft that is connected to a compressor wheel that forces air into the motor. Turbochargers are not the most efficient form of forced induction, but they are near the top with ratings of 65 to 70 percent.

Contrary to popular belief, turbochargers do not make free horsepower. To develop boost in a street application, you will see about 2.5 psi of back pressure for every psi of boost. At 6 psi of boost, the back pressure would be 15 psi. If you try to run that much back pressure on a normally aspirated motor, it will choke and die. The turbocharger does not provide free horsepower, but it does manage to overcome its own drive losses.

Turbochargers fall into a class of forced induction called centrifugal compressors. With a centrifugal compressor, the delivery air volume increases as the square of the rotational speed of the impeller. At lower turbine speeds the turbo will make relatively little boost, but at higher turbine speeds it can easily develop too much. This explains why turbos must be carefully sized to the motor and the application. The lack of boost at lower rpm is sometimes referred to as turbo lag, although this term more properly refers to the amount of time between when the accelerator is opened and when the turbo can pressurize the intake system.

Three factors determine the amount of boost delay in a turbo system. First, it takes a moment for the turbine to spin up to speed. And because of the relationship between boost and turbine speed, low speeds mean low boost. Second, when the engine is at idle or low rpm there is not much energy in the exhaust. The velocity is down, as is EGT. This is why you feel the turbo really kick in once you get the rpm up and the engine is working harder. Third, the bigger the pressure drop between the throttle valve and the air-metering unit, the longer the delay. When the throttle is opened suddenly, a pressure wave is created in that area of the intake tract. Until that pressure wave reaches the air metering unit and everything becomes equalized, the engine does not know what to do.

If that were the least of a turbocharger's problems, we would all own one. In spite of what anybody tells you, turbochargers, with their peaky adiabatic efficiency graph, are not well suited for automobile use. For example, suppose a turbocharged motor running at 3,000 rpm is getting just the right amount of air it needs and the turbine is spinning at X rpm. On accelerating up to 6,000 rpm, assume that the turbine speed doubles as well, to 2X rpm. The motor needs twice as much air as it did at 3,000 rpm, but the turbine is supplying four times as much air!

These numbers are hypothetical, but they are indicative of what happens. There will be rpm ranges when the turbo is supplying too little air, times when it is supplying too much air, and times when it supplies the right amount of air. When there is too little air or just the right amount, there is not much that can be (or needs to be) done. When too much air is supplied, the turbo system needs to vent off some of the boost through a safety valve called a wastegate.

A turbo being pushed to the limit on a dyno.

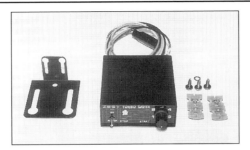

This timer keeps the engine running even after the ignition is switched off and the key removed, to maintain oil flow through the turbo bearings while the housing cools, preventing premature turbo failure.

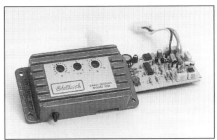

This water injection controller regulates manifold vacuum set point, rpm set point, and liquid delivery.

A wastegate is installed in all modern street turbo systems to limit the amount of boost to a reasonable level. The wastegate is needed because until someone perfects a variable inlet turbine, all the exhaust gas has to flow through one hole after it leaves the cylinder head and tries to get into the turbocharger housing. The size of that hole is critical to the performance of the turbocharger. If the hole is too large, the exhaust gas velocity will be low and boost will come in only at a higher rpm (as it does in the Porsche 930). The opposite happens if the hole is too small; the boost will come in sooner, but it will run out sooner as well.

Turbo systems are usually designed with the hole a little on the small side. When the back pressure builds up beyond a certain point the wastegate opens, venting much of the heat energy and exhaust gas velocity that the turbo would otherwise use.

Turbocharger compressor sizing is also a problem. Because of the peakiness of its adiabatic graph, you can size the turbo smaller and get a more linear response (as the rpm climb from low to high) at the expense of ultimate high-rpm power, or you can size the turbo bigger and give up some of your low-rpm driveability. For a street motor, a fair compromise seems to be to run a higher compression to keep the low-rpm response up and run a big turbocharger timed to deliver maximum flow at the engine's torque peak to augment the high-rpm power.

A variable-inlet turbine housing would address these problems the correct way, letting us get away from the wasteful wastegate. Another solution that so far has not been applied to a Volkswagen turbo system is the twin-scroll turbocharger. Although not as efficient as a variable-inlet turbine, it does a much better job of matching the exhaust flow to the needs of the turbine than does a single-scroll unit, and it is much more simple to design than a variable-inlet turbine.

Another problem with turbochargers involves the conditions under which they run. One half of the turbocharger works in the hot exhaust gas stream, while the other half works in the relatively cool intake air stream. With turbine speeds up to and over 100,000 rpm, it is no wonder that turbo bearings and oil seals are prone to failure.

To minimize the negative aspects of exhaust heat, some turbocharger housings incorporate water jackets through which

The NOS sandwich plate mounts downstream of the throttle body on this supercharged engine. One of the feed lines is nitrous, the other gasoline.

coolant runs. In sophisticated applications, there is even a separate water pump to circulate coolant through the turbo water jacket after the motor has been turned off. Keeping the housing cool goes a long way toward eliminating heat soak, the term used to describe what happens when a red-hot turbo is shut off and the heat cooks the lubricant in the turbo bearing into a dry, hard compound called coke. Coke-covered bearings, oil feed lines, and oil drain lines restrict the flow of lubricant vital to the turbo bearing, and turbo failure is quick to follow.

Another key to longevity in a turbo involves cooling the motor off after use. The simplest way is to let the engine sit at idle for two to five minutes before turning off the key. At idle the exhaust temperature is greatly reduced, giving the turbo housing, the turbo bearing, and the engine oil time to stabilize and cool down. This is required because for many years turbos used plain bearings. Some of the new turbos now use roller or ball bearings. It's too soon to know if these will have better resistance to coking, but they should have much better longevity due to the superior load-bearing attributes of roller or ball bearings compared to plain bearings especially in combination with water-cooling of the turbo housing.

Few people will spend the five minutes sitting there waiting for the car to cool down, however. The Turbo Saver is a

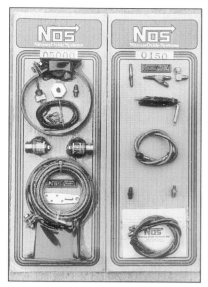

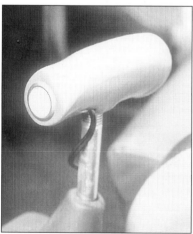

Typical bottle of nitrous oxide.

The NOS kit contains all the pieces you need to add 50 horsepower to your car.

The extra fuel for the fogger nozzle comes from a tap off the fuel distributor.

Mount the nitrous button in an easy-to-reach spot.

the oil. Early noncross-flow heads (with the exhaust and intake manifolds on the same side) are not ideal for turbocharging. Heat from the turbocharger will soak into the head, the valve guides, the valves, and the intake manifold, and nothing can be done about it. (Maybe this is one of the reasons Volkswagen gave up on turbochargers and switched over to mechanical superchargers.)

One final oiling consideration on the turbocharger unit is that the Volkswagen motor can produce extreme oil pressure when started on a cold morning with thick oil in the crankcase. This high pressure can and will blow out turbocharger oil seals. The feed line to the turbocharger must have a properly sized restrictor in it to prevent this from happening.

The placement of the turbocharger is pretty much fixed in the Volkswagen because of space and other considerations. A custom exhaust manifold allows it and the wastegate to hang off the back of the motor. This turns out to be a good location, as the turbo response is best when the turbo is close to the source of the hot, fast-moving exhaust gases that spin the turbine.

The tricky part is plumbing the pressure side of the turbocharger. When running an intercooler and all of its associated piping, the engine compartment can become crowded.

I'm trying to stay away from specific recommendations because turbo kits come and go like the wind. Not one of the kit makers from my first book was in business within two years of that book's release, and they were pretty well-funded (for example, Callaway, GMP, and Arkay).

Superchargers

Mechanical superchargers pressurize air to gain the same effect as the turbocharger, but there are some big differences between the two.

Mechanical superchargers (also known as blowers) use direct drive to spin their impellers, usually in the form of a belt run off the crankshaft or camshaft. There are many more types of mechanical supercharger than there are turbocharger, with three different types available for the Volkswagen.

One of the biggest differences with superchargers is that some of them are what is known as positive-displacement types, meaning that in theory the same amount of air is delivered to the engine per revolution regardless of speed. The most common type of mechanical supercharger is the Roots design, which runs 35 to 60 percent efficient. The Eaton unit used in New Dimensions supercharger kits is an example of this type.

Because positive-displacement mechanical superchargers deliver roughly the same amount of air per engine revolution, it becomes relatively easy to size the blower to the needs of the motor without having to rely on a wastegate. Another aid to correct sizing is that once you find a supercharger that is close in size, you can fine-tune the output by varying the ratio between the drive sprocket and the driven sprocket. As a side benefit to this correct sizing, throttle response across the rpm range is far more linear than with a turbocharged motor.

Blown motors will benefit from head flow work and from

device that allows the car to idle for a preset period of time, freeing the driver to go on his or her way. Another handy item is the Turboluber, sibling of the Preluber mentioned in "Prelubrication." The Turboluber can be preset to pump engine oil through the turbo for several minutes after the key is turned off, as well as to provide prelubrication on start-up.

The issue of heat is not confined to the turbocharger and

A boost gauge can also reveal problems with idle vacuum or boost leaks.

The old Autotech supercharger.

free-flow exhaust systems. Stay away from radical camshafts, however, as a long overlap period will allow the blower to push the incoming air/fuel mixture right out the exhaust valve without waiting for it to be burned. The Volkswagen G-lader supercharger (discussed later) uses a camshaft with far less overlap than you will find in a normally aspirated motor. (A more complete discussion of supercharger camshafts can be found in "Supercharger Camshafts.")

One possible drawback of this design is that at higher altitudes a supercharger will not produce as much boost as a turbocharger. A supercharger provides the same percentage of boost; a turbocharger provides the same amount of boost, plus it benefits from the lower density of the ambient air.

To illustrate, David Singer of General Motors found that when a supercharger and a turbocharger were both calibrated to a pressure ratio of 1.4 and were taken to an altitude of 3,650 feet (at Warren, Michigan), the supercharger maintained its 43 percent pressure increase. The turbocharger pressure increase climbed to 71 percent; however, running more boost hastened the onset of detonation.

The familiar Roots blower has two- or three-lobe straight or curved impellers to shove the air into the motor. (The New Dimensions blower use three curved rotors.) Because of its design, even if a Roots blower were as efficient as a turbocharger, it would still heat the air more. How is this possible?

A Roots blower is a constant-volume supercharger. Air enters the Roots blower at atmospheric pressure. The lobes

carry the air around the inside of the blower housing and deposit it in the intake manifold *without* changing the air pressure. Air compression starts only when the newly arriving air joins the air that is already in the intake tract.

The high-pressure air in the intake tract constantly tries to escape back out the way it came in, past the rotors that are dumping in ever more unpressurized air. As a result, the air in the intake tract is beaten back and forth by the rotors, creating additional heat. Instead of the temperature increase constant being $r^{0.283}-1$, it is closer to $r^{0.4}-1$ (remember that r is the pressure ratio, as described earlier).

This higher temperature increase constant was derived in tests done years ago with straight two-lobe rotors; there appears to have been little testing of modern Roots designs utilizing better materials and construction techniques, and spiral three-lobe rotors. However, this temperature increase constant can be used to illustrate the point. As the accompanying chart shows, a difference in the temperature increase constant makes a difference in the amount of heat in the intake air charge.

Supercharger Heat Gain Due to Compression Pressure
Supercharger Compressor Efficiency Ratio

	40%	50	55	60	65	70	75	80	85%
1.00	70.0	70.0	70.0	70.0	70.0	70.0	70.0	70.0	70.0
1.05	96.1	90.9	89.0	87.4	86.1	84.9	83.9	83.0	82.3
1.10	121.5	111.2	107.4	104.3	101.7	99.4	97.4	95.7	94.2
1.15	146.1	130.9	125.4	120.8	116.9	113.5	110.6	108.1	105.8
1.20	170.2	150.1	142.9	136.8	131.7	127.2	123.4	120.1	117.1
1.25	193.6	168.9	159.9	152.4	146.1	140.6	135.9	131.8	128.2
1.30	216.5	187.2	176.6	167.7	160.2	153.7	148.1	143.3	139.0
1.35	238.9	205.1	192.8	182.6	173.9	166.5	160.1	154.4	149.5
1.40	260.8	222.6	208.7	197.2	187.4	179.0	171.7	165.4	159.8
1.45	282.2	239.8	224.3	211.5	200.6	191.3	183.2	176.1	169.9
1.50	303.2	256.5	239.6	225.4	213.5	203.2	194.4	186.6	179.7
1.55	323.7	273.0	254.5	239.2	226.1	215.0	205.3	196.9	189.4
1.60	343.9	289.1	269.2	252.6	238.6	226.5	216.1	206.9	198.9
1.65	363.7	305.0	283.6	265.8	250.7	237.8	226.6	216.8	208.2
1.70	383.1	320.5	297.7	278.7	262.7	248.9	237.0	226.6	217.4
1.75	402.2	335.8	311.6	291.5	274.4	259.8	247.2	236.1	226.3
1.80	421.0	350.8	325.3	304.0	286.0	270.6	257.2	245.5	235.2
1.85	439.5	365.6	338.7	316.3	297.4	281.1	267.0	254.7	243.9
1.90	457.6	380.1	351.9	328.4	308.5	291.5	276.7	263.8	252.4
1.95	475.5	394.4	364.9	340.3	319.5	301.7	286.3	272.7	260.8
2.00	493.1	408.5	377.7	352.1	330.4	311.8	295.7	281.6	269.1

In theory, the positive-displacement blower delivers the same amount of air to the engine for each revolution. This is not completely true, because as the speed of the blower increases from 2,000 rpm to 10,000 rpm, the volumetric efficiency rises from about 40 percent to about 60 percent, as a result of gains from moving the air at a higher velocity. So even though you have some boost at 1,500 rpm, the instant you put your foot down, you still see maximum boost at maximum rpm.

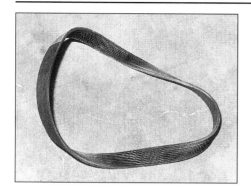

The poly-V belt.

The poly-V drive, as used on the Autotech supercharger, provides positive drive to the blower, and makes it easier to vary the blower drive ratio than a sprocket drive.

Nitrous oxide injection can also be set to turn on automatically at a preset rpm in racing applications.

charge and helps push the piston along. This phenomenon is not as strong with a turbocharger, which is why the supercharger is said to have a positive gas exchange loop while the turbocharger has a negative gas exchange loop. The ratio between the intake pressure generated by the turbo and the back pressure needed to create that intake pressure can be as important to efficient turbocharger use as can overlap.

If superchargers are so good, why aren't they used in more forms of racing? There are three answers to that. First, when building a street machine we are not necessarily concerned with what is done in a race machine, because there are lots of techniques racers use that simply do not work in a street rod. Everything from spring rates, cam profiles, and compression ratios, to types of fuel used must be chosen with the end purpose in mind. In racing, you might be at full throttle more than 60 percent of the time. In a street car, such behavior would result in someone's death or at the very least the suspension of your driving privileges. Race engines typically have narrow power peaks that would be miserable to try to live with in a street car. A supercharger, because it does not typically deliver the same narrow power peak, makes for a much more satisfying performance enhancement for the street.

For the second reason, consider an old Formula 1 engine needing 43 psi of boost. A Roots blower is not going to do the trick because in spite of its flat adiabatic graph with respect to speed, as boost pressure increases, efficiency plummets. The limit appears to be approximately 14 psi of boost, which is more than enough for a street machine. That is why Formula 1 engines made use of special turbochargers that develop 1 psi of boost for every 0.75 psi of back pressure. You will never see a turbocharger that efficient on a street vehicle, and such a vehicle is going to be very difficult to drive.

The third reason has to do with heat. A turbocharger dumps a lot of heat into the oil, and a supercharger does not. In a motor that is run continuously for most of its life, this heat can

This instantaneous boost is what makes blowers so nice to drive. Volkswagen did a study in which two engines of equal displacement were compared. One was equipped with a turbocharger and the other with a supercharger. Both engines made 88 horsepower at 6,000 rpm and 110 lb-ft of torque at 3,700 rpm, but the supercharger-equipped engine produced 96 lb-ft of torque at 2,000 rpm while the turbocharged engine produced only 70 lb-ft of torque. This test showed that the supercharger-equipped engine responded to abrupt full-throttle acceleration in one-third of the time taken by the turbocharged engine. The study also showed that least 90 percent of maximum torque was available from 2,500 to 6,000 rpm.

Another benefit of blowers is that the exhaust tract is essentially untouched, and there is no extra back pressure to deal with. This may not be a cause for much concern for individual hot-rodders, but for a manufacturer like Volkswagen it means that existing emissions technology will work with only minor modifications.

The lack of back pressure in a supercharged motor brings up another plus: Positive work is carried out on the piston during the intake cycle. As the air is forced into the motor it both relieves the piston of the job of pulling in the fresh air/fuel

This turbo has a water cooling jacket to cut down on turbo bearing failures.

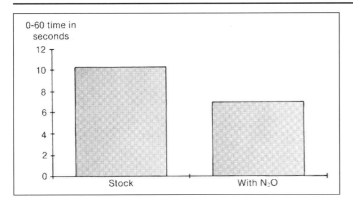

The effect of nitrous on acceleration.

Table 26: Superchargers vs. turbochargers		
Characteristic	Supercharger	Turbocharger
Performance	equal	
Octane needed	equal	
Emissions	✔	
Response	✔	
Exhaust temp.	✔	
Fuel economy	equal	
Altitude compensation		✔
Ease of installation	✔	

Superchargers vs. turbochargers: A properly done supercharger has a lot going for it, even compared with a turbocharger.

be dealt with. A street car does not run continuously, and when the motor is shut down that heat must be allowed to escape. Race motors are also rebuilt much more often than street motors, so longevity must be taken into consideration as well.

Volkswagen G-Lader

The G-lader supercharger design is used in the Corrado. The *G* is for the shape of the unit, and *lader* is the German word

Turbo heat gain due to compression

Pressure ratio	Turbocharger compressor efficiency								
	40	50	55	60	65	70	75	80	85
1.00	70	70	70	70	70	70	70	70	70
1.05	88.4	84.7	83.4	82.3	81.3	80.5	79.8	79.2	78.7
1.10	106.2	99.0	96.3	94.1	92.3	90.7	89.3	88.1	87.0
1.15	123.4	112.7	108.9	105.6	102.9	100.5	98.5	96.7	95.1
1.20	140.1	126.1	121.0	116.7	113.2	110.1	107.4	105.1	103.0
1.25	156.3	139.1	132.8	127.5	123.1	119.3	116.0	113.2	110.6
1.30	172.1	151.7	144.2	138.0	132.8	128.3	124.4	121.0	118.0
1.35	187.4	163.9	155.4	148.3	142.2	137.1	132.6	128.7	125.2
1.40	202.3	175.8	166.2	158.2	151.4	145.6	140.6	136.1	132.3
1.45	216.8	187.5	176.8	167.9	160.4	153.9	148.3	143.4	139.1
1.50	231.0	198.8	187.1	177.3	169.1	162.0	155.9	150.5	145.8
1.55	244.9	209.9	197.2	186.6	177.6	169.9	163.3	157.4	152.3
1.60	258.4	220.7	207.0	195.6	185.9	177.7	170.5	164.2	158.7
1.65	271.6	231.3	216.6	204.4	194.1	185.2	177.5	170.8	164.9
1.70	284.6	241.7	226.0	213.0	202.0	192.6	184.4	177.3	171.0
1.75	297.2	251.8	235.3	221.5	209.8	199.9	191.2	183.6	176.9
1.80	309.7	261.7	244.3	229.8	217.5	206.9	197.8	189.8	182.8
1.85	321.8	271.5	253.1	237.9	225.0	213.9	204.3	195.9	188.5
1.90	333.8	281.0	261.8	245.8	232.3	220.7	210.7	201.9	194.1
1.95	345.5	290.4	270.4	253.7	239.5	227.4	216.9	207.7	199.6
2.00	357.0	299.6	278.7	261.3	246.6	234.0	223.1	213.5	205.1

The calculated temperature of the intake charge for a turbocharger when the ambient temperature is 70 degrees Fahrenheit. As you can see, intake charge temperature is more sensitive to compressor efficiency than it is to pressure ratio, so doubling the efficiency of the turbocharger means you can double the boost pressure and get less temperature gain.

for blower. The G-lader (or G-charger, as it is also called) is based on a steam engine design that was patented in 1906. As a steam engine it never succeeded, but as a supercharger it does quite well.

While G-lader is the generic name, the actual article comes in different sizes. The smaller unit for the Polo in Europe is called the G-40. This stands for a G-lader with a 40-millimeter scroll. The G-60 unit has the same G shape with 60-millimeter deep scrolls.

These scrolls do the same job as the lobed rotors found in the Roots blower. The inner scroll is moved relative to the outer scroll by means of a dual eccentric drive. The motion described by the inner scroll alternately uncovers the intake port to take in air at atmospheric pressure and then uncovers the outlet port for the discharge cycle.

Because the air feed is essentially constant, only weak pulsations occur on the intake of the supercharger, thus keeping noise to a minimum. The soft openings and closings also eliminate heavy pulsations in the intake tract. Because of the shortness of the scrolls, the G-lader has no internal compression. This makes the G-lader a high-volume, low-pressure device.

Still, the G-lader can make 0.8 bar of boost, and it does so fairly efficiently. When working at 0.5 bar of boost, efficiency is rated at 65 percent. This is further enhanced by the intercooler that drops the intake charge temperature 131 degrees Fahrenheit.

The G-lader currently runs 72 percent overdrive, for a supercharger speed of just over 10,000 rpm at an engine redline of 6,000 rpm. Maximum speed for the G-lader is 13,000 rpm.

Extended testing by Volkswagen showed that the internal engine components were adequate for the 50 percent additional power. For reasons of reliability, however, the supercharged engine uses special block, top piston rings, sodium-filled exhaust valves, and a heat-treated cylinder head. The basic compression ratio is set at 8.0:1. European versions use the Heron head.

As an autorotator, the G-lader is quite poor. Volkswagen designed around this by including a feedback loop that returns the output of the G-lader back to the inlet side when there is

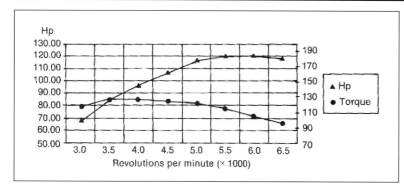

Horsepower and torque for the 1.8-liter Golf, supercharged with 6 psi of boost.

Supercharger heat gain due to compression

Pressure ratio	Supercharger compressor efficiency								
	40	50	55	60	65	70	75	80	85
1.00	70.0	70.0	70.0	70.0	70.0	70.0	70.0	70.0	70.0
1.05	96.1	90.9	89.0	87.4	86.1	84.9	83.9	83.0	82.3
1.10	121.5	111.2	107.4	104.3	101.7	99.4	97.4	95.7	94.2
1.15	146.1	130.9	125.4	120.8	116.9	113.5	110.6	108.1	105.8
1.20	170.2	150.1	142.9	136.8	131.7	127.2	123.4	120.1	117.1
1.25	193.6	168.9	159.9	152.4	146.1	140.6	135.9	131.8	128.2
1.30	216.5	187.2	176.6	167.7	160.2	153.7	148.1	143.3	139.0
1.35	238.9	205.1	192.8	182.6	173.9	166.5	160.1	154.4	149.5
1.40	260.8	222.6	208.7	197.2	187.4	179.0	171.7	165.4	159.8
1.45	282.2	239.8	224.3	211.5	200.6	191.3	183.2	176.1	169.9
1.50	303.2	256.5	239.6	225.4	213.5	203.2	194.4	186.6	179.7
1.55	323.7	273.0	254.5	239.2	226.1	215.0	205.3	196.9	189.4
1.60	343.9	289.1	269.2	252.6	238.6	226.5	216.1	206.9	198.9
1.65	363.7	305.0	283.6	265.8	250.7	237.8	226.6	216.8	208.2
1.70	383.1	320.5	297.7	278.7	262.7	248.9	237.0	226.6	217.4
1.75	402.2	335.8	311.6	291.5	274.4	259.8	247.2	236.1	226.3
1.80	421.0	350.8	325.3	304.0	286.0	270.6	257.2	245.5	235.2
1.85	439.5	365.6	338.7	316.3	297.4	281.1	267.0	254.7	243.9
1.90	457.6	380.1	351.9	328.4	308.5	291.5	276.7	263.8	252.4
1.95	475.5	394.4	364.9	340.3	319.5	301.7	286.3	272.7	260.8
2.00	493.1	408.5	377.7	352.1	330.4	311.8	295.7	281.6	269.1

Supercharger heat gain due to compression
Here is shown the calculated temperature of the intake charge for a supercharger when the ambient temperature is 70 degrees Fahrenheit. Although these figures were arrived at using a two-lobe straight Roots blower, virtually any compressor that does not have internal compression will create more heat in the intake charge than one that does.

Table 24: Horsepower loss due to altitude		
Altitude in ft	Altitude in mi	HP
0	0.00	100
328.1	0.06	99.00
656.2	0.12	98.01
984.2	0.19	97.03
1312.3	0.25	96.06
1640.4	0.31	95.10
1968.5	0.37	94.15
2296.6	0.43	93.21
2624.6	0.50	92.27
2952.7	0.56	91.35
3280.8	0.62	90.44
3608.9	0.68	89.53
3937.0	0.75	88.64
4265.0	0.81	87.75
4593.1	0.87	86.87
4921.2	0.93	86.01
5249.3	0.99	85.15
5577.4	1.06	84.29

Horsepower loss due to altitude: For every 300 feet in altitude, you lose 1 percent of your horsepower.

pulley (to increase the amount of overdrive), and a different fuel pressure regulator to boost fuel delivery to match the higher boost level. Autotech also offers a neat one-way valve for the idle air stablizer circuit that eliminates the effect of wear in the control valve, maintaining boost.

Another way to get more horsepower from your G-Lader is to have New Dimensions rebuild it. With special internal coatings and techniques, you can gain an impressive amount of additional boost at the same shaft speed.

Advanced Motorsport Solutions Supercharger

Even though most superchargers are positive-displacement devices, they don't have to be. Advanced Motorsport Solutions offers a Rotrex centrifugal supercharger for the VR6 that resembles the compressor half of a turbocharger. Instead of being driven by exhaust gases, it is driven by a serpentine belt. The kit comes with a special chip that was developed by AMS.

The compressor is sized to the engine so that it is delivering maximum boost (8.5 psi) at the horsepower peak, so it needs no wastegate. Because the engine can be left stock, you still have the normal VR6 engine performance at low rpm when boost is low, and the way AMS has sized the compressor, boost comes in very smoothly. It feels as if you are driving a car with a much bigger normally aspirated engine, rather than a car with a noticeable bump in acceleration as the compressor starts working.

no demand for the extra power. This does reduce the power demand from the engine, but it also gives the intake air charge more time to pick up heat from the compressor.

You can increase the performance of your G-60 with more aggressive camshafts, an engine management chip, a smaller

Table 25: Air pressure drop due to altitude		
Altitude in feet	Air pressure in PSI	Altitude in meters
0	14.7	0
656	14.3	200
1000	14.2	305
1641	13.9	500
2000	13.7	610
3000	13.2	914
3281	13.0	1000
4000	12.7	1219
5000	12.2	1524
6000	11.8	1829
6562	11.5	2000
7000	11.3	2134

Air pressure drop due to altitude: As you go up in altitude, the air pressure drops. If it drops too much, you might feel you need forced induction for day-to-day driving, let alone high performance.

Compared to a positive-displacement supercharger, the AMS setup creates less heat in the intake air, but an intercooler is available for more power still.

Advanced Motorsport Solutions claims 100 horsepower in what is essentially a bolt-on part. (The work can be done in about 12 hours.) This is a pretty good deal in and of itself, but it becomes even more attractive when it is compared to your alternatives. You can spend a lot of money on parts to increase the displacement of your VR6, and to make the head and intake system flow more air (including the cost of new cams). After you have the parts, you still have to do, or pay for, the labor. Some tuners promise up to 300 horsepower for the complete package, which is seriously expensive, with less than 10 percent more horsepower than the AMS supercharger delivers. This assumes, of course, that the workmanship on your 300-horsepower VR6 was all done properly, including the head work, so you really are making that much horsepower.

With the supercharger, none of that laborious porting and polishing matters, because you are forcing the air through the passages, instead of relying on the piston to suck the air into the motor.

Given the VR6's reputation for head gasket problems, you may want to consider installing Raceware or ARP head studs to keep the cylinder head in place at the higher cylinder pressures.

Autotech Supercharger

Although now discontinued, the Autotech Supercharger worked just the way you would expect a supercharger to work.

Unlike blowers for many American cars, the Autotech blower ran dry (in other words, pumping only air, instead of air *and* fuel). This gave it 8 to 11 percent better power, because adding fuel increases the density of the air, creating drag within the compressor housing. The Autotech blower also used hollow rotors for lower rotational inertia. This blower required so little horsepower at full boost that the small Woodruff keys holding the cam belt sprockets to the crankshaft and camshaft in the early cars were strong enough to drive the blower without shearing off.

The later kits used a poly-V belt instead of the cogged belt found in its early kits. This allowed more leeway in sizing the driven pulley on the supercharger to set the boost pressure. The stock system came with a 1.4:1 pulley setup that made 8 psi of boost, and replacement pulleys were available up to 1.6:1 to make 12 psi of boost. Although Autotech recommended running low compression (8.5:1) with its blower, Griffin Motor Werke in Berkeley used the Autotech blower setup with 16V motors running 10.0:1 compression.

One nice feature of the Magnason blower Autotech used is that of all the mechanical supercharger designs, it is the best autorotator. In other words, when the blower is not making boost, the engine vacuum is enough to cause the rotors to rotate on their own. This reduces the load on the blower bearings, the drive belt, and other components. Autorotation helps because even the heaviest lead-foot is going to be in boost only 10 percent of the time or less. The other 90 percent of the time, you are not using the blower.

The Magnacharger's straight lobes may be noisier, but its design is efficient enough at autorotating that the car can be driven with the belt off (although performance would suffer).

Fuel Enrichment

Under boost, the supercharged motor needs a lot more fuel than a normally aspirated motor. If for no other reason, the 1987-and-later programmable electronic fuel injections are great because you can tell the computer how much fuel to put in and when to do it.

CIS is another story. CIS injection supplies adequate fuel for the additional horsepower a blower demands up to about 130 horsepower, but it can run short in a higher-performance motor. Back in the early days, we rigged up switches in parallel with the cold-start enrichment system, but this was crude and experimental.

For the K-Jetronic blower kit, Autotech used an Audi 5000 Turbo warm-up regulator, which was plumbed to produce rapid response to changes in manifold vacuum and pressure.

For the KE-Jetronic, Autotech has developed an add-in circuit board and pressure sensor for continuously variable modification of the control pressure through the differential pressure regulator.

If you are putting together your own system or if you run into problems, you will have to spend some time dyno testing and taking EGT and oxygen sensor readings until you get everything straightened out. Things are not as bleak as they

A supercharger atop a 10.0:1 16V Scirocco motor. With 6 psi of boost, this car makes close to 180 horsepower and runs to 60 miles per hour in the low seven-second range.

For a while, VW was experimenting with turbocharging, but then scrapped the project in favor of supercharging.

For the early cars with warm-up regulators, use the Audi Turbo unit on the left to fool the injection into supplying extra fuel.

seem, however. Although you can easily run a motor into meltdown on the dyno by keeping it in boost for several minutes, in real life, you will be lucky to stay in boost more than a few seconds at a time. This is one reason why fuel enrichment systems that seem all wrong theoretically can provide a sufficient margin of safety for street applications.

One rumor about supercharged CIS motors is that the CIS cannot supply the fuel needed by the motor because the fuel pressure to the injectors is kept at a constant while the boost pressure rises. The example usually given is that if you had 6 psi of fuel pressure and 6 psi of boost, the pressure differential across the injector would be zero, so you would get no flow. Although this is an extreme example, if it were true it would mean that the fuel injection's ability to operate gets worse at the precise time the motor needs fuel the most.

As it turns out, this is not the case. The dynamics of injecting a fluid into a gas are fairly complex, but suffice to say that because air is compressible and fuel is not, the injectors will work fine at any boost level you are likely to use.

A basic rule of thumb for figuring this out is as follows:

$$\frac{\text{manifold pressure}}{\text{fuel pressure}} < 0.5$$

For this formula to work, both manifold pressure and fuel pressure must be expressed in terms of absolute pressure (psia), or the measured pressure plus the atmospheric pressure. At sea level, the atmospheric pressure is 14.7 psi, so if you have a boost (manifold) pressure of 7 psi, adding 14.7 psi gives you 20.7 psia. For fuel pressure, CIS runs at a minimum of 68 psi. Adding 14.7 psi gives you 82.7 psia. This works out to:

$$15\ 1.4 - 70 \times 0.8 = 81.4 \times 0.8 = 65.12$$

$$151.4 - 65.12 = 86.28 \text{ degrees Farenheit}$$

This is well under the 0.5 limit. As long as you keep the boost-pressure-to-fuel-pressure ratio under 0.5, the amount of boost will have no appreciable effect on fuel delivery. Above 0.5, the relationship is not linear, so this formula will no longer approximate the effect of a lower pressure differential across the injector.

In the example with 6 psi of fuel pressure and 6 psi of boost, the formula tells you that the ratio is 1, meaning no flow. In real life the injector would still work, although less efficiently. Playing with the numbers a little, you can determine that the stock CIS fuel injection is good to 27 psi of boost in this respect. Of course, with that much boost you have lots of other things to consider.

While on the subject of fuel delivery, one thing to watch out for on CIS cars with superchargers of any kind is that the fuel injectors are held in the heads by nothing more than the friction of the rubber fuel injector O-ring. Under lots of boost or during a backfire, the injectors can be popped out of their holders. With the resulting massive air leak, the car will run very poorly at low rpm, although it sometimes will smooth out at higher rpm as the percentage of air leaking into the system becomes small compared with the overall volume of air. If your car exhibits poor running at low rpm (such as at idle), check to see that the injectors are fully seated. (See "Injector O-Rings.")

The European 1.3-liter Polo with the 40-millimeter G-lader supercharger.

Pressure ratios and heat gain		
Pressure ratio	Turbocharger factor	Supercharger factor
1.10	0.027	0.039
1.15	0.040	0.057
1.20	0.053	0.076
1.25	0.065	0.093
1.30	0.077	0.111
1.35	0.089	0.128
1.40	0.100	0.144
1.45	0.111	0.160
1.50	0.122	0.176
1.55	0.132	0.192
1.60	0.142	0.207
1.65	0.152	0.222
1.70	0.162	0.236
1.75	0.172	0.251
1.80	0.181	0.265
1.85	0.190	0.279
1.90	0.199	0.293
1.95	0.208	0.306
2.00	0.217	0.320

Pressure ratios and heat gain: Assuming the theoretical factors are accurate, you can see the difference in the intake charge temperature multiplier between a compressor with internal compression and one without.

Ignition

Even if you are running a low-compression engine and do not get carried away with the boost, you must have some way of backing down the ignition advance under boost. Force-inducted motors can melt down in minutes from detonation. Again, with the programmable Digifant and Motronic systems, this is a matter of reprogramming the engine management chip.

With CIS cars that have vacuum-actuated distributors, the easiest way to control the advance is to route your vacuum hoses so that under boost the ignition timing progressively becomes more retarded. This is accomplished by connecting a manifold port to the advance side of the distributor vacuum can (the vacuum can must also have a retard side port so it can breathe). When the supercharger is not producing boost, you will have some vacuum advance. As you roll into boost, the advance will gradually go away, eventually being replaced by retard.

Make sure you use hose clamps on all vacuum fittings, or the boost will blow them right off.

Intercoolers

If you are pumping 6 psi of boost or less into a motor with less than 8.5:1 compression, you can get by without an intercooler. Those of you with more boost or more compression, read on.

An intercooler sits between the turbo or supercharger and the cylinder head, and cools the intake charge. There is a price for this feature, and it is called pressure drop. Proper intercooler sizing and construction will minimize pressure drop.

Intercoolers also have efficiency ratings, just like everything else. If you used an 80 percent efficient intercooler in the turbo system in the preceding example, the intercooler would remove 80 percent of the heat above ambient temperature from the system. The calculations look like this:

$$15\ 1.4 - 70 \times 0.8 = 81.4 \times 0.8 = 65.12$$

$$151.4 - 65.12 = 86.28 \text{ degrees Farenheit}$$

This works out to a substantial drop in intake charge temperature, due to the intercooler. For turbo-charged cars, the intercooler must be at least 70 percent efficient and have a pressure drop of less than 2.5 psi to be worth the trouble of mounting it. Otherwise, your car will be just as fast or faster without it.

The mathematics that prove this are involved, but basically they show that in a typical street turbocharger system, for each additional psi of boost you will add roughly 18 degrees Fahrenheit to the intake air temperature. If you lose 3 psi of pressure and you need 6 psi in the intake, you will have to make 9 psi of boost at the turbo outlet.

That 3 psi of extra boost is going to cost you 54 degrees Fahrenheit of additional temperature in the intake charge. If the intercooler is less than 70 percent efficient, it will not be able to remove enough of that additional heat to keep the charge density from being thinner than it would be on a system that has less restriction, and thus less heat, in the intake tract to begin with. However, because superchargers do not have a problem

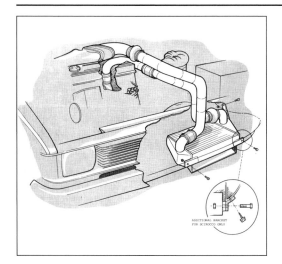

Suggested positioning for an intercooler in turbo cars with air conditioning.

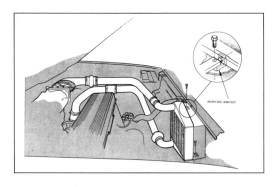

Suggested positioning for an intercooler in turbo cars without air conditioning.

with back pressure, even an inefficient intercooler is better than nothing. You just have to find room to put one.

The simplest intercooler to plumb in is the air-to-air intercooler, in which ambient air carries the heat away from the intercooler as the heat is picked up from the intake charge.

Cartech has had some interesting experiences with air-to-water intercoolers, in which a separate cooling system is used instead of air to cool the intercooler. An air-to-water intercooler is much more complex to install, but because of the superior thermal reserve of the water the unit can be much smaller. The water has a far greater ability to transfer heat away from the intercooler surface than does air, leading to increased intercooler efficiencies.

One fallacy about intercoolers used with turbochargers is that if there is a loss across the intercooler, you can make up for it with more boost. This is not the way it works. For every pound of boost, your back pressure must increase by 2.0 to 2.5 psi. This is known as fighting a losing battle. It helps to not have the loss in the first place.

Water Injection

Water injection is an idea that never really caught on because of the maintenance it requires.

Here is how it works. The water that enters the combustion chamber acts to boost octane because it does not burn. (Remember that octane is the rating of a fuel's ability to resist compressive detonation. That's why EGR increases octane

too.) It also expands when turned to steam by the heat of the gasoline being ignited, which helps force the piston downward. As it changes from water to steam, it absorbs heat out of the combustion chamber, which helps lower the temperature there, and it will help clean the combustion chamber of carbon build-up and then keep it clean.

Water injection is so effective that you will get more power from it than you would from injecting an equal amount of extra gasoline. If you inject too much water, however, it will cool the combustion process too much, robbing you of power.

The correct way to connect water injection (so it works under periods of low vacuum) is to have a pressure-sensitive switch controlling a water pump and an rpm sensor to tell the water injection how much water is needed. When the switch detects that the manifold vacuum has risen to a certain level, it should turn on the pump.

As mentioned earlier, water injection does have a couple of drawbacks. Unlike an intercooler, water injection requires that you keep water in the tank. The better units have a water level warning control, but you still have to stop and fill up. Also unlike an intercooler, water injection puts a lot of extra water into the motor. Some of this water can find its way into the crankcase (accelerating sludge formation); some of it can attack the rings, valves, valve seats, and exhaust system (hot metal oxidizes faster than metal at ambient temperature); and some of it can attack the aluminum of the head.

Nitrous Oxide

Nitrous oxide, or N_2O, is also used to increase the density of the intake air charge, only in a radically different way. N_2O provides an instant, neck-snapping acceleration. A conservative nitrous oxide system that can be operated in complete safety (as far as the engine components are concerned) will add 50 to 60 horsepower on a 100 horsepower engine.

N_2O is sold bottled under high pressure. As it is released into the intake system, the nitrous oxide expands. In the process of expanding, there is a pronounced cooling effect due to the latent heat of vaporization as the nitrous changes states from liquid to vapor. This in turn rapidly cools the intake charge, making it much denser. In a normally aspirated motor, the temperature drop is around 50 degrees Fahrenheit. In a supercharged motor, the temperature drop can be up to 100 degrees Fahrenheit.

The purpose of injecting nitrous oxide is not to get more fuel into the cylinder. What you are after with nitrous is the oxygen. As you may remember from science class, combustion that involves pure oxygen is extremely violent. The nitrogen in nitrous oxide acts as a buffer, releasing the oxygen at a more gradual rate. Therefore, nitrous oxide is actually better for our purposes than pure oxygen.

With all this extra oxygen, you also need to augment the amount of fuel entering the motor. It is critical that the motor *never* be allowed to go lean when using N_2O. Not ever. Not even for a little while. The pistons and piston rings would melt in the resultant detonation.

Too much boost with too little good-quality fuel. The top ring was completely gone.

The guts of a turbocharger. The compressor side is on the left, turbine on the right. This one got too hot, and the turbine-side bearing was damaged.

The oil return line from the turbocharger must be above the oil level in the crankcase.

Traditional Setups

The traditional method of introducing nitrous into the engine utilizes a plate that bolts up between the throttle body and the intake manifold. The plate holds two tubes, one that meters nitrous into the intake and one that meters gasoline to keep the motor from going lean.

This is a poor way of introducing nitrous into a fuel-injected engine. The Volkswagen intake manifold is described in the parts list as an "air distributor" and was never meant to carry fuel. When you hit the nitrous button, the air mixture rushing into the manifold suddenly has to share its limited space with the nitrous and the gasoline.

On top of that, the gasoline molecules are heavier than the air or the nitrous molecules. In the A1 cars, the momentum of the gas molecules tends to carry them toward the end of the intake plenum that feeds the No. 1 and No. 2 cylinders. The air and nitrous turn the corner into cylinders No. 3 and No. 4, but the gasoline does not. This creates a lean condition on 3 and 4 that melts pistons. It also puts a combustible mixture into the intake manifold, and if this ignites it can blow the intake boot off the fuel distributor so hard it can dent the hood and curl back the edges of the air sensor plate.

Fogger Nozzles

A better way of adding nitrous to a Volkswagen engine was used by Autotech, which mounted an NOS (Nitrous Oxide Systems) nitrous system on its blown Project Golf using a sandwich plate with what is called a fogger nozzle instead of a twin-tube setup. The fogger nozzle atomizes the nitrous/fuel mixture to the extent that distribution of the mixture is much more even across all cylinders.

Because of the relatively short duration of N_2O injection into the motor, the stock crankshaft, rods, pistons and so on are more than equal to the additional stresses involved, even though horsepower output far exceeds stock levels.

Individual Injectors

The best way to introduce nitrous into the Volkswagen motor would be through individual fogger nozzles at each cylinder, the same way the fuel is delivered. NOS offers a wide

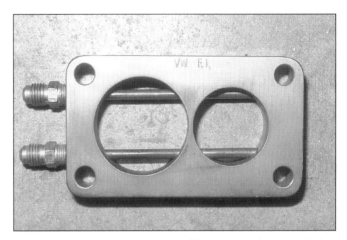

An old-style nitrous sandwich plate. It is much better to have individual nozzles at each cylinder.

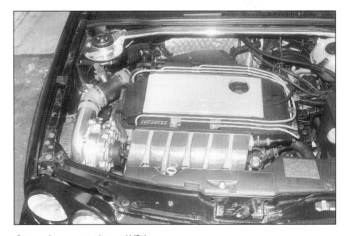

Super-clean supercharged VR6.

range of drop-in jets to allow sizing of the nozzles for setups such as this. It has been estimated that a well-thought-out four-injector nitrous oxide setup would double the output of a 100 horsepower engine. Without the individual fogger nozzles for each cylinder, you risk getting uneven fuel distribution, which will lead to engine meltdown.

Fahrenheit to Rankine Conversions
Degree Fahrenheit

	0	.1	.2	.3	.4	.5	.6	.7	.8	.9
30	489.7	490.7	491.7	492.7	493.7	494.7	495.7	496.7	497.7	498.7
40	499.7	500.7	501.7	502.7	503.7	504.7	505.7	506.7	507.7	508.7
50	509.7	510.7	511.7	512.7	513.7	514.7	515.7	516.7	517.7	518.7
60	519.7	520.7	521.7	522.7	523.7	524.7	525.7	526.7	527.7	528.7
70	529.7	530.7	531.7	532.7	533.7	534.7	535.7	536.7	537.7	538.7
80	539.7	540.7	541.7	542.7	543.7	544.7	545.7	546.7	547.7	548.7
90	549.7	550.7	551.7	552.7	553.7	554.7	555.7	556.7	557.7	558.7
100	559.7	560.7	561.7	562.7	563.7	564.7	565.7	566.7	567.7	568.7
110	569.7	570.7	571.7	572.7	573.7	574.7	575.7	576.7	577.7	578.7
120	579.7	580.7	581.7	582.7	583.7	584.7	585.7	586.7	587.7	588.7
130	589.7	590.7	591.7	592.7	593.7	594.7	595.7	596.7	597.7	598.7
140	599.7	600.7	601.7	602.7	603.7	604.7	605.7	606.7	607.7	608.7
150	609.7	610.7	611.7	612.7	613.7	614.7	615.7	616.7	617.7	618.7
160	619.7	620.7	621.7	622.7	623.7	624.7	625.7	626.7	627.7	628.7
170	629.7	630.7	631.7	632.7	633.7	634.7	635.7	636.7	637.7	638.7
180	639.7	640.7	641.7	642.7	643.7	644.7	645.7	646.7	647.7	648.7
190	649.7	650.7	651.7	652.7	653.7	654.7	655.7	656.7	657.7	658.7
200	659.7	660.7	661.7	662.7	663.7	664.7	665.7	666.7	667.7	668.7
210	669.7	670.7	671.7	672.7	673.7	674.7	675.7	676.7	677.7	678.7
220	679.7	680.7	681.7	682.7	683.7	684.7	685.7	686.7	687.7	688.7
230	689.7	690.7	691.7	692.7	693.7	694.7	695.7	696.7	697.7	698.7
240	699.7	700.7	701.7	702.7	703.7	704.7	705.7	706.7	707.7	708.7

Degree Rankine

Fahrenheit to Celsius Conversions
Degree Fahrenheit

	0	1	2	3	4	5	6	7	8	9
30	-1.1	-0.6	0.0	0.6	1.1	1.7	2.2	2.8	3.3	3.9
40	4.4	5.0	5.6	6.1	6.7	7.2	7.8	8.3	8.9	9.4
50	10.0	10.6	11.1	11.7	12.2	12.8	13.3	13.9	14.4	15.0
60	15.6	16.1	16.7	17.2	17.8	18.3	18.9	19.4	20.0	20.6
70	21.1	21.7	22.2	22.8	23.3	23.9	24.4	25.0	25.6	26.1
80	26.7	27.2	27.8	28.3	28.9	29.4	30.0	30.6	31.1	31.7
90	32.2	32.8	33.3	33.9	34.4	35.0	35.6	36.1	36.7	37.2
100	37.8	38.3	38.9	39.4	40.0	40.6	41.1	41.7	42.2	42.8
110	43.3	43.9	44.4	45.0	45.6	46.1	46.7	47.2	47.8	48.3
120	48.9	49.4	50.0	50.6	51.1	51.7	52.2	52.8	53.3	53.9
130	54.4	55.0	55.6	56.1	56.7	57.2	57.8	58.3	58.9	59.4
140	60.0	60.6	61.1	61.7	62.2	62.8	63.3	63.9	64.4	65.0
150	65.6	66.1	66.7	67.2	67.8	68.3	68.9	69.4	70.0	70.6
160	71.1	71.7	72.2	72.8	73.3	73.9	74.4	75.0	75.6	76.1
170	76.7	77.2	77.8	78.3	78.9	79.4	80.0	80.6	81.1	81.7
180	82.2	82.8	83.3	83.9	84.4	85.0	85.6	86.1	86.7	87.2
190	87.8	88.3	88.9	89.4	90.0	90.6	91.1	91.7	92.2	92.8
200	93.3	93.9	94.4	95.0	95.6	96.1	96.7	97.2	97.8	98.3
210	98.9	99.4	100.0	100.6	101.1	101.7	102.2	102.8	103.3	103.9
220	104.4	105.0	105.6	106.1	106.7	107.2	107.8	108.3	108.9	109.4
230	110.0	110.6	111.1	111.7	112.2	112.8	113.3	113.9	114.4	115.0
240	115.6	116.1	116.7	117.2	117.8	118.3	118.9	119.4	120.0	120.6

Degree Centigrade

Celsius to Fahrenheit Conversions
Degree Centigrade

	0	.1	.2	.3	.4	.5	.6	.7	.8	.9
0	32.0	33.8	35.6	37.4	39.2	41.0	42.8	44.6	46.4	48.2
10	50.0	51.8	53.6	55.4	57.2	59.0	60.8	62.6	64.4	66.2
20	68.0	69.8	71.6	73.4	75.2	77.0	78.8	80.6	82.4	84.2
30	86.0	87.8	89.6	91.4	93.2	95.0	96.8	98.6	100.4	102.2
40	104.0	105.8	107.6	109.4	111.2	113.0	114.8	116.6	118.4	120.2
50	122.0	123.8	125.6	127.4	129.2	131.0	132.8	134.6	136.4	138.2
60	140.0	141.8	143.6	145.4	147.2	149.0	150.8	152.6	154.4	156.2
70	158.0	159.8	161.6	163.4	165.2	167.0	168.8	170.6	172.4	174.2
80	176.0	177.8	179.6	181.4	183.2	185.0	186.8	188.6	190.4	192.2
90	194.0	195.8	197.6	199.4	201.2	203.0	204.8	206.6	208.4	210.2
100	212.0	213.8	215.6	217.4	219.2	221.0	222.8	224.6	226.4	228.2
110	230.0	231.8	233.6	235.4	237.2	239.0	240.8	242.6	244.4	246.2
120	248.0	249.8	251.6	253.4	255.2	257.0	258.8	260.6	262.4	264.2

Degree Fahrenheit

Pressure and vacuum

	PSI	Inches of Hg	Bar		PSI	Inches of Hg	Bar	Boost (psi)
	0	0	0	Sea level	14.70	29.93	1.01	
	0.50	1.02	0.03		15.00	30.54	1.03	0.30
	1.00	2.04	0.07		15.50	31.56	1.07	0.80
	1.50	3.05	0.10		16.00	32.58	1.10	1.30
	2.00	4.07	0.14		16.50	33.59	1.14	1.80
	2.50	5.09	0.17		17.00	34.61	1.17	2.30
	3.00	6.11	0.21		17.50	35.63	1.21	2.80
	3.50	7.13	0.24		18.00	36.65	1.24	3.30
	4.00	8.14	0.28		18.50	37.67	1.27	3.80
	4.50	9.16	0.31		19.00	38.68	1.31	4.30
	5.00	10.18	0.34		19.50	39.70	1.34	4.80
	5.50	11.20	0.38		20.00	40.72	1.38	5.30
	6.00	12.22	0.41		20.50	41.74	1.41	5.80
	6.50	13.23	0.45	Pressure	21.00	42.76	1.45	6.30
	7.00	14.25	0.48		21.50	43.77	1.48	6.80
	7.50	15.27	0.52		22.00	44.79	1.52	7.30
	8.00	16.29	0.55		22.50	45.81	1.55	7.80
	8.50	17.31	0.59		23.00	46.83	1.58	8.30
	9.00	18.32	0.62		23.50	47.85	1.62	8.80
	9.50	19.34	0.65		24.00	48.86	1.65	9.30
	10.00	20.36	0.69		24.50	49.88	1.69	9.80
	10.50	21.38	0.72		25.00	50.90	1.72	10.30
	11.00	22.40	0.76		25.50	51.92	1.76	10.80
	11.50	23.41	0.79		26.00	52.94	1.79	11.30
	12.00	24.43	0.83		26.50	53.95	1.83	11.80
Vacuum	12.50	25.45	0.86					
	13.00	26.47	0.90					
	13.50	27.49	0.93					
	14.00	28.50	0.96					
	14.50	29.52	1.00					

Chapter 9

Exhaust Systems

ollowing the theory that the engine is an air pump, and that the more efficient it pumps air the more horsepower it will make, the exhaust becomes a key part of the overall picture of boosting the horsepower. However, there is more to a great exhaust setup than sheer size, especially in Volkswagens with oxygen sensors.

Because pollution control equipment and vehicle inspections are so prevalent, a good way to start understanding exhaust systems is by looking at some of the factory air pollution controls.

Pollution Control Equipment

Generally, as the engine is run leaner, CO and HC are gradually reduced, but oxides of nitrogen are increased. As the mixture richens, oxides of nitrogen are increased slightly, then fall off somewhat. This means that mixture control does not provide the total answer to pollution reduction.

Exhaust Gas Recirculation

With exhaust gas recirculation (EGR), a portion of the exhaust gas is fed back into the intake manifold, where it acts to reduce the peak combustion temperature, and thus the oxides of nitrogen. With air injection, atmospheric oxygen is injected into the exhaust, where it serves to oxidize any unburnt fuel. The reason the unburnt fuel is there in the first place is because the timing is run slightly retarded, allowing combustion to continue taking place after the exhaust valve opens. Without the EGR, the HC and CO values would be far too high, so the engine is tuned to eliminate oxides of nitrogen at the expense of the other two emissions, which the EGR takes care of afterward.

Catalytic Converter

In a catalytic converter, heat and chemical reactions combine to reduce pollutants. Catalytic converters work best in systems in which the percentage of pollutants in the exhaust fall within a narrow range, which is where the oxygen sensor and "closed loop" injection systems come in.

Catalytic converters can be damaged if contacted by raw fuel (which happens when there is a misfire, or the engine is running very rich). Catalytic converters are also vulnerable to impact and vibration damage, which typically breaks up the ceramic substrate, and creates a rattling noise from the converter housing. More catalytic converters will break apart

For racing or off-road use or for use with leaded fuels, the catalytic converter is often replaced with a straight pipe.

For racing, the rear muffler is also replaced with a straight pipe. The angle cut on the pipe reduces the strength of the reflected pulse.

rather than clog, but they can clog, too, and when they do they act as a restrictor in the exhaust. If your engine just won't rev, and the exhaust note sounds muted, check to see if the catalytic converter is clogged and in need of replacement.

If you do need a replacement, Techtonics and some of the German tuners offer aftermarket cats that flow more air than stock, but are still street legal.

On the subject of rattles, the catalytic converter creates a lot of heat, which is why there are heat shields surrounding it. If these shields work loose or become cracked, they make an irritating racket. Usually, tightening up the four bolts that hold the shield beneath the catalytic converter eliminates the noise. If not, jack up the car and tap on the exhaust system with a soft hammer, listening for rattles. There aren't too many bolts, or places for the shields to crack, so you should be able to locate the source of the rattle fairly quickly.

Oxygen Sensor

With the introduction of the oxygen sensor and closed-loop control, Volkswagen was able to control emissions while ensuring that the engines ran well. Compared to earlier attempts to control emissions, this was a big break-through. Oxygen sensors continually test the exhaust gas to determine the amount of oxygen in the exhaust gas. If the car runs lean,

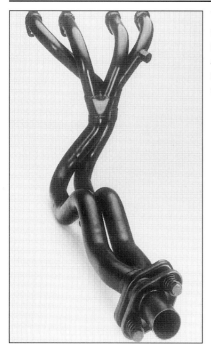

The SuperSprint four-into-two-into-one tube header for the 1974—1984 VW. Always use a firmer front motor mount on A1 cars with tube headers.

The Borla stainless steel exhaust offers good performance and great longevity.

the oxygen sensor tells the fuel injection to richen the mixture. If there is too little oxygen in the exhaust the car is running rich, and the fuel injection is instructed to trim the fuel allotment.

With the three-way catalyst and closed-loop control, CO and HC are at a minimum when the air-fuel mixture is just slightly more lean than stoichiometric. Oxides of nitrogen are virtually eliminated when the air/fuel ratio is slightly richer than stoichiometric. By maintaining the air/fuel mixture within a hair's breadth of stoichiometric, the combination of the three-way catalyst and the oxygen sensor can almost totally eliminate pollution. It is a little like having a mechanic under your hood constantly tinkering with the mixture adjustment so it will always be just right.

Oxygen sensors can be damaged by silicone lubricants and sealants. If you must use a silicone product in your oxygen-sensor-equipped engine, make certain the silicone cannot get to the sensor. The silicone bonds with the sensing surface of the sensor probe, rendering it worthless. (Even though it is not silicone-based, antiseize compound can ruin a oxygen sensor too.)

Headers

Just as with the intake manifold, the size of the exhaust is critical. Too small an exhaust will be restrictive, too large an exhaust will lose too much energy and thus horsepower.

The length of the header is also critical. Exhaust pulses have a frequency, meaning that as with sound waves there are areas of compression and areas of rarefication. When the exhaust design causes an area of rarefication to help "suck" out the area of compression that follows it, the design is referred to as tuned. Because the frequency of the pulse changes in proportion with the change in rpm, exhaust timing works best over a narrow range of rpm.

It was once common practice to remove everything from the head back, bolt on a short- tube header and free-flow exhaust, and feel as if you had some real horsepower. In fact, some of the stock manifolds were better than a short-tube header and made more horsepower.

Headers are constructed of tubing instead of cast iron, which in addition to making them lighter also makes it easier to play around with diameters and lengths. Unfortunately, the thinness of the material used in headers makes them far less resistant to cracking than cast-iron manifolds. With the amount of flex in stock Volkswagen motor mounts, this means trouble.

Headers can be either short-tube or long-tube four-into-one style or tri-y. In the four-into-one design, the four primary tubes run from the cylinder head to a common collector, where the tubes are arranged so that the exhaust pulses will be next to each other in the circle. Thus, starting at the tube for cylinder No. 1, the tube next to it would be the tube for cylinder No. 3. Next to that, and diametrically across from the tube for cylinder No. 1, would be the tube for cylinder No. 4. Between this tube and the No. 1 tube would be the tube for cylinder No. 2.

Short-tube headers make power at higher rpm than long-tube headers. As an example, a Super Vee motor uses headers 28 inches long. For a street car, a short-tube header is less than ideal because the length helps neither the high end nor the low end. The long-tube header is a little better, with the understanding that it will not flex enough to prevent cracking.

At one time, antireversionary headers were available for the Volkswagen. This design features an exaggerated mismatch in port openings, so that a smaller port empties into a larger one. This makes it more difficult for the pulse to be sucked back into the motor, as it then has to move from a larger port to a smaller port. Unfortunately, the antireversionary header was prone to cracking because of the elaborateness of the design. Also, even with theory on its side, antireversionary headers were never as efficient as tri-y headers.

The tri-y design can also be referred to as a four-into-two-into-one exhaust. Each exhaust port has its own tube, but is paired with one other cylinder. Cylinders 1 and 4 share a collector, as do cylinders 2 and 3. These two collector tubes then merge into one tube. The distances from the cylinder head to the first collector and from the first collector are selected to tune the exhaust to the desired rpm range of the engine. Tri-y headers

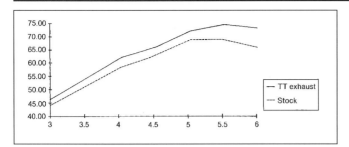

On a 1,600-cc motor, replacing the exhaust improved horsepower across the board. On engines with more restrictive exhausts (such as the 1983 or 1984 GTi), the improvement would be even better.

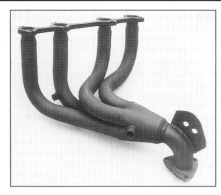

The famous four-into-one header.

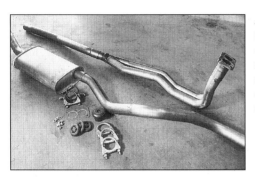

A typical free-flow aftermarket exhaust. Note that the front motor mount is included with the system.

tend to be longer, so they don't fit in every situation, although they work marginally better than the four-into-one design.

Cast-Iron Manifolds

The factory uses cast-iron manifolds. With the exception of the 1982 Scirocco and all the 1983 and 1984 U.S. cars, the factory manifolds work well. The 1983–1984 manifold is easy to identify, as it was the first manifold that used clips instead of threaded fasteners to hold the downpipe.

Clips or not, the 1982 Scirocco and the 1983 and 1984 Rabbit, Scirocco, and Jetta manifolds are just about as bad as you can get, so if you have one of these cars by all means replace the manifold. The most popular replacement has been either an earlier manifold (for example, from a 1982 Jetta) or a Euro GTi manifold. The two are internally identical, the difference being that the Euro version has heavier flange where the downpipe attaches. You will also need the matching downpipe, which will give you 10 percent more horsepower than the stock setup.

Aftermarket Manifolds

There are many good aftermarket manifolds and exhaust systems available, from a wide variety of tuners. With a little shopping, you will be able to find one that is well made from good materials, and which the dyno shows makes good horsepower. Brosal's Brospeed even comes with a high-temp ceramic coating and a warranty.

Porting and Gaskets

As with the intake manifold, you should match port the exhaust manifold with the exhaust ports on the cylinder head. If you have opened up the exhaust ports, you will need to either port the entire manifold (in the case of a cast-iron

manifold) or blend it in. Porting cast iron is very time consuming, so you will probably want to blend the ports instead, which involves opening up the header to match the port in the cylinder head, and then tapering off the grinding to match the original diameter of the manifold runner. Do your blending at least 1 inch deep into the exhaust manifold.

There are three types of exhaust manifold gasket. The first type is the well-known stock gasket. The next is the turbo gasket, which incorporates more metal and is thus more resistant to blowing out under the heat and pressure created in turbo applications. The third is a very narrow gasket, designed to allow the maximum porting of the cylinder head and still allow a gasket to seal. The thinner the gasket, the more problems there are with sealing

If you are racing, you can get away with using High Temp RTV silicone sealer "blue silicone" instead of a gasket. Be careful around oxygen sensors, because the silicone will neutralize the ceramic, making it necessary to buy a new sensor.

A3 Exhaust Rattle

The four-cylinder A3s—even the newest ones—have a tendency to develop a rattle in the exhaust that is most audible when the engine is warm, and you are driving at between 2,500 and 3,500 rpm. The noise is coming from the heat shield on the exhaust manifold, which has a spot weld that breaks. An easy and inexpensive fix is to drill out the spot weld and put in a bolt and a self-locking nut to reclamp the heat shield.

High-Performance Exhausts

Finding an exhaust system that flows well and is fairly well tuned is not much of a problem. The trick is in either trying to get a free-flow exhaust that incorporates the catalytic converter, or mixing and matching the various years and styles of exhaust components, usually done in an effort to retain the converter. Removing the catalytic converter gains horsepower and reduces exhaust temperature. It is also illegal in many states and doing so contributes to pollution. If for any reason you do remove your catalytic converter, replacing it with a center resonator will cure the "raspberries" that occur at certain rpm.

With the general high quality of a lot of the exhaust systems out there, it is easy to find a system that will work well with your car, either with or without the catalytic converter. One thing you can't evaluate beforehand is the sound of the

A European header can be drilled and tapped for an oxygen sensor....

...Just make sure the hole goes through to both ports, so the sensor gets an accurate reading.

exhaust system. Some exhausts make your car sound like an old Fiat, while others have a deeper sound, or are more muted.

Another factor to consider is that a stainless steel exhaust, such as those sold by Tectonics and Borla, are going to last a lot longer. Here in Southern California, where the climate is mild, it doesn't matter much one way or the other, but in other parts of the world, a stainless steel exhaust will last where others don't. If you have an A3, you have a stainless steel exhaust already.

Flex Couplings and Motor Mounts

As mentioned earlier, one problem with the transverse engine is that the motion of the engine can put a lot of stress on an exhaust system. This is different from the normal vibration that is caused by having a straight four—which is much smoother in a longitudinal position—oriented transversely.

To combat this, Volkswagen has tried a variety of different flexible couplings. The aftermarket has been busy on this problem too, with the result being the development of the exhaust ball joint. Different exhaust systems require different flex couplings, so find out what you need when you buy your system.

You will definitely need a flex coupling, however, if you hope to get the maximum life from your system.

The Techtonics exhaust system takes a slightly different approach to this problem. Darrell crimps his downpipe flange in such a way that it takes more flex than the 1976–1984 European GTi setup.

One thing that really helps cut down on exhaust flex in the pre-1985 cars is to replace the front motor mount, as described in "Motor Mounts," although you might want to replace the front motor mount for other reasons anyway.

Muffler Hangers

High-quality exhaust systems are heavy, and the stock muffler hanger breaks under the weight of the stock factory exhaust. They're not that difficult to replace, but you can avoid the problem by using reinforced muffler hangers. The best ones have a chain molded within the rubber, although you can also buy hangers made of different materials, which last a little longer than the stock pieces.

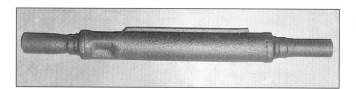

After removing the catalytic converter, you may need to use this resonator pipe to reduce "raspberries."

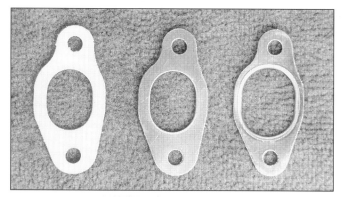

From left to right are a stock exhaust gasket, a heavy-duty turbo gasket and a special gasket for ported heads. Room temperature vulcanizing (RTV) silicone works well for short periods of time in race engines.

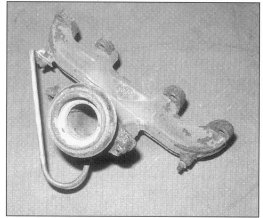

The dreaded 1983—1984 exhaust manifold.

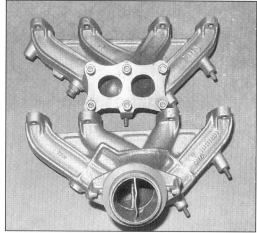

The European manifold (top) flows about the same as the slightly larger late-model U.S. manifold.

This aftermarket front motor mount for A1 cars allows less engine movement, which means less flex for the exhaust.

This aftermarket A2 front motor mount limits engine travel without increasing harshness . . .

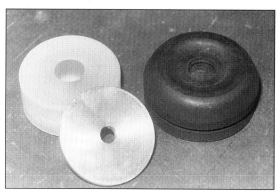

. . . as does this aftermarket A3 front motor mount.

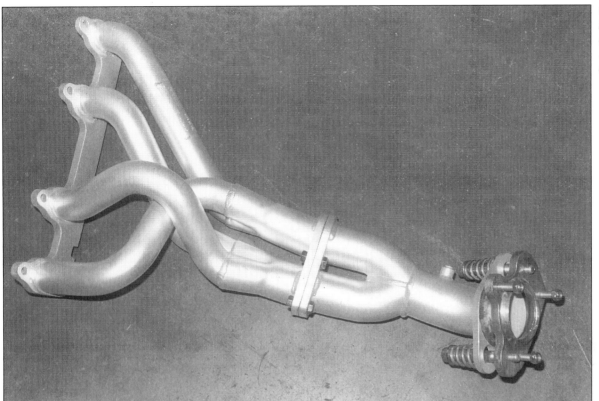

Ceramic-coated header and downpipe for 1992—1995 cars, with flex joint.

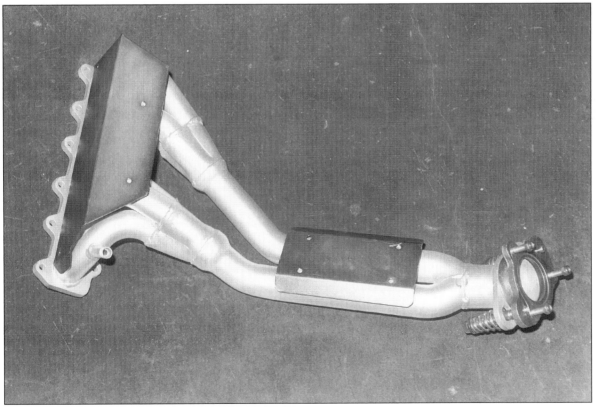

Ceramic-coated heading and downpipe for VR6, with flex joint and heat shields.

Cooling

Many feel that the Volkswagen engine runs hotter than is prudent. The reason Volkswagen designs the car to run that hot is to help meet fuel emissions and economy standards.

That is fine for a car that has to pass federal inspection, but for the car in your garage—the one you want to keep for several trouble-free years—too much heat means reduced longevity and more problems along the way. Seals dry up and blow away, oil bakes out to a thick sludge, heads warp, and close fits lose tolerance. For these and other reasons, many choose to give up some of the fuel economy of the hotter motor in favor of long-term savings in engine repairs.

This does not mean you should run your engine as cold as it will go. After a point, the colder the engine is the worse it runs. For example, the engine must be hot enough to evaporate the volatile contaminants out of the oil.

What you are aiming for, then, is the right balance between longevity and usability.

Water Cooling
Fan Switches

The stock fan switch turns the radiator-mounted electric cooling fan on at 194 to 199 degrees Fahrenheit. A better setup seems to be a fan switch one step colder, one that turns on at around 180 degrees Fahrenheit. If you go too cold with the fan switch, your fan will run all the time, even after you turn off the motor. This will create a drain on the electric system that will ultimately cause the battery to go dead (and your fan will wear out).

Thermostats

The only problem I ever have with the thermostat occurs when refilling the cooling system after it has been drained. My guess is that an air pocket develops around the thermostat so it does not get warm enough to open. As you might expect, the motor gets extremely hot when this happens. If this happens in you car, keep adding coolant, making sure that the coolant level is right up to the top of the filler neck. This allows coolant to get to both sides of the thermostat through the small tube at the top of the radiator, breaking the air pocket. Once the thermostat opens, set the coolant level as you normally would.

The thermostat is just about the last thing you should need to replace in a hot rod Volkswagen. With a good oil cooler, a slightly lower fan switch, and synthetic oil (if necessary), you should not have any heat problems.

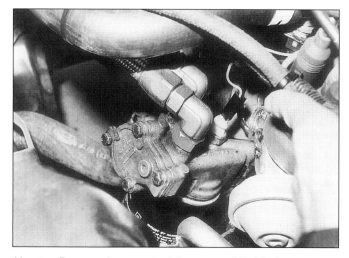

Here is a European thermostatic oil filter mount drilled for American fittings. Compare the restrictive right angles of these fittings to the curved hoses on the factory setup.

Here is a typical oil cooler mount in a Golf. Sturdy brackets such as these go a long way toward minimizing vibration and failure.

If you do everything and still have a heating problem, as might be the case in a turbo motor, check your EGT before changing the thermostat (see "Exhaust Gas Temperature Readings" for a discussion of this). If your EGT is too high, changing the thermostat is not going to help.

Radiators

The stock radiator is aluminum with plastic end caps. It works fine in every conceivable street application, but it is somewhat fragile. Many aftermarket radiators are available that are constructed of 100 percent steel. You give up a little in weight and gain a little in strength, usually at a lower cost. The diesel cars have a copper radiator that is very nice and that is also unnecessary for anything putting out less than 200 horsepower. For cars putting out more, an oil cooler can help take some of the load off your radiator.

If you are racing, also go to the hardware store and buy some metal screen like that used in screen doors to put in front of your radiator. This extra layer of protection helps keep rocks from putting holes in your radiator.

Water Pumps

The stock water pump works fine right out of the box, which is fortunate, considering there are no aftermarket high-performance pumps available. If your engine is suffering from overheating at speed but is cooling okay at idle, and the coolant seems to be circulating through the radiator when you look into the filler neck, the impeller vane may be no longer solidly attached to the pump shaft. At low rpm it will go along for the ride, but when it is asked to do some real work it simply spins on the shaft. This does not happen very often, but it can.

Special Coolants

We all know that a mixture of ethylene glycol (also known as antifreeze) and water is used because it freezes at a lower temperature and boils at a higher temperature than straight water, and the standard cooling system is pressurized to further raise the boiling point. Ethylene glycol also protects the engine from the corrosive combination of water and heat, and there are special coolants formulated for engines with aluminum components. As the coolant protects the engine parts, some of its additives become depleted, making it necessary to change the antifreeze every year or two to maintain protection.

As well as this system has worked over the years, there is another type of coolant coming to the market that is significantly different.

First a review. For the purpose of this comparison, consider the characteristics of the coolant when the engine is up to operating temperature. Boiling occurs locally in all circulating-liquid engine cooling systems at critical areas where the heat flux is greatest, such as around the exhaust valves in the cylinder head. The vapor that is created must then be condensed into the surrounding bulk liquid.

The problem with water-based coolants is that the vapor generated is primarily water vapor; the ethylene glycol (or whatever additive is being used) remains a liquid. Under high ambient temperatures with heavy loads, the bulk of the coolant can be so close to the boiling point of water that the vapor will not readily condense. Conventional cooling systems catastrophically fail when the bulk coolant temperature cannot be maintained below the boiling point of water for the pressure of

 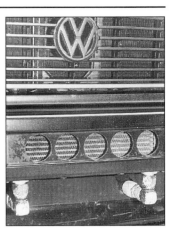

The wax element oil thermostat from the Porsche 911, which will fit into the European oil cooler filter housing, opens earlier than the Volkswagen element.

Here's an interesting place for an oil cooler in a GTi. One wrong bump, though, and you're on foot.

the system (250 degrees Fahrenheit with a 15 psi cap). In other words, the whole system gets so hot that the water remains vaporized, forming large vapor pockets that become hot spots.

Enter anhydrous propylene glycol (*anhydrous* means no water is added). Propylene glycol is a substance so low in toxicity that it is an ingredient in some foods. Its boiling point is 369 degrees Fahrenheit and it has a pour point of minus 71 degrees Fahrenheit.

Propylene glycol coolant, with the additives required for automotive use, has been developed by Dow Chemical but is not available for general use. Industrial-grade propylene glycol is okay for experimentation, but it is not recommended for long-term use. Do *not* use the propylene glycol sold by recreational vehicle dealers, which is intended for mixing with water—it has the wrong additives. The technology of propylene glycol coolant is very promising, and someone is sure to develop this product.

A patented engine-cooling process, invented by Jack Evans, president of Mecca Development and marketed by National Technologies, takes advantage of the characteristics of anhydrous propylene glycol. Because the boiling point of propylene glycol is so high and most coolant is maintained far below this boiling point, Evans' "hybrid engine cooling process" avoids the creation of hot spots by preventing pockets of vapor from lingering. Any vapor that is generated locally immediately condenses into the surrounding coolant. Thus, the propylene glycol continues to cool the engine even when the motor is turned off.

The system is "hybrid" in the sense that it combines features of boiling-liquid systems (the Model T Ford, for example, used a straight-vapor system, relying on the heat lost through boiling the water to cool the system) and circulating-liquid cooling systems (found in modern cars). The coolant jacket is not pressurized, but rather is vented to the atmosphere through an overflow tank. The cooling system, not bound by

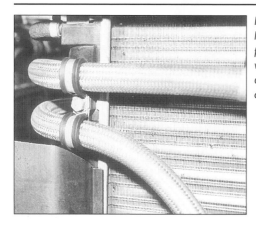

Fasten braided lines securely to prevent them from wearing through other components.

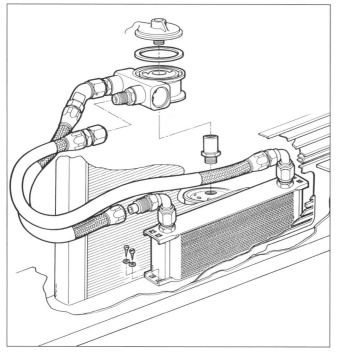

This is the traditional location for the oil cooler in cars without air conditioning.

the limitations of water, can function up to and beyond 300 degrees Fahrenheit without failure.

Water has served us long and well because it has the largest latent heat of vaporization (calories/gram) of any substance. Evans identified, however, that the heat of vaporization must be viewed on a molar basis (calories/mole) rather than on a mass basis (calories/gram) to be of significance. The problem in the cooling system is due to the volume occupied by vapor, not to the mass of the vapor. On a molar basis, propylene glycol has a heat of vaporization 25 percent greater than water.

Critics point out that propylene glycol has a much lower thermal conductivity than water, and a lower specific heat. Evans' studies show that at critical areas the mechanism of heat transfer is by boiling, not by conduction. Although propylene glycol is less effective at transferring heat from itself to the

radiator, the bigger problem has always been the transfer of heat from the radiator to the air.

Specific heat refers to the amount of heat needed to raise a given quantity of the liquid 1 degree Celsius. Comparing specific heats, if water has a value of 100, then propylene glycol rates a 73. In other words, it requires less heat to increase the temperature of the propylene glycol. However, cooling systems using a 50/50 mix of ethylene glycol and water rate an 88 on this scale, making propylene glycol's value an 83 compared with 50/50 ethylene glycol and water. This 15 percent disadvantage is more than made up by the benefits of using propylene glycol.

The bad news is that ideally, the cooling system should be modified to realize the full benefits of propylene glycol. Evans' favorite configuration is to reverse the coolant flow direction so that the coolant enters the cylinder head first. The head runs cooler, and as the coolant flows into the block it gives up some of its heat, reducing the demand on the radiator. When used this way, it is also possible to run the motor much hotter for better efficiency and lower emissions. With the coolant running hotter, radiator efficiency is also improved because the difference in temperature between the radiator and the ambient air is greater. Even without this, though, propylene glycol works better than water and anti-freeze, and it's non-toxic.

The good news is that propylene glycol also can be used as a coolant in conventional flow systems. Either way, it is important that the coolant jacket not be pressurized. Engine temperatures are a function of the boiling point of the coolant (unless vapor pockets form). Propylene glycol already has a high boiling point, and pressurization would drive it too high. The conventional flow direction is a compromise because some pressurization (by action of the coolant pump) is unavoidable.

The Volkswagen cooling system requires very little modification to be adopted for use with propylene glycol, because the by-pass-type thermostat is located at the input side of the pump. There is no restriction at the outlet from the top of the engine to the radiator. A recovery condenser, vented to the atmosphere, must be added to communicate with the top of the radiator or expansion tank. This prevents the system from becoming pressurized, and allows the creation and condensation of vapor without losing coolant.

Coatings

The reason the Volkswagen owner's manual recommends that you change your coolant periodically is that coolant changes chemically as it ages. Eventually, it starts attacking the metal parts in the cooling system, especially aluminum parts. Aluminum does not rust, but it does oxidize in other ways, and the result is the same: The part can become ruined.

G&L Coatings has a resin you can have applied to the water jacket in the cylinder head and block that not only promotes cooling but also protects the metal from oxidizing. This same company can also coat the outside of your motor against corrosion, with the same benefit of added cooling.

Oil Cooling

Of the three engine-cooling systems (air, water, and oil), oil cooling is the most promising for getting big cooling gains with relatively little effort. Many Volkswagen owners with oil temperature gauges decide to install an oil cooler.

For every 18-degree-Fahrenheit increase in temperature, the oxidation rate of oil doubles. In fact, the rate of reaction in any homogeneous system is approximately doubled with each 18-degree-Fahrenheit increase in temperature. This does not normally pose a problem for your oil until you hit 200 degrees Fahrenheit of so. This works out well because under normal conditions you want to run the oil between 180 and 212 degrees Fahrenheit. Any colder and the volatile contaminants (fuel, water) that find their way into the oil and not evaporate off. Any higher, and the oil will oxidize too fast, seals will get baked out, and hot-start problems will begin to crop up.

Unless you live where it is really cold most of the time, consider getting an oil cooler. And unless you live in the tropics, include an oil thermostat in the system. The oil thermostat prevents oil from circulating through the oil cooler until the temperature exceeds a preset temperature.

In addition to helping the motor run cooler, an oil cooler increases the thermal reserve of the cooling system as a whole. With the extra quart of oil and the additional cooling surface, it will take longer for your car to reach meltdown when running under extreme load conditions.

Calibrating the Oil Temperature Gauge

Before you dismiss the idea of purchasing an oil cooler because your oil temperature gauge reads just where you want it to, calibrate your oil temperature gauge so you know it is telling you the truth.

To calibrate your oil temperature gauge, first remove the sender from the motor. You are going to need to drop the sender into boiling water, so arrange for some convenient way of doing this, and also arrange to have the sender plugged in. You may have to fashion a temporary extension to the oil sender lead to do this. You will also need to ground the sender to the block. You can use a test lead with alligator clips at each end, and make certain that the connectors are secure.

Water boils at 212 degrees Fahrenheit at sea level, lower as altitude increases. When the water boils, note the reading on your gauge. Where the needle falls is 212 degrees Fahrenheit, no matter what the printing on the face of the gauge tells you. Your reading will be more accurate if you do not allow the sender to rest against the hot bottom of the pan in which you are boiling the water.

Types of Oil Coolers

One of my least favorite oil cooler setups is the factory oil-to-water arrangement. First, I do not trust it. I have seen problems with similar setups in Audi 5000 transmission fluid coolers and Porsche 944 oil coolers that allow coolant to mix with the oil. Second, I do not like the idea of using the same radiator area to get rid of heat from both the coolant and the oil.

Here's one way of mounting a nonfactory oil cooler in the factory position. This engine is also turbocharged, so space is at a premium. The bracket next to the oil cooler is for an engine compartment stress bar.

On the plus side, the oil warms up more quickly than it would normally and when in good condition it seems to work fine. If you have one, you do not need to replace it, but watch it carefully. Keeping your coolant fresh and ready to combat corrosion makes good sense too.

On cars with air conditioning, a cursory examination of the engine compartment will reveal that there is not much room for the oil cooler. The solution is to extend the radiator mounting brackets by welding some extra metal to the end, then drilling new mounting holes 1/2 or 3/4 of an inch farther back. This leaves plenty of room in front of the radiator for the oil cooler. (Moving the radiator back, when done cleanly, can also be a great source of merriment to your turbocharger installer, who will not be able to figure out why the intercooler plumbing fits with room to spare on everybody else's car except yours.)

For 1985-and-later cars, the European-GTi-style filter mount with the built-in oil thermostat works fine, as it does in the earlier cars. It will not work on the 1983 and 1984 models because the air conditioner brace cuts across right where the filter mount needs to be. The only solution for these cars is to use a sandwich plate adapter.

The Euro GTi setup is very compact, but it comes from the factory with the oil thermostat set to open at 230 degrees Fahrenheit, which seems a little warm. Darrell Vittone claims that he has no problems with the thermostat opening that late, and that is the temperature at which it is fully open, so there will be some flow before that. If you want to use the Euro GTi mount and have the oil thermostat open sooner, Autotech sells a 190-degree thermostat with its Euro GTi filter mount.

Another possible modification of the European GTi mount is to drill and tap the DIN fittings for American-size threads. This is what Autotech does for its oil cooler kits, and it works well as long as you do not overtighten the fittings. Drilling the housing reduces the thickness of the metal in the casting, so

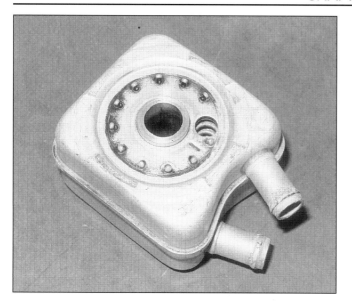

The stock oil-to-water cooler. With these, cooling system maintenance is a must to prevent corrosion.

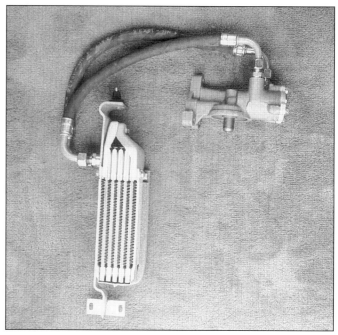

European oil cooler setup for mounting to the right of the radiator. Note the rounded 90-degree adapters, much less restrictive than the sharp 90-degree connectors.

caution is advised. With the American fittings, you have available a wealth of different shapes, sizes and efficiencies of oil cooler. You also will have available a wealth of fittings. Bear in mind that a 90-degree angle fitting is as restrictive as 10 feet of hose. Use bent-tube right-angles if you can find them.

When you buy your oil cooler kit, you may be offered the choice of rubber hose or braided stainless hose. The braided stainless lines are more popular because they do not give as many problems as rubber hose, but a commercial-grade heavy-duty rubber hose should give you no problems. Make sure the rubber hose you get is rated to at least 150 psi, as the Volkswagen motor when cold can develop very high oil pressure. If you lose a hose while driving and do not notice it, your motor will be history in a hurry.

If your motor does blow up when you are running an oil cooler, the cooler must be thoroughly cleaned, or replaced. If you do not get the scrap metal out, it will come out later after you put your motor back together again, ruining everything.

Most shops simply flush the oil cooler with solvent for hours on end, shaking it and swishing it around to try to dislodge as many of the pieces as possible. While this may work, the best way to clean the cooler is with an ultrasonic cleaner, you will have to find someplace that performs this service. The alternative is to buy a new, clean one.

Chapter 11

Transaxles and Drivetrain

There are two basic Volkswagen manual transaxles. The easiest way to tell them apart is that one uses linkage between the shift lever and the transaxle, and the other uses cables between the shift lever and the transaxle.

The first is the 020, a version of which came installed in everything except Corrados, VR6s, and the A4. From 1975 through 1977, the 020 was available only as a four-speed. In 1978, 020 five-speeds started appearing and are now available with a variety of gear ratios. In 1987, 16Vs and select other models came with strengthened versions with a larger diameter input shaft.

Volkswagen brought out the first of the cable-shifted transaxles, the 02A, in 1989, to mate up to the Corrado G-60 and all VR6-equipped models. In addition to its other differences, the 02A comes with a hydraulically operated clutch. Most recently, Volkswagen has unveiled the related 02J gearbox in the New Beetle and other A4s.

Clutches

As engine size and power output increase, Volkswagen increases the size of the clutch. However, car buyers won't put up with high clutch pedal effort, so in some cases, Volkswagen has increased the size of the clutch, without increasing the clamping force. In other words, if you have 100 square inches of clutch surface, with 20 pounds of clamping force per square inch, you have a total clamping force of 2,000 pounds. If you increase the surface area of the clutch by 10 percent to 110 square inches, but you want the clutch effort to remain the same, simple math shows that you will have only about 18 pounds per square inch of clamping force.

This doesn't necessarily mean that the larger clutch in this example is worse than the smaller clutch, because the increase in surface area creates a clutch that will last longer. It's another one of those engineering trade-offs.

If pedal effort were not a consideration, you would have the smallest possible clutch with a very high clamping force. The smaller clutch would have less rotating mass than a larger clutch, which would give you "free" horsepower in the form of a quicker-revving engine. (For a more in-depth explanation of this "free" horsepower, see the discussion on "Selecting Wheels.") With less friction surface and a high clamping force, the amount of pressure per square inch of friction surface becomes formidable.

This is why the Sachs 190-millimeter sport clutch was for a while considered to be the hot tip for early A1 cars with high-output motors. With a 30 percent stiffer spring and a relatively small surface area, it resisted slip quite well, and it

If you like the stock shifter but it is starting to feel sloppy, a factory bushing kit such as this one will do the trick for you.

With your stock drain plug, a magnet from Radio Shack and some epoxy, you can make your own magnetic transmission drain plug.

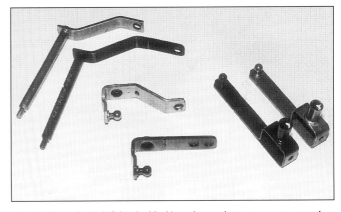

Comparing a short-shift kit (in black) to the stock parts, you can see that there are some major changes in the lengths of the arms.

could be used with the existing flywheel and pressure plate.

The 210-millimeter clutches hold up to 180 horsepower with no problems, but if your car has a 190-millimeter clutch, obviously you need to change the flywheel and pressure plate to run the larger clutch disk. There's not much that can be done about the price of the flywheel, but when you replace the clutch disk, you are supposed to replace the pressure plate and throw-out bearing at the same time, so you can save yourself a few bucks by making the switch when your old clutch wears out.

There are four distinctly different 210-millimeter clutches, so make certain you either get all matching components, or that you deal with someone who knows how to mix and match for optimum performance.

Clutch Availability

Engine	Clutch
1.6-liter (1975–1982)	190-millimeter (four- and five-speed)
1.7-liter Euro (1983–1984)	190-millimeter (four- and five-speed)
1.7-liter U.S. (1983–1984)	200-millimeter (four- and five-speed)
1.8-liter 8V (1983–1997)	210-millimeter (four- and five-speed, and five-speed with nickel hub disk)
16V (A1 and A2)	210-millimeter (five-speed and five-speed with nickel hub disk)
2.0-liter (A3)	210-millimeter
G60	228-millimeter
VR6	228-millimeter

For cars with more than 300 horsepower, the only choice is a four-puck clutch, so called because instead of continuous friction material it uses metallic pucks. These are unpleasant to drive on the street, but for racing they really hold on.

Reinforcing the Transaxle

Unless you are hard on transaxles, this may be an area in which you can save some money. People with high-performance Volkswagens have gone both ways with street machine transaxles, fully prepped and totally stock, with equal results. You may feel better about putting 200 horsepower through a transaxle that has been thoroughly massaged, but experience shows the stock transaxle works great. If you swap out your old engine for a new one, you should, however, swap the newer transaxle too, not only for longevity but also because of better matched gear ratios. There is more about gear ratios coming up later in this chapter.

If you have a four-speed box and want more strength, you can switch to virtually any of the 1985 and later 020 transaxles from the four-cylinder 8V cars, or to the 16V transaxle, which has a stronger input shaft and larger clutch splines. In addition to strength, all the later transaxles offer five speeds. For maximum strength, the 1989 and later 02A transaxle from the G-60, VR6, and A4 cars easily handles 178 horsepower and then some.

If you have to pull your transaxle apart, there are things you can do to boost its tolerance for abuse. As with any other machined part, gears have a wealth of stress risers that can lead to failure. The fillets at the roots of the teeth that are especially prone to cracking, and therefore would be strengthened by shot peening. In addition to the normal benefits of shot peening, the indentations caused by the peening process create reservoirs that hold gear lube for better lubrication. If you want shot peening and smooth gear teeth, the gears can be lapped after shot peening, as long as no more than 10 percent of the surface depth is removed.

If you want gears that are stronger to begin with, special heat-treated gears in limited ratios are available from Autotech

Installing a short-shift kit: Unclip the plastic rod ends and pry them off their pivots.

and Abt Motorsports. For racers, straight-cut gears can be had, as well. The noise makes these unacceptable for street use, but they are stronger.

Differential Problems

There are two big problems with Volkswagen transaxles. First, the ring gear is attached to the differential with eight rivets, and second, the shaft for one set of the differential gears (aka spider gears, the bevel-cut gears inside the gear carrier that enable the differential to work) is retained by these goofy stamped-steel cups that are themselves held to the gear carrier by two of the aforementioned rivets.

Sometimes, the heads of these rivets will break off, which means there can be big chunks of metal floating around among the gears in your transaxle. These chunks can make a mess of a gear, if they become caught between the teeth.

If the rivet that breaks off is one of those holding the spider gear shaft retainer, not only do you have floating metal chunks, but you also have the spider gear shaft wandering out of its bore. Once it wanders far enough out, it will start machining the transaxle housing from the inside out. It can actually cut through the housing, at which time gear lube will leak from the (new) hole.

Amazingly, Volkswagen knows about this, and sells a repair kit that consists of eight bolts to replace the rivets, and snap rings for the spider gear shaft (yes, the shaft is already machined to accept snap rings!). You can save a few bucks by purchasing the aftermarket equivalent, such as the one developed by Gary Peloquin for Velocity Sport Tuning. The Peloquin/Velocity kit has two sets of snap rings: regular-duty and heavy-duty. The heavy-duty snap rings are more difficult to install but hold better. Remember that snap rings are directional, and the sharp edge should face outward.

The cost of the kit is minor compared to the cost of labor for installing it. The transaxle has to come apart so the differential can be disassembled, and the rivets drilled and then punched out. Most do-it-yourselfers won't be able to do the job right, which means paying a mechanic to do it. Be aware that some mechanics replace only the broken rivets, leaving the rest of the rivets in place to break later. Do not let one of these mechanics do the work on your car.

Transaxle Swap: Five Speeds in Place of Four

One thing you should consider on an early car with the four-speed transaxle is swapping it for a five-speed. Whereas the four-speed just barely seems to cover the bases, the five-speed gives you much more latitude in gear ratios. With the five-speed, for example, you can have four close-ratio gears on the bottom for racing and an overdrive fifth gear for cruising. Or you could make first just low enough so you do not stall it coming off the line and have four close-ratio gears up top.

The point is that there are possibilities with the five-speed, and it is not difficult at all to install one. You should be able to find a good used five-speed at your local wrecking yard for a reasonable fee. Make sure you get the clutch pushrod that goes with the transaxle; the five-speed pushrod is different from the four-speed pushrod. Also try to get the mounts that go with it, and if you are really lucky you may even get the linkage too. If these three items do not come with the transaxle, you can get the pushrod from a dealer, and some aftermarket tuners have kits that include the mounts and all the linkage pieces you will need for the conversion.

Examine the pushrod before you install it. A bent or damaged pushrod should never be used, as it will hang up and alter the clutch engagement. If you suspect it, or if your clutch is giving problems, replace it with a new one from the dealer.

Shift Points

Volkswagen does some sophisticated modeling when selecting gear ratios. It makes use of a computer program that factors in air resistance and drivetrain losses, among other things, with an eye toward what it calls engine elasticity, which has to do with the car's performance in passing gear. Passing gear is defined as the gear one below top gear. In a five-speed box, that would be fourth gear.

Volkswagen looks for the best passing time (the time it takes for the car to accelerate from 40 to 60 miles per hour) while maintaining some semblance of fuel economy. This choice is tempered by the gear ratios that are available for fourth, as well as by the need to match shift points both to and from fourth.

There are, however, other methods of choosing gear ratios. In his book *Tune to Win* Carroll Smith gives a complete explanation of how to gear a transaxle to any given track. The digested version of his information is this: Fifth gear (in a five-speed gearbox) is selected so that the top speed you will see at the track corresponds with your horsepower peak, and second gear is chosen such that the motor is just coming up on the torque peak of the motor at the slowest point of the course. Third and fourth are chosen to best span the in-between area. First gear is used only to start the car from a dead stop, so neither the ratio nor the torque drop between first and second is of critical importance.

Another factor to consider for the track, where your top speed will be fairly high, is that air resistance increases sharply as speed rises above 60 miles per hour. You would therefore want to make your shift points a little closer together on top to compensate. You should do this when setting up a street transaxle too, but with the low maximum speed limit in the United States, acceleration is a bigger consideration than top-speed performance.

Volkswagen Transaxle Codes and Ratios

Application	Final	1st	2nd	3rd	4th	5th
TDI (1997)	3.16	3.75	2.12	1.36	0.97	0.76
TDI (1996–1997)	3.24	3.78	2.12	1.35	0.97	0.76
VR6 (1996–1997)	3.39	3.78	2.12	1.46	1.032	.084
VR6 (1994)	3.39	3.30	1.944	1.31	1.032	0.84
Corrado SLC (1994)	3.65	3.30	1.944	1.31	1.032	0.84
1.8-liter 8V	3.667	3.455	2.118	1.444	1.129	0.894
16V	3.667	3.455	2.118	1.444	1.129	0.912
1.8-liter 8V	3.667	3.455	1.944	1.370	1.032	0.745
2.0-liter 8V (1994–1997)	3.667	3.455	1.944	1.286	0.97	0.81
1.8-liter 8V (from 1990)	3.667	3.455	1.944	1.444	1.129	0.894
New Beetle (TDI)	3.89	3.50	1.944	1.23	0.84	0.68
1.6-liter gasoline (through 1980)	3.89	3.455	1.944	1.286	0.97	0.76
1.6-liter gasoline (from 1981)	3.89	3.455	1.944	1.286	0.909	0.71
1.6-liter gasoline (through 1980)	3.89	3.455	1.944	1.286	0.97	—
Pickup (from 1981)	3.89	3.455	1.944	1.286	0.909	—
1.6-liter gasoline (1981 on except Pickup)	3.89	3.455	1.944	1.06	0.70	—
1.6-liter gasoline (through 1979)	3.90	3.455	1.944	1.370	0.97	—
1.6-liter diesel (1985)	3.941	3.455	1.944	1.370	1.032	0.745
1.6-liter diesel (1986–1990)	3.941	3.455	1.944	1.286	0.909	0.745
1.6-liter diesel (1990)	3.941	3.455	1.944	1.444	1.129	0.894
Four-cylinder (through 1979)	4.17	3.455	1.944	1.286	0.97	0.76
New Beetle (gasoline)	4.24	3.78	2.12	1.36	1.03	0.84
1.6-liter diesel (ECO)	4.250	3.455	1.944	1.286	0.909	0.745

Remove the selector lever. Be on the lookout for any other worn or broken parts so you can replace them at the same time.

Remove the relay shaft rod. When reinstalling, note that the 90-degree bend goes with the relay shaft. The 95-degree bend goes with the selector shaft.

Replace the stock selector shaft with the one from the kit.

Install the relay shaft that came in the short-shift kit.

Lubricate the selector shaft from the short-shift kit with moly grease and put it into position.

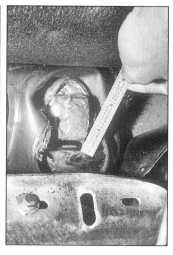

To adjust the linkage, put the shift lever in neutral, aligned with the 3-4 gate. There should be 1/2 inch of clearance. If not, rotate the shift rod on the selector lever until there is. Don't get frustrated; shift linkage adjustment always seems to work backward from the way you expect it to.

Gear Ratios and Shift Points

So there you are with your turbocharged 2021-cc 16V motor. You spent every waking hour for the last seven months working on it and just about every spare nickel as well. You are obviously interested in acceleration, but did you know when you should upshift to maximize the power that your engine is putting out?

For maximum acceleration, you want to upshift when the torque available at the driving wheels is going to be greater in the next higher gear than it is in the gear you are using. If you shift too late, you will be underutilizing the power available in the next lower gear. If you shift too early, you will be running in an rpm range at which the engine is not making full power.

There are two ways of determining where your shift points should be. (Note: You can also use this method to determine what gear ratios would be best for your engine

output.) Neither method takes into account drivetrain losses, rotational inertias, air resistance, or other subtleties, but even so you can get pretty close.

For now, assume that you are interested in maximum acceleration. Before you do anything else, get your engine's torque curve from your engine builder. If you are running a stock engine, you can use the factory-supplied charts; they will be close enough.

Method 1

The first method uses gear charts to figure out either where your shift points should be or what gears you should be using. This method will appeal to those of you without a computer. If you have a computer or have access to one, use it. Calculating shift points with gear charts is possible, but only barely.

Because gear charts for the Volkswagen are difficult to obtain, you may want to make your own. You will need a few large pieces of graph paper and a straight-edge. If you have access to a pocket calculator or a slide rule, things will go much faster.

Consult the list of available gear ratios, and look up the height of the tires you are using from the chart. Also, consult the list of final drive ratios and pick one to start with. You will need to make a separate chart for each final drive and tire diameter you are considering using.

The formula you will be using is:

$$mph = \frac{rpm \times tire\ diameter \times \pi}{final\ drive\ ratio \times gear\ ratio \times 1056}$$

You already know the tire diameter in inches, the value of pi and the final drive ratio, so you can make things go much quicker by choosing an rpm point (5,000, for example), and doing all your calculations from that rpm. You will then have one data point for each gear. Instead of calculating another data point for each gear, make sure your chart starts out at 0 rpm/miles per hour. At 0 engine rpm, the car will not be moving so you have an automatic and highly accurate second data point for all the rear ratios, and you do not have to do any calculations. When you draw your gear lines on the chart, you do not have to stop at 5,000 rpm. Extend the line up far enough to cover whatever redline you are using for your shift point analysis.

The calculations will go quicker still if you multiply the three values on top, multiply the final drive ratio by 1,056 on the bottom, and then divide the value you just got for the bottom. Then all you have to do to get the miles per hour with any gear ratio is to divide this subtotal by the gear ratio, and you will get the speed in that gear at the rpm you have chosen. With a 5,000-rpm redline, a tire diameter of 22.76 inches and a 3.90 final drive, this works out to:

$$mph = \frac{5000 \times 22.76 \times 3.14}{3.90 \times gear \times 1056}$$

$$= \frac{357,332}{4118.4 \times gear}$$

$$= \frac{86.8}{gear}$$

To get your upper data points, divide 86.8 by the gear ratio.

Once you have all your data points, label the Y-axis (on the side of the chart) rpm and label the X-axis (at the bottom of the chart) miles per hour. The bigger the piece of graph paper you start with, the more accurate you will be able to make your chart. The most important thing is to have the axes cross at the zero point. Now take the values you calculated for each gear and graph them on your paper.

Get out your dyno sheet. If it does not have horsepower figures on it, you will have to calculate the horsepower from the torque figures, using the formula:

$$hp = \frac{torque \times rpm}{5250}$$

On a separate piece of graph paper, draw a representation of your horsepower curve. Then make photocopies of it; this allows you to mark all over your horsepower curve drawing without ruining the original. You are now ready to calculate your shift points.

Read across the side of the gear chart until you come to the highest rpm your car can attain. Follow this line across. There will be several gear lines crossing it, but you are looking for the one that crosses nearest to the horsepower peak of the engine. A little under is fine and so is a little over, as long as it is not above your redline. The gear ratio line that crosses at that point is your ideal high-performance fifth gear.

In selecting the rest of the gears, you will get to mark up your horsepower curve drawings. What you are looking for is the maximum area under the curve. You do not want to shift at the horsepower peak. To visualize what happens when you shift to the next higher gear, take one copy of your horsepower graph and draw a vertical line straight down from the horsepower peak, and extend it until it touches the X-axis.

When you upshift, the rpm in the higher gear is less than the rpm in the lower gear. Suppose your rpm falls off by 1,800 rpm when you upshift. Subtract 1,800 rpm from 6,500 rpm, and draw another vertical line downward from 4,700 rpm. The area on your graph that is surrounded by the two vertical lines, the X-axis and the horsepower curve, is called the area under the curve, or the power you have available when you shift at this rpm.

Now assume you hold off shifting until the rpm reaches 7,500. Draw a vertical line downward from 7,500 on your graph. At this higher rpm, you will have more of an rpm drop when you shiftÑfor example, 2,000 rpm. Subtract 2,000 rpm from 7,500 rpm, and draw a vertical line downward from 5,500 rpm. There is much more area under the curve now than in the first example, so it will be better to shift on the other side of the horsepower curve than right at the horsepower peak.

If you next want to explore the differences it would make to change final drives, you have to make up another whole gear chart with all new numbers and lines. If you do not drive your car all winter anyway, and you need a project to work on while you are waiting for spring, you can figure out the proper transaxle ratios using gear charts. Otherwise, check out the second method.

Method 2

This method uses a computer, so if you neither have a computer nor have access to one, the first method will have to do. The program demonstrated here is written in BASIC. It has been run on a personal computer using GW-BASIC under MS-DOS as is, and on a NOVA-compatible minicomputer using Business BASIC under IRIS with the CLS statements changed to PRINT CS. With a few changes, you should be able to run it on any computer.

This program was written by Jack Broomall, an engineer with Chrysler. Instead of a gear chart it makes use of one additional equation that calculates the torque available at the drive wheels:

Front wheel torque =
engine torque x gear ratio x final drive ratio

```
100 REM SHIFTPOINT OPTIMIZER PROGRAM
105 REM Jack Broomall Racing
110 CLS
115 DIM R(30)
120 DIM T(30)
125 PRINT "Shift Point Optimizer Program"
130 FOR A=1 TO 1000
135 NEXT A
140 CLS
145 GOTO 195
150 CLS
155 PRINT "Note: It will be necessary to re-enter all data points."
160 FOR W=1 TO 30
165 R(W)=0
170 T(W)=0
175 NEXT W
180 PRINT
185 PRINT
190 GOTO 200
195 CLS
200 PRINT "Input Torque vs. RPM Information from Dyno Testing"
205 PRINT
     "+++++++++++++++++++++++++++++++++++++++++++++
     +++++++"
210 N=1
215 PRINT "Data Point" N
220 PRINT
225 INPUT "Engine Speed (RPM): ";R(N)
230 PRINT
235 INPUT "Engine Torque (lb-ft): ";T(N)
240 PRINT
245 CLS
250 PRINT "If you wish to enter another data point enter 1"
255 PRINT
260 PRINT "If you wish to run the program enter 2"
265 INPUT "1 or 2";I
270 IF I>1 THEN 295
275 N=N+1
280 CLS
285 GOTO 215
290 CLS
295 CLS
300 PRINT "Please check that torque/RPM data points are cor-
     rect"
305 PRINT
310 PRINT
315 PRINT "Data points entered this run:"
320 PRINT
325 PRINT "Data," "RPM," "Torque"
330 PRINT "Point,", "(lb-ft)"
335 PRINT "—————————————————————."
340 FOR J=1 TO N
345 PRINT J,R(J),T(J)
350 NEXT J
355 FOR A=1 TO 1000
360 NEXT A
365 PRINT
370 PRINT
375 PRINT "If data is correct as displayed, enter 1 to continue"
380 PRINT "If data is incorrect enter 2 to make corrections"
385 INPUT "1 or 2";I
390 IF I>1 THEN 150
395 CLS
400 GOTO 420
405 CLS
410 PRINT "Note: It will be necessary to re-enter all gearing &
     tire info."
415 PRINT
420 PRINT "Input Transmission Ratio Information"
425 PRINT "—————————————————————————"
430 PRINT
435 PRINT "Please enter information as requested."
440 PRINT
445 INPUT "Number of forward gears: ";G
450 FOR T=1 TO G
455 IF T=1 THEN 475
460 IF T=2 THEN 495
465 IF T=3 THEN 515
470 IF T>3 THEN 535
475 PRINT
480 PRINT "First gear ratio: "
485 INPUT G(1)
490 GOTO 550
495 PRINT
500 PRINT "Second gear ratio: "
505 INPUT G(2)
510 GOTO 550
515 PRINT
520 PRINT "Third gear ratio: "
525 INPUT G(3)
530 GOTO 550
535 PRINT
540 PRINT T "fourth gear ratio: "
545 INPUT G(T)
550 NEXT T
555 CLS
560 PRINT "Input differential ratio"
565 PRINT "————————————————————"
570 PRINT
575 PRINT "Differential ratio: "
580 INPUT D
585 CLS
590 PRINT "Input tire diameter"
595 PRINT "———————————————-"
600 PRINT
605 PRINT "Tire diameter (inches): "
610 INPUT T1
615 CLS
620 PRINT "Please check that the following input data is entered
     correctly."
```

```
625 FOR A=1 TO 1000
630 NEXT A
635 PRINT
640 PRINT
645 FOR B=1 TO G
650 PRINT "Gear " B " is " G(B) ":1"
655 PRINT
660 NEXT B
665 PRINT "Differential ratio is "D ":1"
670 PRINT
675 PRINT "Tire diameter is "T1 " inches"
680 PRINT
685 FOR A=1 TO 1000
690 NEXT A
695 PRINT "If data is correct as displayed, enter 1 to continue"
700 PRINT "If data is incorrect, enter 2 to make corrections."
705 INPUT "1 or 2";I
710 IF I>1 THEN 405
715 CLS
720 PRINT "For maximum torque at front wheels, make upshifts
      as follows:"
725 PRINT "_____
    _____."
730 PRINT
735 FOR F=1 TO (G-1)
740 G1=G(F)
745 G2=G(F+1)
750 FOR U=R(1) TO R(N) STEP 20
755 FOR C=1 TO (N-1)
760 IF U>=R(C) AND U<R(C+1) THEN 770
765 NEXT C
770 T2=T(C) +(T(C+1)-T(C))*((U-R(C))/(R(C+1)-R(C)))
775 T3=T2*G1*D
780 U2=U*(G(F+1)/G(F))
785 IF U2<R(1) THEN 840
790 FOR K=1 TO (N-1)
795 IF U2>=R(K) AND U2<R(K+1) THEN 805
800 NEXT K
805 T5=T(K)+(T(K+1))*((U2-R(K))/(R(K+1)-R(K)))
810 T4=T5*G2*D
815 IF T3<T4 THEN 825
820 GOTO 850
825 PRINT "Make "F "-" (F+1) " shift at " U " rpm."
830 PRINT
835 GOTO 860
840 NEXT U
845 U=U-20
850 IF U=R(N) THEN 825
855 GOTO 840
860 NEXT F
865 PRINT
870 PRINT "END OF OUTPUT"
875 END
```

This program not only tests for proper shift points at the rpm and torque figures that you enter, but it calculates what the

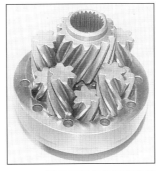

Torque is transmitted from one side of the Quaife differential to the other via the 10 smaller planetary gears.

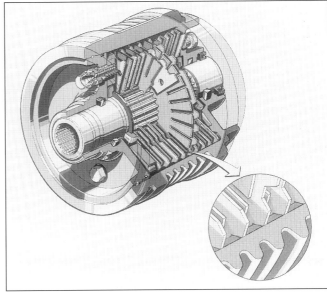

The VW viscous limited-slip differential (Syncro).

torque and road speed will be at rpm in between the given data.

To test the program, start off with some known quantities. Plugging in the torque figures for a stock 1983 GTi, along with the stock gear and final drive ratios, this is what you should get:

NUMBER OF GEARS: 5
GEAR 1 : 3.45
GEAR 2 : 2.12
GEAR 3 : 1.44
GEAR 4 : 1.13
GEAR 5 : 0.91
DIFFERENTIAL RATIO : 3.90
TIRE DIAMETER : 22.76 INCHES
For maximum torque at the front wheels make upshifts as follows:
MAKE 1-2 SHIFT AT 6,500 RPM
MAKE 2-3 SHIFT AT 6,300 RPM
MAKE 3-4 SHIFT AT 5,940 RPM
MAKE 4-5 SHIFT AT 5,880 RPM

From looking at the output you might divine that the factory did things pretty well with the exception of first gear, which is at redline. Otherwise, each upshift matches the torque in the next higher gear with the torque in the lower gear for a smooth acceleration curve throughout the speed range. This is probably one reason you bought a Volkswagen.

Cut-away view of the Syncro.

A phantom view of the Golf Syncro.

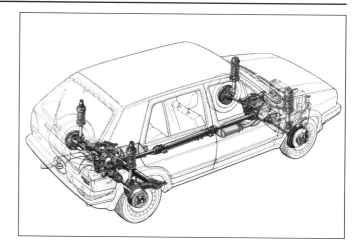

Now "build up" the motor and try those same ratios again. Taking the stock torque figures, add five lb-ft to each number and plug them into the program. your results should be as follows:

For maximum torque at the front wheels make upshifts as follows:

MAKE 1-2 SHIFT AT 6,500 RPM
MAKE 2-3 SHIFT AT 6,380 RPM
MAKE 3-4 SHIFT AT 6,000 RPM
MAKE 4-5 SHIFT AT 5,940 RPM

The gearbox works better with the built-up motor as long as the torque curve follows the factory curve. As the GTi and 16V became more powerful, they were able to use the same gearbox because Volkswagen concentrated on preserving the low-end torque. The more powerful motor also allowed Volkswagen to eventually use the overdrive 0.89 fifth gear.

Now test the program with a difficult example: a strong-running turbo motor with a torque peak at 4,000 rpm and a horsepower peak at 7,000 rpm. Remember that you are still running this motor with the stock gearbox, as many people do. Turn on the computer, load the program, and plug in the numbers. You should see the following:

For maximum torque at the front wheels make upshifts as follows:

MAKE 1-2 SHIFT AT 7,500 RPM
MAKE 2-3 SHIFT AT 7,500 RPM

MAKE 3-4 SHIFT AT 7,500 RPM
MAKE 4-5 SHIFT AT 7,500 RPM

Clearly, something undesirable is happening here. Each shift is at redline, leaving you to guess what is going on. Now you miss the manual gear chart that tells what the rpm drop is and whether or not the transaxle is working for you or against you.

One way around this limitation is to use the formulas with a spreadsheet program (if it can perform calculations) to generate charts from which you can pick out the information you need. If is less accurate than the BASIC program at picking shift points, but both a spreadsheet and a programmable database can, with very little programming, approximate the actual shift point while showing some of the things missed by abandoning the manual gear charts.

Setting up a spreadsheet to do these calculations is easy. Setting up a database program is a little more difficult, but not much. Spreadsheet programs such as Excel have more flexibility and slightly better accuracy than databases. If you run the same numbers with Excel that you ran with the BASIC program, starting off with the stock motor, you should get the following data on front wheel torque. Because of the flexibility and slightly better accuracy of the spreadsheet, let's take it from the top again and run the same numbers with Excel that we did with the BASIC program. Starting off with the stock motor, we get the following figures for speed at each rpm point (mph), and front wheel torque (fwt):

Shift-Points with Stock Motor

	First		Second		Third		Fourth		Fifth	
rpm	mph	fwt	mph	fwt	mph	fwt	mph	fwt	mph	fwt
2,000	10	1,278	16	785	24	534	31	419	38	337
2,500	13	1,359	20	835	30	567	38	445	48	358
3,000	15	1,386	25	852	36	578	46	454	57	366
3,500	18	1,372	29	843	42	573	54	450	67	362
4,000	20	1,319	33	810	48	550	61	432	76	348
4,500	23	1,292	37	794	54	539	69	423	86	341
5,000	25	1,251	41	769	60	522	77	410	95	330
5,500	28	1,157	45	711	66	483	85	379	105	305
6,000	30	982	49	604	72	410	92	322	114	259
6,500	33	821	53	504	78	343	100	269	124	216

Note that you can enter as many rpm points as you have data for.

This program gives two pieces of information that the BASIC program did not tell you: the rough rpm drop at the shift point (2,500) and the speed at each shift point.

Here is Round 2, with the additional five lb-ft at each torque point. The figures confirm that the car is quicker and that everything else has stayed right in line, the way you wanted it.

Shift Points with Higher Output Motor

rpm	First			Second			Third			Fourth			Fifth		
	mph	fwt		mph	fwt		mph	fwt		mph	fwt		mph	fwt	
2,000	10	1,346		16	827		24	562		31	441		38	355	
2,500	13	1,426		20	876		30	595		38	467		48	376	
3,000	15	1,453		25	893		36	607		46	476		57	383	
3,500	18	1,440		29	885		42	601		54	472		67	380	
4,000	20	1,386		33	852		48	578		61	454		76	366	
4,500	23	1,359		37	835		54	567		69	445		86	358	
5,000	25	1,319		41	810		60	550		77	432		95	348	
5,500	28	1,224		45	752		66	511		85	401		105	323	
6,000	30	1,049		49	645		72	438		92	344		114	277	
6,500	33	888		53	546		78	371		100	291		124	234	

What about the turbo motor? With the stock gearbox it looks something like this:

Shift Points with Turbo Motor

rpm	First			Second			Third			Fourth			Fifth		
	mph	fwt		mph	fwt		mph	fwt		mph	fwt		mph	fwt	
2,000	10	2,295		16	1,411		24	958		31	752		38	605	
2,500	13	2,543		20	1,563		30	1,061		38	833		48	671	
3,000	15	2,590		25	1,592		36	1,081		46	848		57	683	
3,500	18	2,624		29	1,612		42	1,095		54	859		67	692	
4,000	20	2,560		33	1,573		48	1,069		61	839		76	675	
4,500	23	2,480		37	1,524		54	1,035		69	812		86	654	
5,000	25	2,360		41	1,450		60	985		77	773		95	622	
5,500	28	2,247		45	1,381		66	938		85	736		105	593	
6,000	30	2,178		49	1,339		72	909		92	713		114	575	
6,500	33	2,119		53	1,302		78	885		100	694		124	559	
7,000	35	2,018		57	1,240		84	842		108	661		134	532	
7,500	38	1,790		61	1,100		90	747		115	586		143	472	

The horsepower peak at 7,000 rpm makes this an inflexible engine for street use. Every time you shift, even at redline, you are losing a lot of torque. (Most people would not even miss it with this much power, but in spite of the fact that the car is fast, you are throwing away horsepower you spent good money for because the transaxle will never let you fully exploit it.) And with over 2,000 lb-ft of torque being transmitted to the front tires all the way from 2,000 to 7,000 rpm, you will be lucky to keep the car on the ground.

To get the most from this motor, you would need to build up a transaxle using gears that do not yet exist. Just for fun, let's "construct" a gearbox using an available first gear and final drive, and arrange the other gear ratios to allow full use of the acceleration latent in this engine. The resulting gear set looks like this:

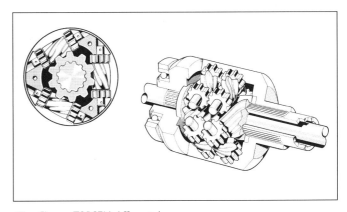

The Gleason TORSEN differential.

145

"Ideal" Turbo Motor Gear Set

Gear	Ratio
First	2.50
Second	2.16
Third	1.86
Fourth	1.60
Fifth	1.38
Final	3.00

Plugging these ratios into our spreadsheet gives us:

Shift Points with "Ideal" Gear Set

rpm	First mph	First fwt	Second mph	Second fwt	Third mph	Third fwt	Fourth mph	Fourth fwt	Fifth mph	Fifth fwt
2,000	18	1,280	21	1,105	24	952	28	819	33	706
2,500	23	1,418	26	1,225	30	1,055	35	907	41	782
3,000	27	1,444	31	1,247	36	1,074	42	924	49	797
3,500	32	1,463	37	1,264	42	1,088	49	936	57	807
4,000	36	1427	42	1,233	49	1,062	56	913	65	788
4,500	41	1,382	47	1,194	55	1,028	63	885	74	763
5,000	45	1,316	52	1,137	61	979	71	842	82	726
5,500	50	1,253	57	1,082	67	932	78	802	90	691
6,000	54	1,214	63	1,049	73	903	85	777	98	670
6,500	59	1,181	68	1,021	79	879	92	756	106	652
7,000	63	1,125	73	972	85	837	99	720	114	621
7,500	68	998	78	862	91	742	106	638	123	551

Dropping the final drive ratio from 3.90 to 3.00, and changing the first gear ratio from 3.45 to 2.50 has brought the front wheel torque more down to earth; with the stock gear set, there was more front wheel torque available in second gear than this "ideal" box has in first. This combination of first gear and final drive gives about the same front wheel torque as the improved GTi motor in the second example. From second gear on up, however, the turbo motor keeps charging while the GTi motor starts falling off.

This is a true close-ratio box, as the 1,000-rpm drop at red-line will attest. The top end suffers, however, and freeway cruising at 3,500 rpm in fifth gear is bound to be a little buzzy. When these figures are run through the BASIC program, you get 7,400 rpm as the shift point for all gears. It should be noted, however, that these calculations are designed to help understand the relationship between engine output and gear ratios, not as a search for the ultimate gear box. The ratios calculated for this "turbo motor" won't necessarily work for any other motor.

If this sounds like too much work, some tuners such as Autotech will, for a fee, create a custom gear chart for you. Autotech also sells a number of different ring-and-pinion ratios, as well as two different close-ratio gear sets (all from Hor Technologie). If optimizing your five-speed box doesn't do the trick, then you have to start looking at a six-speed conversion, which was first developed by VL Enterprises.

Six-Speed Transaxle Conversions

As can be deduced from the examples above, value of the six-speed conversion is not that your car will somehow have a much higher top speed than it would with a four- or five-speed transaxle, but rather that by closing up the rpm drop between shifts, you have a better chance of maximizing acceleration by keeping the engine in the most powerful portion of the torque curve.

You may have heard the expression that a highly modified engine is "peaky." This is a reference to the fact that, in order to obtain a maximum horsepower figure, the engine builder has, through a combination of techniques, created an engine that continues to make torque at higher rpm. From the formula for calculating horsepower, you know that torque is multiplied by rpm (before division by 5,280). Thus, if the engine continues to make significant torque at higher rpm, the horsepower figure will shoot upward.

It can't shoot upward forever, of course, and eventually pumping losses and internal engine friction bring it down, and quickly. Thus, you have a horsepower curve that rises dramatically, and then falls the same way. You can imagine that a 1.5-liter engine making 1,000 horsepower (as Formula 1 engines did back in the turbo era) is going to have an extremely narrow horsepower peak and is going to be very difficult to drive smoothly.

One of the ways to make a peaky, high-performance engine more driveable is to tailor the gear ratios around the horsepower curve, with gears close enough so that at least one gear allows you to drive with the engine in the fat part of the power curve at all times.

There are a couple of different ways of getting a six-speed transaxle. EIP Tuning in Maryland does it by retaining your original first two gear ratios, replacing third through fifth, and then adding sixth. You can then tailor the ratios more closely to your engine output by replacing the final drive. For example, for closer ratios, you could change to a numerically higher final drive. For a strong motor (such as a turbo) that was aiming for top speeds, you would go for a numerically lower final drive. EIP, Eurospec, and others also offer an even simpler kit that adds sixth gear only.

The Autotech SportTuning approach works only with the 02A "cable shifter" transaxles that come with VR6 engines and the 02J transaxle in the New Beetle and Golf/Jetta IV, and involves replacing the mainshaft and all fifth existing gears and adding sixth. The kit also comes with a new nose cone to hold sixth gear, and with the internal linkage required to make the shifts. The ratios are:

A fifth-gear conversion kit, complete with parts, gasket, and special tool.

Autotech Six-Speed Transaxle Ratios

Gear	Ratio
First	2.727
Second	1.929
Third	1.500
Fourth	1.200
Fifth	0.956
Sixth	0.800
Final	3.667 (stock)

Note that the first gear ratio is closer to the original second gear ratio than it is to the original first gear ratio, fifth gear is only a little higher than the 0.91 fifth, and sixth gear is almost the same ratio as one of the "economy" fifth gears. (Others offer a 0.75 sixth gear.) Even though the 1983 GTi figures used in the previous examples don't really apply (because the six-speed conversion won't work with the early transaxle), if we use them one last time for the sake of continuity, we get:

Autotech Six-Speed Shift Points

rpm	First mph	fwt	Second mph	fwt	Third mph	fwt	Fourth mph	fwt	Fifth mph	fwt	Sixth mph	fwt
2,000	14	950	19	672	25	523	31	418	39	333	46	279
2,500	17	1,010	24	714	31	556	38	444	48	354	58	296
3,000	20	1,030	29	729	37	567	46	453	58	361	69	302
3,500	24	1,020	34	722	43	561	54	449	68	358	81	299
4,000	27	980	38	693	49	539	62	431	77	344	92	287
4,500	30	960	43	679	55	528	69	422	87	337	104	282
5,000	34	930	48	658	62	512	77	409	97	326	115	273
5,500	37	860	53	608	68	473	85	378	106	301	127	252
6,000	41	730	57	516	74	402	92	321	116	256	138	214
6,500	44	610	62	431	80	336	100	268	126	214	150	179

Our BASIC program confirms what the spreadsheet tells us:
For maximum torque at the front wheels make upshifts as follows:

MAKE 1-2 SHIFT AT 6,200 RPM
MAKE 2-3 SHIFT AT 5,980 RPM
MAKE 3-4 SHIFT AT 5,900 RPM
MAKE 4-5 SHIFT AT 5,920 RPM
MAKE 5-6 SHIFT AT 5,800 RPM

As indicated, these calculations use the stock final drive. Autotech also sells two numerically higher (lower geared) final drives for the 02A/02J transaxle, 3.94:1 and 4.24:1. The shift points are the same with any of these three final drives, of course, although the speed will be different with each. With the stock 3.667 final drive, your shift from fifth to sixth comes at around 112 miles per hour. With Autotech's 3.94 final drive, your speed would be around 102 miles per hour, and with the 4.24 final drive it would be around 97 miles per hour. Autotech also offers a race-only version with yet different ratios.

If acceleration is paramount, you could change the final drive ratio to the lowest geared (highest ratio) combination you can find, and even run "shorter" tires. The low final drive will reduce the rpm drop between gears, but it will also limit your top speed. The shorter tires will help lower your center of gravity, but unless you are autocrossing, these are desperate measures.

Overdrive Fifth-Gears

In the GTi transaxle chart, the 0.91 gear has a different spacing than the rest of the gears, hence the lower shift point. Volkswagen did this because with the 55-mile-per-hour legal speed limit in the United States when these cars were introduced, top-end speed was not nearly as important as passing speed. The 0.91 and 0.89 fifth gears deliver enough torque to the front wheels that often you do not need to shift down to pass or go up grades.

There are a couple of stock Volkswagen factory fifth gears that have the "right" spacing for the GTi gearbox. The 0.76 fifth gear predated the 0.91 fifth gear in the earlier Formula E cars because of the great fuel economy it gave. Subsequently, Volkswagen came out with a 0.745 fifth gear, which is the one currently sold by Autotech SportTuning, Neuspeed, and the dealer. If you plan to do a lot of upshifting into fifth at 100 miles

Preassemble the thrust washer, gear, synchro, hub, and operating sleeve before reinstallation.

per hour, these are the gears for you.

For the rest of us, the 0.745 gear presents too great a drop in front wheel torque when shifting from fourth to fifth. With the 0.91 gear there is between 60 to 80 lb-ft of front wheel torque lost shifting from fourth to fifth at 55 miles per hour, roughly half of the loss of torque for that same shift using the 0.745 fifth gear. Along those same lines, the even taller 0.71 fifth gear is too tall for all but the stoutest motors.

Overdrive Fifth Gear

| rpm | Fourth | | Fifth | |
	mph	fwt	mph	fwt
2,000	31	419	47	276
2,500	38	445	58	293
3,000	46	454	70	299
3,500	54	450	82	296
4,000	61	432	93	285
4,500	69	423	105	279
5,000	77	410	117	270
5,500	85	379	128	250
6,000	92	322	140	212
6,500	100	269	151	177

This does not mean that the 0.745 gear is worthless, however. If you know you will be driving more than 25,000 miles in fifth gear over the life of your car, a 0.745 gear will save you money based on fuel costs alone. As a bonus, you will also get reduced engine wear (the motor will not have to turn as many rpm to get you where you are going) and a quieter car. The BASIC program for optimum shift points shows that the shift from fourth to fifth should be made at 6,400 rpm for maximum acceleration. Autotech sells a 0.745 fifth-gear conversion for the 8V engines and a 0.80 conversion for the 16Vs.

Limited-Slip Differentials

Back in the days of 70-horsepower Volkswagens it was not necessary to worry too much about getting the "power" to the ground. Nowadays, however, it seems fairly commonplace to come across a Volkswagen with 140 or more horsepower, and in a front-wheel-drive car this much horsepower can prove to be a real handful, especially in a corner.

Weight transfer works against good traction. Under acceleration, the weight transfer is to the rear (off the front wheels), and in a corner the weight transfer loads one side greater than the other. This means that one of the front wheels has very little weight on it, making it easier for that wheel to spin when torque is applied.

Previous solutions included detent-type locking differentials and friction plate limited slips. The detent locking differentials were great for building up pectorals and biceps, and because they work in an on/off manner (they are either locked or spinning) they are very hard to drive. The friction-type limited slips were only marginally easier to muscle around, but because of their construction they tend to wear

Disconnect the CV joints in preparation for lowering the transmission. Have a friend step on the brakes to help hold the axle from turning.

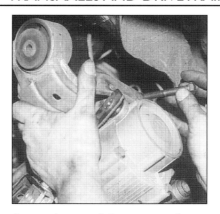

Remove the transmission mount to allow the nose cone to drop down for easier access.

With the nose cone off, fifth gear is exposed. Do not allow the selector rod to come out of the transmission.

Measure the shift fork adjustment before dismantling. This allows you to set the shift fork accurately upon reassembly.

Remove the bolt on the end of the main shaft with the same 12-point wrench used for cylinder head bolts.

Pry up the lock-tab on the late-style transmissions. The early-style lock requires minor grinding.

The special tool is now needed to remove the threaded sleeve that retains the fifth-gear shift fork.

Slide the old fifth gear, synchro, and gear hub off the main shaft (the operating sleeve, fork, and dogs have already been removed).

Remove the circlip for the pinion-shaft half of fifth gear. Note that the indicator groove on this gear faces outward.

Too much horsepower can break these transmissions.

Three different sizes of four-puck racing clutch discs.

A stock spring-center disc on the left and a prototype Marcel-type solid-center disc on the right, for better driveability in a heavy-duty clutch.

out in use, losing effectiveness.

GTi "Minislip"

When the GTi came out in 1983, one of the first things we noticed was turning one of the front wheels when both wheels were in the air caused the other to turn in the same direction—just as if there were a limited slip in the transaxle. The transaxle

drive flanges were different, too, and upon pulling them off we discovered that there were springs behind them applying pre-load. Immediately the word went out that this was a secret limited slip.

As it turns out, Volkswagen did this not to provide a limited slip but to eliminate a problem it was having with vibrations in the drivetrain. The "break-away" torque was only 3 to 5 lb-ft, so it was hardly worth retrofitting to any car that didn't come with it.

Gary Peloquin in California, however, saw the possibilities, and designed a version of the "minislip" that builds on what Volkswagen did, but Peloquin's version (sold through Velocity Sport Tuning) yields 85 lb/ft of breakaway torque. This may not be enough for a pro rally car, but it does reduce torque steer and increases stability in low traction conditions, such as when the pavement is a little wet. Once you get used to it, you can actually feel when it starts to slip and back out of the throttle a little until it bites again.

Like any traction device that works due to friction, the "minislip" can and does wear out. Longevity depends on your driving habits.

Perhaps the best things about this "minislip" are that it is affordable, and you can install this yourself, which can't be said for any other limited slip.

Torque Biasing

A couple of years ago, Gleason introduced a new type of limited slip differential that had automotive writers the world over scratching their heads for a way of explaining its operation. But as complex as the Gleason design is, it works, and Audi uses it in the Quattro. The whole idea is that gears inside the Gleason allow the differential to apply torque proportionally to wheels that are spinning at different speeds, or to one wheel even when the wheel on other side of the car has lost traction. Thus the name, TORSEN for Torque Sensing. (TORSEN is a registered trademark of Gleason Power Systems.)

The Gleason has one main drawback, however. Gleason only sells to original equipment manufacturers, not to the aftermarket. A small firm in England, however, has come up with a torque biasing differential for the Volkswagen that is available to the enthusiast, the Quaife. The Quaife differential uses helical cut gears as opposed to the Invex cut gears in the Gleason.

On either side of the differential, each stub axle connects to its own large helical gear. There is no direct connection between these two large helical gears. Each of the two large helical gears drives five smaller-diameter helical gears (for a total of ten). The smaller gears from one side of the differential mesh with their counterparts from the other side of the differential.

In a corner, the outside wheel must turn faster than the inside wheel. The Quaife (and the Gleason, for that matter, as they both work essentially the same) allows this speed differential. But because the axles are connected through the smaller planetary gears, both axles receive the proper amount of torque.

In practice, the Quaife differential does increase the steering effort slightly in low-speed maneuvers. This stiffness is the result of the application of torque to both wheels, not because of any loss of differential action. And unlike detent, viscous, friction

Changing the ring and pinion alters overall ratio but leaves gear spacing the same.

Steel synchros (left) are heavier duty than the stock brass version, but they tend to accelerate wear on other components.

plate, and other limited slips, the Quaife limited slip does not "snatch" (slip a little and then catch). This makes it more pleasant to drive, and it is easier on tires and other drivetrain components. In fact, a Formula 1 car equipped with a limited slip of the same design was able to run an entire race on the same tires, an impressive testimony to the smoothness of this differential.

The design is the result of five years of development, with "test vehicles" provided by various police agencies and ambulance firms. Under these conditions, the differentials have gone more than 100,000 miles without wearing out. Either of these two torque sensing differentials can be used with ABS, which is not true for detent or locking differentials.

In addition to the cost of the differential you must include the cost of removing your transaxle, tearing it down, rebuilding it with the Quaife installed, and reinstalling it in the car. This means that the Quaife differential will appeal mostly to those at the high end of the performance spectrum. However, if you are running a Volkswagen with more than 150 horsepower, this might prove to be the icing that lets you enjoy the cake.

Detent

Here is a truly unpleasant unit to live with, although it is fairly easy to set up. And back when it was one of the few units around, you either put up with it or did without. It is different from the torque biasing unit in that it is either locked or unlocked. There is no "slip" per se. The percentage of lock is determined by the number of spring-loaded detents you install. With just a few detents there is a little bit of locking power; with the differential fully loaded with detents, you have a substantial percentage of lock.

The reason it is so unpleasant is that when the grip of the two driven tires is approximately equal, the unit locks up, sending the same amount of power to both sides. As traction is reduced on one tire relative to the other tire, the detents come under stress to pop out of their detented position. When the difference in traction becomes enough to pop the detents out of their pockets, power to one side is lost until the detents pop back into their pockets again. Each time the detents pop out and back in again, one side of the car unloads and then loads. And if the detents skip across the top of the pockets before reseating, you feel that too.

Friction Clutch

This is a traditional construction for a limited slip. Volkswagen used them in early versions of its racing cars, and you

can still get a clutch-type limited slip for either the 020 or 02A transaxles from Eurospec. An arrangement of plates (some with a smooth finish, some with a friction surface) are interleaved to obtain the desired amount of slip. Unlike a torque biasing differential, the friction clutch has the amount of torque transfer preset (for example, at 40 percent) so that when one drive wheel breaks loose, a preset amount of the otherwise lost torque is applied to the other wheel. Like most things that rely on friction to operate, the clutches wear out, necessitating replacement.

In addition to replacing the clutch discs every 10,000 to 25,000 miles, you can vary the amount of slip by using shims of different thicknesses. The harder you set the differential and the harder you run it, the more often you will have to replace the clutch disks.

If you have one of these differentials and it is making noise, it may be the gear lube you are using, as the friction plates are somewhat finicky about what you feed them. A quick fix is to drain out a little of the gear lube and add some General Motors Limited Slip Differential Lubricant Additive, part No. 1052358.

Shimming Values for VW Friction Clutches

Setting	Load in Nm	Shims Used
Mild street	180 Nm	1.9 mm + 1.9 mm + 1.9 mm
Sport	230 Nm	2.0 mm + 2.0 mm + 2.0 mm
Rally	270 Nm	2.0 mm + 2.0 mm + 2.1 mm
Race	310 Nm	2.0 mm + 2.1 mm + 2.1 mm

Viscous

The viscous differential also has interleaved plates, and in fact works because of the viscosity (internal friction) of the silicone fluid that fills the gaps between the plates. The plates therefore do not actually touch one another. The percentage of torque transfer varies with the difference in speed between the two wheels, partly as a result of the plate design and spacing, and partly because of a physical property of silicone fluid that it experiences virtually no change in viscosity when heated. If one wheel is rotating only a little faster than the other, only a little torque transfer occurs. When there is a big difference between the speeds of the two wheels, the viscous differential will transfer up to 95 percent of the torque to the wheel with traction.

Because of the difficulties in handling the silicone fluid, servicing a viscous differential can be accomplished only with special equipment. The silicone fluid is under pressure, and there is an air bubble of known (and controlled) volume included in the differential casing. Any deviation from the correct amount of pressure or air bubble volume can radically change the characteristics of the differential.

Stick with helical-cut gears for street use. Straight-cut gears are stronger but make a lot more noise. Helical gears can be either shot peened or heat treated if additional strength is needed.

With some scrap aluminum, a bolt and some Zerk fittings, you can make your own front wheel bearing packer.

Volkswagen uses viscous differentials in its Syncro.

Antislip

The antislip system is tied in closely with antilock brake systems. It is an in-between system that allows you to use the big horsepower in a front-wheel-drive car without having to go to the expense of a torque biasing differential. The catch is that the car must have ABS and electronic throttle control.

Here is how it works: On acceleration, a computer measures relative wheel speed, just as it does when braking. If one wheel starts spinning, the computer will sense this and will then tell the ABS to apply braking force to that wheel, but it also transfers the excess torque over to the wheel with traction. If neither wheel has traction, the computer will send out a signal to the throttle to cut back on engine power until traction is achieved.

How does it back off the throttle? The throttle is not connected to the accelerator pedal. The accelerator pedal is connected to a potentiometer. As you depress the accelerator pedal, the potentiometer sends a signal to the computer to open the throttle. No throttle cable! With the physical connection between the accelerator pedal and the throttle butterfly eliminated, the computer can then adjust the throttle to its liking.

Lubrication and Maintenance

Transaxle lube in some ways has it easy compared with motor oil, because there are no combustion by-products to contend with. But gears and bearings still wear, creating millions of little pieces of garbage for the gears, bearings, and gear lube to contend with—and thus far, changing gear lube has proven easier than rigging a filtering setup.

Transaxle lube also is subjected to shear forces that are far in excess of those found in a motor. You can prove this by draining the gear lube and replacing it with motor oil for a couple of days. The motor oil will shear down, and shifting will become progressively more difficult. Do not put transaxle lube in your motor, though, as the extreme-pressure additives tend to attack bearings.

In addition to conventional gear lubes, there are fine synthetic gear lubes available. Typically, they reduce friction, allowing the transaxle to run cooler (while not affecting shifting), and protect longer. If you have a magnetic drain plug in your transaxle, synthetic gear lube is a good investment, after allowing your transaxle a break-in period of a few thousand miles.

Magnetic Drain Plug

In the Beetle, Volkswagen was careful to use magnetic drain plugs to trap at least the ferrous wear particles in the transaxle.

With the water-cooled generation, this practice seems to have been dropped. I recommend that you use a magnetic drain plug in your transaxle. Although you can use two magnetic plugs (one for the drain and one for the fill), you need only one.

When you take out your drain plug, you will see a little hole on the inside where the magnet is suppose to go. You can clean the drain plug and epoxy a magnet to it, or just buy a magnetic drain plug ready to go. The magnet doesn't have to fit into the hole, so you should be able to find something that will work at any hardware store.

Constant-Velocity Joints

Volkswagen constant-velocity joints are not a problem as long as they are kept clean and lubricated. Inspect your CV boots early and often, and immediately replace any torn or leaking boots. The factory uses metal bands to retain the boots; everybody else uses big tie-wraps, and they work great.

If you have never disassembled and reassembled a CV joint, be very careful. They go back together two ways. One way is the correct way. The other way causes the joint to lock up tight, and you may not be able to get it unlocked. If in doubt, mark the inner and outer pieces so you can get them back together the same way they came apart. The shop manual contains an illustration showing the correct orientation of the pieces. (Those with late model cars with automatic transaxles don't have to worry about this, as the CV joints are completely different in construction.)

When you buy a new CV joint, it comes with a new boot, a new boot clip and a little blue bottle of CV joint grease. This grease appears to be the same brand used as the factory fill, and is not to be trusted. In every CV joint I have ever taken apart, the grease is runny and uninspiring. I recommend repacking your CV joints with Swepco moly grease or something similar. Never attempt to roll your car without the CV joint stub axle firmly in place in the front wheel bearing, as this damages the wheel bearings and you will be forced to replace them.

Wheel Bearings

Wheel bearings rarely fail, but it has been known to happen. The Hacker Brothers used to have problems with the sealed Volkswagen front wheel bearings until they started repacking them with a high-quality grease that is, unfortunately, no longer on the market. Repacking requires a special bearing packer that they made themselves, but between the special grease and the repacking, they eliminated bearing failures.

If you are going to be subjecting your wheels' bearings to

To repack the front wheel bearings, first carefully remove the outer seal, . . .

. . . then the inner seal, . . .

. . . then clamp on the bearing packer and force in the new grease until you can see that all the stock (white) grease has been displaced.

extreme use, you should consider repacking them. First find (or fashion) a bearing packer. Then use a blunt screwdriver to carefully pop out both seals on both sides of the bearing. Set these aside for later; you are going to reinstall the same seals. Force the new grease into the bearing until the old grease (the factory

grease is a clear white color) has been pushed out the other side and you can see the new grease coming in behind it. Replace the seals the same way they came out, and you are done.

For street use, this is all you should need to do. For racing, it is a good idea to carry an extra set of bearings and repack them periodically just to be on the safe side.

Rear wheel bearings should be treated to the same routine maintenance required by any open roller bearing.

Front Hubs

For street use, the front hubs will work just fine and never wear out. For racing, they seem to break right at the shoulder where the hub emerges from the wheel bearing. This is the only part in the drivetrain that tends to fail under race conditions. That tendency argues eloquently in favor of proper CV joint maintenance, which most racers perform religiously.

Under race conditions, hubs can reach a 90 percent failure rate, but some racers do have a cure. After tightening the stub axle bolt to the proper specification, they get a big wrench and add as much extra torque as they have people available to stand on the wrench handle. I shudder to think what the final torque reading must be, and removal is a chore, but the failure rate drops to less than 20 percent. Follow this procedure at your own risk, and only when conditions demand it.

Linkage

If you have ever examined the shifter linkage at the transaxle, you may have wondered how in the world it works with all those levers and rods running hither and yon. Replacing the shift rod with a pair of cables in the A3 cars doesn't make the linkage any more explicable.

The most important thing to keep your car shifting properly is to make sure all the bushings are in good shape. If the bushings are okay, but you find the shift throw to be excessive, there is a solution: the short-shift kit.

A short-shift kit changes the fulcrum points and lever lengths of the shift linkage to reduce shifter throw. The disadvantage is that the effort required to make a shift is increased. Yet even with half the shifter throw, the effort is not so bad that anyone should steer clear of a short-shift kit.

Many aftermarket suppliers now offer short-shift kits. The Abt kit comes from Volkswagen Motorsport's rally program and offers a straightforward 50 percent reduction in shifter throw. Other kits give you a choice of either 30 percent reduction or 50 percent reduction. I have not tried the 30 percent reduction, but the 50 percent reduction is enough to make it seem that there is little motion involved in shifting gears.

Weighted Shift Rods

The Golf III came with weighted shift rods, and now aftermarket suppliers are offering them as a retrofit for other transaxles. They don't seem to make shifts shorter, quicker, or easier, but the weight does add inertia to the shift linkage, which makes shifts feel more positive.

In race cars, the front hubs fail in the shoulder area. The "cure" seems to be to overtighten the hub nut.

This spider gear shaft retainer has been hammered almost to the point of failure by loose parts floating around in the transaxle.

Here's the source of those loose parts: broken rivets.

These aircraft-quality fasteners replace the rivets with bolts and the spider gear shaft retainer with circlips.

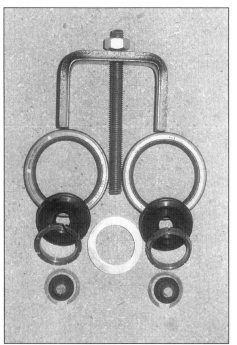

A "minislip" aftermarket modification is a cheap way to improve traction under acceleration.

Chapter 12

Suspensions and Steering

Tools and Techniques

There is good news and bad news about the Volkswagen suspension. The bad news is that many things cannot be adjusted—things that it would be nice to be able to adjust for ultimate performance.

The good news is that with fewer adjustments, fewer things can go wrong. Most people will not spend the hours of testing it takes to dial in a suspension, but they will crawl under the car with a wrench and crank in some more roll stiffness, without knowing if the car needed more roll stiffness, or even without knowing what roll stiffness is!

This does not mean nothing can be done with the Volkswagen suspension. One just has to approach it a little differently than a race car that has adjustable everything.

It is beyond the scope of this book to describe slalom testing, but you might be able to do some skid pad testing. Skid pad testing tells you only the car's ability to corner on a flat surface at a constant speed, so it is not indicative of the way the car will ultimately handle or ride. It is, however, if you so desire, one aspect that can be measured, pondered, and improved upon.

The first thing you need is a skid pad. The pad area should be level and as free from irregularities as possible. The best size for a skid pad is 200 feet in diameter. This is big enough to make the steering angle less significant and small enough to avoid involving aerodynamics during the test.

When running a skid pad test, run both clockwise and counterclockwise, and take the average of the two times. Your counterclockwise times will always be better than your clockwise times, because the weight of the driver is on the inside of the car.

You will also need an accurate way of measuring the time it takes to drive around the skid pad. After you have run around the pad both directions and have an average number, the formula you use is

$$\frac{1.226 \times r}{t^2} = g$$

In this formula, r is the radius of the skid pad, t is the time you measured and g is the g-rating of the car. Driving around the skid pad, you can see that only rarely, if ever, will you reach your car's maximum lateral acceleration while driving on the street. Still, skid pad testing can give you a feel for your car, and for what it will do at and beyond the limit of tire adhesion.

Shocks

To understand why gas shocks evolved in the first place, look at what happens in a hydraulic shock, the type your car probably came with from the factory.

Dozens of makes of hydraulic shocks exist, including Koni, Boge and Sachs. Although it is called a shock absorber, that duty is really carried out by the spring. The thing we call a shock absorber is actually a damper—it damps excessive spring reactions to driving surface irregularities. Rather than rock the boat, however, I will refer to them as shocks.

Shocks are filled with a fluid, usually oil. As the suspension is compressed and extended, this oil is forced through metered holes (valves) in a piston attached to the end of the piston rod. The oil slows the movement of the piston rod. The oil slows the movement of the piston, and thus damps the otherwise uncontrolled spring action of the suspension springs. Some hydraulic shocks incorporate another set of valves at the bottom of the shock that serves to make the shock react progressively. This can improve both ride comfort and handling, because a progressively valved shock will provide a good ride when you are riding over a smooth freeway or traveling at low speeds, and it will also provide good handling when the piston velocity is high (such as would be the case over rough roads or at high speeds).

As the piston travels through the oil, two things happen. First, heat is generated by the friction of the oil passing quickly through the valves. Heat can cause the oil to boil or give off gaseous by-products. When this happens, the shock absorber's response characteristics start to change rapidly, and handling will become unpredictable. Second, the piston leaves a wave in the oil, similar to the way a boat leaves a wake in the water as it passes. A mild amount of turbulence creates a harshness in the

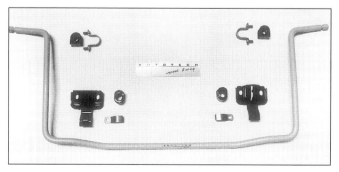

An aftermarket antiroll bar for an A1 chassis. This aftermarket setup uses polyurethane bushings.

A typical lower stress bar with some adjustability built in. Forward-mounted antiroll bar is less effective than other designs because of front end flex. Note the stress bar tying together the lower A-arm pivot points.

The suspension from 1985 on has the large subframe and redesigned A-arms, and the antiroll bar is behind the engine. A-arm bushings for this suspension minimize unwanted suspension geometry changes without sacrificing the ride characteristics.

shock absorber, and excessive turbulence will lead to cavitation, even more harshness and loss of controlled damping. Although the undemanding driver might never notice the effect heat and turbulence make in shock response, the enthusiast would—and thus was born the gas shock.

The first gas shock design to successfully attack both problems was the de Carbon, which surfaced in 1950. This system, employed by Bilstein, is also referred to as a high-pressure gas shock because nearly 300 psi of nitrogen gas (N_2) is sealed inside the shock absorber housing. The effect of the nitrogen gas on the oil is to raise the temperature at which the oil will boil, much as a pressure cooker does. It also eliminates air pockets, where hot, foamy oil might cause problems in a regular shock. More important than that, the de Carbon system stops cavitation, so erratic handling is much reduced.

This does not mean the de Carbon system is perfect. Because of its construction, a de Carbon shock has only one set of valves. A de Carbon shock absorber might be a comfort shock or a performance-valved shock, but not both.

Because the gas chamber is put at one end of the shock absorber, a de Carbon shock will have less travel than a conventional shock of the same dimensions. Finally, there is the matter of the gas pressure. If all the gas pressure were only on one side of the piston, the shock would be very stiff, as it would have 300 psi of preload pushing the piston to its full extension. Therefore, the gas pressure must act on both sides of the piston.

But one side of the piston must connect to the piston rod, and this reduces the surface area of the piston by the radius of the piston multiplied by pi. Because the area of the piston on the side opposite the piston rod will always be more than that of the side with the piston rod, there will be more area for the gas pressure to push against on one side of the piston. This causes the piston to slowly grow to full extension when relieved of outside compression. It also means that the piston rod is normally of a smaller diameter than the piston rod on an equivalent hydraulic shock.

In most cars, this is no problem, but in the Volkswagen it is, because these cars incorporate MacPherson struts in the front suspension. In a MacPherson strut suspension, the shock absorber (which is called the strut in this application) is subjected to many types of side loading not found in other suspension geometries. With a reduced piston rod diameter, many feel that the de Carbon-style shock absorber is at a disadvantage. Even so, the positives outweigh the negatives, and until recently the de Carbon system was considered the best possible way to go.

Modern advances in shock absorber technology have resulted in designs that retain the advantages offered by the de Carbon system, while eliminating the disadvantages. This new generation of shocks, developed by Tokico, are referred to as low-pressure gas shocks. They feature a state-of-the-art pressure seal that allows more latitude in designing the internal components and damping characteristics than with a high-pressure shock. They offer shock travel, piston rod diameter, and valving equivalent to those of a hydraulic shock, and the cavitation and foaming control of a de Carbon shock. Since they were first introduced to the U.S. aftermarket in 1981, low-pressure gas

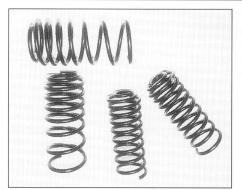

Winding the spring with the coils closer together at one end makes the spring rate progressive.

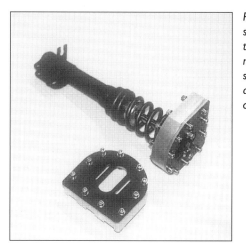

Pulsar Racing's front strut housings lower the car while maintaining suspension travel, and they add a camber adjustment.

The Pulsar Racing strut extender mounted in the car. Note how it reinforces the top of the strut tower.

shocks have made quite an impression on the shock absorber industry, and now nearly every serious shock manufacturer is offering a low-pressure gas shock.

If you change both your shocks and your springs at the same time, and the resultant ride is too harsh, the normal reaction is to blame the springs. My experience with the Volkswagen is that the shocks have more of an effect on the ride of a street car than do the springs.

Therefore, be very careful about the shocks you choose, staying either with original equipment replacement shocks or with low-pressure gas shocks. The regular nonadjustable Tokicos are very nice, and for a lot more money the adjustable ones are, too. Unlike earlier adjustable shocks that would compensate only for wear, the Tokicos adjust both bounce and rebound. If you get the adjustable Tokicos, do not get carried away. The Hacker Brothers set theirs at number 2 in the front and number 1 in the rear in their race cars.

One last word on shocks. The amount of stiffness you can put up with in your suspension is not only a function of your mindset, it is also determined by the roads you must normally travel. A stiff suspension that feels perfect in California, Tennessee, or Texas may be very uncomfortable in Ohio, Arkansas, or New York. Rather than try to do everything with shocks, use softer shocks and springs, and heavier antiroll bars.

Springs

The stock Volkswagen up to 1984 has just under 4 inches of suspension travel before it bottoms out, which is why most aftermarket springs lower the car about an inch or so. Any more than that and you will run out of suspension just about anywhere you drive, causing the shocks to blow out. Stock suspension travel was increased in 1985 to 5 inches, but the principle remains the same. Because of this it is difficult to lower the center of gravity a significant amount for a street vehicle.

Springs can be either single-rate or progressive-rate, depending on their construction. A single-rate spring offers linear response across all levels of compression. A progressive-rate spring becomes stiffer as it is compressed more. This allows the spring to deliver a good ride for normal street use and then stiffen up when the going gets rough.

Early Volkswagens had the single-rate springs. The 1977 Scirocco introduced a trick taper-ground progressive-rate spring. The taper-ground spring is a nice way to go, but in the United States, taper grinding of spring wire is expensive, so most of the taper-ground springs come from abroad.

An alternative to using taper-ground wire is to wind the springs with different spacing between the coils (for example, closer together at the top than at the bottom) or with a different diameter at one end than at the other.

With lowered springs and reduced ground clearance, you need more spring rate to keep your car from bottoming out. With a single-rate spring this objective is easy to achieve, but at the expense of ride comfort. With a progressive-rate spring you can preserve at least a little of the ride comfort and still keep your oil pan off the ground in a dip.

Most of the better aftermarket springs are now made of chrome silicon that has been cold wound. These are far superior to the mandrel-bent, oil-tempered steel springs we used to have to put up with.

With all the good chassis springs around, it is not necessary to butcher a set of stock springs, either by heating and bending or by cutting off coils. Heating and bending will not give you a predictable spring rate, and cutting off a coil makes the spring stiffer and far from progressive.

Another problem with shortening chassis springs is that when the suspension is at full droop (that is, when the suspension is as far down as it can be), you want the springs to be still touching both the bottom and the top spring perches. If the spring is not touching the top perch, spring action becomes unpredictable.

If you wish to lower your car more than an inch for racing, you will need to either find a shortened shock absorber

Prematched suspension components help take some of the guesswork out of selecting a suspension.

Lowering the car even 1 inch greatly helps handling. If you are running sticky tires, you need to lower your car to prevent rollovers.

(good luck!) or extend your shock towers upward. Extending your stock towers allows you to retain the full suspension travel while moving the chassis (and center of gravity) closer to the ground. Another benefit of extending the shock tower is that you can give yourself some camber adjustment up top, instead of at the bottom of the strut only. One of the easiest methods for doing this is by changing the upper spring perches so the spring mounts higher. ABD Racing sells billet aluminum spring perches for just this purpose.

Remember to have your headlights realigned any time you change the ride height of your car.

Kits

Springs are often sold in kit form, so you do not have to figure out what rates and heights are going to work on your car. Although many kits come with just the springs, there are kits available that include fully assembled front struts as well. The cost is higher, but you do not need a spring compressor to install them; you unbolt your current springs and shocks, and bolt in the new parts. If your shocks are due for replacement when you upgrade your springs, a preassembled kit will make your job much easier.

Just remember that any time you take apart your front suspension, you will need to have it realigned. One nearly new set of Comp T/A radials wore down to the belts in 700 miles because the owner did not have the car aligned after lowering it.

Front Suspension

After toying with different front suspension settings (some literally by accident!), we have found that the stock settings work very well. The difference really shows up when you put some torque through your front end. James Sly's 180-horsepower turbo Rabbit at one point was almost too "squirrelly" to drive hard, in spite of three alignments. After changing the settings back to stock, the problem disappeared.

For racing, the best setting is about 1/8 inch of toe-out and up to -2.5 degrees of camber. This much negative camber helps control understeer and improve turn-in response. Tire wear with these settings will be high. Camber can also be asymmetrical (for racing only) to better match the course. For example, at Riverside where all the important turns are right-handers, the Volkswagen racers used to run 2 degrees of camber on the left side and 1 degree of camber on the right side.

You can get more camber than the stock adjustment will normally give by loosening the adjustment bolts and having a compatriot pull out at the bottom of the tire and push in at the top of the tire. This gives you the benefit of all the slop inherent around the adjustment bolts. Make sure the adjuster bolt is turned to allow maximum camber. It is harder to get the camber equal from side to side this way, but you can squeeze out a few extra points if you need them.

Those with 1985-and-later cars with the revised suspension who need more front camber than the adjustment will allow can get 1 degree more camber by changing the top adjustment bolt to Volkswagen part no. N10076601. This bolt is the same as the stock bolt everywhere except the shank, which is 1 millimeter thinner to allow more movement at the adjustment point. If you still do not have enough camber, the lower bolt may be changed too.

To fine-tune your front suspension settings, you will need a tire pyrometer. (For details, see "Tire Pressure.")

The three stages for suspension adjustment are Stage 1, the stock settings; Stage 2, for hot street rods; and Stage 3, for all-out racing, in which tire wear isn't as important as traction. Note that the caster setting is not adjustable through normal means. In the A4, camber can be equalized side-to-side by sliding the subframe back and forth. One solution if you need more camber in A1, A2, and A3 cars is to install camber plates from Euro Sport at the tops of the front struts.

Front Camber Settings

Model	Stage 1 (stock)	Stage 2	Stage 3
A1	+20 ft ± 30 ft	-1 degree 30 ft ± 10 ft	up to -2.5 degree
A2, A3	-32.5 ft ± 30 ft	-1 degree 30 ft ± 10 ft	up to -2.5 degree

Front Toe Settings

Model	Stage 1 (stock)	Stage 2	Stage 3
All	-15 ft ± 10 ft (1/16 in)	-15 ft ± 0 ft (1/16 in)	1/8 in

Antiroll Bars

Over the years, antiroll bars have been variously called antisway bars, sway bars, roll bars, and so on. For the purpose of this book they are called antiroll bars because technically that is what they do—counteract body roll.

After much deliberation I have come to the conclusion that the best arrangement for the front bar is the factory GTi style. Many aftermarket suppliers have adopted this mounting system as well, so it should not be difficult to find a good set of antiroll bars. If you have a GTi, you can simply unbolt your stock bar and bolt in whatever size bar you desire. Keep in mind that the bigger the bar the harsher the ride will be, although it will not be nearly as harsh as it would be with springs heavy enough to keep the body from rolling.

For racing use, the hot setup is to leave an antiroll bar in the stock location and mount another bar right beneath it. Alternately, the stock front bar is replaced with a 1 1/8-inch bar. If you plan to do much exploration into custom antiroll bars, you can make your own bars using stressproof steel (in whatever diameter you choose) and a torch. The stressproof steel can be heated and still retain the properties it needs to act as an antiroll bar. Production bars should all be cold-formed on mandrels.

If you watch much Volkswagen racing (or race yourself), you know that a stock Volkswagen wants to lift its inside rear tire in tight, fast turns. This is the case with most front-wheel-drive cars, because of the inherent understeer that comes from having steering, braking, and power all applied at the heavy end of the car.

Understeer is a situation in which increasing the steering input does not change the direction in which the car is traveling. In other words, the car is sliding off the road front-end first. (Oversteer is what happens when the rear end of the car wants to slide while the front of the car can still steer.)

To balance out your car's handling, you can increase or decrease either the understeer or the oversteer. There are many ways to do this, not all of which are easy or even possible.

To reduce understeer (increase oversteer), try one or more of the following:
- Increase weight transfer at rear by increasing rear roll stiffness
- Reduce weight transfer on front by reducing front roll stiffness
- Increase aerodynamic downforce on the front tires
- Reduce aerodynamic downforce on the rear tires
- Use wider front tires
- Use narrower rear tires
- Reduce front spring rate
- Increase rear spring rate
- Use a lighter front antiroll bar
- Use a heavier rear antiroll bar
- Move some weight toward the rear of the car
- Use softer front shocks
- Use harder rear shocks
- Use more negative camber in the front
- Use more positive camber in the rear
- Raise the front tire pressure
- Lower the rear tire pressure
- Make the front track wider
- Make the rear track narrower

To reduce oversteer (increase understeer), try one or more of the following:
- Reduce weight transfer at rear by reducing rear roll stiffness
- Increase weight transfer on front by increasing front roll stiffness
- Reduce aerodynamic downforce on the front tires
- Increase aerodynamic downforce on the rear tires
- Use wider rear tires
- Use narrow front tires
- Use heavier front springs
- Use lighter rear springs
- Use a heavier front antiroll bar
- Use a lighter rear antiroll bar
- Move some weight forward
- Use softer rear shocks
- Use harder front shocks
- Use more negative camber in the rear
- Use more positive camber in the front
- Lower the front tire pressure
- Raise the rear tire pressure
- Make the rear track wider
- Make the front track narrower

Upper stress bars tie the tops of the strut towers together for extra rigidity.

This racing front antiroll bar has both an adjustable link for preload and multiple settings to change the rate of the bar. For all but the most specialized applications, the antiroll bar should have no preload.

High-Performance Bushings

Suspension bushings come in stock, hot street and metal-to-metal strengths. For street use, the metal-to-metal versions are much too harsh; these are for race only. Depending on the condition of the roads where you live, the hot street bushings, which are often made of poly instead of the standard-issue rubber, can be a blessing or a curse. When used with very high horsepower applications, high-performance bushings can help you maintain control, although you will have to put up with a harsher ride.

Whether or not you choose to go with high-performance bushings, keep an eye on the front strut bushings. They tend to deteriorate and take the edge off the otherwise sharp handling your car is capable of. Replace them when they clunk or get loose.

Boxing the Lower A-Arms

The idea of boxing (or reinforcing) the lower A-arms is something inherited from the 914 and 924 racers, especially because the 924 front lower-A-arm is so close in design to that of the Volkswagen.

I usually advocate using stronger suspension pieces, but I have not yet seen a big problem with Volkswagen A-arms flexing or completely failing. Boxing the A-arms does increase unsprung weight (which is not good) and provides some wonderful hiding places for corrosion (which is not good either). This modification is not recommended unless you discover that you need it.

Front Stress Bars

If you have ever looked underneath the front end of your pre-1985 car, you may have been amazed at the way the front of the lower suspension pickup points seems to float in midair. This is not the best setup for hard cornering.

The lower stress bar was developed to strengthen this crucial area. If you have enough money to buy only one bolt-on suspension piece, the lower stress bar should be it.

The first lower stress bar was a simple affair: a nearly straight bar attached to the two front mounting points, using the stock pickup point bolt. Now, however, lower stress bars have grown more complex and seem to work even better. The two styles include one with a built-in provision for mounting the front antiroll bar and one with a triangulated mounting scheme. Either one will provide some handling benefits.

One word of caution: Never put a floor jack underneath the stress bar and try to lift the car with it. Eventually, this *will* lift the car, but in the meantime the stress bar will develop a permanent bend, ruining its usefulness and pulling your alignment out of whack. If someone else works on your car, specify to *not* support the car on the stress bar before you leave the premises.

Upper stress bars provide less dramatic improvements in feel, but can cut the amount of body flex in the early cars significantly. In 1985, Volkswagen made extensive changes to the chassis that reduce the need for stress bars. Make sure the top stress bar you buy will clear the motor, radiator overflow tank, and so on, and still allow the hood to close. There are so many different engine configurations that suppliers have had to develop a multitude of stress bars to accommodate all the cars—just look until you find one that fits.

Rear Suspension
Antiroll Bars

As shown in the handling lists, changes at one end of the vehicle often produce different handling characteristics at the opposite end of the car. That is why using a stiffer rear bar will not help keep the inside rear tire planted on the ground in a fast corner; this is the job of the front bar.

In the Volkswagen it is more important to have both front tires in contact with the pavement than both rear tires, although the ideal situation would be to use all four tires all the time. Keeping the front tires on the ground is the job of the rear antiroll bar, which also counteracts the tendency of the Volkswagen to understeer. For the best-balanced handling, you will need both a front and a rear antiroll bar. The 1985-and-later Volkswagens, for example, have a built-in rear antiroll bar to complement the front antiroll bar.

Tokico started the trend toward low-pressure gas technology. This five-way adjustable Illumina is Tokico's top-of-the-line shock. Shocks for the A4 adjust at the bottom of the strut.

The adjustment on the rear Tokico Illumina shock.

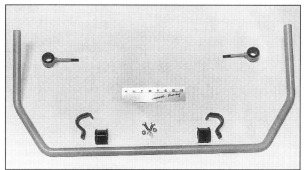

The Autotech rear antiroll bar has sliding ends that eliminate binding but still provide reinforcement against trailing arm deflection.

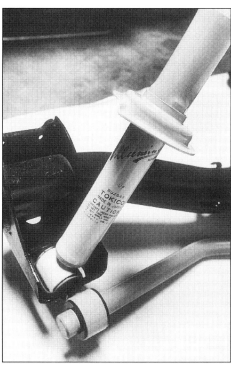

An installed view of the Autotech sliding rear antiroll bar mount.

This APS antiroll bar features Heim joints at the ends to adjust the fit.

Some rear antiroll bars require that you drill two rather large holes in your rear torsion beam for the bracket bolts. The metal in the beam is tough, so start with small bits and work your way up slowly. Trying to get done too fast will result in burned and dull drill bits, and you may eventually become convinced that you will never get the holes drilled.

When mounting the bar to the torsion beam on some pre-1984 cars (such as the Cabriolet), it is impossible to get the bolt, nut, and bracket attached to the torsion beam; there simply is not enough room. The way around this is to temporarily drop the torsion bar down by removing the four pivot bolts (two per side). Be sure you have a jack underneath the torsion beam when you lower it, or it will drop down and hang itself on the brake lines. You will need to lower it only a little bit to get access. Make sure you don't stress the brake lines at any time, and when you are done be sure to snug up the pivot bolts.

Rear Stress Bars

As in front, the tops of the shock towers in the rear are separated only by air, and they appear to be prime candidates for reinforcement. However, the rear shock towers do not locate the rear suspension the way the front shock towers locate the front suspension, so any gains from reinforcement probably would be subtle. I am in favor of reducing chassis flex whenever possible, but I would put off installing a rear stress bar until last, unless you have an A2, where they make a noticable difference.

Steering

If the stock-ratio steering rack is not quick enough, you can buy a quick-ratio steering rack that reduces the lock-to-lock rotation by a full turn (about 25 percent). The drawback to the manual quick-ratio steering rack is that steering effort goes up sharply. If you try to combine a quick-ratio rack with smaller-diameter steering wheel, you will be able to put away your Jane Fonda workout video as long as you commit to driving a few miles each day. A 15-inch steering wheel is highly recommended with the quick-ratio manual steering rack.

This APS rear antiroll bar has an adjustable link that allows you to remove (or dial in) preload.

The New Dimensions aluminum mount (right) provides positive location of the steering rack.

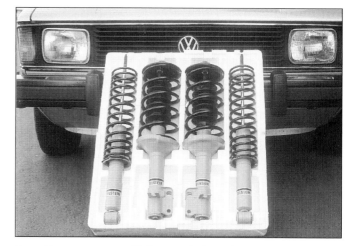

Some kits come preassembled, so you don't need a spring compressor to install them.

The 1985-and-later VW has a much different rear torsion beam setup, including a special bushing for better tracking. Note the nonadjustable rear antiroll bar.

This auxiliary front antiroll bar runs in metal bushings, in addition to a stiffer version of the stock bar, for a racing application. The welded-on collars prevent the bar from wandering from side to side under load.

In racing applications, the power steering reservoir can overflow. The remedy is to provide an overflow bottle so the excess fluid will be automatically recycled back into the system as it cools down, similar to the way a coolant recovery tank works on a radiator.

Weight Redistribution

One obvious way to improve the handling of your car is to redistribute the weight so the car isn't so nose heavy. The only component that easily qualifies for relocation is the battery. But, is what you get from moving the battery to the trunk worth the effort of doing it?

Fortunately, you can calculate what the resultant weight differences will be from moving the battery before you make the decision. For this example, assume you are working with a car that has a gross vehicle weight of 2,300 pounds, a front weight bias of 62 percent, and a battery that weighs 40 pounds. (This must be a later-model car, as the early cars weighed just under 2,000 pounds.)

With its 94.5-inch wheelbase, this 2,300-pound Rabbit will have 1,426 pounds on the front axle and 874 on the rear axle. The center of gravity is 35.91 inches behind the front axle, or about where the shifter is.

Moving the 40-pound battery to the trunk, directly over the rear axle, moves the center of gravity back only about 1.9 inches. But the combination of moving the weight *and* the center of gravity at the same time gives you a bigger difference in weight distribution than you might expect. Now, the front axle is supporting 1,380 pounds and the rear axle is supporting 920 pounds.

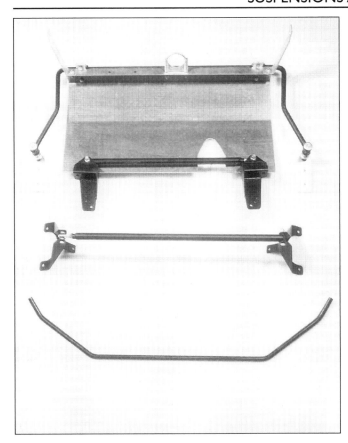

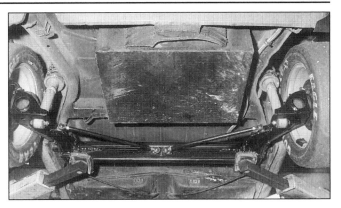

Another Pulsar Racing piece is this set up for preventing rear wheel toe-in under hard cornering. Note the fuel cell.

For off-road use, this set up includes antiroll bars, upper and lower stress bars, and a bash plate.

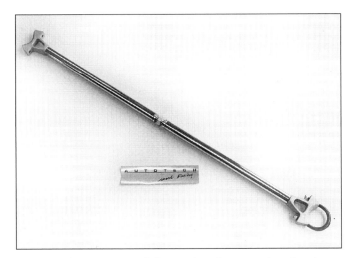

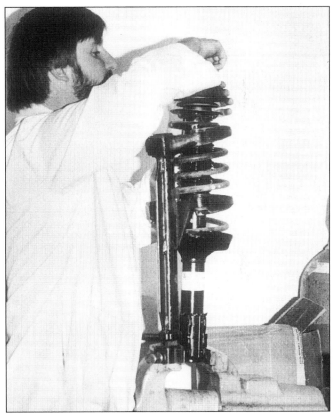

There are many types of spring compressors for working on MacPherson struts. Do not attempt to disassemble a MacPherson strut without one.

Rear stress bars are not needed as much as front stress bars, but they do lend strength to the chassis.

While all this was going on, the polar moment of inertia has also been changed from its old value of 4,839,124 lb/in to a new, higher value of 4,929,744 lb/in, a difference of 90,620 lb/in. (The polar moment of inertia is calculated by multiplying the weight of the car's components by their distance from the center of gravity.) Raising the polar moment of inertia in a car that weighs as much as the

Volkswagen is not necessarily a bad thing, and you have transferred 46 pounds away from the front end, reducing understeer in the process.

If moving the battery sounds better than going on a diet to accomplish a similar end, here is what you will need: a plastic battery box with a top, two battery terminal ends, 250 inches (or so) of 8-gauge wire (or larger), and some cable splices. The

Polyurethane suspension bushings can firm up the handling without destroying the ride.

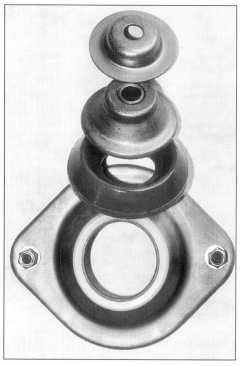

When replacing your front struts, check the upper strut bearings too. If they have been clunking, replace them at the same time.

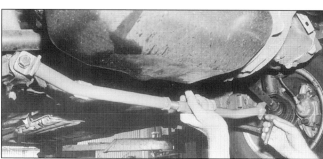

(A1 only) Installing a lower stress bar can be very simple, and the improvement in handling is amazing.

plastic battery box should be available at a boating supply store, if you cannot find one elsewhere. Bolt it down so it does not slide around in your trunk. The top is necessary so you can put things in your trunk without subjecting them to battery acid. The heavy-gauge wire can usually be found at a welding supply store. Heavier wire is more difficult to work with and is more expensive, but the greater the diameter of the wire the less voltage drop you will have and the better your electrical system will work. (By the way, if you are planning to put large stereo amplifiers in the trunk, having the battery right there to power them is quite convenient.)

Corner Balancing

Corner balancing involves adjusting the weight on each wheel for maximum handling. For example, if the desired weight distribution is 54 percent in the front and 46 percent in the rear, you would raise or lower each end of the car until you achieved this balance. The weight would then be adjusted evenly between the right and left wheels at each end of the car for best all-around handling. Weight balancing is done with the driver in the car, and the maximum difference from side to side should be no more than 30 pounds.

The suspension on the Rabbit is not conducive to easy weight adjustments. Although you can jack weight into the car by preloading the antiroll bars, this is not the correct method for corner balancing the chassis, and the car will handle strangely as a result (this method is better suited for oval-track work).

For true corner balancing, you will need either a bunch of chassis springs that have been precalibrated (so you can swap springs until the weight distribution is correct) or a set of the sophisticated (and expensive) shocks with adjustable spring perches. You will also need a set of special scales for weighing the corner by corner, and a lot of patience.

Even the hottest street machine usually will not require corner balancing; however, if you are racing your car, consider contacting someone who can help ensure that your car is handling at its maximum potential.

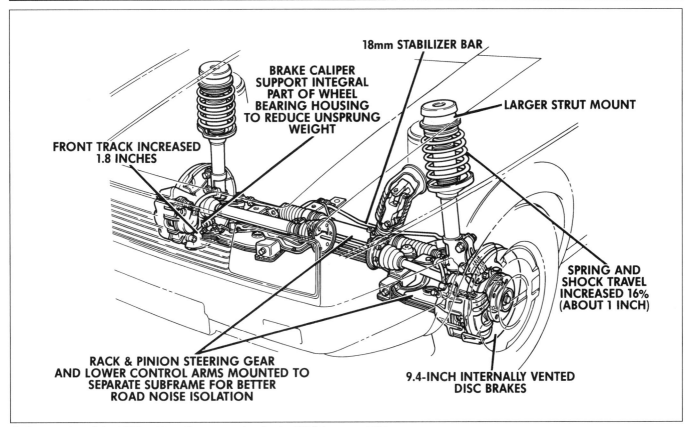

18mm STABILIZER BAR

LARGER STRUT MOUNT

BRAKE CALIPER SUPPORT INTEGRAL PART OF WHEEL BEARING HOUSING TO REDUCE UNSPRUNG WEIGHT

FRONT TRACK INCREASED 1.8 INCHES

SPRING AND SHOCK TRAVEL INCREASED 16% (ABOUT 1 INCH)

RACK & PINION STEERING GEAR AND LOWER CONTROL ARMS MOUNTED TO SEPARATE SUBFRAME FOR BETTER ROAD NOISE ISOLATION

9.4-INCH INTERNALLY VENTED DISC BRAKES

A phantom view of the 1985-and-later front suspension for the GTi, Scirocco, and GLi.

A phantom view of the 1985-and-later rear suspension for the GTi, Scirocco, and GLi.

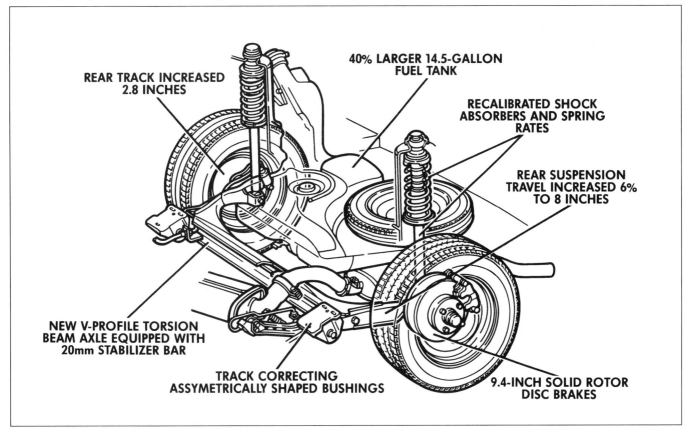

REAR TRACK INCREASED 2.8 INCHES

40% LARGER 14.5-GALLON FUEL TANK

RECALIBRATED SHOCK ABSORBERS AND SPRING RATES

REAR SUSPENSION TRAVEL INCREASED 6% TO 8 INCHES

NEW V-PROFILE TORSION BEAM AXLE EQUIPPED WITH 20mm STABILIZER BAR

TRACK CORRECTING ASSYMETRICALLY SHAPED BUSHINGS

9.4-INCH SOLID ROTOR DISC BRAKES

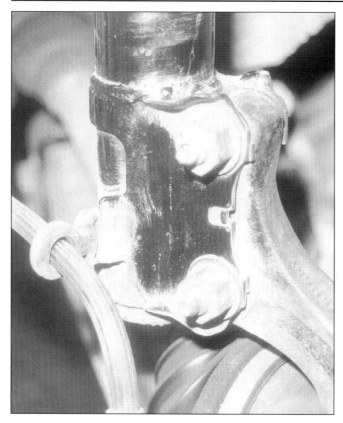

These two bolts can be replaced with bolts having thinner shanks, to get more camber adjustment in the 1985-and-later cars.

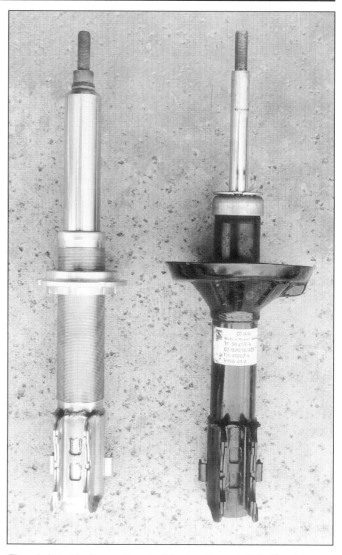

Threaded strut bodies, such as the Bilstein unit on the left, allow for maximum adjustability (including corner weighting).

The bolt on the right allows more camber adjustment than the stock bolt on the left.

Upper strut bearing for 1985-and-later racing suspensions.

The lower control arm bushing can be replaced with this precision bearing (race only).

The rear torsion beam pivot can also be upgraded with this solid pivot for racing applications with the later cars.

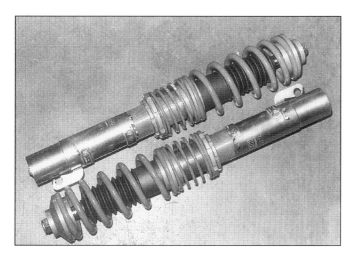

Adjustable height aftermarket gas shocks for the A4. The use of two different rate springs gives them a progressive nature. Shock valving is adjustable from the bottom of the strut housing.

A full-height aftermarket rear spring for the A4 on the left, with a trick adjustable perch setup to its right. The adjustable perch can be adjusted over a range of nearly 1.5 inches.

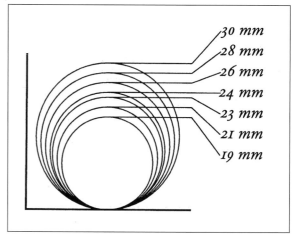

Even 1 or 2 more millimeters in antiroll bar diameter represents a big increase in stiffness.

A4 front suspension showing subframe and pendulum motor mount.

D97/699

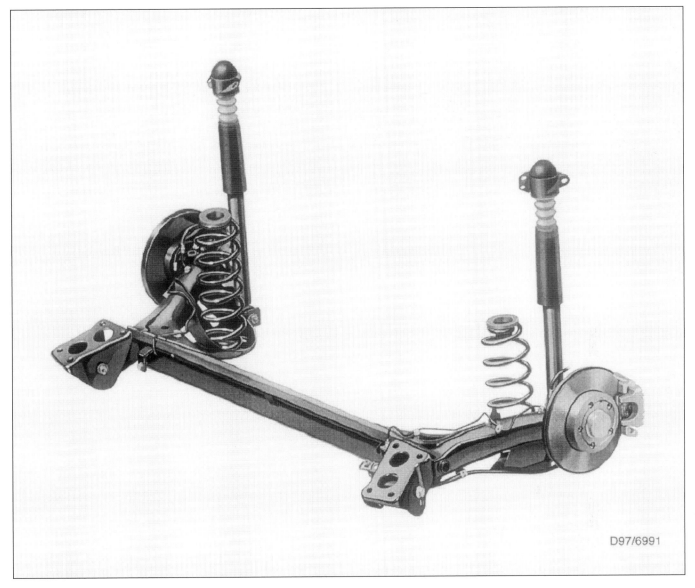

D97/6991

A4 rear suspension showing track-correcting pivot bushings and separate chassis springs, instead of the coil-over set up of previous years.

Chapter 13

Tires and Wheels

One of the easiest ways to improve your Volkswagen's performance is to mount a set of high-performance tires. If you buy a set of tires the same size as the original equipment, they are obviously a direct replacement. In many cases, you also have the choice of tires that fit your existing rims, but are wider than the original equipment. This is referred to as the Plus concept (described below).

If your budget allows it, you can also replace the stock wheels with aftermarket wheels. Typically, rather than buying aftermarket wheels the same size as the original wheels, you would choose wheels that are either wider than stock, larger in diameter than stock, or both. If you increase wheel diameter by 1 inch, this is referred to as the Plus 1 option; it's called the Plus 2 concept if you increase wheel diameter by 2 inches and so on.

The Plus Concept

The best starting point for demonstrating the Plus concept is the 13-inch wheel. The stock tire on this wheel was at one time a 155R13. This is called an 80 series tire, because the measurement of the tire from the bead to the thread is 80 percent of the measurement from sidewall to sidewall (this relationship is referred to as the aspect ratio). This makes it a tall, skinny tire.

To maintain the same sidewall height but with a wider tire, you have to change the aspect ratio. For every increase in tire width (155 millimeters to 175 millimeters, 175 millimeters to 195 millimeters, and so on), you must also decrease the series (80 to 70, 70 to 60, and so on). The rule of thumb is that for every 10 percent reduction in series, you add 20 millimeters to the tire size. Thus, a 175/70R13 has roughly the same rolling radius as a 155R13 (although not explicitly stated, the aspect ratio is 80). With the lower aspect ratio, the replacement tire is wider, but retains the same overall diameter.

One misconception is that with a wider tire you achieve better handling because you have more rubber touching the pavement. Not so.

No matter what size tire you have on your car, the *footprint* of the tire will be the same. Assuming that the same weight presses down on the narrow tire as on the wider tire, the amount of tire deformation will be the same. In other words, a 155R13 tire will have the same amount of rubber touching the ground as does a 195/50VR15. By changing to a wider tire, you are, however, changing the shape of the *contact patch* (where the tire meets the pavement). With a 155R13 tire, the contact patch is long and narrow. With a 195/50VR15, the contact patch is short and wide.

The 13-inch original factory alloy for the VW.

In a corner, the 155R13 tire with its tall sidewalls will squirm all over the place in response to side loading. As it pushes out, the tread is pulled away from the pavement, reducing traction and causing the tire to skid. A wider tire, with shorter sidewalls, is not as prone to this, so it is better at maintaining the shape (and thus stability) of the contact patch.

This all works very well on dry surfaces, but in wet conditions there are other things to consider. As a tire rolls over a wet surface, the first third of the contact patch shoves the water out of the way, the second third squeegees the road surface of excess water, and the final third provides the actual grip. With a skinny tire like the 155R13, the long contact patch means that each third of the contact patch has more time to do its job. The 195/50VR15, on the other hand, has a much shorter contact patch, leaving each (shorter) third of the contact patch much less time to get the water out of the way and provide traction. This is one reason wide tires are not as good in the rain as narrow tires, and why they tend to hydroplane (skim along the top of the water instead of forcing through to the road surface) easier.

VW introduced this 14-inch rim on the American GTi.

These Panasports were stronger, lighter, and bigger than the factory rims, three great qualities.

One-piece Ronal R-8 spoked wheel.

Therefore, if most of your driving is done in the dry, a wide tire will do you the most good. If you drive in water, snow, or ice, a narrower tire would better suit your needs. It used to be that if your situation demanded it and you can afford it, you had one set of wheels and tires for summer use and another set for winter use. Now, the wider, high-performance tires have incorporated a lot of technology from racing tires that greatly improves their ability to remove water from the area of the contact patch, so for all but fairly extreme conditions, one set of the correct performance tires is all you need for year-around use.

The Plus I and Plus 2 Concepts

Once you have exhausted the possibilities of mounting wider tires on the stock rims, the next step is to increase the rim size. Wheels are available for the Volkswagen from 13- to 19-inch sizes, so no matter what size you start with, you can add up to 3 inches to your wheel diameter, depending on clearance. Adding 1 inch (going from a 13 to a 14, or from a 14 to a 15) is referred to as Plus 1. Adding 2 inches (going from a 13 to a 15) is referred to as Plus 2.

To maintain the overall height of the tire, the aspect ratio must again be reduced when upgrading to a Plus 1 or Plus 2 size. The rule of thumb for the Plus concept usually works here, too, but it is better to consult a tire spec sheet for actual dimensions, especially when several similarly sized tires are in your target range. You may need to refer to the tire dimensions eventually anyway, as even two tires that have the same advertised size can have small dimensional differences. In extreme cases, one tire will fit, while another tire of the same advertised size will not. If you buy your tires and wheels from an aftermarket firm that is knowledgeable about Volkswagens, the people there should be able to help you avoid clearance problems.

In addition to a wider contact patch, a Plus 1 or Plus 2 tire has the high-performance advantage of a shorter sidewall. Shorter sidewalls flex less, so the tread maintains better contact with the pavement. With a Plus 1 or Plus 2 tire, the wheel extends to where the sidewall of the tire used to be, and the rim is much stiffer than the tire, which also reduces the amount of flex in this area.

Aside from the high cost of a set of Plus wheels and tires, this additional high-performance advantage comes at the expense of wet-weather performance (as previously noted) and ride characteristics.

This brings up the subject of the relative performance of wider tires on stock rims versus a Plus 1 or Plus 2 setup. There are linear relationships for ride, handling, ruggedness, and cost. Ride and ruggedness will be best with 13-inch rims because of the cushioning effect of the sidewall. Larger-diameter tires not only ride worse but do a poorer job of protecting the rim from pothole damage and so on. Handling will be best with the larger diameter tires and wheels, although you may prefer the ride quality of a wheel and tire combination that is a step or two down from the ultimate.

Modular wheels, such as these Ronal RC-2s, allow you to custom-fit rims to the car by bolting together sections that fit your application.

One-piece rims, such as this Ronal R-10, are better suited for day-to-day street use than two- or three-piece rims.

Balancing

It seems so simple, and yet it causes so many problems. To be truly balanced, your wheel must have weights both on the inside and on the outside—not just on the inside. To determine the location of the inside and outside weights (they are almost never at the same point on the rim), you must spin-balance the tire and wheel together: static balancing won't work. If the tire has worn irregularly due to suspension misalignment or really bad shocks or struts, even spin balancing won't work.

Rotating

The whole point behind rotating your tires is to squeeze more miles out of tires that are wearing unevenly. It works, too, although you may not want to do it. Instead, it is better to fix the reason the tires are wearing unevenly in the first place. If you don't rotate your tires, your front tires should wear out before the rear tires. This allows you to replace two tires at a time, rather than having to buy all four at once. Still, you will want to rotate your tires to even out the wear if you are attempting to stretch the life of an existing set in preparation for changing over to a set of Plus concept wheels and tires.

If you prefer to rotate your tires, make *sure* you check with the tire manufacturer to see what constitutes an acceptable rotation pattern and what does not. As radial tires evolve, and depending on the spare tire that came with your car, suggested rotation patterns have changed too.

Tire Pressure

In most situations, the factory-recommended tire pressures will be adequate for your driving. As just discussed, the weight of the car remains the same no matter what tire you put on, so you will need only the recommended tire pressure.

Where tire pressure becomes critical is in racing. Whereas street tire pressure is checked and adjusted only when the tires are cold, at the track it is adjusted when the tires are at operating temperature. To do this accurately you will need a tire pyrometer in addition to your tire pressure gauge. If you already own a digital multimeter, check to see if there is a temperature probe available for your meter before you buy a pyrometer. You might be able to save some money.

With the tire pyrometer, you can check your alignment as well. Here is how it works:

After running the car on the course, bring it in and immediately use the pyrometer to take the temperature of the tires, checking the outside edge, middle, and inside edge. After about 30 seconds, the temperature will be too low for an accurate measurement, so hurry.

Insert the point of the pyrometer just underneath the tread of the tire and wait for the reading to stabilize.

The tire will be hottest where it is working the hardest. For example, if the inside edge is hotter than the middle or outside, you have too much negative camber. If the middle is hottest, the tire pressure is too high. (If the middle is cooler, the tire pressure is too low.) If the outside is hottest, there is too much positive camber.

Momo road wheels, with the gas cap cut to match.

VW rim from the 1987 Scirocco 16V. Despite the way it looks it is not directional, and it is fairly heavy, compared with other rims.

Checking tire temperatures with a tire pyrometer.

As strange as this may sound, shaving the tire actually makes it last longer. With less tread, there is less tread squirm and thus less heat. A full-depth tread on a race tire will lose huge chunks of rubber, throwing the tire out of balance and shortening its life. For racing use, tire shaving is mandatory.

Selecting Wheels

While for many years, all Volkswagens had four-bolt wheels, many of the newer cars now come with five-bolt wheels. In both cases, the bolt diameter is the same at 100 millimeters.

The standard offset of the 4 1/2- and 5-inch-wide Volkswagen wheel is 45 millimeters. With the introduction of the 5 1/2-inch-wide wheels, it changed to 38 millimeters. Offset is designed into the wheel to complement the negative roll radius built into the front suspension. Negative roll radius causes the car to automatically steer in the direction of a skid caused by unequal front wheel traction and makes it easier to control the car should you lose pressure in a front tire.

As desirable as it may be to retain the wheel offset (and thus the negative roll radius) the factory intended, with the MacPherson strut front suspension there is little room to fit a wider rim on the inboard side of the wheel. That is where Volkswagen chose to put the strut. After a point, therefore, you cannot make the tire any wider without reducing the offset. Because the wheel offset at which the negative roll radius would be lost is about 31 millimeters, you should choose a wheel with greater than 31 millimeters of offset. It used to be difficult to find wide rims with the right offset, but now you should have no trouble finding even really wide rims that still have 35 millimeters of offset.

Certain linear relationships among wheel size, tire profile, cost, and performance are easy to remember, and that can make it much easier to decide what combination is right for you. These relationships are shown in the chart.

You more than likely will be faced with a multitude of different readings, so check and recheck often until you have everything sorted out.

Do not be surprised if your hot tire pressures are much higher than your cold tire pressures. If you are using your car for both the street and occasional autocrosses, be sure to write down what tire pressures you need for both situations, both hot and cold. This will save you time.

Tire Shaving

Shaving refers to the practice of grinding tread off a tire to prepare it for racing. As opposed to a normal street tire, a shaved tire will have only 3/32 to 6/32 inch of tread.

Tire Characteristics

Category	Less	More
Ride	19-inch	13-inch
Handling	13-inch	19-inch
Ruggedness	19-inch	13-inch
Cost	13-inch	19-inch

When using the chart, weigh cost against ride, handling and ruggedness, and make the best decision for your car. After *European Car* editor James Sly, who for years had one of the hottest Rabbits in southern California, moved to the Washington, D.C., area, he soon realized that the difference in road conditions made his 15-inch wheel-and-tire combination much too aggressive for comfortable street use.

His is not an unusual case. In the northern regions, where frost heaves and potholes are the order of the day, you will want a taller sidewall to help soak up the inevitable jolts. Even in southern California, a combination of 15-inch (or larger) rims and stiff suspension can quickly pound out your strut towers, not to mention you and your passengers.

You can get big improvements in handling without going to larger-diameter rims by increasing the width of whatever rim size you want to use. For dry performance, the wider the rim the better the car will handle, as long as everything fits underneath the fender. If you are going for a certain look that demands 18- or 19-inch rims, then you may be willing to put up with the ride harshness, and to drive more carefully on rough roads to avoid damage to the rims or chassis.

Unless you are desperate for a certain offset, backset, or style, stay away from the modulars for street use. Modulars come as either two- or three-piece units. In the two-piece versions, the outer rim is one piece and the inside/center is the other. The inside/center is chosen with both clearance and offset in mind, while the outer rim is chosen based on how wide you want the rim. In the three-piece versions, there is an outer rim, an inner rim, and a separate center piece. By using different-shaped halves, the manufacturer can vary the clearance and offset while making any diameter or width wheel. Be aware that modulars can leak air at the seams, so keep an eye on those tire pressures.

Another factor to consider with rims is *unsprung weight*. Unsprung weight, as the term implies, is weight that is not supported by the springs. The greater the unsprung weight, the more difficult it is for the springs and shocks to control wheel movement and deliver the best handling on rough surfaces. Unsprung weight is important even on stock Volkswagens, because of the relatively low overall weight of the car and the chassis flex present (albeit this is more of a problem in the A1s than the later ones). It takes only a pound or so increase in weight in each wheel to make a big difference in the way the car rides, handles, and feels. With heavy rims, your car will feel ponderous and rough. They can lead you to spend a lot of time trying to get the right combination of springs, shocks, and antiroll bars, because that's where the

Two identical tires on one specially built rim from JJD. These may have worked in wet conditions, but not in the dry, and they were heavy.

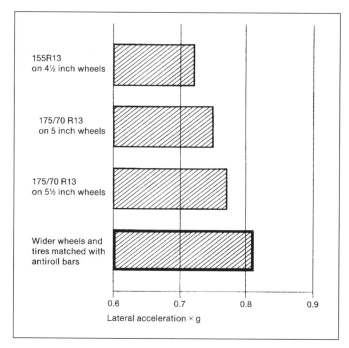

Wider wheels support the sidewalls better and allow you to run wider tires. Antiroll bars keep the tires flatter on the ground, so they work better.

The trailer-style stem stays tucked in, out of harm's way. The rim is a lightweight directional 14-incher from Dino.

problem seems to be. With light wheels, the car feels nimble and responsive and is a real joy to drive.

Unsprung weight is the reason there are alloy wheels. Steel wheels are typically heavier, so switching to an alloy wheel should save weight and give you all the benefits of lower unsprung weight. Where it becomes a bit trickier is in upgrading from one alloy wheel (such as the stock alloys) to another. There is no law that says that a wheel has to be designed with appearance being secondary to performance, so check the weight before you buy.

Another reason to go for a lighter tire-and-wheel combination is that your engine has to accelerate (and your brakes have to decelerate) every extra ounce of weight you bolt on, and this goes double for rotating weight. The total mass of a rotating part—also known as the effective mass of that part—depends on the static mass (the weight), plus the diameter of the part, the weight distribution, and even

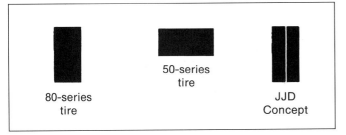

80-series tire	50-series tire	JJD Concept

Although all these tires have different aspect ratios, physics dictate that they all have the same contact patch.

Tire and wheel equivalencies: Plus 1 and Plus 2
For better handling it is possible to increase the rim size, shorten the sidewall, and maintain the same tire diameter making use of the Plus 1 and Plus 2 concepts.

Tire and Wheel Equivalencies

Tire height ⟶ | 13 | 13 | 13 | 14 | 14 | 15 | ⟵ Rim diameter

Tire size	155R13	175/70 R13	205/60 R13	185/60 R14	205/55 R14	195/50 R15
Aspect ratio	80	70	60	60	55	50
Tire designation	P3	P3/70	P6	P600	P600	P7 (P700)
Cross section*	6.26"	7.13"	8.19"	7.44"	7.87"	7.79"
Tire diameter	22.76"	22.76"	22.67"	22.76"	22.91"	22.88"
Revs/mile	917	917	917	917	907	914

NOTE: All cross section widths measured on 6 inch rim except for the 155 R13, which is measured on a 5 inch rim. Cross section will change by approximately 0.020 inch for ever 1/2 inch change in rim width.

the gear ratios of the differential and transaxle. The end result is a number that is bigger, and more important, than the static weight. To put it another way, if you had two sets of tires and wheels that were identical in dimension, but one of the sets was lighter than the other, changing from the heavier set to the lighter set would make the car faster (in addition to the improvement in nimbleness noted above). With the lighter wheels and tires, the engine can more easily accelerate the correspondingly lower effective mass, even with the same engine output. This is just about like getting free horsepower.

If you do get the urge for different wheels and tires but you cannot afford the best of both, skimp on the tires. You will have to live with the rims for years, so that is where you should spend your money. While you are wearing out your cheap tires, you can be putting aside money to get better ones next time around.

Once you have a set of nice rims, always have your tires changed using a European-style changer. The difference in the European-style changer is that there is little contact between the changer and the rim, so the possibility of damage is greatly reduced. Twenty years ago when water-cooled Volkswagen hot-rodding was just getting going, these changers were rare in the United States. Ten years ago, the situation was much better, and today you should have no trouble finding a shop that uses them.

For practical purposes, there are two stages to upgrading your wheels. You could, of course, "upgrade" your wheels by purchasing the same size wheels as you currently have, going for lighter weight or a different look, but normally a wheel upgrade involves increasing the width or diameter of the existing wheels.

The table above lists both four-bolt and five-bolt rims. Not all cars will fit all sizes shown. For example, some Corrados will not fit as much wheel-and-tire as Golfs and Jettas. Even a difference of 1/2 inch can make a big difference in fit. Your supplier should be able to tell you which wheel-and-tire combinations will fit your application.

Selecting Tires

When buying high-performance tires, be aware of hidden cost factors. Tires come graded as to how they will perform in three areas: temperature, traction, and tread life. The tread life rating is the one to be interested in. Most tires that grip the road for improved handling have a softer compound and thus a shorter life span, but a low wear rating does not guarantee that a tire will handle well.

The Work modular wheel.

Handling aside, the wear rating is your clue to how expensive the tires really are. A low wear rating can make an "inexpensive" set of tires expensive, and "expensive" set of tires exorbitant.

Be sure to check the wear rating before you buy, and ask others what kind of life they have been getting from their tires. Also, consider alignment and driving habits. Actual experience may confirm or refute the rating that appears on the tire sidewall. The number on the sidewall is generated by the tire company, and at this point there is no agency or committee whose job it is to ensure these numbers are accurate.

Two other numbers appear on sidewall: traction and temperature. Traction is the tire's ability to maintain grip on a wet surface; temperature is the tire's ability to resist destructive heat build-up. Tires are rated in each of these three categories as A, B, or C. With ratings this broad, its not unusual to find performance tires that have garnered A ratings for traction and temperature. Do not, then, buy tires solely on their traction and temperature ratings. On the other hand, any high-performance tire you buy should score As in these areas.

In addition, there is one other rating, which you will find as part of the tire size. For example, in a 195/50VR15, the V is the rating (the R stands for "radial," of course). This rating refers to the maximum sustained speed for which the tire is deemed safe. You should have no trouble finding a performance tire that far exceeds the maximum sustained speed at which you will be using your tires.

Wheel Upgrades

Model	Stock	Stage 1	Stage 2
A1	4.5 x 13, 5.5 x 13, 6 x 13, 6 x 14	6 x 13, 6 x 14, 6 x 15, 7 x 15	7 x 16, 7.5 x 16, 7 x 17
A2, A3	5.5 x 13, 6 x 13, 6 x 14, 6 x 15, 6.5 x 15	6.5 x 15, 7 x 15	6.5 x 16, 7 x 16, 7.5 x 16, 7 x 17, 7.5 x 17
		6.5 x 15, 7 x 15	6.5 x 16, 7 x 16, 7.5 x 16, 7 x 17, 7.5 x 17
A4	6 x 14, 6 x 15, 6 x 16	7 x 17, 8 x 17	7 x 18, 8 x 18

You may need to run fender flares with really wide wheels, such as the 7-inch Zenders on this car.

Tire Speed Ratings

Letter Rating	For Sustained Speeds Up to
F	50 mph
G	56 mph
J	62 mph
K	68 mph
L	75 mph
M	81 mph
N	87 mph
P	93 mph
Q	100 mph
R	106 mph
S	112 mph
T	118 mph
U	124 mph
H	130 mph
V	130+ mph
Z	150+ mph

When upgrading tires, there are three basic stages. The first stage is to buy tires to fit your existing wheels. The second stage is to buy tires in combination with a set of wheels for improved performance, as is the third stage, with the difference being that you are going all out. Note the previously stated cautions about fit. What fits one car will not necessarily fit another seemingly identical car because of dimensional differences due to manufacturing tolerances. This goes both for wheels and tires separately.

Snow Performance

Wide, low-profile tires will not do you much good in the mud and snow. The ideal snow tire is tall and skinny, just like the stock tires that come with your car. The skinnier tire pushes down through the snow to give you some traction, although even with the best snow tires "performance" is marginal compared to even an average tire on clean, dry pavement.

High-performance street tires have a closed-tread design to put as much rubber against the ground as possible. In a snow tire, you want an open-block tread. Snow will pack into the voids between the blocks of rubber and provide extra traction when it sticks to snow on the road.

If you are serious about snow traction, and your state will allow it, studded tires are the way to go, as they will work on ice better than will simple snow tires. Generally, however, you are going to have to take it easier in the snow than a clean, dry roadway. No matter what you do to improve the snow traction, you will rarely, if ever, see the far side of 0.20 g of lateral acceleration.

If you live in snow country and you have your heart set on steamroller tires for the summer months, keep that set of stock wheels in the garage for when winter rolls around.

Miscellaneous Tips and Techniques

If you race, replace your old tires before they get too worn out. Then, use your old tires for setting up the suspension; if you can get your car to handle well on used-up tires, it will be that much better on new tires.

Also for racing, change your stock valve stems for the shorter valve stems used for trailer wheels. This prevents the valve stems from being torn off accidentally if you get too close to a competitor or a wall, and the sudden loss of air pressure that follows.

Directional wheels are a great idea—if they are directional the proper way. Because the normal path for cooling air through the brake rotor is from the inside out, any directional wheel you buy should be mounted to pull air to the outside of the car. This may increase the problem you have with brake dust, but at least your wheels will be working to increase brake cooling.

Tire Speed Ratings

Letter rating	For sustained speeds up to
F	50 mph
G	56 mph
J	62 mph
K	68 mph
L	75 mph
M	81 mph
N	87 mph
P	93 mph
Q	100 mph
R	106 mph
S	112 mph
T	118 mph
U	124 mph
H	130 mph
V	130+ mph
Z	150+ mph

Tire Characteristics

Category	Less	More
Ride	19-inch	13-inch
Handling	13-inch	19-inch
Ruggedness	19-inch	13-inch
Cost	13-inch	19-inch

Tire characteristics: The linear relationships among tire characteristics allow you a great deal of choice and latitude in selecting a combination that's right for your driving.

The race tire on top is feathered and is showing signs of chunking along the edge, due to excess tread depth. The shaved tire beneath it fared much better.

A good-quality tire pressure gauge is a necessity.

Modern computer wheel balancers tell the technician how much weight to put on both the inside and outside of the rim.

Chapter 14

Brakes

Volkswagen is good about supplying brakes adequate for the intended use of the vehicle. As its cars have become more powerful and capable in other respects, the brakes have improved. But if you increase the power output of your engine, you need to increase the efficiency of your brakes to match.

Brakes work by converting productive work to useless heat, which is generated when the brake pads slide against the surface of the brake rotor. This heat then dissipates into the air (and the brake caliper, and the brake fluid, and the road wheel, and the wheel bearing, and the axle, and the CV joint). As you may have discovered, metal does not naturally dissipate heat quickly. In fact, it seems to hold heat rather well when the cooling medium is air. For this reason—and because you do *not* want the heat being transferred to the caliper, fluid, wheel, bearing, stub axle, or CV joint—additional means must be found to dissipate heat from the rotor.

The most common solution is to install vented rotors. A vented rotor is constructed with air passages radiating out from the center of the disc. As heat builds up on the outer surfaces of the rotor, it is dissipated both from the outside surfaces and through the air channel between the two friction surfaces of the rotor. The natural cooling process is aided by the fact that as the rotor spins, air in the channel is thrown out by centrifugal force, with cool air being sucked in to replace it through the center of the rotor. Next time you see a race car, note that the brake-cooling air ducts feed the center of the rotor, instead of blowing on the friction surface of the rotor, for this very reason.

Brake Pads

The stock brake pads are designed to wear out before the rotors. They are soft and do not squeak much, and if you are lucky they do not make much dust, either. For high-performance use they will do, but there are other options.

The most common choice is the so-called semimetallic pad. These pads are harder than the stock pad and may squeak a little more, but they do last longer and stop better. The drawback is that the harder the pad is the quicker the rotor wears out. You can use a harder pad if fade is a problem, but the harder the pad the more time it takes to warm up, and the more aggressively it wears the rotor.

Brake Squeak

Some brake squeak comes from the normal interference between the pad and the disk. There is not much you can do

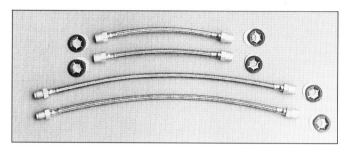

A braided stainless brake line set for an A1. Later sets require five or six lines to replace all the rubber brake lines. Get lines with swagged ends, so no adapters are required.

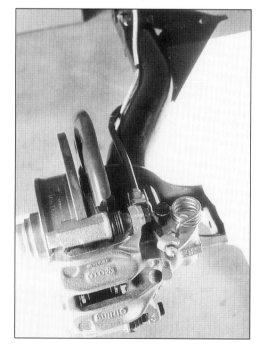

Cars with rear drums can be upgraded to rear disc brakes using all factory parts, with the addition of a proportioning valve.

about this, however, a considerable amount of the noise comes from the backs and sides of the pad where it touches the caliper. This noise you can do something about.

Use high-temperature moly grease to lightly coat the back and sides of the brake pad backing plate, as well as the mounting hardware, such as the pins and spreaders. This eliminates most of the noise. Perma-Tex and others make special compounds for this use. Whichever you choose, *do not* get any on the pad material.

Slotting the Pads

When you apply the brakes, the friction between the pad and the rotor creates heat and brake dust. Some of this dust finds its way between the pad and the rotor and decreases braking efficiency. Most Porsche pads come with a slot in the middle to allow this dust and heat to escape. Some Volkswagen pads do not have this feature, but it is easy to add with a hacksaw if you cannot locate pads that come already slotted.

Bedding the Pads

Brand-new pads (and shoes) need to be broken in before they will work properly. For street use, you might never notice the difference between bedded and unbedded brake linings. For racing, bedding the pads is a *must*. Bedding the pads may also help avoid glazing on the rear pads of newer cars.

The process for bedding brake pads is not new, and a good treatment of the subject can be found in Carroll Smith's *Prepare to Win*. He recommends warming up the pads with a couple of medium-strength stops, then following up with a high-speed "burn-in" conducted someplace where you have enough room both in front (in case the pads do not bed) and behind (to prevent being rear-ended). Visual examination is required to determine if the pads are bedded or not. The top 1/8 to 3/16 inch of a properly bedded pad will be a gray-brown, in contrast to the normal gray or black color that is found with new pads.

Drilling or Slotting the Rotors

Drilling the rotors is an expensive way to avoid slotting your pads, but it does look trick, and hundreds of racers cannot be all wrong. The holes also provide more surface area for the rotor to promote cooling.

One problem with drilled rotors is that they tend to develop heat cracks. Even on the Porsche rotors that have the holes cast in place, you can sometimes see heat cracks. Drilling the rotor creates stress risers (small areas that are prone to crack) everywhere on an already stressed surface. Heat cracks are inevitable.

Nowadays drilled rotors are readily available through the aftermarket. If you have a set of drilled rotors that are heat cracked, be sure the cracks do not extend through to the inside of the cooling vent. Even if the cracks do not look serious, take the wheels off often to check on their progress.

If you decide to drill your own rotors, follow a 3-2-3 pattern, drilling between the webs (if you have vented discs). The holes must be chamfered both for stress reasons and to avoid the cheese grater effect that unchamfered holes have on brake pads.

Because of these and other problems, drilled rotors are taking a second place to slotted rotors. Slotting the rotors helps vent the dust and hot gases from the pad, which increases braking efficiency. Cooling isn't improved, as it is with drilling, but slotting is preferable for street use because you don't have to replace the rotors as often.

Remember that the brake rotor is a rotating assembly, so after you remove metal you will need to get the rotor balanced again. This can be the most difficult part of the

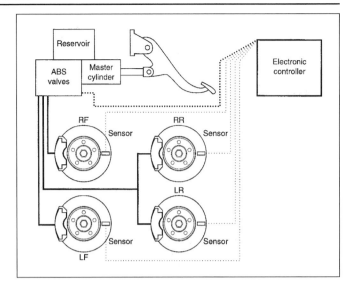

ABS systems monitor wheel rotation in case wheels lock up during braking.

Although expensive, rear disc brakes are an easy bolt-on.

operation; it might be a good idea to locate someone who can balance a rotor before you plunge into this project. Also, keep track of your brake wear for the first few thousand miles or so, as the holes cause the pads to wear faster, chamfered or not.

Once you have installed drilled or slotted rotors, you may notice that brake pedal effort is marginally higher for the same braking effect, due to the slight reduction in surface area touching the brake pad, compared to a smooth rotor.

Upgrading the Front Brakes

The easiest and least expensive way to upgrade your brakes is to replace worn parts with better-quality parts during normal maintenance and repair. Therefore, Stage 1 consists of replacing worn brake pads with semimetallic pads, flushing and

This homemade drilled rotor really reduces stopping distances, but it also tends to crack.

The 10.1-inch vented front rotor from the 16V.

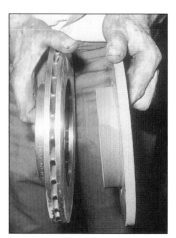

Vented rotors versus solid rotors.

bleeding the brake system using high-quality brake fluid (see "Brake Fluid"), and replacing cracked or otherwise suspect brake lines. For more on selecting brakes lines, see "Braided Stainless-Covered Teflon Brake Lines."

If you are planning to upgrade the rear brakes from drums to rotors, you may need to change the master cylinder to match, which is something to consider if your master cylinder goes bad. If you find yourself in the situation where you need to service your master cylinder but you aren't ready to spring for the whole front and rear upgrade, master cylinders can be rebuilt with care. Many repair shops won't do this type of work because of the liability involved, but with care and a couple of tools, you can safely rebuild your existing master cylinder so it will get you through until upgrade time.

A1 Front Brakes

Where front brakes are concerned, the A1 chassis designation includes all Rabbit, Scirocco, Jetta 1, and Fox automobiles. Where Stage 1 optimizes the brakes you already have, Stage 2 involves the installation of 9.4-inch vented rotors on cars with drums or solid rotors. On cars sold through the middle of 1980 with the small brake pads, you also will need to replace your calipers, and 1975–1976 cars with Girling calipers will need new brake lines. The later cars with the "banana" pads will accept the wider vented rotors fine, although you must use thinner pads. These upgrades can be purchased from the dealer, but it is usually less expensive to buy them as a kit from an aftermarket performance house.

The third stage is for drivers who are serious brake users. This involves trading in your current setup for the 16V rotors and calipers, or for the even larger 11-inch aftermarket rotors. The 10.1-inch rotors offer nearly 25 percent more swept area for braking, and will really stop you in a hurry. One drawback is that clearance between the caliper and the inside of the wheel may be a problem. The 13-inch steel wheels will rub, so you must use at least 14-inch wheels. The 11-inch rotors require at least 15-inch wheels, although not all 15-inch wheels will clear, so check first before buying. As a rule of thumb, 15-inch (or larger) wheels designed to fit the Corrado G-60 should work. You can also have these rotors cross-drilled for better venting and increased resistance to fade, although this does shorten rotor and brake pad life.

A2 Front Brakes

Cars with A2 front brakes include the Golf 2, Jetta 2, and Corrado. On these cars, the caliper attaches to the wheel bearing housing in such a way that changing to a larger rotor requires replacing the housing as well. Fortunately, there is enough clearance in the stock components to allow for easy change-over from the thinner solid rotors to the thicker vented rotors without having to change anything else. As always, 11-inch rotors require at least 15-inch wheels, and cross-drilling is an option.

When upgrading from the 9.4-inch brakes (solid or vented), 1985–1988 Golfs will also require new front hubs and new lower ball joints, as will the 1985–1987 Jetta 2.

Slotting the pads allows brake dust and hot gases to escape from between the pad and rotor for better braking.

A3 Front Brakes

A3 models include the Golf 3 and Jetta 3. At this level, the hot setup starts with the late-model VR6 rotors and adds special high-performance dual-piston calipers. The advantage of dual-piston calipers is that the trailing piston can be larger than the leading piston. This equalizes the pressure applied to the back of the brake pad, which not only improves braking, but also maximizes pad life. The 11-inch rotors need wheels that will clear; the 11.3-inch rotors require five-bolt wheels which, if you don't have them already, means you will need to upgrade the rears to match so you don't have different bolt patterns at the front and rear of the car. For extreme use you can have the rotors cross-drilled.

A4 Front Brakes

Judging by the brakes on the New Beetle, the Golf and Jetta IV will have 10.6 inch rotors up front, with five-bolt wheels.

Bigger brakes seem to be the wave of the future. EIP Tuning, for example, now offers a monstrous 13-inch brake kit, for which you will need 17-inch wheels for clearance.

Upgrading Rear Brakes

Weight distribution of the car at rest is heavily biased toward the front. During deceleration, even more weight is transferred to the front, resulting in very little weight in the rear. Therefore, putting a set of force-cooled vented rotors on the rear of the car will not perk up the braking performance by very much. You can check this by keeping track of how fast your rear brake shoes need adjustment or wear out. Typically, you will go through five or more sets of front pads before the rear shoes need attention. Rear rotors will fade less than rear drums, however, making them very handy for those occasional canyon runs, slalom events, and road courses.

For front brakes, you can easily and inexpensively upgrade their performance by switching to high-performance pads. For the rear drum brakes, "high-performance shoes" is an oxymoron. Because of the front weight bias of the VW under braking, however, the stock rear shoes work fine as long as they are in proper adjustment.

This still leaves two stages to upgrading the rear drums. The first stage involves fitting the larger 200-millimeter rear drums, backing plates, and shoes from a Dasher, Pickup, or Audi Fox. This method allows the use of the existing wheel cylinders and parking brake cable.

For Stage 2, rear rotors are the only way to go. The kits are expensive, because the conversion requires new rotors, calipers, stub axles, brake lines, brake cables, carriers, dust shields, and other hardware. The conversion also requires proportioning valves.

Proportioning Valves

With upgraded front rotors and rear drums, your car will stop great—the first couple of times. If you are hard on brakes and are experiencing fade, it is time to consider trading in the rear drums and shoes for rotors and pads. Because calipers and rotors work differently than shoes and drums, the brake balance needs to be adjusted when you upgrade from rear drums to rear rotors. This is typically done with a proportioning valve. Without the proper proportioning valve, the rears will lock up before the fronts, putting you wildly out of control as the rear end of the car passes the front of the car on its way to the accident you are about to have.

Another aspect of brake performance that is related to weight distribution is the effect of the proportioning valve that is found on some Volkswagens. This little item, located near the rear axle, senses any decrease in ride height from stock, and then increases the rear brake bias on the assumption that the decrease in ride height is due to a heavy load of cargo in the trunk. If you lower your car, the proportioning valve will be tricked into thinking that there needs to be more rear brake bias. If you find you are locking up the rear brakes in your lowered car during panic stops, this is the reason.

Master Cylinders

The stock master cylinder will be fine as it is, unless you upgrade the rear drums to rotors, in which case some cars will need to upgrade to a 22-millimeter master cylinder as well. The larger diameter makes it possible for the master cylinder to provide enough pressure to the calipers without excessive pedal travel. Although this master cylinder bolts up to the later German-built cars, some of the earlier German-built A1 cars will need a replacement vacuum booster and fluid reservoir, and the brake pedal linkage will need to be modified (or replaced) on U.S.-built A1 cars. Check with the supplier of your rear rotor conversion kit to see if a larger master cylinder is called for in your application.

Solid rotors drilled in a 3-2-3 pattern.

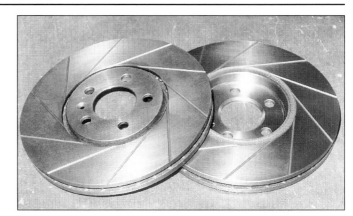

Slotting rotors improves braking, with fewer problems from cracking, compared with drilled rotors.

Vented rotors are drilled so the holes do not penetrate the webs.

Braided Stainless-Covered Teflon Brake Lines

Stock rubber lines are fine and will last for many years before needing replacement. However, being rubber, and being that the braking system sees pressures on the far side of 300 psi when you apply your foot to the brake pedal smartly, the insides of the lines are going to deflect at least a little, absorbing some of the energy that you are contributing with your foot.

The braided stainless lines use Teflon instead of rubber, and Teflon does not deflect nearly as much as the rubber does. Hence, the energy of your pushing on the brake pedal is transmitted with more fidelity to the calipers. The brake pedal feels firmer too.

Replacing the front brake lines is easy. The job will be much less messy if you depress and hold the brake pedal before and during this time you have the brakes lines off. This prevents the brake fluid in the reservoir from running out all over the floor. Always use line, also called flare-nut, wrenches, rather than common open-ends, when working with brake lines.

Replacing the rear lines, especially the right rear line on A1 cars, can be difficult. Be patient, use line wrenches for maximum grip and minimum damage, and if all else fails put the car on jack stands, place a jack beneath the rear torsion beam and remove the four bolts holding the torsion beam to the chassis. *Carefully* lower the torsion beam until you can get to the rear brake lines.

Once you can reach the line itself, you may find that it is still difficult to break the fitting loose. There is little room for two flare-nut wrenches, so if the fitting does not yield easily you will have to take more drastic measures. I do not normally recommend this as a procedure, but you can cut the brake line and use a deep socket to grab one end of the fitting.

When you're through, thoroughly bleed the brakes until the pedal is firm again. Remember to monitor the brake fluid level in the reservoir while you bleed the brakes; if the reservoir runs dry and you start pumping air through the braking lines, you will have to completely bleed the brake system all over again.

Before you take the car off the jack stands to go for a test drive, wipe all connections dry with a rag, and then ask a friend to apply the brakes steadily while you crawl underneath and look for leaks. It is embarrassing to make a mistake working on an engine. It is deadly to make a mistake working on the brakes.

One thing to watch out for with the braided stainless lines is that they will wear right through whatever they come up against. Route the lines in such a way that they do not interfere with any other components.

There is no DOT (Department of Transportation) approved braided stainless brake line, while the factory rubber lines are DOT approved. However, braided stainless lines rarely come apart.

Still, because of their abrasiveness, their lack of DOT approval, and their cost, braided stainless-cover Teflon lines are not for everyone, and the average enthusiast will get great performance from a set of stock rubber brake hoses in good condition.

Wherever you buy your lines, you should not have to put up with adapter fittings. Look around until you find brake lines that mount up the same way the factory lines do.

Brake Fluid

For a while, silicone brake fluid seemed to be the hope of the future. It does not absorb moisture out of the air the way glycol-based fluids do, its boiling point is higher and it is mild on seals. Silicone fluid has been rated DOT 5 by virtue of its physical properties.

The higher boiling point is nice, but the really great thing about silicone brake fluid is that it is not hydroscopic, as DOT 3 and DOT 4 fluids are. When water gets into your brake fluid not only does the boiling point plummet, but your internal brake parts are wide open to corrosion.

When upgrading to rear discs it, is critical to correct the front-to-rear brake bias with a proportioning valve, such as this one.

Table 51: A1 front brake upgrades

Stock	Stage 2	Stage 3
9.1" drums	9.4" vented rotors, calipers, carriers, and pads. Early cars (1975-6) may require new brake lines.	10.1" or 11" vented rotors, with new calipers, carriers, and pads. (See note about wheel clearance.) Optional: cross-drill and/or slot the rotors.
9.4" solid rotors with small pads		
9.4" solid rotors with "banana" pads		
9.4" vented rotors with "banana" pads	No change needed.	
10.1 vented rotors		11" vented rotors, etc.

A1 front brake upgrades.

Table 52: A2 front brake upgrades

Stock	Stage 2	Stage 3
9.4" solid rotors	9.4" vented rotors and pads.	10.1" or 11" vented rotors, with new calipers, bearing housings, and pads. Optional: cross-drill and/or slot the rotors.
9.4" vented rotors		
10.1" vented rotors	No change necessary.	11" vented rotors with new calipers, bearing housings, and pads. Optional: cross-drill and/or slot the rotors.
11" vented rotors		Optional: cross-drill and/or slot the rotors.

A2 front brake upgrades.

Table 53: A3 front brake upgrades

Stock	Stage 2	Stage 3
10.1" vented rotors	11" vented rotors, with new calipers, bearing housings, and pads.	11.3" vented rotors, with dual-piston calipers, carriers, adaptor brackets, and pads. Optional: cross-drill and/or slot the rotors.
11" vented rotors		
11.3" vented rotors	No change necessary.	Dual-piston calipers, carriers, adaptor brackets, and pads. Optional: cross-drill and/or slot the rotors.

A3 front brake upgrades.

Table 54: A4 front brake upgrades

Stock	Stage 2	Stage 3
10.6" vented rotors	Cross-drilling and/or slotting.	11.3" vented rotors, with optional cross-drilling and/or slotting.

A4 front brake upgrades.

These big brakes need the clearance afforded by the Abt two-piece 17x7.5-inch rims.

Rear disc brakes with drilled rotors.

So silicone brake fluid (DOT 5) is demonstrably better than glycol-based brake fluid, but if ever there was a product aimed narrowly at the enthusiast market, this is it.

Because DOT 5 fluid must be miscible with DOT 3 and DOT 4 fluid by law, you can mix DOT 5 fluid with either of the other types. This is a long way from saying that you can simply pour silicone fluid in on top of your old DOT 3, however. Every drop of DOT 3 or DOT 4 fluid that is left in the system will reduce the positive characteristics of the silicone fluid by that much.

The worst area, and the area for which most people are switching to silicone brake fluid, is the wheel cylinders. Tests conducted by a major automobile manufacturer show that even after a complete flush, there are still pockets of old fluid in the wheel cylinders. Because silicone brake fluid floats on top of glycol-based brake fluid, the remaining glycol-based brake fluid in the system will allow corrosion to continue.

The bottom line is, if you are going to use silicone fluid, you must disassemble everything and thoroughly clean all traces of old fluid before switching over. This includes flushing the brake lines. This can be a real problem because whatever you use to flush with also must be removed. If you use alcohol and then blow out the lines with an air gun, keep in mind that many air tanks and air lines have a lot of moisture in them, so you could be blowing water back into your nice clean brake lines.

Once you decide to take everything apart, you might as well go to the dealer and purchase all new seals. If you do the job right, this will be the last time the brake system will be apart.

Bleeding a brake system that uses silicone fluid is yet another challenge, but at least you are nearing the end. Silicone brake fluid is more viscous than glycol-based brake fluid, so it will trap and hold air bubbles for a lot longer time. When you decant the silicone brake fluid into your system,

exercise extra care not to aerate the fluid. As a precaution, you can carefully pour the silicone fluid through a clean piece of screen to remove air bubbles.

The bleeding process itself should be done slowly to minimize aeration of the silicone fluid. In spite of all your precautions, there is a good possibility that you will be left with a spongy pedal. If so, bleed the brakes again every couple of days until the sponginess is gone, or until you get tired of the whole mess and switch back to glycol-based fluid and yearly maintenance. In some cases it is just not possible to get the air bubbles out of the fluid.

It is things like this for which they invented the category of "trick" stuff. Trick stuff is stuff that works great, but is so expensive or time-consuming that almost nobody will do what it takes to use it.

The reason silicone fluid is not installed at the factory is ABS. The Bosch ABS has small fluid passages through which response time is critical if the ABS is to function properly. The higher viscosity of silicone fluid is not ideal for this application.

For the near future, automotive engineers are working on a DOT 4+ fluid that will be better than the current DOT 4 while retaining compatibility with ABS. This new fluid might approach DOT 5 in many of the performance areas—and if there is still a problem with moisture absorption, you can always continue flushing your brakes once a year.

In the meantime, if you are not ready to experiment with silicone fluid (or you have a car with ABS), there are some great "conventional" brake fluids such as Castrol LMA (Low Moisture Absorption) and Lucas Girling DOT 5.1. Volkswagen recommends changing the fluid every two years, but it doesn't hurt to do it more often, and if you have spent a small fortune on brake upgrades, a shorter service interval is cheap insurance. Remember to change your fluid more often if you live in an area that is humid or has frequent rainfall.

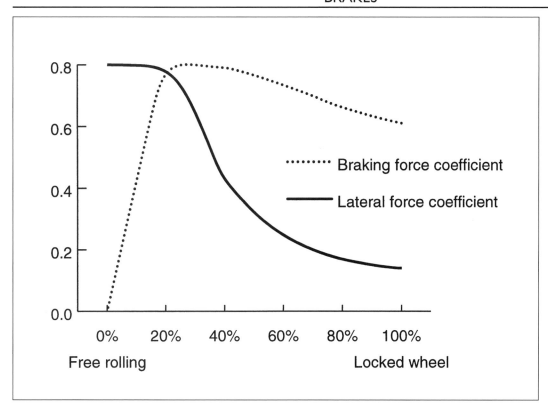

Maximum braking and cornering mean keeping the tires from slipping. Traction goes down as the wheels lock up.

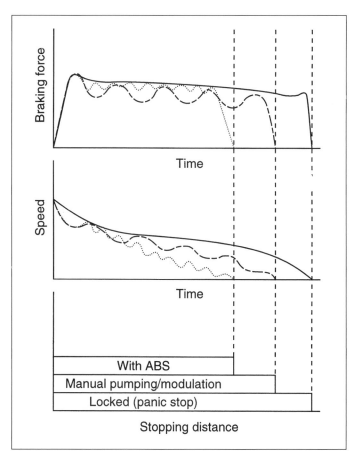

Modulating the brake pedal produces shorter stopping distances than stomping on the pedal and holding it, and ABS systems modulate the brakes faster and more accurately than any human.

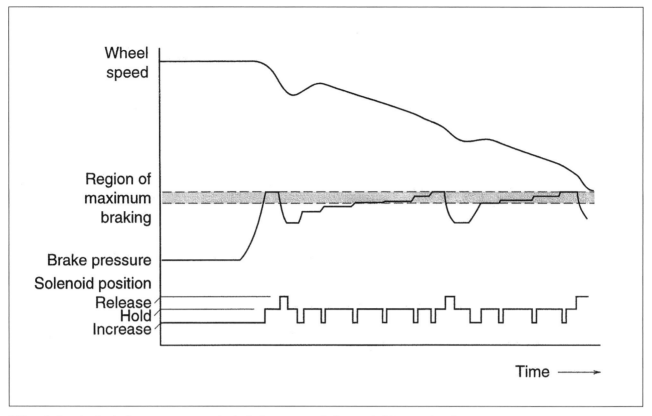

ABS works by releasing brake pressure to any wheel cylinder to prevent lock-up, optimizing stopping distances.

Silicone brake fluid has its uses, but for most street applications, it's too much trouble.

Keeping the brake pedal depressed minimizes brake fluid loss when you open the brake lines.

Chapter 15

Body and Chassis

Straightening Your Car After a Wreck

With the unibody construction of the new cars, such as the water-cooled Volkswagens, straightening everything back out after a collision is something not every collision repair shop can handle.

When shopping for a collision repair facility, make sure the shop you choose has a piece of equipment called a *bench*. With a bench, the car can be precisely measured and pulled back into alignment so it won't drive down the street sideways. If the chassis of your car has been bent in a collision, it is almost impossible to fix it without a bench.

Another consideration when having a major repair done on your car (such as installing a *clip*, when a large piece from another car is used to replace a damaged piece on your car) is that the collision repair shop use MIG (Metal Inert Gas) welding equipment. MIG welding uses an inert gas to flood the spot where the welding is taking place. This inert gas prevents oxygen from getting into the weld and reducing the strength of the joint. Gas welding is not adequate because it is impossible to gas weld and maintain the integrity of the metal. Remember, without a frame, the chassis has to withstand all the stress itself. Do not accept a major repair to your vehicle that does not make use of a bench and MIG welding, and don't even think about buying a used vehicle that was repaired after a major accident without the use of a bench and MIG welder.

For racing and other high-stress use, you will want to strengthen the chassis to reduce body flex. The factory adds inner fender panels on its rally cars, and seams (especially on the front shock towers) are fully welded (as opposed to spot welded). A properly designed and installed roll cage will triangulate the chassis from front to rear, making everything stiffer, contributing to better handling.

Stress Bars

Stress bars were in demand in the A1 cars because there was so much chassis flex, and the suspension pick-up points were not supported very well. With each new chassis type, Volkswagen has added strength to the chassis, but if you really push your car, you need to consider adding stress bars to reinforce the suspension pick-up points. For details on using stress bars to reinforce the suspension, see "Front Stress Bars" and "Rear Stress Bars."

These full leather Recaros can even make long-distance drives comfortable.

A roll cage should fit tight against the roof.

Body Kits

One of the most difficult things to test properly is a body kit that is to be used on a street vehicle. The changes in performance are usually subtle, the kits can be fairly trying to

189

With deep side and seat bolsters, these Scheels are more difficult to get into and out of, but they do provide more lateral support for high-performance cornering.

A body kit with fender flares and side skirts.

install properly, and to really understand what is happening, you need a wind tunnel.

In lieu of a wind tunnel, buying German body kits is the best way of ensuring that you are not ruining the aerodynamics of your car. In Germany, the government tests all kits for several qualities, including one that specifies that the body kit not degrade the fuel economy of the car as delivered from the factory. This does not mean the kit will help your car, just that it will not hurt it.

If you decide to install body parts, there are a few things to consider. First, between the manufacturing tolerances of your car and the manufacturing tolerances of the body kits, some discrepancies are bound to arise. This means that you should not start installing your full-body kit at four o'clock in the afternoon so your car will look sharp for your evening date. Leave yourself plenty of time. This also means that if you start to mount a kit part and it does not seem to fit very well, it is up to you to make it fit. Sending it back for an exchange more than likely will not solve the problem. Be ready to do some fabrication and fitting.

Second, plan ahead. Do not assume that if you buy an air dam today, in six months you will be able to buy front fender flares that integrate beautifully. Some parts are not meant to be used in combination with other parts, even when all the parts are from the same firm. If you want the whole kit, buy the whole kit—or be ready to do some fabrication.

Third, keep in mind that every time you drill a hole in your sheet metal for a sheet metal screw or a rivet, you are inviting rust to attack your car. If you must drill, clean the inside and outside surfaces of the sheet metal before drilling, and when installing the fastener coat it with silicone caulk (RTV). The silicone will help seal out the moisture and protect against corrosion.

Fourth, prepare yourself for the inevitable wreck. Fiberglass or hard-plastic body panels can be very resilient, but once their stress limit is exceeded they do let go, making it necessary to replace or repair them. If you have a fiberglass body kit, however, you may be able to do at least some of the repair yourself, with a little fiberglass and resin.

Air Dams

Although the air dam increases the frontal area of the car, it still manages to work as an aerodynamic device because it keeps air from getting underneath the car and creating drag. In fact, some air dams are so effective that brake-cooling ducts must be incorporated into the air dam to prevent the front rotors from cooking to death. Before the introduction of the Golf body style (which features subtle aerodynamic tailoring along the hood mating line), some enthusiasts were also blocking off as much of the front grille as possible to keep air from wandering through the engine compartment and causing trouble. Every little bit helps.

The factory chin spoiler that is common on the early Sciroccos is good for a 10 percent increase in gas mileage. The factory duckbill spoiler found on the early GTis is also very effective, although it will not fit American-built cars after 1978.

The factory Golf GTi spoiler available on the 1986-and-later cars is a very nice piece that incorporates brake-cooling ducts. This spoiler will fit the 1985 cars, because the body shape is similar, but it is more difficult to mount. On the 1986 cars that did not come with this spoiler (such as the Jetta), the sheet metal is formed to accept the spoiler easily, with no body modifications needed.

Wind Splits

Wind splits mount on the top edge of the front fenders or on either side of the hood. They work on the principle that directed air is smoother than air that chooses where it wants to go. By providing channels for directing the airflow over the top of the car, wind splits can theoretically help aerodynamics.

A-Pillar Fairings

A-pillar fairings first appeared on the Formula E (economy) cars, but they can be used on any early car that does not have the flush-mounted windshields and redesigned rain gutters.

A Rabbit spoiler where it will do the most good.

Volkswagen cleaned up the airflow in this area starting with the A2. On the A1 cars, however, the A-pillar fairings eliminate a good amount of drag from this problem area.

Rear Spoilers

Rear spoilers help the aerodynamics by keeping the airflow over the car attached as long as possible. Without an effective rear spoiler, the airflow wants to detach from the car soon after passing over the rear edge of the roof. This creates a turbulence and thus a drag at the rear of the car.

The problem with some spoilers is that they are so far out of the airflow that they cannot help do anything except make your car look different from someone else's. On a Rabbit, for example, a rear spoiler that is mounted below the rear window is not going to get enough air to make much of a difference to the airflow. A much smaller spoiler above the rear window will be much more effective.

A good example of this can be seen in the factory rear spoilers mounted on the Sciroccos. A small rear spoiler down low would not have done the job, so the factory used a fairly stout spoiler well up in the airflow. (Volkswagen has one of the best wind tunnels around, so it is not a surprise that the design works.) The factory Jetta GLi rear spoiler, although not very big, works because on the sedan there is still some airflow across the rear edge of the trunk.

Side Skirts

Side skirts not only make the car look lower, they can also help keep the sides of the car clean by preventing mud from splashing up off the road. As previously mentioned, it is a lot easier to buy the side skirts at the same time you buy the front spoiler and so on, to ensure that everything will fit together and that the overall effect will be what you want.

The air stream detaches coming over the back edge of the roof, so the spoiler must be high enough to be in the air stream.

If you don't need a passenger seat, putting the battery box here is a lot better than putting it in the trunk.

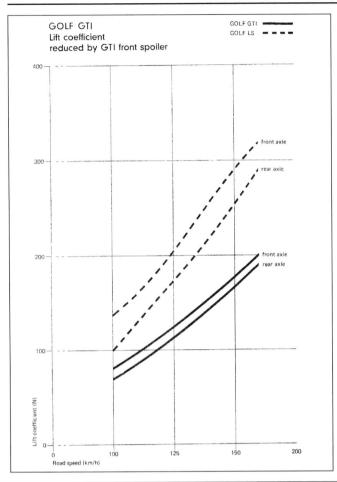

GOLF GTI
Lift coefficient
reduced by GTI front spoiler

GOLF GTI ——————
GOLF LS – – – –

A properly designed front spoiler helps reduce lift at both ends of the car.

Painting plastic surfaces

Type of part	Pre-treatment	Priming	Painting		
			One-step paints	Two-step paints	
			Non-metallic	Metallic base	Clear coat
Fiberglas	1. Wash off with soap and hot water 2. Roughen and with fine Scotch-brite 3. Rinse	Plasto-flex primer	Paint	Metallic base paint	Clear coat
ABS		Plasto-flex primer	3 paint to 1 flex	Metallic base paint	3 clean to 1 flex
Primed poly-urethane		Flexprime (if required)	2 paint to 1 flex	9 metallic paint to 1 flex	2 clear to 1 flex
Semi-hard polyurethane foam		Plasto-flex primer	2 paint to 1 flex	9 metallic paint to 1 flex	2 clear to 1 flex
Soft polyure-thane		Plasto-flex primer	2 paint to 1 flex	9 metallic paint to 1 flex	1 clear to 1 flex

Painting plastic surfaces

Chapter 16

Electrical Systems

Once you get used to working with Volkswagen electrical systems, you find that they are not at all unpleasant to deal with. Most German cars conform to the DIN standard for wiring numbers and functions, so in a pinch you might even be able to lend a hand to that Mercedes or BMW owner who finds himself stranded.

It is beyond the scope of this book to explain how to read a wiring diagram, but a few pointers on the descriptions of terminals are included in the following chart.

Volkswagen Electrical Terminal Numbering

Terminal	Description
4	High voltage (ignition coil, distributor)
15	Switched positive from battery or ignition switch output
30	Input direct from the battery positive terminal
31	Return direct to battery negative or ground
84	Combination relay contact and relay coil input
85	Relay coil ground
86	Relay coil hot
87	Relay contact, break when activated
88	Relay contact, make when activated
B+	Battery positive terminal
B-	Battery negative terminal
D+	Charging system positive output
D-	Charging system negative or ground
DF	Charging system field terminal

Ignitions

The electronic ignitions on the later cars is satisfactory for all but the most demanding use. In the newest cars, the ignition is integrated into an "engine management system," which also runs the fuel injection (and sometimes, other aspects of the car's operation as well), so modification or replacement is that much more difficult (modifications usually take the form of reprogramming the Engine Control Unit chip). If, however, you are running an early car with a points-condenser-coil ignition, you owe it to yourself to convert to a breakerless ignition, whether or not you are interested in high performance.

With an electronic ignition you can set it and forget it, and it will deliver peak performance for thousands and thousands of miles. In contrast, a points ignition begins to deteriorate almost from the moment it is installed.

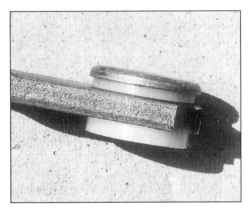

These two-piece Delrin bushings are stronger than the stock rubber item, and they don't melt away, so they last longer too.

If you have a points distributor and you do not trust electronic ignitions, at least treat yourself to an ignition that uses the points only as a trigger. This extends the life of the points and gives you some benefits due to improved ignition performance. Some of these systems allow you to revert back to the stock points-condenser-coil-setup in a few minutes.

Most units on the market use points, a photocell, or a magnet to trigger the ignition. Here are a few of the more popular setups.

Allison/Crane

The Allison ignition completely replaces your points with a photo-optical sensor and has a black box that mounts outside of the distributor to control the coil. The Allison is a little difficult to install in the Bosch distributor but once you get it in, it is fairly rugged. The Allison uses a red LED (light-emitting diode) as a light source, and it is very hard to get it to misread, even when the inside of the distributor is filthy.

The light beam is interrupted by a control rotor that slides onto the distributor shaft just underneath the distributor rotor. Because of the way the slots are cut in the control rotor, the Allison will tolerate a great deal of wobble in the distributor shaft. If you have a mildly worn-out distributor, the Allison might be able to extend its life.

Mount the black box in a cool place (under the cowling is fine) and make sure it is well grounded; you can get a shock from touching it while the motor is running.

Perlux

The Perlux Ignitor is a drop-in component that replaces your points, containing all the necessary electronics inside its

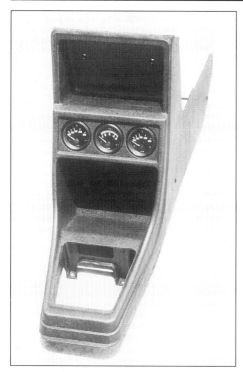

This stock early Scirocco center console fits early Rabbits with only a little modification and provides space for mounting three gauges.

Hella offers many different products for the VW, including map lights, electric horns, and, my favorite, the four-light grille for the early Rabbit.

and a condenser. You can keep a set in a plastic bag in the glovebox just in case.

If you are suspicious that a piece of electronic equipment could be subjected to the heat inside a distributor and still function perfectly, join the crowd. However, Perlux has millions of miles of experience with this unit, as the U.S. Postal Service utility vehicles all have Audi motors outfitted with Ignitors.

MSD

MSD stands for "multiple spark discharge." The principle behind its operation is that although a capacitive discharge (CD) ignition has a fantastic ability to deliver a high-energy spark to the spark plug, it does so over too short a time. The time is so short that the total area under the curve of a CD spark is less than with other types of ignition systems. MSD compensates for this lack of area under the curve by triggering the spark plug to fire multiple times at each spark instead of just once.

If this is the way it really worked it would be great, but multiple spark occurs only at low rpm. By 3,000 rpm, the typical street version of the MSD ignition is putting out only one CD-style spark.

MSD does makes same radical units for race use, but they are for race use only and are not recommended for street use.

Factory Breakerless

If you have an early car with a point-activated ignition, a reliable upgrade can be found in your local junk yard in the form of the later-style factory breakerless ignition. This system is more complex than the points-actuated setup, but with the shop manual you should be able to muddle through. Dyno tests show that this ignition is good up to 7,500 rpm without missing a beat.

Factory Knock-Sensor Ignition

This is currently the hottest ignition you can buy for Volkswagen. Using a digital "map," the knock-sensor ignition computer knows how much to advance the spark based on all the engine variables that fed into it. If it receives a signal from a small piezoelectric crystal that is mounted to the engine, it knows that detonation is taking place and it retards the spark in steps until the detonation disappears. It then constantly checks to see when it is all right to advance the timing again.

This ignition first appeared in 1985 on the GTi, the GLi, and the Audi 4000. On the Volkswagen motors it had a checking value of 14 degrees plus the ignition point at 4,300 rpm; Audi used 16 degrees plus the ignition point at 3,000 rpm. With more timing earlier on, the Audis had the edge in horsepower, just as if they had a recurved distributor. On top of this, the Audi rev limiter cut in between 6,570 and 6,630 rpm, much higher than the Volkswagen limit of 6,200 to 6,400 rpm. On the spec sheets, the Audi motor made 2 horsepower more. Because of the different advance curve, however, there was much more than a 2 horsepower difference in driving feel.

Here is the secret. Both cars used the identical ignition system. Audi felt that with its longitudinal motor it could get

black control head. The only clue from the outside of the distributor that something is different is that there are two wires coming out instead of one.

The Ignitor is triggered by a magnetic control rotor, which again slides on underneath the distributor rotor. Perlux includes a nonmagnetic feeler gauge to set the gap between the control head and the control rotor. This gap is somewhat critical, so your distributor has to be in good shape for best operation.

Because it uses the same mounting holes as the points, the Ignitor is very easy to install. If it ever fails, it should be a simple matter to remove the control head and install a set of points

The stock lighting setup can certainly be improved.

With quartz-halogen lights, the view ahead is remarkably better, side illumination is improved, and light scatter is reduced, as can be seen on the trees in the distance.

away with more spark advance. Volkswagen, with its transverse engine, was not sure it could. The ignition computer used in both cars has two different maps in it. To change your car from the Volkswagen map to the Audi map, pin 11 on the knock-sensor control unit (normally connected to ground) must be disconnected.

Is this safe to do? Apparently so. In 1986, Volkswagen started using the Audi map.

The knock-sensor ignition is available through your dealer, but at a list price of around $1,400. The junk yard is probably the best place to look for one.

If you are running an engine with the same combustion chamber dimensions and the same compression ratio as the factory motor, you will get the most from this ignition. If you are running stock compression you will not see much benefit from this setup, and for the cost and aggravation you should concentrate on other areas in your search for more horsepower.

If you are running anything different you may not see any benefits either. The ignition map is very precisely tailored to the engine it is mounted on. If you are using a much bigger cylinder bore, the flame front must be started earlier by the spark plug than in a small-bore engine. Thus, the knock-sensor ignition might actually be retarded from the position at which it would run best—unless you cranked in some more lead.

On the other hand, if you mounted this ignition on a motor with a smaller bore than the motor on which it came stock, the flame front would start too early, giving too much advance and really giving the knock sensor a workout—unless you cranked in less lead.

Bosch, which designed this ignition system, has over 2,000 engineers on the payroll working on nothing but automobile-related stuff, so it's a good bet that most do-it-yourselfers are not going to have the sophistication needed to mix-and-match the knock-sensor ignition with various engine configurations.

Distributors

The section on bolt-on horsepower mentioned that a recurved distributor was a good modification for a stock compression engine. Here is why. Advancing the timing improves the torque and helps mileage by fooling the motor into thinking the compression ratio is higher than it is. If the timing is advanced too much, however, detonation will occur. The earlier the spark plug fires, the earlier the flame front starts, so the higher the temperature of the combustion process. This increased oxides of nitrogen, which is why the early cars with EGR ran the timing retarded.

Even with the recurve, notice that the vacuum canister is retained. You may have seen advertised distributors for the Volkswagen that are referred to as the "009 version for the Rabbit." These distributors, like their Beetle counterparts, have no vacuum canister. The reason given is that you will get more horsepower with a straight mechanical advance distributor. I have not found this to be true for a couple of reasons.

First, the vacuum retard allows you to set the timing with enough initial lead to get the car off the mark in a hurry and without having to put up with a high idle. The vacuum retard works only when the throttle is closed, so it does not affect performance, and setting the idle on your car without a vacuum retard can sometimes be frustrating.

The vacuum advance comes in only when there is high vacuum in the intake manifold, which means only during part-throttle conditions. This additional advance extends mileage and makes the car run much nicer. When you plant your foot, the manifold vacuum goes away and you are right back to the mechanical advance, so you are not giving up anything.

The mechanical advance distributor is not recommended except for racing use, where it does have a slight advantage over the more complex vacuum-assisted distributor.

If you are running a modified distributor (so the factory specifications do not apply to you), aim for about 36 degrees of total advance. With a 009 distributor, this means running about 14 degrees of initial.

The ideal lighting setup; fog lights are low enough to see over but high enough for ground clearance; driving lights are higher for better "throw."

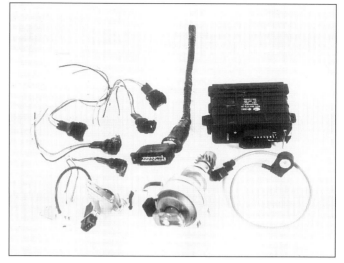

This is the way you might buy a factory knock-sensor ignition from the junkyard. From the dealer, this ignition is expensive.

After setting the timing, warm up the engine and try a couple of hard acceleration runs. If you can hear any detonation at all, back the timing off in two-degree increments until it goes away. Listen carefully; detonation can be difficult to hear over the other noises in the car, especially when the pinging is just beginning to come in.

Servicing

It is amazing how many people fail to service their distributors. It is also unfortunate, because they last a lot longer with a little care. All you have to do is pop off the distributor cap and rotor, and put a couple of drops of motor oil on the felt pad. The oil eventually trickles down and keeps the inner shaft free so your timing can advance and retard the way it is supposed to.

If you have a distributor with points in it, never install a set of points without lubricating the points cam with Bosch points grease. It comes in black-and-yellow tubes and can be found just about everywhere. A tube will last forever unless you work on cars for a living, and then you should not expect to get much more than four or five years out of it.

If you perform your own periodic maintenance, it takes only a second to pop the cap and check to see if the points cam is lubed. Your points will stay set longer because the rubbing block won't be wearing away as fast. In some cars, the points cams become so dry that the rubbing block squeaks loudly. Don't let this happen to yours.

Installing

Unless you are swapping your early ignition for one of the late knock-sensor ignitions, it is pretty simple to remove and replace the distributor. A special wrench used to be available from Snap-On (it was meant for a Pinto, but it fit the Volkswagen, too) that made it a much easier job to get to the distributor hold-down bolt. If you plan on doing a lot of work

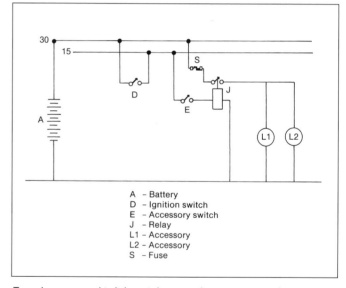

A - Battery
D - Ignition switch
E - Accessory switch
J - Relay
L1 - Accessory
L2 - Accessory
S - Fuse

To make sure your big lights, air horns, and stereo gear get the power they need, run them off relays. The wire to the relays should be good and thick, and the distance between the relay and the accessory should be as short as possible.

on Volkswagens bend, weld, or fabricate a wrench to the same general dimensions.

Before you remove the distributor, turn the engine to TDC. If you remove the distributor cap, you can watch the rotor. Turn the engine until the rotor points to the mark on top of the distributor housing.

Remove the points wire or wires, remove the hold-down bolt and clamp, and pull the distributor out. Notice as it comes out that the rotor turns slightly so it no longer points exactly at the mark on the distributor housing. This is normal.

Have your points grease handy if you are working with a distributor that uses points. It takes only a little smear of Bosch

The Crane ignition uses a slotted control rotor, instead of points, to trigger the photocell.

grease to radically extend the life of your points rubbing block. Also check the area around the distributor drive hole to see that there is no dirt there waiting to fall into your motor.

Line up the rotor just the way it was after you pulled it out. In other words, it won't be pointing right at the mark on the distributor housing, it will be off to one side. Remember that the gears on the intermediate shaft and the distributor are cut at an angle, so as they mesh the rotor will want to turn.

Normally, you can simply slide the distributor in, and if you have lined up the gears the right way, the rotor will point at the mark on the distributor housing when the distributor is all the way down in the hole. If not, pull the distributor out and try again until it lines up.

Once in a while, the distributor will go down to within about 10 millimeters of being all the way in and stop. Pull it out, and check to see that the oil pump shaft drive tang is pointed in such a way that it can engage the drive slot in the bottom of the distributor. When the engine is at TDC, the tang should be parallel to the axis of the crankshaft.

When you get the distributor all the way down, check to see that none of your timing marks has moved and that the rotor is still pointing at the mark in the distributor housing. If so, replace the hold-down clamp and bolt, reconnect all the electrical connections, and replace the cap.

Spark Plugs

Can you read a spark plug and determine how the engine is running? If so, you are better than most. All those color charts in the shop manuals and spark plug catalogs fail to tell you two important things that you must know before you will be able to read a spark plug.

First, unleaded gas will give you a much more subtle spark plug picture than will leaded gas. Unleaded gas works differently in a motor than leaded gas, and the charts that appear in

the shop manuals usually show spark plugs that have been run on leaded. If you are using unleaded gas you are going to have to work harder to read the plugs.

Second, you can't just pull the plugs out any time and look at them. You need to run the engine under load (preferably under the load conditions that are causing you to check the plugs in the first place), then immediately shut it off and coast to the workshop (or pit) area.

Once you learn to read them though, keeping an eye on the condition of your plugs will allow you to anticipate problems.

A normal plug will have light tan deposit on the insulator nose. Fresh plugs have sharp corners on the center electrode. When those corners get rounded off, it's time for new plugs.

An overheated plug will have blistered or chalky deposits, and there may even be some glue showing between the center electrode and the insulator where it has melted out. The metal in the electrodes may also show heat discoloration.

An oil-fouled plug will have black, wet-looking deposits covering the insulator. The deposits will not easily rub off. This does not mean that your valve guide seals are leaking; your plugs will not show oil fouling even when you are going through a quart of oil every 250 miles. Oil on the plugs may, however, mean a worn guide, or a broken or unseated piston ring.

A fuel-fouled plug will have dry, fluffy black deposits that will wipe off.

As far as spark plug choices are concerned, it is very difficult to do better than the Bosch plug that is specified for your engine. For example, the much-advertised SplitFire plug seems to work better at first—which is logical, based on the fact that it has much more of the sharp "edge" on the ground electrode than a standard spark plug—but performance can drop off rapidly thereafter, and the quality of the plug itself is nowhere near that of a Bosch.

If you want to experiment with other plugs, make certain that the plugs you try have rolled threads rather than cut threads. If the threads are rolled (that is, the threads are formed by rolling the spark plug body between thread-shaped rollers), the threads will be smoother, which translates to less wear and tear on your aluminum cylinder heads. Cut threads are made with a die, and you can see the jagged edges on the threads. Die-cut threads are usually found on cheaper, mass-produced spark plugs.

Another thing you can do to preserve the spark plug holes in your cylinder heads is to use a little antiseize compound on the spark plug threads during installation. Note that if you use the same amount of torque to tighten a spark plug that has antiseize on the threads as you would with a bare plug, the plug with the antiseize will actually be tighter in the cylinder head because there is less friction during the tightening process. Therefore, set your torque wrench to the low side of the torque spec, just to be on the safe side.

Engine Management Chips

Between the growing concern over engine exhaust emissions and the seemingly opposing desires for more horsepow-

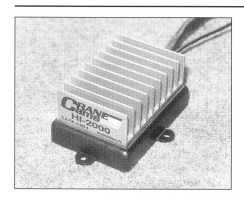

Crane's high-quality transistorized ignition replaces the points and gives a hotter, more reliable spark.

This is the stock Perlux mounting plate. In some distributors, the point at the top of the plate hits the vacuum-advance arm.

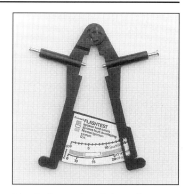

The flash test doesn't have the sophistication of a diagnostic scope, but for its small price, it tells you a lot about your ignition.

er and lower fuel consumption, the days of the carburetor were numbered. If you've ever compared the underhood view of a modern, fuel-injected, computer-controlled engine with that of a late-1970s carbureted engine, with all its vacuum lines, you will be glad they "don't build them like they used to." Stiffer emissions standards forced automakers to add so many extra components to the engine to compensate for the deficiencies of the carburetor that it sometimes seemed you couldn't even see the engine beneath all the emissions control equipment. The modern engine—even with all its sensors, control harnesses, and separate fuel injectors for each cylinder—seems stripped by comparison.

The advantage of all the sensors, control harnesses, computers, and other fuel injection components is that rather than asking a simple device such as a carburetor to control the increasingly complex parameters of an internal combustion engine in the modern age, you can have a sophisticated, fast-acting, computer control just about everything that needs controlling.

In order to do this, the computer must control not only the fuel injection, but also the ignition. By monitoring engine temperature, intake air temperature, engine speed, throttle position (or the amount of air entering the engine), the composition of gasses in the exhaust, and other metrics of engine status, the computer can calculate the correct amount of fuel and spark advance for just about every imaginable situation.

As amazing as these engine management systems are, there's more to them.

To start with, they are set by the automaker to deliver acceptable performance over a wide range of conditions, using a wide range of octanes, without allowing engine emissions to deteriorate for 50,000 miles. If they program the computer incorrectly and engine emissions are excessive before the 50,000-mile mark, they can be heavily fined by various government entities, and made to recall and repair all other similar vehicles. This is powerful inducement to err on the side of caution. Furthermore, although some of these systems are "adaptive," meaning they learn about peculiarities of the engine

and adapt to compensate, they don't have enough latitude to compensate for engine modifications such as free-flow exhaust, a more aggressive camshaft, etc. However, the chip that controls the engine can be modified, as well.

When these chip-controlled engine management systems were first introduced, only the automakers had the equipment to program (or "burn") the chips. With the proliferation of computer-controlled engine management systems, however, has come the proliferation of aftermarket sources for reprogrammed chips. This is just as well, because even though the technology for burning chips has filtered down to the hot-rodder, it can be very difficult to develop a better engine-management program. To put it another way, even if you could easily grind your own camshaft, you probably wouldn't do it because of the difficulty in coming up with a workable cam lobe profile. Programming these chips is best left to those with the time and inclination to spend the hours necessary to do the job right.

When the job is done right, several factors are taken into consideration. First and foremost, aftermarket chip providers take advantage of the fact that they know you are going to be using 92 octane fuel all the time, where automakers have to leave some slack for cars running 87 octane.

Higher octane means the engine can accept a more aggressive ignition advance curve without melting down. However, the computer controls all aspects of engine performance, and the programmer can put in more advance just where it is needed, leaving the driveability the same for smooth part-throttle performance.

The chip also controls the amount of fuel fed to the engine, but this doesn't mean that an aftermarket chip dumps fuel in and expects the engine to somehow make horsepower. Instead, the fuel delivery is fine-tuned for performance driving, so you can achieve the elusive goal of having more power and equal or better drivability without sacrificing fuel economy. Of course, if you change the way you drive, you will more than likely change your fuel economy. Unlike a bigger engine that uses more fuel all the time whether or not you are demanding more from your engine, a properly set up chip can virtually

The ground mounting plate should fit easily without touching the advance arm.

To install the Perlux, first remove the points and check the internal ground strap. The condenser comes off next.

duplicate your existing mileage, but still have more horsepower on tap whenever you need it.

Another reason why chip programmers don't simply dump in a lot more fuel and hope for the best (in addition to the fact that this could be fatal for your catalytic convertor and even your engine) is that in order to be sold legally in states with tough emissions laws, such as California, the "chipped" engine still has to pass emissions testing. Too much fuel means too much pollution to pass the "smog" test.

In addition to all this, many chips also reset the rev limit of the engine to a higher point—which is particularly welcome on modified engines—and some chip programmers remove the speed limiter in the chip. The rev limiter can be eliminated too, but leaving it in helps safeguard your engine.

Aftermarket chips are available for most Volkswagens from 1990 and newer, equipped with Digifant or Motronic injections. There are a lot of sources for off-the-shelf chips, but if you need a custom chip for an unusual combination of engine components, Advanced Motorsport Solutions is the place to go.

Wiring Modifications

Years ago, Bob Cousimano at CMW Racing noticed that seemingly small voltage drops between the engine and chassis, the engine and battery, and the chassis and battery in the Porsche 911 were causing significant reductions in horsepower due to the inability of the ignition and charging systems to function properly. These voltage drops don't show up in normal tests of the charging system, so if you didn't know what

you were seeking, you could spend a lot of time trying to find missing horsepower.

The reason for the voltage drops is deteriorated connections between the ends of charging system cables and the cable ends themselves. The cable ends can look and feel fine, while still not performing correctly. This is because a good electrical joint has two properties: physical integrity and electrical integrity. Typically, even the oldest connections have physical integrity; internal corrosion (oxidation), however, may have reduced the electrical integrity.

This syndrome is most likely to surface on older cars, but any car can benefit from resoldering the crimped connectors in the charging system loop, which includes the connection between the alternator and battery positive and the connection between the battery negative and chassis ground. An additional ground can also be run between the battery negative and the alternator housing.

New Dimensions' approach is to replace the alternator-to-battery and battery-to-chassis harnesses with new, larger-gauge harnesses. New Dimensions also offers an auxiliary cable to connect the battery negative to the alternator housing.

To test for this problem, you will need a volt/ohm meter. First measure voltage between the alternator output and the battery positive terminal while the engine is running. If you see more than a fraction of a volt, you have a voltage drop problem. Second, measure between the negative terminal of the battery and the alternator housing. Again, any significant voltage reading means that the cables aren't doing their job. Finally, measure between the battery negative terminal or the

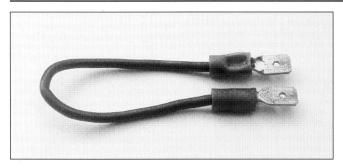

A homemade jumper for activating the fuel pump without the relay. I keep one in my toolbox and one in my glovebox.

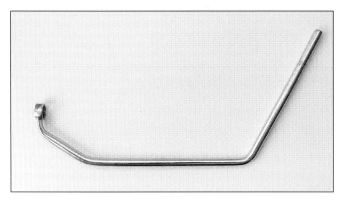

An angled wrench such as this makes it easier to adjust the distributor timing.

engine block and a good chassis ground. (On vehicles that connect the alternator to the battery positive by way of the starter, don't overlook the connections at the starter.)

Resoldering the cable ends is difficult to do with an electric soldering gun because you will need to heat the connection hotter than the electric soldering gun is capable of achieving. A better way is to use either one of those "personal size" butane torches or an acetylene torch. Before you solder, check to see that the connection between the cable and the cable end is physically tight. Also remember to use rosin-core solder, rather than acid-core. Get the connection hot enough that the solder "wicks" into the connection. Once the solder has wicked into the connection, do not move the connection until the solder has cooled enough to solidify. Moving a solder joint while the solder is still molten will result in a "cold solder" joint, which looks almost like a properly soldered joint, but which does not pass current as it should.

If your cables are in good physical condition, resoldering works surprisingly well. If the cables are questionable, or if you have a 90-amp alternator or a big stereo system, the heavy-gauge cable replacements are a better way to go. Either way, getting your charging and ground cables working properly will eliminate a host of potential problems.

Gauges

Volkswagen gauges are for the most part well placed and legible. With all the different trim levels and options over the years, there is no standard equipment in the way of gauges, however.

Instrument clusters from one Volkswagen will often bolt right into another Volkswagen, as long as the shape of the cluster is the same. For example, on the early Rabbits you can upgrade to the Scirocco instrument cluster (which includes a tachometer) by snapping out the stock unit and snapping in the Scirocco version (along with the necessary extra circuit board). All the wiring is there, ready to go. Likewise, the 120-mile-per-hour speedometer in the 1984 cars will drop into the 1983 cars with no other changes, and the 140-mile-per-hour instrument cluster from the 16V will replace the Scirocco instrument cluster. The parts can often be found at the junk yard.

VDO, the manufacturer of all these gauges, also offers an overwhelming assortment of other gauges in many sizes and styles. Several aftermarket suppliers offer three-across gauge panels that make it relatively simple to mount your most-needed gauges.

No two people will agree on what gauges are important, but I like to have a tachometer first, temperature gauges next (oil and exhaust gas), and then electrical (amps and volts). Supercharged motors should have boost pressure gauges.

Beyond that, the choices seem endless, considering the amount of space you have to fit them all into. Outside temperature gauges can be nice in colder climates for predicting the onset of road icing, vacuum gauges can help with engine problem diagnosis and fuel economy, and an engine-hour meter will impress your pilot friends.

Although VDO gauges are generally high quality, it is a good idea to calibrate the gauge when possible. Water and oil temperature gauges can be calibrated by dropping the sender into boiling water while it is connected to the system (remember to rig up a ground wire). Water boils at 212 degrees Fahrenheit at sea level. Voltage gauges can be checked against a test meter, as can ammeters, although a stand-alone ammeter is more difficult to find unless you know someone with an AVR (amp, volt, resistance charging system) tester.

The whole point of having gauges is to get better information for making certain decisions. If the information is wrong, you may make the wrong decisions, so make sure your gauges are accurate.

Lights

Headlights have two main characteristics: light output and pattern. Output refers to how bright the lamp is; pattern refers to the way the reflector disperses that brightness.

The output of the stock sealed-beam headlight (required on all U.S. cars since the 1930s) is relatively low, making it easy to out-drive your lights at night. Out-driving your lights occurs when you cannot see far enough ahead to allow yourself time to react at the speed you are driving. Europe has several good-quality kits available to convert to quartz-halogens headlights, but these are illegal in the United States. Fortunately, both GE and Sylvania offer sealed-beam halogens that are legal for use in the United States.

As poor as the traditional sealed beams are in terms of output, they are also wasteful in terms of pattern. The normal sealed-beam pattern sprays light in every direction, further degrading their effectiveness. For halogen headlights, the most popular (and useful) pattern is one with a very sharp horizontal cutoff to keep the light out of other people's eyes and down on the roadway where you need it. Some halogens also have an angled cutoff to the right of the horizontal cutoff for better illumination of the roadside.

Headlights are one of the three types of light that can be mounted at the front of the car, the other two being driving lights and fog lights. Each of these is a special-purpose lamp not to be confused with the other.

Driving lights typically have reflectors designed to project the beam a great distance down the road in a long, thin pattern. This is in addition to the greater amount of light they provide.

Fog lights are designed to be mounted low on the car. Having the lights low allows you to look out over the top of your lights, rather than through the light that is being reflected back at you. Fog lights are also lower powered than driving lights, but it is their position you are interested in, not their output. Too bright a fog light will merely add to the amount of reflected light, obscuring your vision as normal headlights do.

A fog light is also available for the rear, in the form of an auxiliary brake light. This is usually a single large light that produces very bright light for better visibility in the fog. You will not make many friends using this in stop-and-go traffic or in the city, however.

Another interesting brake light improvement is to convert the normal brake lights to use quartz bulbs. Automotive Performance Systems sells these, although I would recommend them only in situations where brake light visibility is a real problem.

Whether you opt for the more sedate legal halogens or the quad-bulb flame throwers you found at a Group B rally team's garage sale, you must have them properly aligned. A normal headlight is bad enough when pointing in people's eyes. A misaligned halogen can be deadly. This is true in day-to-day use as well as when you load up the rear of the car with heavy items and alter the ride angle of the car. You must also realign your headlights whenever you change the ride height.

Aside from the legal aspects of using halogen lights, there are other limitations to how much light you can run, based on the electrical system's capacity to provide power. The lights cannot, for example, draw more power than the alternator can produce, without draining the battery.

Generally, you never want to load your charging system to more than 80 percent of its full rated output. Thus, if your alternator is rated at 50 amperes, 40 amperes is the most you should consider drawing out of it for very long. From this 80 percent figure (whatever it turns out to be in your case) you subtract the needs of the car—ignition, running light, radio, and so on.

Assume your car needs 5 amperes to run. With a 50-ampere system, you would be left with 45 amperes for your lights. Since watts equal amperes times volts, in a 12-volt system you have

The distributor machine shows how much advance there is over the rpm range.

540 watts to play with. If the only other accessory you are running is the lights, this should be no problem—540 watts provides a *lot* of light. Just be careful when you have your dual 100-watt high beams on at the same time you are blasting tunes out of your 200-watt, 60 percent efficient stereo.

Assuming your electrical system can provide the power, if you think the existing wiring might be marginal, you should run the lights through relays.

Remote Relays

If you are satisfied with the stock lighting and horns, read no further. The stock wiring will power these items quite satisfactorily. When you feel the need for some 100-watt flame throwers, extra driving light, or industrial-duty horns, you will soon find that the stock wiring is not up to the amperage demands that these devices can place on the electrical system.

The normal electrical pathway starts at the battery, goes back to the dashboard where the switch or button is mounted, and then goes back to the accessory. The factory does it this way for reasons of cost, ease of assembly, and simplicity, but it makes it more difficult to upgrade the system. The small wires and the long distances involved limit the flow or amperage, possibly leading to overheating and failure.

The way around this problem is to install an electrical relay near the accessory that is drawing a lot of power. By locating the relay close to the accessory and using heavy-duty wire, you can eliminate any overheating problems in the wiring without having to redo your entire wiring harness. The original wiring is used to trigger the relay (tell it when to turn on). The trigger signal is much less than the original use the wires were intended for, so longevity is increased. When triggered, the relay connects the accessory directly to the battery through a much shorter route, and you can use a heavier-gauge wire to ensure that the accessory gets the juice it needs.

Left to right are Bosch WR5CP (platinum), Bosch W7DCT Super (1986 GTi), Bosch F6DTC (16V) and Champion G-63 (Oettinger).

The distributor on the 16V engine is driven off the exhaust camshaft.

These hardened intermediate shaft and distributor drive gears will solve any problems you have with breakage.

If you want the accessory to be off whenever the ignition is off, wire it in. If not, connect the accessory switch to a wire that is always hot (if it is not that way already).

The wire from the battery to the relay and from the relay to the accessory should be heavy-gauge wire. If you are running a lot of current through it, keep the distance as short as possible too. Although this is usually used for lights and horns, you could also use it to supply power to a big stereo amplifier.

Intermittent Wipers

If your car does not have the intermittent wiper option, it can be added anytime. The Volkswagen number for the relay is 191.955.529, and it plugs into the relay board where the jumper is. The only other thing you will need to do then is to break out the small plastic tab underneath the wiper actuator arm, so the arm can move downward to the intermittent wiper position.

Roof-Mounted Antennas

The 1987-and-later GTi roof-mounted antenna has been a popular retrofit, but in 1994 Volkswagen changed the design. The new version has only a single cable for both the signal and antenna amplifier power. The old version is no longer stocked, and the new radio has been changed internally for the difference in wiring. The table below shows which combinations of antenna, radio, and cables are compatible.

Radio/Antenna Compatibility

Antenna	Radio	Cables	Compatible?
New	New	New	Yes
Old	Old	Old	Yes
New	New	Old	Yes
Old	New	Old	Yes
Old	New	New	No
New	Old	New	No
Old	Old	New	No
New	Old	Old	No

Chapter 17

Accessories

Alarms

Alarms have come a long way since the late 1970s, when there were only a few companies competing in the automotive security aftermarket. Now you get an alarm at a stereo store, a mobile phone store, a specialty alarm store, a department store, and even through the mail.

At the same time, the level of sophistication of the average alarm has risen. In addition to door switches and motion sensors, sound discriminators can "listen" for the sound of the glass being broken (or the squeak of a lug bolt being loosened). Instead of settling for a siren, you can have your alarm yell, "Burglar! Burglar!" in a loud, synthesized voice. Alarms are available that will arm themselves automatically after a certain period of time, will lock the door automatically when armed, or will tell you if and why the alarm went off while you were away. Some will do all this and more. There are so many different types of alarms that it would be nearly impossible to cover them all here. There are some general things to look for, however.

The first thing to require in an alarm is that there is no entry delay. If the alarm lets you open the door, sit down and compose yourself before entering the code on a keypad, the thief is going to have that much time too, and a thief works *fast*; he will be gone before your alarm makes its first sound.

The second thing you should do is install the alarm in as remote a location as possible. Try to find the most radically different installation you can think of, because an experienced thief has an advantage in that he figures out alarms for a living. If you put yours where everybody else puts theirs, you just wasted your money. This is especially true for alarms installed by professional installers, who usually use a standard alarm layout. If you have an alarm professionally installed, rewire it after you get it home. At the very least, put the siren someplace where it would take Houdini to reach it or the wires leading up to it.

A lot of people put decals on their window to inform would-be burglars that the car is equipped with an alarm, but there is no evidence that the burglars pay any attention to these. Still if you do not mind the look of a decal it may not hurt. The only drawback is that if the decal specifies the type of alarm installed, it can give the thief an idea about what he is up against before breaking in. Remember, the thief is the pro and does not need much of an edge to win at this game.

One way of slowing down a burglar is to install plates around the door handles where burglars usually pry their way

It's better to have an extinguisher in your trunk than none at all, but your primary unit should be closer at hand.

in. This is effective, although there is nothing to prevent a thief from breaking a window or slashing your Cabriolet top. The alarm that comes as standard equipment with the American A3s is a good-quality, midlevel alarm. One problem with any mass market alarm, however, is that thieves know the locations of all the components in advance, as well as how best to circumvent or defeat the system. There's not much you can do

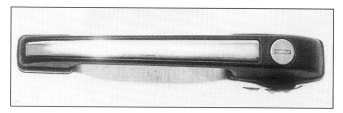

Thieves can pry open your car by inserting a screwdriver here.

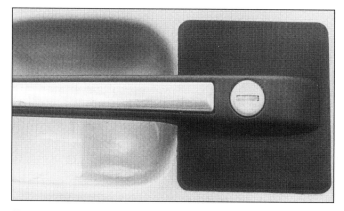

The Armor door plate foils them.

with the factory alarm to mitigate this situation, but if you install your own system, try to come up with an innovative way of mounting and interconnecting the components. Anything novel will slow down the thief, and every moment counts.

Radio Lock

For the first few years of their existence, Rabbits, Sciroccos, and Jettas were prime targets for radio thieves. This essentially stopped with the introduction of antitheft radios from the factory. When stolen, the radio "forgets" how to work, and it will remember only after the proper code is entered in.

If you install a different radio, however, you may have to consider some way of retaining it. Radio locks are a step in the right direction, although they are difficult to install. One negative trade-off is that the burglar may wreak more damage in the attempt to get at your radio than if you didn't have a lock in the first place.

Removable radios are another almost-good idea. For the first week or so you will always take the radio with you when you leave your car. After that, you probably won't, putting you right back where you started—except that the thief will not have to brutalize your dash to steal your radio.

Wheel Locks

Wheel locks are designed to delay the thief long enough to make your wheels a less inviting target. If your motion detector is set right, it will detect someone jacking up your car, and sound before he begins removing the tires and wheels. It is still a good idea to use wheel locks, though, because you are

not always close enough to hear your alarm, and it is doubtful anyone else will respond to the sound of your car alarm.

Vehicle Retention

If the thief is determined to take the whole car, you have a much better chance of foiling him, although hanging onto your car can be a real problem in some areas. Volkswagens are nowhere near the top of the most-stolen list, but that is not much of a consolation when *your* car disappears or is broken into.

Just about anybody with a nice car has at one time or another said those fatalistic words: "If they really want your car, they're gonna get it one way or another." Unfortunately, this is true. It is up to you to make it as difficult for them as possible. The thief may do some damage, but it is better to have a slightly tattered car than no car at all.

There are ways of wiring an ignition and fuel pump cutouts so that as long as your alarm is armed, the car cannot be started. Depending on the sophistication of the setup, these can be very effective.

There are two problems with these setups. The first thing you need to find out is what happens when the system fails. If there is no way for you to by-pass the system in the event that the whole thing malfunctions, you are going to need to know the number of the local tow service. On reliable systems this may not be much of a concern, but they always seem to quit at the worst possible time.

The second problem is more serious. My good friend Randy Michel once had his car stolen at gun point. The thief waited until Randy opened the door and then stuck a gun in his face. Taking the keys, the thief invited Randy to crawl under a nearby car, and then drove off. Randy was lucky he did not have an ignition or fuel pump cutoff, because if he had the thief would have found out about it soon enough, and he probably would have wanted to chat about it.

If this possibility bothers you but you still hate the thought of someone simply driving away in your Volkswagen, find a time-delay ignition or fuel pump cutout. These let the car run for a couple of minutes even if you don't push the button to deactivate it. This lets the thief get far enough away so you do not have to deal with him on his terms if you do not want to.

The hope is that the thief will stall the car right in the middle of an intersection while a police officer looks on. The drawback to this system is that thieves are often quite good at finding hidden switches and buttons. Still, it can be extremely difficult to find a microswitch hidden behind the stock door panel fabric, or back under the rug on the tunnel between the seats. If it sounds as if I am being vague, you are right. If I tell you all my trick hiding places for microswitches, they won't be secrets anymore! You should be able to develop your own secret switch locations with no trouble.

Fortunately, most cars are not taken this way, leaving you with some other methods for making your car just too much trouble to fool with.

One of these methods is to prevent the steering wheel from turning even if the normal steering wheel lock has been

A radar detector only needs to save you from one ticket to pay for itself.

The VC-200 Performance Computer will give you read-outs on time to distance, distance to speed, and peak g-force, all of which are extremely valuable for testing the effectiveness of engine modifications.

disabled. The first devices to do this were called *canes*, in reference to their general shape. They locked the brake or clutch pedal to the steering wheel so neither could be used.

The second generation of this idea is a device called The Club. It locks across the steering wheel, extending out from the steering wheel so that the end of The Club interfers with the windshield, the console, the door, your legs, and every-

thing else if you try to turn it.

The Club has three advantages over a cane. First, it is more visible, so it serves as a better deterrent. Second, it is quicker and easier to put on, so you will use it more often than you might use the cane. Third, no amount of bending the steering wheel will allow the thief to remove The Club (a cane can be removed that way).

The Club is not perfect, however, because the steering wheel can still be removed and a different one installed. This falls into the category of "if they really want it," however. How many thieves are going go carry around a spare steering wheel? A bigger problem is that a thief can cut the wheel rim fairly easily and remove either device.

When installing either a cane or The Club (or any time you park your car), always point the nose of the car into a corner and then crank the front wheels fully to the left or right. This makes it much more difficult to tow your car without getting into it and defeating the steering lock mechanism.

That brings up the next device: a removable steering wheel. Race cars have these, and now so can you. Again, the chances of a thief having a replacement steering wheel are pretty remote. The drawback is that you have to carry around your steering wheel everywhere you go.

One last thing you can do is immobilize your car so it cannot be towed, pushed, or dragged off. This forces the thief to pick all four tires off the ground to move your car. The way to accomplish this is with a brake line lock. This is a device that is plumbed into your brake system. Each time you leave the car, you turn the key on the line lock and push on the brake pedal. The line lock acts as a one-way valve that maintains the pressure in the lines, keeping the discs and drums locked tight. Apparently, this has no adverse effect on the braking system.

Another way to use the line lock is to turn the key without pushing on the brake pedal. The next time the pedal is depressed, the line lock will keep the brakes applied until the key is used to unlock them. This might allow a thief to get to the end of the block before discovering that you were just kidding when you let him or her take the car.

Fire Extinguishers

An automotive fire must be dealt with quickly because of the large amount of readily available combustible material involved. That means having your extinguisher mounted close at hand. Under the driver's seat, on the rear seat floor, or inside the glovebox are the best locations. Some people prefer a location on windshield A-pillar, but that blocks the entryway and is a possible safety hazard in a collision. Avoid any trunk mounting location except for back-up extinguishers; it will take too long to reach in an emergency.

There are different types of fire extinguishers, each of which specializes in a certain type of fire. A car fire extinguisher, for example, has to be safe for use around electrical wiring and oil and gasoline, in addition to the normal flammable materials inside the passenger compartment. In the case of

The G-analyst works best for setting up suspensions for at the track.

an engine fire, the fire extinguisher must not cause any damage to the engine as it is extinguishing the fire. Dry powders, for example, will get into the motor and ruin piston rings, valve seats, and bearings. Some of the other chemical extinguishers will attack hot aluminum and electrical wiring on contact.

Carbon dioxide (CO_2) extinguishers are popular with racetracks because they are a "clean" way to fight fires (leaving no residual gunk) and are relatively inexpensive to recharge. On the other hand, they release a very cold fluid (minus 100 degrees Fahrenheit) that could cause thermal shock to hot underhood components.

Whichever type of extinguisher you choose, make sure it is mounted close at hand and is charged. You hope you never will have to test its effectiveness, but if you do need it, you will need it immediately.

Radar Detectors

Police radar is a major weapon in the law enforcement arsenal to ensure compliance with posted speed limits. Federal, state, and local authorities have all aligned themselves on the use of radar for this purpose, with the result that police departments across the United States use hundreds of radar units every day in the line of duty. This puts the number of radar-equipped police officers you are likely to encounter during a 3,000-mile cross-country trip about equal to the number of fast food establishments you will see along the way. For long-distance travel, therefore, you may want a radar detector.

About a dozen manufacturers produce radar detectors for sale in the United States. They typically range in price from about $200 to nearly $400 and give different levels of radar detection. Modern radar detectors warn of X-band, K-band, Superwide Ka-band, and laser broadcasts, and some even track multiple broadcasts simultaneously. Evaluating these devices is beyond the scope of this book, but enthusiast magazines such as

Car and Driver usually test all the better units nearly once a year. Their in-depth and timely testing makes them required reading if you hope to stay on top of the radar detector market.

There are three types of radar detectors: remote, standard, and compact. The remote units are the most covert and are to be considered if you drive in "radar-prohibited" states, where the police will not only give you a ticket but confiscate your radar detector, as well.

The standard units are single-piece construction (as opposed to the remote units), approximately 5x7 inches in size. The famous Escort was one such unit. Although the standard-size units worked fine, their larger size makes them more difficult to mount and more easy for the police to spot.

The compact units are the most advanced (and costly) of the three designs, dimensionally about the same as two audio cassette tapes stacked atop one another. The Passport 7500 is an excellent example of the compact detector. The technical sophistication of these units is stunning. The better ones will even discriminate between true radar traps and the almost identical collision avoidance radar.

Another type of device that stirs the imagination is a radar jammer, for which there are several configurations. Because of the questionable legalities involved with building and using radar jammers, jammers are nowhere near as easy to purchase as detectors, and companies that were here today are often gone tomorrow. When they work, the results are awe-inspiring, but units that work are few and far between. You are probably better off with a good-quality radar detector for the time being.

Steering Wheels

The small-diameter steering wheels you see in the Formula 1 cars look trick, but they are not the hot tip for a Volkswagen. Although there are many wonderful aftermarket steering wheels out there, I prefer factory wheels for three reasons.

First, the stock wheel affords the best view of the gauges. If you are of average height, you might be able to see the gauges even with a smaller wheel, but it is worth checking out before you buy.

Second, I find that the steering effort is just about right with the stock-diameter wheel. A smaller steering wheel makes the effort too high, and a larger steering wheel makes it seem as if you are driving a tractor or a 1960s muscle car.

When the steering effort is just right it is much easier to pass the wheel between your hands, as taught in driving school. This factor is far more critical than the steering ratio in finding the fast way around a turn (or a series of turns).

Third, I enjoy having the horn buttons near the rim of the steering wheel. Having to move a hand to the center of the wheel to actuate the horn button is sometimes not the best way of maintaining control of your automobile.

If you decide to go steering wheel shopping, keep in mind that ergonometric studies have shown that the proper steering wheel does *not* have a smooth, thin rim. A thicker rim with bumps on the back is far less fatiguing to drive. Better still, if you can find one you like, are the sculpted wheels that dictate

A four-point harness is recommended for racing applications.

For high-performance cornering, you need a seat with higher bolsters to prevent you from sliding around.

where you put your hands. They are not for everybody, but once you get used to them they are very nice.

Seating

The stock Volkswagen seat is not designed for maximum lateral support during high-g maneuvers. One exception is the optional sport seat in the Scirocco. The sport seat in the Corrado, GTi, and GLi had better bolsters, and the 1987–1992 16V GLi came with genuine Recaros. Less bolstered, the sport seats in A3 GTis and GLXs represent a good compromise between a flat seat that allows easy entry and exit and a sport seat that offers good support in corners. This might be hard to appreciate until you find yourself faced with a million errands to do in one day in a car with high side bolsters.

Even with a wide variety of seats available in the aftermarket, recommendations are difficult to make. Preferences in seating are a personal matter, and the wrong seat can make life miserable.

When you contemplate the purchase of a seat, first check to see that it fits you. Check also to see that the mounting hardware is of high quality. Recaro supplies excellent mounting hardware, and you should expect no less from whatever seat you choose.

One final thing to keep in mind is that the roofline on the Scirocco or Corrado is lower than on the Rabbit or Jetta. This will make it that much more of an effort to climb over a high bolster, so plan accordingly.

Putting the more laid-back Scirocco or Corrado seats into a hatchback or sedan is easy, as long as you like riding a little lower. On the other hand, putting hatchback or sedan seats into your Scirocco or Corrado will just about eliminate headroom for all but the very shortest members of society. If you are faced with this situation, you can switch the seat rails from one type of seat to the other, so you can adapt one style of seat to work in a chassis for which it was not designed.

Analysis Methods
Stopwatch

It is surprising what you can do with a stopwatch or two and some mathematics. The November 1970 *Road & Track* has an interesting article by Ronald F. Brown on just this subject. The article is much too extensive to repeat (or even summarize) here, but if you are interested you can request a copy from your local library. Not everyone can afford his own dyno, but no hot-rodder should be without a stopwatch.

If it is too much time and trouble to calculate horsepower using a stopwatch, at the very least you can use one to tell if your car is faster or slower than it was before you made your last change. All you have to do is remember to measure your car's performance before each modification, so you have something against which to check afterward.

It is a tough habit to develop, but if you run against the stopwatch before you make a change and then again afterward, you can make sure that you are always headed in the right direction.

Computers

One tool that wasn't available to hot-rodders who didn't work at NASA in 1970 is the modern computer. The chapter on transaxle gearing shows some of what a computer can do for the average hot-rodder. Here's something else.

If you know your vehicle's weight and road horsepower, you can estimate both the elapsed time (ET) and trap speed for your car at the drag strip, using a couple of different formulas.

The first are the "quick" formulas, which are more simple to work with, at the expense of accuracy. The quick formula for 1/4-mile elapsed is:

$$\text{1/4-mile ET in seconds} = 5.825 \times \left(\frac{\text{vehicle wt}}{\text{road hp}}\right)^{0.3333}$$

The quick formula for 1/4-mile trap speed is:

$$\text{Trap speed in mph} = 234 \times \left(\frac{\text{road hp}}{\text{vehicle wt}}\right)^{0.3333}$$

Don't bet your pink slip on the basis of what these formulas tell you, as they can be as much as a full second off on ET and 6 miles per hour off on trap speed.

Using a computer to "curve fit" performance data published in the major car magazines, I arrived at these two formulas, which have proven more accurate. In both of these formulas, engine horsepower is represented by x, and vehicle weight is represented by y. For these formulas, engine horsepower is as stated by the manufacturer, that is, engine dyno horsepower, not chassis or road dyno horsepower. For 1/4-mile elapsed time in seconds, the formula is:

$ET = 27.5531495 + (-0.0948251x) + (-0.005154y) + 0.00010768x^2 + 2.4552\text{E-}05xy + 1.1652\text{E-}06y^2 + 5.6525\text{E-}08x^3 + (-2.409\text{E-}08yx^2) + (-3.13\text{E-}09xy^2) + 1.531\text{E-}11y^3$

For 1/4-mile trap speed in miles per hour, the formula is:

$\text{Trap speed} = 4.53092116 + 0.37237133x + 0.05715395y + (-0.0007074x^2) + 6.209\text{E-}06xy + (-2.159\text{E-}05y^2) + (-6.276\text{E-}07x^3) + 2.5635\text{E-}07yx^2 + (-1.791\text{E-}08xy^2) + 2.5258\text{E-}09y^3$

From the data I have examined, the figure you get for ET should be within about 0.25 second of an actual, measured run against the clock, with not more than 0.6 second maximum discrepancy for all cars, from the front-wheel drive Geo Metro to the rear-wheel drive Dodge Viper. Actual measured trap speed should be within 2.5 miles per hour, with a maximum discrepancy of not more than 4 miles per hour.

Computers are handy for doing the calculations, but for that matter many inexpensive hand-held calculators can do that, as can a slide rule. Where you really get the benefit of using a computer is when your spreadsheet program has the

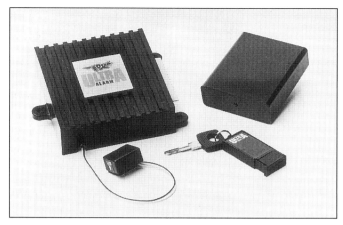

Modern alarm systems feature remote control arming and disarming, motion detection, sound detection (such as the squeak of wheel bolts being removed), and even proximity sensors. Remember that any alarm that gives you an entry delay gives that same delay to the thief.

ability to "back calculate," that is, to look at the results of an equation and change the variables until the results match a pre-determined number. In Microsoft Excel, this facility is called "Goal Seek."

For best results, you need to be as accurate as possible with the weight, ET, and trap speed. You can weigh your car at a public scale for a couple of dollars. Set your car up as closely as possible to the condition in which it will race (tank full, spare parts and tools out of the trunk, and so on.), and don't forget to add your body weight. The drag strip should be able to provide you with timing slips, which show the ET and trap speed.

Armed with this information, the only uncertain variable is the horsepower figure. Using the formulas above, plug in your vehicle weight and rated horsepower and see how close the ET and trap speed are to the actual measured ET and trap speed. If there is a discrepancy, use the "Goal Seek" function to back calculate the horsepower based on the real-world measurements. (Obviously, this works only if you have set up each variable in its own cell on the spreadsheet.) The resulting figure you get for horsepower can then be used as a base rating against which all other modifications can be compared. It doesn't even matter if your calculated horsepower figure is 1 or 2 horsepower high or low, because all your calculations from then on will be relative, that is, higher or lower than your base rating.

Accelerometers

Using a stopwatch, drag strip, and computer as described above, you can approximate horsepower based on quarter-mile times. Still, with all this you might want more, or you might want the same, only easier. Or you may not have a drag strip convenient to where you live. Fortunately, a couple of companies now sell accelerometers. An accelerometer works by measuring the acceleration of a known weight. Then, using calculus, it calculates the speed and distance over which this acceleration occurred.

A dead pedal is used as a foot brace when cornering. It should be at the same height as the clutch pedal.

If you are going to be putting a lot of miles on your car, an engine-hour meter will help you schedule repairs and maintenance.

Another way of measuring performance is with a radar gun, which can also help you calibrate your speedometer.

Built-in fire-control systems are expensive, but for racing, they're a must.

One unit is the G-analyst. Depending on the mode you select, the G-analyst will graphically show you acceleration and deceleration, side-to-side g-forces or all four (using the concept of the friction circle), and it provides numbers to go with the graphs.

Other accelerometers are sold by Vericom (the VC-200) and Tesla Electronics (the G-Tech/Pro). These are better suited for acceleration and deceleration, although they can be used for lateral acceleration as well. Neither has a graphics display, but they will tell you time to speed, distance to speed, and peak g-force at the push of a button.

The problem shared by all of these units is that body roll and pitch are also calculated in, unless you trick the accelerometer into compensating by entering in a correction factor. But because there is no accurate way to determine the correction factor for a given car, you must guess. Your guess is then the basis for all the high-powered calculations performed by the accelerometer. This renders the results somewhat less than reliable.

For straight-line performance numbers, the VC-200 and G-Tech/Pro are best, while for setting up a car for a race course, the G-analyst is superior.

Windshield Wipers

The best wiper setup is the stock Bosch blade and insert. The inserts wear out quickly, but they are not expensive or difficult to change. Many people bend the wiper blade prongs to grip the insert, but this just makes it more difficult to change the insert later on. You can leave them comfortably loose without fear of losing an inset. For best results, orient the inset so that the cutoff end is pointing toward the top of the windshield. Point the other end (the end with the tabs for the thin metal inserts) toward the hood.

I do not recommend the double-wiper systems. If you have the same amount of pressure applied through twice as much surface area, your pressure per unit of surface area is going to be half as much. A double-wiper would therefore work half as well as a single wiper.

"The Club" is a highly effective steering wheel lock.

This steering wheel lock hooks onto the brake or clutch pedal to slow down thieves.

Appendices

Volkswagen Engine Information

Over the years, Volkswagen engines have proliferated from a couple of basic engines to a bewildering array of bores, strokes, displacements, outputs, fuel delivery systems, and even configurations.

Year	Model	Engine code	Hp	CC	Bore x Stroke	Notes
1973	Audi 80 GL		98	1471	76.5 x 80	9.5:1 compression
	Audi 80 L		69	1297	75 x 73.4	8.5:1 compression
	Audi 80S, LS		86	1471	76.5 x 80	9.5:1 compression
	Audi Fox		75	1471	76.5 x 80	8.2:1 compression
1974	Audi Fox		75	1471	76.5 x 80	8.2:1 compression
	Dasher		75	1471	76.5 x 80	8.2:1 compression
1975	Rabbit, Scirocco	FC,FG	71	1471	76.5 x 80	Carburetor, solid lifter
	Dasher	XS, XR		1588	79.5 x 80	Carburetor
1976	Rabbit	FC,FG	71	1471	76.5 x 80	Carburetor
	Rabbit, Scirocco	FN	74	1588	79.5 x 80	Carburetor
	Super Scirocco	EE	78	1588	79.5 x 80	CIS, solid lifter
	Dasher	YG,YH,YK	78, *83	1588	79.5 x 80	CIS
1977	Rabbit, Scirocco	EE	78	1588	79.5 x 80	CIS
	Dasher	YG,YH,YK	78, *83	1588	79.5 x 80	CIS
1978	Rabbit, Scirocco	EH	71	1457	79.5 x 73.4	CIS
	Rabbit	FX	62	1457	79.5 x 73.4	Carburetor
	Dasher	YG,YH	78, *83	1588	79.5 x 80	CIS, long down pipe
1979	Rabbit, Convert ible, Scirocco	EH	71	1457	79.5 x 73.4	CIS
	Scirocco	EJ	78	1588	79.5 x 80	CIS
	Dasher	YG,YH	78, *83	1588	79.5 x 80	CIS, long down pipe
1980	Rabbit, Pick-Up, Convertible Scir occo, Dasher, Jetta	EJ	78	1588	79.5 x 80	CIS, oxygen sensor, electronic ignition, idle stabilizer
	Rabbit	FX	62	1457	79.5 x 73.4	Carburetor, 49-state
	Dasher	YG,YH	78	1588	79.5 x 80	CIS
1981	Rabbit, Pick-Up, Convertible Scir occo, Jetta, Dasher	EN	74	1716	79.5 x 86.4	CIS, solid lifter
	Rabbit	JF	65	1716	79.5 x 86.4	Carburetor, solid lifter
1982	Rabbit, Pick-Up, Scirocco, Convert ible Dasher, Jetta	EN	74	1716	79.5 x 86.4	CIS

	Rabbit	JF	65	1716	79.5 x 86.4	Carburetor, Oxygen Sensor closed loop
	Quantum	WT	74	1716	79.5 x 86.4	CIS
1983	Rabbit, Pick-Up, Jetta Convertible, Scirocco from 83 1/2	EN	74	1716	79.5 x 86.4	CIS
	Rabbit	JF	65	1716	79.5 x 86.4	Carburetor, Oxygen Sensor closed loop
	GTI, Scirocco after 83 1/2	JH	90	1781	81 x 86.4	CIS, solid lifter, 144 mm rods
	Quantum	WT	90	1781	81 x 86.4	CIS, 144 mm rods
1984	Rabbit, Pick-Up, Jetta	EN	74	1716	79.5 x 86.4	CIS
	Rabbit	JF	65	1716	79.5 x 86.4	Carburetor, Oxygen Sensor closed loop
	GTI, GLI, Scirocco, Cabriolet	JH	90	1781	81 x 86.4	CIS, solid lifter, 144 mm rods
	Quantum	KX, WE		2226	81 x 86.4	5-cylinder
	Quantum	JN	90	1781	81 x 86.4	CIS lambda, 144 mm rods
1985	Golf, Jetta	GX	85	1781	81 x 86.4	KE-Jetronic, hydraulic lifters
	GTI, GLI	HT	100	1781	81 x 86.4	10:1 compression KE-Jetronic, knock sensor
	Scirocco, Cabriolet	JH	90	1781	81 x 86.4	CIS, 144 mm rods
	Quantum	KX		2309	82.5 x 86.4	5-cylinder
	Quantum	JN	90	1781	81 x 86.4	CIS
1986	Golf, Jetta	GX	85	1781	81 x 86.4	CIS
	GTI	RD	102	1781	81 x 86.4	New timing, 10:1 compression, KE-Jetronic
	GLI	RD	105	1781	81 x 86.4	10:1 compression, new timing, dual manifold/down pipe KE-Jetronic
	Scirocco, Cabriolet	JH	90	1781	81 x 86.4	CIS, 144 mm rods
	Quantum	KX		2309	82.5 x 86.4	5-cylinder
1987	Golf, Jetta	GX	85	1781	81 x 86.4	CIS
	Golf, Jetta	PF, RV	100	1781	81 x 86.4	Digifant II
	GLI, GT	RD	105	1781	81 x 86.4	10:1 compression, new timing, dual manifold/down- pipe, KE-Jetronic
	Scirocco, Cabriolet	JH	90	1781	81 x 86.4	CIS, 144 mm rods
	GTI 16V	PL	123	1781	81 x 86.4	

	Fox	UM, JN	81	1781	81 x 86.4	CIS (restricted exhaust)
	Quantum	KX		2309	82.5 x 86.4	5-cylinder
1988	Golf, Jetta	GX	85	1781	81 x 86.4	CIS
	Golf, Jetta	RV	85	1781	81 x 86.4	Digifant II
	Golf, GT, Jetta, Carat	PF	105	1781	81 x 86.4	Digifant II, dual out let manifold and down-pipe
	Carat	RD	105	1781	81 x 86.4	10:1 compression, dual manifold/ down-pipe, KE- Jetronic
	GLI 16V, Scirocco 16V	PL	123	1781	81 x 86.4	KE-Jetronic
	Cabriolet	JH	90	1781	81 x 86.4	Digifant II, Hydrau lic lifter
	Fox	JN	81	1781	81 x 86.4	CIS (restricted exhaust)
	Quantum	KX		2309	82.5 x 86.4	5-cylinder
1989	Golf, Jetta	RV	100	1781	81 x 86.4	Digifant II, also a 105 Digifant II with dual down pipe
	Golf, GT, Jetta, Carat	PF	105	1781	81 x 86.4	Digifant II, dual out let manifold and down-pipe
	GTI 16V, GLI 16V	PL	123	1781	81 x 86.4	KE-Jetronic, rifle-drilled rods
	Cabriolet	JH	90	1781	81 x 86.4	CIS, 8.5:1, 144 mm rods
	Fox	JN	81	1781	81 x 86.4	CIS (restricted exhaust)
	Corrado G-60	PG	158	1781	81 x 86.4	Supercharged Digi fant I
1990	Golf, Jetta, Carat	RV	100	1781	81 x 86.4	Digifant II
	Golf, Jetta, Carat	PF	105	1781	81 x 86.4	Digifant II, dual out let manifold and down-pipe
	GTI 16V, GLI 16V, Passat	9A	134	1984	82.5 x 92.8	KE-Motronic injec tion, smaller intake port, reshaped exhaust, 42 mm intake manifold, 10.8:1 compression with dual knock sen sors
	Cabriolet	2H	90	1781	81 x 86.4	Digifant II
	Fox	JN	81	1781	81 x 86.4	Digifant II (restricted exhaust)
	Corrado G-60	PG	158	1781	81 x 86.4	Supercharged, Digi fant I

1991	Golf GL, Jetta GL, Jetta Carat	RV	100	1781	81 x 86.4	Digifant II
	GTI	PF	105	1781	81 x 86.4	Digifant II with dual down pipe
	GTI 16V, GLI 16V, Passat GL, Passat Wagon	9A	134	1984	82.5 x 92.8	KE-Motronic injec tion, smaller intake port, reshaped exhaust, 42 mm intake manifold, 10.8:1 compression with dual knock sen sors
	Corrado G-60	PG	158	1781	81 x 86.4	Supercharged, Digi fant I
	Cabriolet	2H	94	1781	81 x 86.4	Digifant II
	Fox	ABG	81	1781	81 x 86.4	Digifant II (restricted exhaust)
1992	Golf, Jetta	RV	100	1781	81 x 86.4	Digifant II
	Golf, Jetta	PF	105	1781	81 x 86.4	Digifant II with dual down pipe
	GTI, GLI, Passat	9A	134	1984	82.5 x 92.8	Motronic injection, smaller intake port, reshaped exhaust, 42 mm intake manifold, 10.8:1 compression with dual knock sen sors
	Cabriolet	2H	90	1781	81 x 86.4	Digifant II
	Corrado G-60	PG	158	1781	81 x 86.4	Supercharged, Digi fant I
	Corrado VR6	AAA	178	2792	81 x 90.3	Motronic with dis tributor, high flow cat
	Fox	ABG	81	1781	81 x 86.4	Digifant II (restricted exhaust)
1993	Golf III, JettaIII	ABA	115	1984	82.5 x 92.8	Cross-flow Motronic 2.0, "tall block" with 159 mm rods
	Passat VR6	AAA	172	2792	81 x 90.3	Motronic with dis tributor
	Corrado VR6	AAA	178	2792	81 x 90.3	Motronic with dis tributor, high flow cat
	Fox	ABG	83	1781	81 x 86.4	Digifant II (restricted exhaust)
1994	Golf III, JettaIII	ABA	115	1984	82.5 x 92.8	Cross-flow Motronic 2.0, "tall block" with 159 mm rods
	Corrado SLC	AAA	178	2792	81 x 90.3	Motronic distributor less, high flow cat

	Jetta GLX, Passat GLX (VR6)	AAA	172	2792	81 x 90.3	Motronic distributor less
1995	Golf III, JettaIII, Cabrio	ABA	115	1984	82.5 x 92.8	Cross-flow Motronic 2.0, "tall block" with 159 mm rods
	Passat VR6	AAA	172	2792	81 x 90.3	Motronic distributor less
	GLX	AAA	172	2792	81 x 90.3	Motronic distributor less
1996	Golf III, JettaIII, Cabrio	ABA	115	1984	82.5 x 92.8	Cross-flow Motronic 2.0, "tall block" with 159 mm rods
	Passat VR6	AAA	172	2792	81 x 90.3	Motronic distributor less
	GLX, GTI (VR6)	AAA	172	2792	81 x 90.3	Motronic distributor less
	Passat 4 cylinder	ABA	115	1984	82.5 x 92.8	Cross-flow Motronic 2.0, "tall block" with 159 mm rods
1997	Golf III, JettaIII, Cabrio	ABA	115	1984	82.5 x 92.8	Cross-flow Motronic 2.0, "tall block" with 159 mm rods
	Passat VR6	AAA	172	2792	81 x 90.3	Motronic distributor less
	GLX, GTI (VR6)	AAA	172	2792	81 x 90.3	Motronic distributor less
	Passat 4-cylinder	ABA	115	1984	82.5 x 92.8	Cross-flow Motronic 2.0, "tall block" with 159 mm rods
1998	Golf III, JettaIII, Cabrio	ABA	115	1984	82.5 x 92.8	Cross-flow Motronic 2.0, "tall block" with 159 mm rods
	New Beetle	AEG	115	1984	82.5 x 92.8	Cross-flow Motronic 2.0, "short block" with 141 mm rods
	GTI, GLX (VR6)	AAA	172	2792	81 x 90.3	Motronic distributor less
	Passat 4-cylinder	1AT	150	1781	81 x 86.4	5-valve turbo
1999	Golf IV, Jetta IV (V5)	?	151	2324	81 x 90.2	Similar to a VR6 engine with one fewer cylinders

Missing from this list is the "WR12" engine, two VR6 engines siamesed at a 72-degree angle—12 cylinders in total—sharing a single crankshaft, with 5.6 liters putting out 420 horsepower in street trim. Although it is being shown mounted longitudinally in the midengine W12 show car, rumors have it slated for everything from a future version of the Audi A8 to super high-end luxury cars (now that Volkswagen has bought Bentley), to a giant-killer racing machine. It's bound to be heavy and thirsty, but can you imagine what hot-rodders are going to be able to do with a 12-cylinder Volkswagen engine?

Volkswagen has also been working on a W18 engine, which is rumored to be appearing in an upcoming Bugatti.

Volkswagen Chassis Information

Volkswagen uses several different chassis (or platforms) on which they build their different models. These different chassis types are known by their internal designations, such as A1, A2, A3, A4, and so on. Throughout this book, these internal designations are used as a shorthand method of referring to classes of Volkswagens for purposes of understanding which modifications work with which cars. There is also a B series of chassis, which applies to the Dasher, Quantum, and Passat, which are not normally thought of as performance cars (although that is changing with the new Passats).

Chassis reference chart

Chassis	Volkswagen model
A1	Rabbit, Rabbit Pick Up, Rabbit Convertible, Cabriolet, GTI, Jetta I, Scirocco I, Scirocco II
A2	Golf, Golf GTI, Golf GT, Jetta II, Jetta, GLI, Jetta GLI 16V, Jetta Carat, Corrado G-60, Corrado VR6,[1] Corrado SLC
A3	Golf III, Jetta III, GTI VR6, Jetta GLX, Cabrio
A4	New Beetle, Golf 4, Jetta 4
B1	Dasher
B2	Quantum
B3	Passat to 1997
B4	1998-on Passat from 1998 (Audi-based)

A1 Chassis

The A1 chassis appeared with the first Rabbit and continued on in various guises for more than 10 years. The A1 is a straightforward "unibody" car, which means there is no frame underneath the body: The body itself is designed to have all necessary structural strength without the need for a separate frame. The Cabriolet used the A1 chassis after other models had been upgraded to one of the newer chassis. Note that the Volkswagen Fox, although built on a different chassis, does have some components in common with the A1 cars, as does the Pickup.

Volkswagen Models Using the A1 Chassis

Model	Years
Cabriolet	1984–1993
Convertible	1980–1984
GTi	1983–1984
Jetta	1980–1984
Rabbit	1975–1984
Scirocco	1975–1981
Scirocco (second generation)	1982–1989

The first engine to appear in the A1 was 1,471-cc (76.5x80 millimeters). With the head off, the block can be easily identified because there are no steam holes between the cylinders, as in all later blocks. The later motors also have siamesed cylinder bores for greater strength, something missing from this block. With the reduced cylinder wall clearance, this block cannot be honed to more than 79.5 millimeters. This is a fine motor to sell to someone else who is not interested in hot-rodding.

The motor that really helped Volkswagen gain its reputation was the 1,588-cc (79.5x80 millimeters), commonly referred to as a 1.6-liter. The motor is strong and has all the basics necessary for performance tuning, so that outputs of more than double its stock 70-plus horse-

power were possible. Super Vees use a variation of this engine and get over 170 horsepower, albeit at very high rpm.

Another version of this 1,588-cc motor made 100 horsepower running 9.5:1 compression in the European GTi. To get the increased compression ratio, the GTi motor uses dished pistons and a flat head surface, so instead of the combustion chamber being in the head it is in the piston. On an early car, you too can bolt on 28 percent more horsepower by swapping your flat-top pistons for the dished pistons and your head for the Heron type of the Euro GTi. At the time these engines came out they were considered the best. Lately the trend has been more toward motors that make their power lower in the rpm range.

Combine a fuel crunch with strict emissions standards, and you get the 1,457-cc engine (79.5x73.4 millimeters). The crankshaft was changed from the forged unit to a weaker cast piece that is not fully counterweighted. If you are shopping for a core motor, be aware that the stamping on the back of the block still reads "1.6." Pull the pan before you plunk down your money.

The 1,700 motor (1716-cc, 79.5 x 86.4 millimeters) continued the tradition of the 1,600 engine, and the aftermarket jumped all over it as well. The increase in stroke makes this the best choice of the early motors for hot-rodding. The 1,700 block has the letter H stamped on the back. If you come across a block that has 1.7 stamped on the back, you have a block out of a Chrysler Omni or Horizon. Volkswagen sold motors to Chrysler for a couple of years, and if you are buying a motor from a junk yard you may be offered one of them. The Omni block can be used in any build-up, with two caveats. First, it does not have the drilled and tapped pads for mounting the air conditioner bracket, so you cannot use this block in any application that requires air conditioning. Second, the Chrysler products came with carburetors only, so to run fuel injection you will need to switch heads.

The 1,800 engine (1781-cc, 81x86.4 millimeters) showed up in the first American incarnation of the GTi in 1983. The rods are 144 millimeters in center-to-center length, compared with the 136-millimeter length of the rods in the early cars, the wrist pin is smaller at 20 millimeters, and the rod journal is larger (all this, even though the stroke is the same as that of the earlier crankshafts). The valves are spaced a little farther apart than in the earlier motors, and there is an additional oil return drain to complement the large drain located front and center. The heads from this motor can be made to work on the earlier blocks, but some modification is required. The blocks are marked 1.8. These blocks have enough internal clearance to accept a 91-millimeter crankshaft as a bolt-in.

Not shown on the chart above is an engine that appears only in Europe in a version of the Jetta that runs carburetors and 9.0:1 compression. This 1,595-cc powerplant (81x77.4 millimeters) uses the cylinder head from the 1,800 motor, along with the rods and block.

In 1985, Volkswagen introduced hydraulic lifters in the Golf and Jetta; the Cabriolet did not get them until 1988. All 16V engines, which appeared in mid-1986, come with hydraulic lifters.

Crankcase oil jets are common on turbo motors, and the 16V motor has them as well. Small squirters are mounted in the block, pointing up at the bottom of the piston. When the engine oil pressure reaches approximately 30 psi, oil is sprayed on the underside of the pistons to help transfer some of the heat away.

A2 Chassis

In 1985, Volkswagen introduced the A2. The chassis is stronger than the A1, thanks to computer modeling that shows where the chassis flexes so reinforcement can be added where it is most needed (which saves weight). The A2 also has a subframe, to which the engine and transaxle mount.

The suspension mounting points were radically changed, as well. The new version features special bushings with built-in deflection characteristics that make the cars ride nicer and handle better. Because of this design change, none of the suspension pieces are interchangeable across this dividing line. Engine mounting points are, however, so newer engines will bolt into older chassis, leaving only plumbing, electrical, and some other odds and ends that need attention. See "Engine Swaps" for details.

Volkswagen Models Using the A2 Chassis

Model	Years
Corrado G60	1990–1992
Corrado VR6	1993–1995
Golf	1985–1992
Jetta II	1985–1992

The A2 wheelbase is 2.6 inches longer than the A1, as is the body, which is also wider. With the change in chassis also comes an improvement in aerodynamics. In 1990, the bumper covers were enlarged, and 16V engines from 1990 to 1992 are 2.0-liter instead of 1.8-liter. As for the Corrado VR6, it is said to be on an A3 chassis, but it looks virtually identical to a Golf chassis, and it has an A2-style subframe. It does have the "Plus Axle" front suspension (longer axles, longer control arms, and different steering knuckles), however, which was introduced with the A3 chassis.

A3 Chassis

The A3 continues the trend set by the A2, in that the chassis are stronger thanks to computer modeling. The engine again mounts to a subframe, which is slightly different than that in the A2.

Volkswagen Models Using the A3 Chassis

Model	Years
Cabriolet	1993–
Golf 3	1993–
Jetta 3	1993–

With the A3, Volkswagen also introduced the 2.0-liter engine. When doing any serious work on the engine, many find access easier after removing the front bumper.

For the 1994 model year, the GTi and GLX received a new roof antenna with a single cable for both power and signal.

The B4 Passat offers a "1AT" engine, which is said to be coming to the Golf, Jetta, and new Beetle if not others. This 1.8-liter, five-valve turbo four-cylinder engine, rated at an already amazing 150 horsepower stock, can easily be "chipped" to gain 50 horsepower (in conjunction with a free-flow air filter), and with cylinder head porting, bigger turbo, improved intercooler, different wastegate, and chip, puts out nearly 400 horsepower. This combination is said to be extremely driveable on the street, and requires no modifications to the lower end of the engine. This is why some are calling the 1AT engine the engine of the future for Volkswagen street performance.

A4 Chassis

The A4 is brand new as this is written. It is worth noting that there is no correlation between the Volkswagen chassis numbering system and Audi model designations. That is to say, the Audi A4 is not built on a Volkswagen A4 chassis, (although the Audi TT is).

The A4 Golf is 5 inches longer and 1.18 inches wider than the A3, with 39 millimeters more wheelbase.

Volkswagen Models Using the A4 Chassis

Model	Years
Golf 4	1999–
Jetta 4	1999–
New Beetle	1998–

As with previous incarnations, the A4 chassis is stronger still. The engine mounts are of a new "pendulum" type that allows the engine to swing front to back slightly for better control of noise and vibration. The 2.0-liter engine in the New Beetle is also 18 millimeters shorter than its predecessor (for better hood clearance), with correspondingly shorter connecting rods. The new engine also eliminates the intermediate shaft (the oil pump is moved to the front of the engine, where it is chain-driven off the crankshaft, with a spring-loaded tensioner for the chain). The

coolant pump housing is built into the engine block, and there is a new coolant thermostat housing. The new aluminum oil pan bolts both to the engine block and to the transaxle housing for more rigidity. The overall effect of these and other changes is a lighter, more rigid engine/transaxle assembly. Also contributing to lightness is the valvetrain, which features a single valve spring instead of the traditional dual springs.

The 2.0-liter oil circuit is different too. The oil pressure control valve is on the "out" side of the oil filter, the oil return cut-off valve is built-into the oil filter mount, and oil pressure is monitored by a single oil pressure switch.

The coolant pump is driven off the camshaft drive belt and has plastic vanes for lighter weight. The camshaft drive belt comes with an adjustable, semi-automatic drive belt tensioner. The 2.0-liter AEG engine uses red G12 coolant and not the green G11 coolant. Mixed coolant must be replaced.

The AEG also has a two-piece manifold. Some aftermarket tuners (such as New Dimensions) have already taken advantage of this, by removing the top piece of the manifold and bolting in a supercharger unit in its place. The exhaust manifold is different too, constructed of stainless steel tubing.

The distributorless ignition fires two spark plugs simultaneously, but because only one cylinder is on the compression stroke, the "extra" plug firing has no effect.

In the front suspension, rather than having a housing into which the struts mount, the bottom of the struts bolt directly to the wheel bearing housing. There is also a new front antiroll bar, with new links at the control arms. Standard wheels are five-bolt, 16-inch. Front camber is no longer adjustable, but can be equalized from side to side by moving the entire subframe left or right. The amount of caster in the front is increased to 40 millimeters, with power steering offsetting the higher steering effort.

In the rear, the springs have been separated from the shocks, so the shocks can be replaced without removing the springs. The rear axle beam also mounts to the chassis at a 25-degree angle, which allows special bushings to provide steering correction and vehicle stability.

Disc brakes front and rear are standard. Rear brake calipers are aluminum for lower unsprung weight.

Door handles in the A4 are reinforced with a metal plate to help prevent thieves from poking a hole in the door to gain access. New door and ignition locks feature an additional "freewheeling" antitheft feature.

The A4 also comes with CAN-Bus (Controller Area Network Bus) electronics, which among other things improve interchangeability of components, such as engines.

Volkswagen Part Numbers

It can be helpful to understand just what the Volkswagen part number means. Consider the example:

Reading VW part numbers

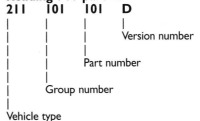

The vehicle type indicates the vehicle (or design project) for which the part was originally designed. This doesn't necessarily mean that this part will be found only on the vehicle for which it was designed, however. The same part (and part number) can sometimes be found on many different Volkswagens, as well as on Porsches and Audis.

The group number indicates what general area of the car the part is used in. Volkswagen has divided the car into 10 sections numbered 1 through 10. The section number serves as the first digit of the group number. For example:

VW Group and Section Numbers

Section number	Covering
Section 1	Engine
Section 2	Fuel delivery and exhaust
Section 3	Cooling
Section 4	Transmission
Section 5	Suspension and steering
Section 6	Tires, wheels, and brakes
Section 7	Linkages
Section 8	Body
Section 9	Electrical
Section 10	Accessories

Engine parts are normally in section 1, so their group numbers are in the 100s. Carburetors and most fuel injection components fall into section 2, so their group numbers are in the 200s, and so on.

The part number is just that—the part number. Part numbers that end in 98 (such as 198, 298, and so on) are kits.

The version number helps keep track of the revisions and improvements to the parts.

There is no number that indicates the vehicle year for which the part was designed. There is also no way of knowing just by looking at the part number if it is the latest or earliest. For that, you have to refer to the dealer supersedure list.

Two things usually confuse people when referring to Volkswagen part numbers. First, the part number stamped on the part is often not the part number. Confused?

Volkswagen seems to assign part numbers to just about everything. Therefore, a distributor housing, for example, may have a part number all its own. This number is for internal use only, however, so if you try to order one, the parts counter man will tell you that you do not have a valid part number. The stamped-in number can sometimes still be used to identify parts for your own information.

The second thing that can confound you is that every once in a while you will find a part for which the part number seems to fall into a "wrong" group. If you are hoping to get a job as a parts counter man at the Volkswagen dealer, this gives you something to look forward to. For the rest of us, the basics are usually enough to keep us out of trouble and help us sound intelligent when ordering parts from the dealer.

What is Horsepower?

In the world of machines, work is defined in terms of force and distance, or:

$$\text{Work} = \text{Force x Distance.}$$

Force is how hard something is pushed. Distance is how far it is pushed. If the force applied by the worker does not result in a movement on the part of the workee, then no work has been accomplished. As an example, pushing your car up a hill requires a tremendous amount of force; holding it stationary requires none because you could be replaced by a rock. When work is measured over time, the result is power.

$$\text{Power} = \text{Work} / \text{Time}$$

The normal unit of measure when discussing power is horsepower, so called because James Watt, the inventor of the steam engine back in 1765, had earlier taken the trouble to measure the amount of power a horse could deliver. Watt found that a horse could lift a weight of 550 pounds to a height of 1 foot in one second's time. Thus, 550 lb/ft-sec

became 1 horsepower, although it should be pointed out that horses are not able to deliver this amount of power for very long.

In its simplest state, work occurs in a straight line. Inside your engine, the burning air-fuel mixture pushes down on the top of the piston. The motion of the piston is confined to a straight line, making things relatively easy to this point.

Where it becomes complicated is between the piston and the crankshaft, where straight-line motion is converted into rotary motion. With Wankel rotary engines, there is no mechanical conversion at this point; the impulse of the burning fuel is imparted directly to the rotating rotor.

Going back to a piston engine, you can see that the complexity comes from the distance factor. If the piston was floating freely in the cylinder, the distance could be measured directly. In order to harness the energy in the fuel, the force expressed at the top of the piston is transmitted to the crankshaft, which does not move in a straight line.

Now several factors come into play, including rod length and stroke. As the piston moves relative to the crankshaft centerline, the rod angle is constantly changing, therefore constantly changing the leverage exerted on the crankshaft journal by the connecting rod.

This makes it necessary for us either to make thousands of measurements (or calculations) of the momentary force working through the different angles (to be averaged), or to come up with a new definition that describes work (also known as force) that takes place in a circular or twisting motion as torque. To measure time, we will need to keep track of how long it takes the crankshaft to complete each rotation, or the angular velocity. Engineers and scientists express angular velocity using a convenient measurement called radians-per-second. Each time the crankshaft completes one rotation (which you thought equaled 360 degrees), it can also be said to have moved through 6.2831853071796 radians (you can already see how convenient radians are). If you are wondering where this number comes from, it is pi times two, or 2π. Thus, if the crankshaft is revolving one time each second, the angular velocity is

$$\text{Angular velocity} = 2\pi \text{ x } n$$

In this expression, n equals revolutions-per-second. This expression of crankshaft rotation can be even further simplified after converting it from seconds to minutes, when it becomes:

$$\text{Angular velocity} = \pi \times \frac{n}{30}$$

Now we have a name for our force (we are calling it torque), and a measurement of how that force is applied, which is angular velocity. The relationship that torque and angular velocity have to power is:

$$\text{Power} = \text{Torque x Angular velocity}$$

By substitution, this gives us:

$$\text{Power} = \text{Torque} \times \pi \times \frac{n}{30}$$

Solving for Power, we get:

$$\text{Power} = \frac{\text{Torque} \times \text{rpm}}{9.549}$$

We now have a generic power formula. Just about the only step left is to define what units to use to express power and torque, and modify the formula accordingly. Here in the United States it is the common practice to use horsepower as the power unit and the pound/foot as the torque unit. Remembering that 1 horsepower equals 550 lb/ft-sec, we convert from the generic formula to horsepower by multiplying by 550.

$$\text{Power} \times 550 = \frac{\text{Torque} \times \text{rpm}}{9.549}$$

Again solving for power, we come up with:

$$\text{Horsepower} = \frac{\text{Torque} \times \text{rpm}}{9.549} \times \frac{1}{550}$$

$$\text{Horsepower} = \frac{\text{Torque} \times \text{rpm}}{5252}$$

What this formula implies is that horsepower figures are calculated while torque figures are measured, and that is exactly right. Engine dynomometers measure the ability of the engine to apply a twisting force through a tethered moment arm of known length to a calibrated gauge at an observed rpm. (Alternately, water-brake and pendulum dynos are also used). Measurements are taken at several rpms, and the numbers are then converted to horsepower using the formula above.

Conversions

Millimeters to Inches

mm	0	0.1	0.2	0.3	0.4	0.5	0.6	0.7	0.8	0.9
0	0.000	0.004	0.008	0.012	0.016	0.020	0.024	0.028	0.031	0.035
1	0.039	0.043	0.047	0.051	0.055	0.059	0.063	0.067	0.071	0.075
2	0.079	0.083	0.087	0.091	0.094	0.098	0.102	0.106	0.110	0.114
3	0.118	0.122	0.126	0.130	0.134	0.138	0.142	0.146	0.150	0.154
4	0.157	0.161	0.165	0.169	0.173	0.177	0.181	0.185	0.189	0.193
5	0.197	0.201	0.205	0.209	0.213	0.217	0.220	0.224	0.228	0.232
6	0.236	0.240	0.244	0.248	0.252	0.256	0.260	0.264	0.268	0.272
7	0.276	0.280	0.283	0.287	0.291	0.295	0.299	0.303	0.307	0.311
8	0.315	0.319	0.323	0.327	0.331	0.335	0.339	0.343	0.346	0.350
9	0.354	0.358	0.362	0.366	0.370	0.374	0.378	0.382	0.386	0.390
10	0.394	0.398	0.402	0.406	0.409	0.413	0.417	0.421	0.425	0.429
11	0.433	0.437	0.441	0.445	0.449	0.453	0.457	0.461	0.465	0.469
12	0.472	0.476	0.480	0.484	0.488	0.492	0.496	0.500	0.504	0.508
13	0.512	0.516	0.520	0.524	0.528	0.531	0.535	0.539	0.543	0.547
14	0.551	0.555	0.559	0.563	0.567	0.571	0.575	0.579	0.583	0.587
15	0.591	0.594	0.598	0.602	0.606	0.610	0.614	0.618	0.622	0.626
16	0.630	0.634	0.638	0.642	0.646	0.650	0.654	0.657	0.661	0.665
17	0.669	0.673	0.677	0.681	0.685	0.689	0.693	0.697	0.701	0.705
18	0.709	0.713	0.717	0.720	0.724	0.728	0.732	0.736	0.740	0.744
19	0.748	0.752	0.756	0.760	0.764	0.768	0.772	0.776	0.780	0.783
20	0.787	0.791	0.795	0.799	0.803	0.807	0.811	0.815	0.819	0.823
21	0.827	0.831	0.835	0.839	0.843	0.846	0.850	0.854	0.858	0.862
22	0.866	0.870	0.874	0.878	0.882	0.886	0.890	0.894	0.898	0.902
23	0.906	0.909	0.913	0.917	0.921	0.925	0.929	0.933	0.937	0.941
24	0.945	0.949	0.953	0.957	0.961	0.965	0.969	0.972	0.976	0.980
25	0.984	0.988	0.992	0.996	1.000	1.004	1.008	1.012	1.016	1.020

in.

Inches to Millimeters

in.	0.0	0.001	0.002	0.003	0.004	0.005	0.006	0.007	0.008	0.009
0.0	0.000	0.025	0.051	0.076	0.102	0.127	0.152	0.178	0.203	0.229
0.01	0.254	0.279	0.305	0.330	0.356	0.381	0.406	0.432	0.457	0.483
0.02	0.508	0.533	0.559	0.584	0.610	0.635	0.660	0.686	0.711	0.737
0.03	0.762	0.787	0.813	0.838	0.864	0.889	0.914	0.940	0.965	0.991
0.04	1.016	1.041	1.067	1.092	1.118	1.143	1.168	1.194	1.219	1.245
0.05	1.270	1.295	1.321	1.346	1.372	1.397	1.422	1.448	1.473	1.499
0.06	1.524	1.549	1.575	1.600	1.626	1.651	1.676	1.702	1.727	1.753
0.07	1.778	1.803	1.829	1.854	1.880	1.905	1.930	1.956	1.981	2.007
0.08	2.032	2.057	2.083	2.108	2.134	2.159	2.184	2.210	2.235	2.261
0.09	2.286	2.311	2.337	2.362	2.388	2.413	2.438	2.464	2.489	2.515
0.10	2.540	2.565	2.591	2.616	2.642	2.667	2.692	2.718	2.743	2.769
0.11	2.794	2.819	2.845	2.870	2.896	2.921	2.946	2.972	2.997	3.023
0.12	3.048	3.073	3.099	3.124	3.150	3.175	3.200	3.226	3.251	3.277
0.13	3.302	3.327	3.353	3.378	3.404	3.429	3.454	3.480	3.505	3.531
0.14	3.556	3.581	3.607	3.632	3.658	3.683	3.708	3.734	3.759	3.785
0.15	3.810	3.835	3.861	3.886	3.912	3.937	3.962	3.988	4.013	4.039
0.16	4.064	4.089	4.115	4.140	4.166	4.191	4.216	4.242	4.267	4.293
0.17	4.318	4.343	4.369	4.394	4.420	4.445	4.470	4.496	4.521	4.547
0.18	4.572	4.597	4.623	4.648	4.674	4.699	4.724	4.750	4.775	4.801
0.19	4.826	4.851	4.877	4.902	4.928	4.953	4.978	5.004	5.029	5.055
0.20	5.080	5.105	5.131	5.156	5.182	5.207	5.232	5.258	5.283	5.309

mm

Chassis dyno "correction" factor

$$\text{Engine hp} = \frac{\text{Road hp}}{0.8} + 8$$

"Drag strip dyno" formulas

Quick formula for 1/4-mile ET:

$$\text{1/4-mile ET in seconds} = 6 \times \left(\frac{\text{vehicle wt}}{\text{engine hp}}\right)^{0.3333}$$

Quick formula for 1/4-mile trap speed:

$$\text{Trap speed in mph} = 234 \times \left(\frac{\text{engine hp}}{\text{vehicle wt}}\right)^{0.3333}$$

Quick formula for horsepower:

$$\text{Engine horsepower} = \left(\frac{\text{1/4-mile speed}}{282}\right)^{2.49793} \times wt$$

Long formula for 1/4-mile elapsed time in seconds, where x = engine horsepower and y = vehicle weight:

ET = 27.5531495 + (-0.0948251x) + (-0.005154y) + 0.00010768x^2 + 2.4552E-05xy + 1.1652E-06y^2 + 5.6525E-08x^3 + (-2.409E-08yx^2) + (-3.13E-09xy^2) + 1.531E-11y^3

Long formula for 1/4-mile trap speed in miles-per-hour, where x = engine horsepower and y = vehicle weight:

Trap speed = 4.53092116 + 0.37237133x + 0.05715395y + (-0.0007074x^2) + 6.209E-06xy + (-2.159E-05y^2) + (-6.276E-07x^3) + 2.5635E-07yx^2 + (-1.791E-08xy^2) + 2.5258E-09y^3

Exhaust Header Sizing
Diameter of the primary pipes:

$$\text{Primary diameter} = \frac{\sqrt{\text{CID x 1900}}}{\text{length x rpm}}$$

$$\text{Primary length} = \frac{\sqrt{\text{CID x 1900}}}{\text{diameter}^2 \text{x rpm}}$$

Horsepower and Torque
Unit of torque are pound-foot (lb-ft)
Units of work are foot-pounds (ft-lb)

Horsepower

$$\text{horsepower} = \frac{\text{torque} \times \text{rpm}}{5250}$$

Torque in lb-ft:

$$\text{torque} = \frac{\text{horsepower} \times 5280}{\text{rpm}}$$

1 horsepower = 1.0319 PS (German horsepower)
= .7457 kilowatt

1 PS = .98632 hp = .7355 kw

1 kw = 1.3410 hp = 1.3596 PS

$$1 \text{ lb/ft} = 1.35575 \text{ Newton/meters (Nm)} = 0.13825 \text{ kilopound/meters (kpm)}$$

1 Nm = 0.10197 kpm = 0.7376 lb-ft

1 kpm = 7.2334 lb-ft = 9.80665 Nm

Linear measure
1 inch = 25.4 millimeters (mm) = 2.54 centimeters (cm)

1 millimeter = 0.03937 inch

1 mile = 1.60934 kilometer

1 kilometer = .62137 mile

Mass
1 kilogram (kg) = 2.2046 pounds (lb)

1 lb = 0.45359 kg

Pressure and vacuum
1 pound per square inch (psi) = 0.0689 bar = 2.03602 inches of mercury (Hg)

1 bar = 14.5037 psi = 29.5298 inches Hg

1 inch Hg = 0.491237 psi = 0.03386 bar

Skid Pad Formula
Where r = the radius of the skid pad:
Temperature

$$g = \frac{1.226 \times r}{r^2}$$

$$\text{Fahrenheit} = 1.8 \text{ Celsius} + 32$$

$$\text{Celsius} = \frac{5}{9} \ (\text{Fahrenheit} - 32)$$

$$\text{Rankine} = \text{Fahrenheit} + 459.69$$

Theoretical Relationships
1 cfm = 1.6 hp (theoretical) = 1.44 hp (estimate)
1 hp = 0.625 cfm (theoretical) = 0.694 cfm (estimate)

Carburetor sizing in cubic feet-per-minute:

$$CFM = \frac{\text{venturi diameter x rpm x engine efficiency}}{56634}$$

Volumetric efficiency of a gasoline engine in percent:
Volumetric efficiency of an alcohol engine in percent:

$$\text{Gasoline engines} = 5600 \times \frac{\text{hp}}{\text{rpm} \times \text{cid}} \times 100$$

$$\text{Alcohol engines} = 5600 \times \frac{\text{hp}}{\text{rpm} \times \text{cid}} \times 100$$

Transaxle

$$mph = \frac{\text{rpm x tire diameter x } \pi}{\text{final drive ratio x gear ratio x 1056}}$$

Volume
1 cubic inch (ci) = 16.3871 cubic centimeters (cc)
1 cc = 0.06102 ci

Index